"Professor Ronald Barston's volume on the theory and practice of contemporary diplomacy can only enhance his considerable reputation in the study and practice of international relations. His sophisticated analysis is based on an impressive range of relevant sources and the argument will certainly appeal to students, practitioners and scholars with an abiding interest in the complexities of diplomatic negotiation. This exceptional work of scholarship will greatly assist their efforts."

**Jack Spence OBE**, *King's College London, UK*

"Ronald Barston's incisive analysis draws upon his own considerable experience in the world of international diplomacy. The book dissects and illuminates the multi-dimensional aspects of diplomatic methods with great perspicacity that will be of enormous interest to students of international affairs and, just as importantly, to diplomatic practitioners. It provides an invaluable guide about how to think and do diplomacy in the real world."

**Michael Rainsborough**, *Australian War College, Canberra, Australia*

# Diplomatic Methods

This comprehensive volume examines developments in diplomatic technique and changes in the diplomatic and political structures which shape, and are shaped, by international relations and the international order.

It provides a comprehensive foundation for understanding the theory, practice and utility of diplomacy, showing how diplomatic techniques are used in different contexts and the various tools that are available to policy actors to provide a broad yet deep view of the subject area. Organised around a framework of 11 chapters, the book embraces new ideas and fresh perspectives exploring individual methods such as reorientation, replacement institutions to combat decline or ineffectiveness of existing arrangements, summit conferences, contrasting approaches to economic agreements, and use of secret diplomatic methods, among others. Furthermore, it develops new concepts such as logistics diplomacy, counter diplomacy, parallel diplomacy and the "alternative architecture", and is widely illustrated with detailed examples including the diplomacy of geopolitics, the conflict over rules for plastics, marine resource disputes, dark trade and sanctions, and influence and strategic surprise.

This textbook will be essential reading for all those interested in or studying in the fields of diplomacy, comparative foreign policy, foreign policy analysis and, more broadly, to international relations.

**R.P. Barston** is an international relations and contemporary diplomacy specialist. He has previously taught at Lancaster University, London School of Economics and King's College, UK.

# Diplomatic Methods

R.P. Barston

Routledge
Taylor & Francis Group

LONDON AND NEW YORK

Designed cover image: © Shutterstock

First published 2025
by Routledge
4 Park Square, Milton Park, Abingdon, Oxon, OX14 4RN

and by Routledge
605 Third Avenue, New York, NY 10158

*Routledge is an imprint of the Taylor & Francis Group, an informa business*

© 2025 R.P. Barston

*British Library Cataloguing-in-Publication Data*
A catalogue record for this book is available from the British Library

ISBN: 978-1-032-06825-1 (hbk)
ISBN: 978-1-032-06819-0 (pbk)
ISBN: 978-1-003-20403-9 (ebk)

DOI: 10.4324/9781003204039

Typeset in New Baskerville
by Newgen Publishing UK

# Contents

# List of illustrations

## Tables

## Figures

# About the author

Professor R.P. Barston is an international relations and contemporary diplomacy specialist. He previously taught at Lancaster University, London School of Economics and King's College, UK and served in the Foreign and Commonwealth Office. He has extensive international experience including Malaysia (National Institute of Public Administration), as World Bank consultant and south-east Asia, as special envoy to Hanoi and the Caribbean. He is also a maritime safety specialist, including course director of the IMO International Maritime Academy in Trieste, Italy and has longstanding links with the International Maritime Bureau (IMB). He is accredited by the International Maritime Organisation (IMO) for maritime safety regulatory training and coordination with the Paris Memorandum of Understanding (PMOU). His publications include *The Maritime Dimension, The Other Powers: Studies in the Foreign Policies of Small States, International Politics Since 1945*, and *Modern Diplomacy* (fifth edition).

# Acknowledgements

Longstanding thanks are owed to Professor Jack Spence (King's College London) and Professor Alan James for support over many years. Special thanks are given to UCW Aberystwyth, Department of International Politics for proving the stimulus to study and later teach and work in international relations. That interest was sustained by later periods of secondment to the UK Foreign and Commonwealth Office, work in international institutions including the IMO, IMB and International Bank for Reconstruction and Development (IBRD) in Malaysia, and leading diplomatic and trade training in south east Asia, including Malaysia, special envoy to Hanoi and Caribbean. Subsequently, directing the Marine Policy postgraduate programme and teaching International Relations at LSE, helped further ideas on diplomacy, working with Christopher Hill, Fred Halliday, Michael Leifer and other colleagues. Longstanding collaboration with Patricia Birnie helped to draw together international and legal perspectives, along with international political economy and environmental issues, into a broader approach to conceptions of diplomacy. Paul Sharp and Andrew Cooper have both, through their scholarship and support, helped over a long period in shaping ideas and approaches to capturing the essence of diplomacy across a wide range of actors. Professor Colin Gray was a longstanding personal family friend and colleague , dedicated to his work , deep interest in his postgraduate students in strategic studies and above all humour.

At King's College London, grateful thanks are owed to colleagues for their support and discussions at different points of this current project, including Charlie Laderman, Maeve Ryan, Flavia Gasbarri, Nicholas Michelson, and Ben Kienzle. Particular thanks are also due to Professor Michael Rainsborough. Special thanks too are offered to Professor Andrew Lambert (King's College London) who shared maritime interests and was generous of his time and office despite the additional regular student queues outside his office for tutorials with me on diplomacy essays and projects.

Specific thanks are owed to foreign ministries and officials from a number of countries who have discussed issues and helped with treaties and questions on state practice. In the United States, Kevin Baumert and colleagues

(Department of State) and Trevor Gunn (Georgetown). In Malaysia, the Institute of Public Administration (INTAN) in Kuala Lumpur provided a valuable setting for developing multisector diplomatic training programmes at all levels from cadet to ambassador, as part of the reshaping of managing the new external relations for Malaysia. Special thanks are also owed to my wife Pamela and sons Robert and Neill for their unfailing support for the Malaysian work, *Modern Diplomacy* and, later, for *Diplomatic Methods.*

Ambassador Tan Sri Hasmy Agam, later head of the Malaysian Institute of Diplomacy of the MFA, provided significant support and encouragement. In the UK thanks are due to former FCO colleagues including Martin Williams. Ambassador Nicholas Bayne was of invaluable help on both the earlier work on *Modern Diplomacy* and current book. His support helped to bring that wider economic dimension and diplomatic practice to appreciations of the scope of diplomatic craft.

In a work of this type and scope, the support of technical international institutions and agencies is central. In the UK, the FCO Treaty Section was of very considerable assistance in responding to often difficult questions on treaty documentation. This help was critical and highly valued.

Thanks is extended to staff of the UN Dag Hammarskjöld Library for the duration of work on this book and other related work which was exceptional. Thanks too are given to the PMOU Secretariat (Maarten Vlag and all colleagues) and International Maritime Bureau (IMB) colleagues Michael Howlett and Cyrus Mody. Working with the IMB over nearly 20 years and United States Coast Guard (USCG), collaborating on the shipping safety (port state control) annual international inspector training course and other projects entailed maintaining IMBs role as a pioneering centre on teaching internationally applied maritime safety.

For permissions on maps, grateful thanks are extended to Japan for use of the map (Ichinokawa) of spatial distribution of chub mackerel in the Pacific chub mackerel fishery. "Effective time closures: quantifying the conservation benefits of input control for the Pacific chub mackerel fishery-PubMed (nih.gov )", M. Ichinokawa, H. Okamura, C. Watanabe, A. Kawabata, Y. Oozeki (2015). The University of Texas library map section is thanked for further use of the South China Sea map, used initially in *Modern Diplomacy.*

Grateful acknowledgement is made to the State Department for permission to use the map of the Republic of the Marshall Islands, from Limits in the Seas No 145, prepared by the Department of States' Bureau of Oceans and International Environmental and Scientific Affairs (OES), Oceans and Polar Affairs Office and Office of the Legal Advisor.

Jill and Michael Startup for secretarial assistance on this and previous publications. Thanks are extended to production staff at Newgen Publishing, including Jill Harper and colleagues. Frances gave dedicated and excellent support in the production of the manuscript. Finally, thanks are given to staff at Routledge, including Sophie Iddamalgoda, Helen Birchall and above all to Andrew Taylor (editor) for interest and exceptional support on this and my previous books with Routledge.

# Preface

In the autumn following the publication of the fifth edition of *Modern Diplomacy*, thoughts turned to looking over the evolution of the book from its first edition some 30 years earlier. The book had stood the test of time, capturing the essence of diplomacy for students and new practitioners: diplomatic correspondence, groupings, institutions, negotiation and specific sectors such as trade, environment, security and diplomacy in conflict, with chapters on mediation and the concept of normalisation. The basic approach was a combination of theory but with a strong emphasis on concepts and diplomatic practice. The approach would be international as far as possible; the content would move away from narrow conceptions of political diplomacy to embrace a wide range of transactions (political, economic, trade, finance), functional relations, environment and treaties. The underlying thinking behind that book, above all, was to encourage a wide perspective on international relations, institutions and issues representing a more diverse approach, which would also incorporate perspectives of weaker or developing powers in the conduct of diplomacy.

At that point, rather than prepare for a sixth edition of *Modern Diplomacy*, thoughts turned to other possibilities. After looking at options, it became apparent that a book on diplomatic methods, dealing with how diplomacy is undertaken, would be of benefit and value. The area was neglected. There was opportunity to continue the same working assumptions on approach and wide illustration. In this respect, *Diplomatic Methods* introduces several new concepts, particularly parallel and counter diplomacy, the use of time as strategic surprise and for flanking diplomacy, emerging groupings, and little-discussed forms of diplomacy such as trilateral diplomacy in development diplomacy.

*Diplomatic Methods* has provided an opportunity to fill gaps with the introduction of logistics diplomacy, a critical part of diplomatic practice but neglected both in the practice and study of diplomacy. This book is concerned with these and other changes, reflected in how states and other actors have developed approaches and methods in the course of the continued evolution of contemporary diplomatic practice.

Professor R.P. Barston, *Sussex*

# Introduction

The evolution of diplomatic methods is examined in the period after 2000. Diplomatic methods continuously evolve and are subject for the most part to adjustment rather than radical shifts or changes. The four traditional methods of diplomacy – negotiation, conferences, institutions and approaches to international order – have nevertheless undergone significant changes. Linking these changes are three important factors: the erosion of the concept of consensus as a constitutive element of international order, the weakening of multilateralism and the search for alternative mechanisms.

## Diplomatic methods

In this study, the term "diplomatic methods" is used to refer to the approach of states and other actors to a problem, issue or event. The approach may reflect a preference for keeping exchanges bilateral and low key, projecting presence through visit diplomacy, reviving stalled relations, or undertaking new exploratory bilateral relations. For some actors, a traditional route has included multilateral participation in the G77, nonaligned or more restrictive intraregional relations of a regional organisation.

Preferences for particular ways of handling issues tend to become recognised as part of the diplomatic style of a state. Styles vary from undertaking traditional conference drafting committee or facilitator roles in multilateral diplomacy; preferring bilateral alliances in a regional organisation; using flags and ports of convenience in sanctions evasion; developing financial service roles; and acting as a maverick state, or in isolation. In terms of participation, one of the changing diplomatic methods is the use of non-attendance at multilateral or other fora, reflecting the erosion of multilateral processes and the diplomacy of disengagement, which are distinguishing features of contemporary diplomacy. Other

DOI: 10.4324/9781003204039-1

changes in diplomatic methods include the switch from traditional methods (discussion, exchange, negotiation) to approaches which move transactions quickly and dramatically to coercive methods or to the edge of crisis, by linking issues to threats of retaliation unless revisions are made to diplomatic positions and policy.

Diplomatic styles or approaches tend to be relatively stable or fixed elements in the diplomacy of many states, shaped by the continuity of interests or constraints of diplomatic space. Changes in diplomatic style are associated especially with alterations of leadership in autocratic systems, or mixed-orientation states adopting divergent positions from an allied group to switch to an adversary or carry out significant reorientation of external relations.

Shifts in diplomatic methods also occur for several other reasons, including rapid secret moves to acquire assets, ports or other facilities to develop presence; the formation of competing coalitions and alliances; and the diversification of trade or other relations. Shifts in methods have also become associated with the use of strategic surprise to command political and economic space in conflicts and to raise levels of tension to command transactions, shifting diplomacy to the boundaries of coercion (chapters 2, 7, 8).

Methods are influenced by changing priorities, decline in usage or may simply lapse. Shifts in priorities can, however, bring or expose contradictions between objectives and tensions over competing interests, especially between trade and foreign policy, where interests and diplomatic initiatives frequently come into conflict. Reducing or resolving these conflicts is an ongoing part of domestic politics and international diplomacy.

## Areas covered and scope of inquiry

The book explores the evolution of diplomatic methods post-2000 through initial chapters which provide context with discussion on orientation and the widespread use of time as method in a variety of contexts. Specific chapters then focus on developments in particular sectors such as summit conferences, economic statecraft, environmental diplomacy and treaties. The latter looks at the reasons for increasing dissatisfaction with negotiated bilateral and multilateral agreements. Two subsequent chapters on parallel and counter diplomacy explore the grey areas between diplomacy and coercion, in which diplomatic and other actions are at odds with traditional concepts of diplomacy which view it as collective action, cooperation and contributing to international order. The final sections of the book cover three areas: the little-explored but critical subject of logistics and supply chain diplomacy, emerging alternative diplomatic groupings and diplomacy in conflicts.

## Evolution of diplomatic methods

Diplomatic methods in the post-2000 period have undergone consider-able change. Linking the changes discussed in individual chapters are the themes of the decline of multilateralism and the search for other formats to manage relations (chapters 1, 3, 5–8, 10). A key part of these changes is the decline of collective consensus decisions, evidenced in the weaknesses of provisions in multilateral agreements, and gaps in implementation through slow entry into force or non-ratification, which are indicative of disengaged diplomacy (chapters 5, 6). Chapter 5 highlights these difficulties over lengthy delay in achieving multilateral rules governing, for example, high seas fishing and illegal dark fleets, and competing approaches to regulating plastics. In terms of other aspects of governance, summit conferences have all but ceased to exist, though may return, as vehicles for managing primary and major power outstanding issues, with governance transformed into bilateral or regional institutions (chapter 3).

Other governance changes have affected several aspects of diplomatic conferences. Large-scale UN event conferences on topics such as habitat and food security have all but disappeared, for reasons of economy and loss of political interest in the format (chapter 3). In other multilat-eral conferences, the difficulties are in achieving sufficient major actor support for consensus wider than minimum entry into force requirements. Standing and ad hoc multilateral conferences have also been significantly affected by reduced diplomatic travel and a shortage of countries willing to host multilateral conferences on cost and other grounds.

In other multilateral areas, the reduced role of the UN in conflict dip-lomacy and peacekeeping, especially the diminished involvement of the UN Secretary-General in mediation and related good offices, is particu-larly notable (chapter 11). It has left gaps in conflict resolution, filled by competitive external mediation, intervention and unrealistic doctrines of political transition in zones of continuing high-level instability following withdrawal of UN and other forces. In other areas, attempts to reshape global governance included initiatives and summits such as those of the Secretary-General's reform packages on debt coordination, sustainable goals and financial institutions (chapters 1, 3, 11).

At individual state level, a notable development in diplomatic methods is the increase in states using mixed orientation (chapter 1) which becomes important in those instances where states are located in sensitive geostrategic areas. The use of mixed orientation for leverage, whilst some-times bringing advantages in facilitating conflict initiatives can, in pos-itional diplomacy, contribute to bilateral or alliance tension when mixed orientation involves support for adversaries in conflicts.

An unusual perspective on changes in diplomatic methods looks at the use of time as method in differing contexts, especially those linked to par-allel and counter diplomacy, rising tension and coercive moves (chapters 2,

7, 8). In part, the reasons for the expanded use of time-based methods lie in alterations in the level of international tension between primary powers but can also be attributed to other factors such as intraregional disputes in which actors seek to delay, block or reverse decisions or entry into force of trade and other agreements with third parties.

Other noteworthy changes in the use of time which have not been extensively explored involve its use as part of flanking diplomacy and as strategic surprise in economic statecraft to exploit a situation or put an adversary at a disadvantage. These are striking additions to diplomatic methods, illustrating the theme of heightened instability and tension reflecting adversarial flexibility and high intelligence monitoring of opponents (chapter 2). Other features reflecting this general theme are seen in economic statecraft creating mega trade blocs such as the RCEP and CPTPP (chapter 4). Such blocs raise several issues, including their impact on geopolitical tensions, the fragmentation of multilateral institutions and their use in counter diplomacy to limit the trade and political options of adversaries (chapters 6, 11). The growth of parallel diplomacy and counter diplomacy has significantly contributed to the erosion of multilateralism and increased international fragmentation.

## Summary of changes in diplomatic methods

The changes in diplomatic methods post-2000 can be grouped in three areas:

1. Major changes: the shift from consensus as the main approach in multilateral collective diplomacy
   - Decline of multilateralism
   - Growth of ad hoc coalitions and regrouping
2. New forms of diplomatic methods
   - Logistics diplomacy (actors, agreements, forms of cooperation)
   - Mixed actors (SOE, states, financial, infrastructure)
   - Plurilateral groups (in and outside multilateral institutions)
   - Innovative treaties (bilateral, modular, plurilateral, digital agreements)
   - Boundary areas (diplomacy and coercion); parallel and counter diplomacy
   - Coercive (strategic surprise, flanking diplomacy and counter diplomacy)
3. Methods in decline
   - Large-scale UN event and theme conferences
   - Associative diplomacy (inter-regionalism)
   - Detailed multisector rule of law agreements (e.g. trade, strategic cooperation)

# Chapter 1

# Orientation

## Introduction

The subject of this chapter is the methods used by states to change and reorientate their foreign policies. Orientation comprises three main areas: the positioning of a state via choice of allies, partners, security relations; trading relations; depth of engagement (organisation; membership; priorities; value promotion; bilateral relations and operating groups).

Orientations vary in complexity and content, from states with relatively minimal foreign policies dominated by transnational security threats or narrowly focused economic dependence issues, through to more complex middle power, great and primary powers, distinguished by the depth and complexity of transactions making up their external policies. The growth of other categories such as open and covert service providers and states aiming to develop newer roles almost exclusively as internationally accepted event hosts in areas such as multilateral, regional and business conferences and sports diplomacy illustrate the broader usage of diplomacy and soft power.

Orientation is neither immutable nor static, although major changes are relatively rare. A central argument in this chapter is that the frequency of sectoral change, much of it trade related, has increased post-2000 as a result of several factors including the instability and conflict in international relations post-cold war, economic dependence and vulnerability, the growth of bilateralism and the corresponding weakening of multilateralism.

By contrast, major shifts in orientation involving substantial change across several sectors have been less frequent, associated with cataclysmic events or regime change. The end of the cold war, for example, provided contexts for states within the former Soviet political and economic bloc to explore new economic and security groupings with European and other blocs.

DOI: 10.4324/9781003204039-2

Much of restructuring has involved partial change of mainly one sector focused on trade. In international trade the weakening of multilateralism and breakdown of the WTO Doha Round has seen intensified trade disputes and increased use of trade diversification strategies based on various forms of bilateral agreements to secure wider market access and supply agreements.[1] In terms of groupings, the nonaligned lost much of their original raison d'être by the end of the cold war. Subsequent periods of intermittent primary power tension have created an uncertain arena for the membership, preoccupied with regional conflicts, climate and transnational pandemics. Large developing groupings like the G77 and African bloc G90 became unworkable in complex multilateral trade diplomacy during the Doha Round, replaced by the spread of rival mega regional groupings, e.g. the China-led Regional Comprehensive Economic Partnership and the Canada, Japan, Asia–Pacific states-backed Comprehensive and Progressive Agreement for Trans-Pacific Partnership and bilateral hedging diplomacy.[2] Commodity powers enjoyed intermittent economic gains linked to price–supply fluctuations for raw materials, but at a political cost of dependence. For many other smaller powers, sectoral restructuring involved hedging strategies, short-term agreements and bilateral deals to buy time and stave off trade and other economic or security problems.

## Perspectives on foreign policy orientation and change

The study of foreign policy orientation has been significantly influenced by K.J. Holsti's seminal work *Why Nations Realign* on foreign policy restructuring.[3] The focus of Holsti's inquiry was on a particular type of foreign policy behaviour through which governments seek to change, usually simultaneously, the total pattern of their external relations. For Holsti, reorientation involves changes in patterns of partnerships, e.g. trade and types of activity, e.g. withdrawal from an international organisation, "... *where governments seek to change, usually simultaneously, the total pattern of external relations.*"[4]

Critical criteria in Holsti's view are intent in that the alteration is non-incremental, and there is conscious linking of different sectors of foreign policy. The first of these criteria is seen as being important in order to distinguish rhetorical ambition from action. Whilst some sectors may take time to be restructured, the speed of change differentiates these from routine or incremental change. The reasons for possible restructuring are identified as assertion of autonomy, the control of transnational processes, destruction of the residues of colonialism or to escape dependence.[5] This chapter will use reorientation in a wider sense to include partial (sectoral) reorientation, the commonest form of revision, and introduce a category of mixed reorientation to capture states pursuing foreign policies in two or more opposing blocs, which has become an expanding category of designed ambivalence.

A second important contribution to the orientation literature bringing attention to the subject of change in foreign policy is that of C.F. Hermann. His central ideas were presented in the paper "Changing Course" some seven years after Holsti's initial work, in an address to the annual meeting of the International Studies Association in London.[6] Hermann is distinctive in drawing out four types of foreign policy change: adjustment (minimum), programme change, problem/goal change and orientation change. Change agents are delineated from four categories: leader driven, bureaucratic advocacy, domestic restructuring and external shock. In contrast to Holsti, Hermann's focus is on leadership and decision-making processes.

Both works reflect an era of international relations dominated by cold war security threats, transition out of colonial rule and newer issues associated with moving from the cold war and emerging economic interdependence. But there are a number of differences in the two approaches, with Holsti paying greater attention to change variables related to culture and tradition, and economic factors. There is also considerable emphasis for Holsti on mapping, particularly the indicators of change such as diplomatic representation and trade, and establishing categories of orientation.

A further important difference between the two approaches is the conceptualisation of external influences. For Hermann, external factors affecting foreign policy restructuring are conceived as external shocks: "Large dramatic events, with high visibility and immediate impact", for example Sadat's visit to Jerusalem, the Tet offensive in the Vietnam war and US dollar devaluation.[7] Holsti, on the other hand, uses external factors to cover a wide range of issues and processes, including dependency and non-military threats, introducing a variety of influences appropriate to a wider range of actors and settings.

Holsti's framework uses four basic categories for grouping orientation: isolation, self-reliance, dependence and diversification. Whilst this framework helps to provide an initial basis for considering the concept of foreign policy redirection, the continued growth in the number of sovereign states, reordering of issues and changing centres of power all suggest the need for additional or revised categories. For example, nonalignment is no longer a leading or sufficiently authoritative grouping or platform to capture the range of contemporary foreign policy.[8]

Interest in comparative aspects of orientation has continued in the post-2000 literature[9] including revised categories of middle powers, which enjoyed a brief renaissance,[10] commodity powers[11] and maverick regimes. The literature on these latter regimes, which pursue high-risk foreign policies, is valuable for the glimpses it sheds on the "grey areas" of external relations – dark trade, sanctions evasion, arms supply and secret bilateral agreements.[12]

Other studies in single-country literature have examined US administration debates on doctrines and shifts in orientation, such as restructuring US–Latin America relations, the merits of "America First" reorientation versus re-engagement with "like-minded countries" and the Indo-Pacific Economic Framework debates.[13] A similar debate has occurred in the African Union (AU) over whether to concentrate on African continental relations or reorientate the AU into bilateral relations with the EU or other external actors in order to pursue a more global orientation.[14]

In the international political economy literature, particularly important areas addressed are the periodic repositioning strategies of small powers as they move in and out of international aid and financial loan support packages, coping strategies and renegotiation of trade/aid agreements. Hardacre's groundbreaking study of the little covered EU–Africa and EU–Latin America economic preference negotiations (EPAs), illustrated the acute problems of trade dependence associated with EPAs.[15]

The often temporary nature of "breathing spaces" is highlighted by Jessica Byron in her work on Caribbean international loan and trade finance packages, in which small powers have to periodically make significant financial reorientation moves every three of four years international financial and trade packages run out or diminish in effectiveness, prompting a review of strategies.[16]

An allied area of this literature is that of A.F. Cooper on small power coping strategies through which small powers attempt to establish niche roles and functions in regional and international relations for identity, influence and reducing vulnerability.[17]

## Reorientation – concepts and scope of analysis

The overview of approaches to the study of orientation in the preceding sections provides background on reorientation and highlights several strands and recurring themes relating to the reasons for restructuring and the factors shaping implementation of foreign policy change. Among these themes are questions of categories; recognition of the need for new strategies to counter economic decline or threats; limitations on options; different sources of vulnerability and responses; global or regional repositioning; marginalisation; and decline or loss of traditional roles. These and related factors such as types of reorientation give context and shape to shifts in foreign policy.

This chapter focuses on three categories of reorientation: partial or sectoral reorientation, mixed and full reorientation. A fourth category of reorientation failure includes a new subcategory of partial reorientation.

## *Sectoral reorientation*

Sectoral reorientation involves restructuring elements of foreign policy in one or more sectors with a view to making partial adjustments rather than full reorientation. It is used commonly in a wide area of areas including trade diplomacy,[18] weapons supply/acquisition, sourcing foreign loans, transportation and logistics. Other uses include initiatives and shift of emphasis to signal interest in participation, for example, in trade discussions and initiatives at bilateral, plurilateral and multilateral levels,[19] or to project new emphasis in bilateral relations.[20]

## *Advantages of sectoral reorientation*

Sectoral reorientation is a highly flexible diplomatic method. It can be expanded to accommodate differing levels of change. It may be part of another initiative or exist separately in its own right. Another advantage is that sectoral reorientation is relatively immune from attack. A sectoral trade reorientation can be defended from domestic criticism of ineffectiveness or other grounds for quite lengthy periods unlike agreements in mixed or full reorientation. The political cost of limitations or failure depends on the sector but is likely to be generally low and less than mixed or full reorientation failure.

## *Limitations of sectoral reorientation*

Sectoral reorientation in both its open and covert forms is vulnerable to various forms of counter diplomacy, coercion and dispute linkage at national, bilateral and international levels. The enhanced intrusion of external powers on trade and regional negotiations through diplomatic and private monitoring, commentary and parallel initiatives is now an embedded feature of diplomacy. Enhanced monitoring and commentary are designed to generate tension, domestic division and revision of policy.

Asymmetrical states are particularly vulnerable to intermittent counter diplomacy mixed with normalisation moves by adversarial powers aimed at limiting opposing alliance security initiatives; trade negotiations or changing unacceptable policies.[21] Vulnerability is driven by dependence, the meshing of commercial and foreign policy, and entrenched domestic economic interests advocating bilateral trade continuity and trade over foreign policy. Overall, domestic opinion is concerned over undertaking any sectoral changes in security orientation which might affect internal stability, loss of links and being cut off from mainstream political, trade and logistical connections.

### Secrecy and sectoral reorientation

Much of sectoral reorientation is conducted as quiet and secret diplomacy out of unnecessary attention. The subject matter might be domestically sensitive, commercial, or involve security commitments which could provoke an adverse response from an enemy or carry high risk over completion.[22] For these and other related reasons, exchanges and commitments are kept out of the public domain. Secret commitments, understandings and side letters necessarily raise questions over the public's right to know about security or sensitive commitments and the extent of any public disclosure.[23] Both premature and partial disclosure inevitably lead to controversy.

### Incidents and transition

Border clashes and other incidents command immediate attention but also point to other related agreements, raising issues about the value of continued bilateral relations or questioning the rationale for reorientation in those agreements. Incidents raise questions about the level of response and prompt questions over whether some fundamental readjustment is necessary. For example, intermittent clashes have occurred since the 1950s on the Sino-Indian border.[24] However the outbreak of serious clashes in the western sector (south of the Aksai Chin highway) with loss of life[25] were a tipping point in India's decision to reduce links with China and adopt a long-range policy of greater economic self-reliance. The clashes called into question India's earlier high-risk political decisions to join the Shanghai Cooperation Organisation. Although remaining a member of SCO, India began to reorientate its foreign policy more into the difficult terrain of mixed orientation and increasing the diversity of its orientation, balancing even more interests. As Shivshankar Menon puts it: "Diplomacy is about choices".[26]

### Factors shaping shifts to sectoral reorientation

Four broad factors are important as determinants of change: perceptions about the extent of vulnerability; loss of niche role; marginalisation in organisations; and dispute linkage. Perceptions about vulnerability especially in areas such as trade, security and transborder threats have been the major variables in shaping responses to changes in orientation.

Increased economic and trading vulnerability, not just for small powers, has been a major issue running through efforts to reorientate foreign policy. A wide range of states have attempted to diversify substantially trade patterns to reduce trade risk. Large powers such as Canada, UK, India, Turkey, Republic of Korea, Australia, Malaysia and many small powers in Africa, Asia and the Caribbean, face ongoing issues over trade dependence and diversification.[27]

Responses have involved institutional changes enhancing the formal powers of trade ministries; experimenting with revising the role of finance ministries, or, in a few cases creating a combined foreign and trade ministry have all been tried with varying success In an innovative move, Canada created for a brief period a special separate post of Minister of Trade Diversification.[28]

External methods have included refocusing attention to intraregional trade relations or directed to states with whom trade had previously been limited. Barbados, for example, shifted focus to greater domestic (intraregional) trade and bilateral initiatives, by expanding trade representative offices to previously neglected states, as part of its repositioning strategy of reducing the emphasis on inter-regional trade and regional groupings.[29]

In looking at the reasons for regular repositioning every few years, as in the case of Barbados, Byron identified the progressive decline in impact of international institution loan packages in national restructuring packages, resulting from the diminishing effect of domestic support measures and above all traded goods loosing market competitiveness at regional level to larger regional neighbours.[30] In addition, inter-regional trade arrangements such as EU–CARICOM seemed to offer little immediate tangible benefits for a small actor.[31]

The shift in Barbados' trade emphasis to intra-CARIFORUM trade involved new near-neighbour missions and integrating the foreign ministry with private sector Chambers of Commerce. Other initiatives outside the region planned for the revival of faltering trade negotiations with Canada, using the spring IMF/Bank meetings in Washington as part of a diversification strategy. This strategy was subsequently postponed because of the COVID-19 pandemic and cancellation of direct meetings, underlining the vulnerability of small but well-run powers to external crises.[32]

Responding to the problem of non-performing or failed trade agreements is often difficult in that decline may be disguised by modest gains; changes in trade dependence may have developed over a considerable time.[33] Korea, for example, assessed that its bilateral FTA with the EU was not likely to prove a long-term stable platform for its predominantly vehicle exports into Europe. The subsequent shift in trade policy involved major diversification geographically into the Middle East and in particular Gulf states, coupled with modifying Korea's trade profile into information technology and project management. Additional diversification was extended regionally by adding agricultural initiatives such as the Mekong Initiative, based on Korean domestic rural agriculture management, to become part of a more geographically diverse Korean trade profile.[34]

A second factor affecting sectoral reorientation – reduction or loss of a role – has become a more significant aspect of orientation because of the widening range of threats to traditional or specialist niche roles.

Threats to, or loss of, traditional service roles such as shipping registry or offshore financial centres have become acute given limited options of affected states in offsetting loss in the short term. For example, an IMF/ World Bank campaign to outlaw and control Offshore Financial Centres (OFCs), and Tax Havens – the mainstay of Caribbean (e.g. Bermuda) and SIDS (e.g. Antigua, St Vincent, BVI) – had a substantial impact on the external revenue of those powers.[35] Marshall Islands was added to the EU/OECD blacklist of non-cooperating financial jurisdiction along with other Caribbean states extending the dispute into international ship registry services.[36]

In other instances WTO rulings on subsidies and EU environmental regulations have affected small power agricultural exports with phase out and loss of traditional market access or additional compliance costs, making them uneconomic.

Niche roles as event or conference host are affected by global health crises and pandemics such as the COVID-19 pandemic, which have resulted in ongoing cancellation or rescheduling of diplomatic conferences. Diplomatic travel is reduced and finding hosts becomes more problematic. As a result, changes have been made in diplomatic conference methods to try and overcome some of these issues with the use of split sites, which reduce the number of conferences held in major traditional multilateral capitals on public health grounds. It is an unsatisfactory, though perhaps unavoidable, solution which affects attendance, levels of participation and overall multilateral commitment.[37]

Third, marginalisation in international institutions is an increasingly important problem within regional integrative and economic cooperation organisations such as EU, MERCOSUR, CARICOM, PIF and AfCFTA. Factors such as expansion of membership, unequal economic benefits, differences over focus, inner political groups and a desire to break with tradition have influenced moves to redefine sectors. In the Pacific, for example, these concerns were underlying the debate by micro states in the PIF on either keeping traditional ties with Australia and New Zealand, based on the "blue water" model (fisheries, tourism and limited outside contact) or breaking out and seeking different external links.[38]

Similar issues have arisen in other regional arrangements as in the EU, where the Franco–German partnership has shaped perceptions held by both larger and smaller EU members of decision exclusion and marginalisation.[39] Manifestations of this are reflected in the formation of externally oriented breakaway groups linked to the PRC.[40]

Reorientation may be shaped by the perceived need to take high-risk initiatives such as shifts away from a traditional trade partner or political reorientation involving leaving an organisation to develop new links, and re-establish identity and role in international relations through different alignments.[41]

## Mixed orientation

Several different several types of mixed orientation have been developed post-cold war.

Some are primarily economic based, e.g. Japan, in which tensions arise from balancing political and economic issues with regional adversaries with western-linked security interests at bilateral (US) and plurilateral level (Quad).[42] Other mixed orientations involve competing political-security links (US–Jordan–Arab League).[43] A third category comprises embryonic mixed orientation, which is at an early or incomplete stage of construction (e.g. Vietnam post-reunification). In the fourth category are those cases in which a mixed orientation has changed to a dependent orientation. (e.g. Pakistan–China). In category four, resumption of mixed orientation may no longer be an option because of changes of policy by a primary power, downgrading regional orientation as part of its own reorientation; severe domestic economic difficulties in the "mixed" orientation power, or external policies allowed to decay or languish by the "mixed" orientation state.[44]

Mixed orientation reflects the increasing fluidity and secrecy in the conduct of contemporary international relations. Reorientation or elements of it may be part of quiet or secret bilateral or group exchanges not in the public domain. Shifts in orientation may not be publicly evident, especially in sensitive adversarial relations, which involve polarised political and security relations.

Reluctance to commit publicly in bilateral relations can occur in reviews of historic security guarantees or joint defence cooperation exchanges; changes in intelligence sharing may be perceived as highly sensitive for political, trade or security relations because of their domestic impact or reaction of external "interested" states.[45]

In these circumstances revised commitments to an ally on security guarantees, joint defence cooperation or intelligence sharing, might be made privately between leaders or framed as secret side letters in security or other agreements. The existence of informal or formal commitments of this kind are frequently not known beyond a narrow leader decision group.

**Table 1.1** States with mixed orientation

| | |
|---|---|
| Turkey | Costa Rica |
| Egypt | Brazil |
| Israel | Mexico |
| Malaysia | Hungary |
| Qatar | South Africa |
| Saudi Arabia | Kenya |
| United Arab Emirates | Rwanda |
| India | Colombia |

In terms of external effect, an element of ambiguity in a commitment may contribute to the general deterrent effect of such commitments to weak or strategically exposed allies. The strength of private commitments are shaped by security demands by smaller allies for weapons, technical support, intelligence and backing in crises.

The extent and flexibility of mixed orientation is distinguished by political recovery following seemingly serious clashes or other incidents; toleration of ambiguities or contradictions in the relationship are some of the features which differentiate mixed orientation. A further feature is that most transactions, particularly with "sensitive" states are not regularly in the public domain, making these elements of bilateral relations in effect "grey areas" or covert relations.

In other cases, mixed orientation may be at early stage – a first exploratory move (e.g. port agreements between China and Piraeus (Greece)). In the case of the latter, further extension of the hub to Italy, Spain and other Mediterranean ports (with China creating a Europe–Med–Middle East link) began to raise increasing political issues for the EU after the first Piraeus move.[46] Strategic dependence and seeming loss of control over Euro–Middle East connectivity seemed pushed into the background, as European port actors and EU members sought inbound investment or were compelled to conduct fire sales of port and other assets as part of Commission and creditor conditionality in debt crises.[47] Port acquisition and connectivity had received very little strategic and coordinated EU attention at policy and directive level through the Commission or Council. The EU found it difficult to shape a coherent response to port and intermodal connectivity, which is surprising given port and shipping assets under individual European corporate control or jurisdiction and European port professional groups. The need for greater attention to event-rather than rule-making approaches is made by Luuk van Middelaar in his valuable study on EU decision-making and diplomacy.[48] Port development and strategic communications for the EU were very much decentralised issue areas left to ports until sometime after Piraeus. For the EU, the early approach to maritime issues had been shaped by environmental concerns, shipping regulation or building up an EU maritime shipping safety inspectorate in competition with the intergovernmental traditional leader on shipping safety – the Paris Memorandum (PMOU) based in Holland, rather than strategic political-commercial threats.[49]

In such contexts, ambivalence and uncertainty aids adversarial strategies of acquisition, establishing incremental non-obtrusive presence through long-term external probing and acquisition, creating hubs and networks which are difficult to challenge competitively or strategically.

### Strategies of mixed orientation states

For mixed orientation states, the selection of methods is shaped much more than in other orientations by willingness to undertake enhanced risk across core sectors. That is, in its external relations the mixed state chooses to move in policy areas subject to controversy or failure.

The split between orientation sectors tends to increased tension between individual policies. For example, Turkish diplomacy over the issues of Libyan recognition and military support, or the economic deal on Syrian refugees raises questions of whether these actions are compatible generally with Turkey's trade and security relations with the EU and NATO membership. These limits are pushed as far as possible by mixed orientation actors.

Visit diplomacy features highly in the methods of mixed orientation states. In order to sustain an eclectic list of interests and project a presidential image, short-notice visit diplomacy is used periodically by Turkey for political firefighting to dampen down conflict and take issues, at least temporarily, off the EU agenda. Innovative initiatives in the EU migrant crisis, or undertaking the security of Kabul airport to facilitate the airborne withdrawal of residual US and NATO forces from Afghanistan earn credit, but also suggest close attention to diplomatic craft and balancing competing interests.[50]

In terms of the sustainability and coherence of the external policies of mixed orientation states, many however tend to be short term, giving an appearance of fragility and uncertainty. Acting as a broker or securing a grain deal secures only short-term political advantages. Related to this is an increased vulnerability to the effects of linkage. High profile or "frontline" roles of several mixed orientation actors in regional conflicts makes them extremely sensitive and vulnerable to linkage from external shocks or incidents spilling over and affecting core sectors of their external relations.

Different methods have been developed by mixed orientation states to reduce exposure or, conversely, to profit from it. Combinations of methods (facilitator, exchanges, recognition, negotiation) have been used by smaller powers, linked by a common concern to maintain low profiles (Jordan, Lebanon, Oman) or to keep sensitive bilateral relations off the radar (e.g. Jordan–US; Israel–Russian Federation). Oman has been particularly successful at cultivating its role as a venue facilitator for quiet diplomacy for meetings and negotiations of the envoys of adversaries, allies and international institutions, in conflicts including Iran, Iraq and Afghanistan.

In contrast, Egypt has maintained lines across the Arab–Israeli conflict on the Palestine issues, with more active diplomacy. Its longstanding ceasefire and mediatory role has been possible, in the absence of diplomatic relations, through the links between respective intelligence services which in practice have become the means and substitute channels for contact on ceasefire arrangements.[51]

An interesting economic example of diplomatic triangulation is provided by Vietnam's offshore oil licensing boundary dispute methods with China, in which the weaker party, Vietnam, attempted to protect its boundary claim by offering a bloc exploration licence to the Russian state-linked oil company, Rosneft. The move met strong counter diplomacy by the PRC, including high-risk maritime incidents with drilling rigs operating in licensed blocs of the Vietnamese EEZ, to create doubts over external commercial backing and derail the project.[52]


## Full reorientation

Major reorientation involving substantial shifts in all or most sectors is generally as a result of factors such as systemic and ideological collapse of a bloc, internal power struggles (coup), socio-political revolution, breaks with a colonial past, and divided sovereignty (secession). Full reorientation is rare with most reorientation partial (sectoral) or mixed.

Full reorientation involves moves which take the actor from an existing or traditional bloc or grouping to an opposing political, economic, or military group. The process is frequently initiated by normalisation initiatives which reflect radical departures from previous foreign policy and overturning traditional symbols and methods of hostility. Perhaps the largest example in contemporary diplomacy of full shift in alignment and economic structures is captured in the events following the removal of the Berlin wall, the end of the Soviet bloc and transfer of many former members into the European Community and NATO.

At the individual country level, Malaysian full reorientation under Mahathir (1981–2003) is explored by Karminder Singh Dhillon in a valuable and groundbreaking study, which rejects the continuity-partial change view of a number of other preceding accounts.[53] Dhillon's study examines Malaysian foreign policy outputs in seven core sectors (Buy British Last; Anti Commonwealth; Look East; Third World Spokesmanship; Regional Engagement; Islamic Posturing and Commercial Diplomacy), arguing that these areas and associated sub-policies were revolutionary given tradition and previous policies.[54]

Full reorientation may involve change in one core sector of relations between two or more states. It is not technically full reorientation involving major shifts in several categories, since it is largely based on one (political) sector. Change in that core area is, however, of massive and fundamental significance, requiring a basic change in longstanding beliefs, underlying philosophy or normalisation moves between longstanding fundamental adversaries. In Israel–Egyptian relations, Sadat's visit to Jerusalem was a fundamental step to normalisation. Egypt was subsequently suspended from the Arab League.[55]


### Characteristics of full reorientation

Foreign policies of developing countries outside of Europe which are undergoing or have completed the process tend to be charismatic leader-dominated, use doctrines for domestic appeal, thrive on short-run successes, but, as with all reorientation, need sustained economic growth and demand quick returns. High levels of leader rhetoric and doctrine are common features of most full reorientation in this category. The doctrine of Bolivarian hemispheric cooperation under Hugo Chavez or Malaysia's "Look East" policies of Mahathir were used partly for domestic purposes to sustain the profile and power of the leader.[56]

Leader rhetoric tends to envisage the country at a higher level of power than its actual capability, with discourse framed around projects, major initiatives or grandiose vision, as policies are projected to move the country into a new alignment or higher level of development form third to second or first world. Doctrine is correspondingly closely linked to internal economic performance, with adverse economic trends ultimately feeding internal opposition at elite and popular level to unsuccessful orientation.

In full reorientation, changes in individual sectors can occur at different rates, rather than similar degrees of change simultaneously occurring in all core sectors. The early literature of Holsti and Hermann tended to over-emphasise response as sudden and dramatic retaliation to an adverse external event. However, as has been argued in the section on sectoral reorientation, trade and other restructuring after initial action is a slow process taking anything up to five years.

Full reorientation is a mixture of short-term responses and longer time frame policies. Dhillon, in commenting on Malaysian economic development diplomacy, argues that despite some edgy or risky moves:

> The nation's foreign policy moved steadily from the traditional defence and security related one under his predecessors to one which revolved around commercial and development diplomacy. Luring FDI, opening of new markets for Malaysia's growing exports, facilitating reverse investments, increasing trade and acquiring foreign expertise, became the corner stones of Malaysian foreign policy.[57]

The brittle aspect of elements of external policy in regimes undertaking full restructuring is, nevertheless, a notable feature – sudden moves, dramatic reversals, cancellation of negotiated terms or withdrawal from treaties – are all hallmarks of highly personalised leader diplomacy. Foreign and other ministries have to catch up with, interpret and implement current ideas and new initiatives, or defend ideas on which there is scant information and no standard reporting from posts as part of the process of implementation.

The intensive use of high levels of presidential visit and personal diplomacy to project presence tends to contribute to implementation difficulties or contradictory strands of policy. Venezuela's Chavez, for example, visited some 150 countries at an estimated cost of $50 million.[58] Presidential diplomacy relies heavily on air transport, access to foreign leaders for bilateral meetings and frequent attendance at multilateral and regional fora. It is highly vulnerable to disruption from civil conflict, environmental emergencies and COVID-19 type crises, which preclude or seriously limit personal and side diplomacy in multilateral fora and may lead to the cancellation or postponement of visits.

In pandemics, contacts between leaders shift to virtual formats and indeed revert to use of more traditional telephone diplomacy. Ironically the telephone returns to replace the photo op or Zoom.

In addition to the varying timescales in full restructuring, the various sectors of change in full orientation often have differing degrees of success. Individual sub-policies may fail or become ineffective. However, failure of a subset does not necessarily overturn or undermine full restructuring unlike other restructuring. In these instances the range of restructuring gives cover and allows for failure in some areas, at least temporarily, until the next election, constitutional review or coup.

Rather, attention is switched by the leadership to other issue areas or publicity given to other areas to gain diplomatic space. In Malaysian "Look East" policy, the identification of Japan as a work and international role model was eventually dropped after three years because of its limited impact on Malaysian economic performance, and questions over the cultural relevance or "fit" with Malay society, given Malay culture and recent historical memories of Japan in Malaya in WW2.

### Reorientation: alliances and NATO expansion

Changing orientation from one economic or military bloc to another is a major undertaking. Although it is technically sectoral reorientation, in practice it is more appropriate to regard the change as a shift close to full reorientation. Sectoral shifts can become full or close to complete reorientation in cases in which neutrality is abandoned or a previously neutral or nonaligned state joins a bloc as the missing piece in full reorientation.

Modern examples of these types of reorientation are seen in the application of Sweden and Finland for NATO membership.[59] Shifts into a military bloc affect bilateral relations, methods of contact and tacit understandings such as on-off limit areas of foreign policy involving relations with adversarial powers. Other changes for a neutral state are the impact on its traditional role as a mediator or go-between in conflicts involving great powers. Greater flexibility is tolerated in cases of switching or mixed reorientation by nonaligned members, but for the former neutral state the advantages of neutrality are likely to diminish more quickly once absorbed into an alliance.

New membership has geographic implications for an alliance in terms of the contexts and scope of common alliance security commitments. The threat boundary is extended for mutual support in the event of attack or other threats to security by adversaries. Expansion of membership has strategic implications in terms of altered geography and changes to threat perceived by an adversary. It may take the boundaries of an alliance into territories previously under the control of an adversary; or the addition of a new member may lead to perceptions of possible loss of security attention by smaller or particularly vulnerable members on the flanks of a military alliance facing a powerful and revisionist neighbour. For an adversary, sectoral reorientation can pose new strategic threats from forward bases or technological reach essential to mobile modern warfare.

The Swedish and Finland applications for membership of NATO in practice constitute full reorientation. They change defence links from informal security relations to formal treaty-based obligations in NATO. Looking back from the next decade will raise some interesting issues over the case, particularly the extent to which the conditions for successful implementation suggested in the following section on Brexit are met.[60]

## UK Brexit: leaving an alliance – a bridge too far?

Leaving an established regional organisation is a rare and high-risk move in foreign policy. The UK decision to leave the EU faced the UK with major trade and political challenges.[61] Achieving the main ideas underpinning Brexit – breaking from the EU, increasing freedom of action and tilting orientation to Asia–Pacific proved, at least for the first two objectives, increasingly difficult and in many respects, illusory.[62] Achieving the third had some measure of success but appeared more of a disconnected strand from the other parts of British external preoccupations and foreign policy. The political and economic strands of Asia–Pacific reorientation involved raising the political and trade engagement with ASEAN[63] and membership of the CPTPP.[64] The defence input was via security cooperation with ASEAN (counter-terrorism, maritime, anti-piracy), a naval carrier contribution to the Asia–Pacific theatre and tripartite nuclear submarine cooperation with the US and Australia.[65] The naval component was arguably the most important part of the package although, in trade and political foreign policy terms, not easy to translate into hard strategic trade agreements.

Unlike other forms of reorientation, full reorientation needs four elements: quick achievement of main objectives and early tangible evidence of success; limited trade disruption or friction from withdrawal terms; little undue diversion or counter diplomacy against main objectives; and a relatively stable domestic environment. Strong evidence of success in the first of these offsets negative factors in the other three elements, but not the reverse.

The major problems of Brexit have centred on the terms of Withdrawal and TCA agreements and difficulties of effective implementation.[66] Four areas of difficulty can be distinguished: implementing treaty reconstruction, filling the trade gap, trade and political friction over the Withdrawal and TCA trade agreements and loss of focus. The first of these, treaty reconstruction, had been identified as an area presenting a major impediment to Brexit,[67] although this was not as great, at least initially, as anticipated.

To expedite the process, a variety of formal and interim arrangements have been used. These inevitably were in many instances rolled over, provisional, informal or frameworks, leaving gaps in the terms, which increasingly typified trade diplomacy. The agreements included several Economic Partnership Agreements,[68] free trade agreements,[69] interim MOUs[70] and framework agreements[71] to achieve continuity.[72] By 2021 some 68 agreements had been concluded, covering 80% of UK non-EU trade.[73]

These would be the subject of later negotiation and vulnerable to external challenge and counter offers, typifying the increased external monitoring and conflict over trade deals.[74] The treaty reconstruction, however, had two other implications on treaty legacy and the impact of the volume of reconstruction in holding back review of treaty reform and innovation in treaty design. First, time pressures prevented the thinning out of marginal or incompatible EU agreements, such as strategic cooperation agreements with European small states, now part of the UK Treaty List, and also essential reform of the inherited heavily rule-based specialist committee structures and dispute procedures, favoured in EU treaty style. This had a legacy effect in continuing into UK trade negotiations, which mirrored EU negotiating subheads and language ("ambitious agreements") and lengthy negotiating rounds, slowing down the process of building new post-Brexit agreements.

Second, the failure to conclude smart trade agreements quickly with all the future core groups – US, India, Canada, Australia, New Zealand – was one of the key factors in holding back Brexit success. Negotiations with ASEAN and CPTPP followed the political and regional agendas of those organisations.

Brexit needed quick, visible signs of success. Whilst the overall number of secondary agreements for non-EU trade was large, these did not capture sufficient high value trade with India, US and other allied markets to cover the reduction in UK–EU trade. The failure to conclude a US trade agreement underlined the boundaries and limitations of Anglo–US relations: that the relationship was primarily confined to security cooperation.

Third, the level of trade friction over implementation of the Withdrawal Agreement and TCA worked against achieving reorientation. A successful Brexit required limited EU trade disruption or friction arising from the withdrawal terms. Trade continuity with the EU was important, pending the conclusion of agreements with Asia–Pacific and US and rebuilding an external UK role outside of Europe. The lack of provisions with the EU on documentary trade access and mutual goods conformity certification were significant negotiating failures – the hallmarks of an incomplete agreement and sources of later friction across fisheries, goods and the financial services role of the City of London.[75]

A fourth set of factors shaping the implementation of Brexit can be grouped around the loss of UK focus after 2020. These factors included the disruption caused by COVID-19, the impact of the Ukraine war in shifting attention back to Europe, and ongoing political problems over the Northern Ireland Protocol. In this context the lack of bureaucratic support for Brexit, combined with government leadership changes, added to the shift away from the original withdrawal ideas of Brexit. A shift in the conception of Brexit was suggested in the detail of the Windsor Framework and media around the Anglo–French summit.[76]

### *The Brexit balance sheet*

Not all parts of the Brexit reorientation were unsuccessful. The treaty reconstruction was a major achievement and important early negotiating gain, given the volume and complexity. The follow-up depends on sustained negotiation and augmented specialist trade officials. In regional and multilateral institutions, the UK resumed its separate position as a founding member or acceded to particular agreements, e.g. FAO agreements,[77] regional resource organisations[78] and key commodity agreements (e.g. sugar, grain) in which the EU had previously represented the UK as part of re-establishing its international presence and legal personality.[79]

The gradual regaining of international presence[80] contributed to a much better coordinated international involvement, especially through WTO beginning to be integrated into foreign policy with better media coverage linked to the ASEAN bid, use of the WTO process and developing potential trade allies such as Mexico.[81] A new narrative was designed for UK–ASEAN relations – maritime cooperation, security and pandemic cooperation, replacing the traditional soft power English-language training model which, in the context of a bid for membership of ASEAN, had come to look increasingly dated and difficult to mobilise in an ASEAN hi-tech context.[82] A slicker model was needed. The US Smart Cities model for US project finance relations with ASEAN was no doubt noted as a contemporary initiative.[83]

These and other agreements, such as with ASEAN and the CPTPP, constitute parts of the hardware in the orientation of British foreign policy. How these will relate to other strands in the future orientation is uncertain but as Brexit is continuously shaped and redefined, they constitute important assets alongside Asia–Pacific relations and developing relations with the EU signifying the UK's international orientation in a modified Brexit.

## Reasons for failed reorientation

Before looking at some of the general factors which can contribute to the failure of reorientation, separate comment on incomplete reorientation is necessary in order to differentiate this as a fourth category for the study of orientation, alongside sectoral, mixed and full reorientation. Unlike most failed orientation, which continues for some time before it is recognised or accepted, incomplete reorientation is identified quite quickly.

### Incomplete reorientation

The concept of incomplete reorientation is introduced to distinguish those situations in which reorientation is under consideration or is at a relatively early stage but there is doubt or division over whether it meets objectives or poses significant difficulties. The policy change may be under consideration, abandoned or subsequently abandoned because of unworkability or changed political contexts. Four main types of incomplete reorientation can be distinguished: change of diplomatic recognition or links with a politically sensitive regime or adversary considered but not carried through (Obama's Egyptian policy regarding Sisi/Morsi); reorientation progressing in fits and starts through poor implementation (Canada–Brazil trade reorientation); blocked or restricted reorientation by external counter action or slow entry into force of a regional or international agreement (Brexit; Africa subcontinental integration – tripartite agreement); and limited improvement from bilateral trade reorientation (Canada–EU). Incomplete reorientation often occurs in contexts of information or policy uncertainty in political crises, with rapidly changing events overturning policy and strategy papers as lines of action are reviewed.

A second set of factors centre on implementation by officials and non-state actors. In sectoral trade reorientation, whilst reorientation may appear politically valuable, bringing business on board to seek new markets may not be as straight forward. Assessments of whether agreements are working may not be comprehensive or timely.

In the remaining section of the chapter some of the general factors which can influence the scale and extent to which reorientation is successful or not are discussed. First, the main reasons for failure of reorientation are loss of leader credibility, timescale, economic decline or unsuccessful external roles connected with reorientation. In the internal category, the international political influence and role of the leader is central to reorientation – influencing ideas, priorities and external perceptions of the state and its relevance. The leader (and close allies group) is also a key defining link to the implementation agencies (foreign ministry, trade, finance, development, defence) and the extent to which initiatives and ideas are communicated and followed up beyond grand rhetoric.

Second, factors related to the timescale of reorientation are particularly critical in sectoral reorientation, which has identified trade or other vulnerabilities for revision. A trade deal or wider reorientation needs to produce evident results quickly for a divided domestic public.

Third, are factors related to the failure of core assumptions and ideas, and policies. Failure of parts of a reorientation is less critical in major and mixed reorientation than sectoral reorientation. In view of the larger number of initiatives, projects and other components in full or mixed reorientation, there is greater capacity to cover up or minimise failed initiatives by setting up additional projects, switching focus or simply diverting attention. Important factors in this category include loss of diplomatic platforms and decline or loss of traditional roles. Similarly, decline of a particular role such as mediation or third world lead, cultivated as part of wider external policy aspirations, takes out an important element in the overall diplomatic orientation as a middle power. Role and acceptance are difficult to regain once lost, as international relations and leading players change. Immediacy predominates over past achievements.

In the fourth category are factors relating to the capacity of states to carry out reorientation. States and other actors become strategically vulnerable when the extent to degree of dependence on other actors appears to limit or curtail options and critical choice. Strategic vulnerability may not necessarily be evident since shifts in bilateral trade patterns tend to be incremental over a decade or more before indicators suggest dependence or become issues in domestic politics. Trade with key states and groups may remain for some time within a diversified range with imports from key partners in the 10–15% consistent with a diversified trade strategy. Counter action on trade dependencies beyond 20–25% becomes increasingly difficult. In other instances, decisions to halt strategic acquisition of port or other infrastructure are difficult in situations of increasing dependence or lack of priority.

## Conclusion

Orientation in its different forms remains a central part of how states manage their involvement in international relations. It is the vehicle for change and adjustment to problems of dependency, vulnerability, loss of options, regaining influence or resolving longstanding issues. Three main forms of reorientation can be distinguished: sectoral, mixed and full reorientation. Within failed reorientation, partial or incomplete reorientation has developed as a distinct category.

Full reorientation is rare in contemporary diplomacy. It is largely a product of the collapse of communism at the end of the cold war and subsequent switching into western economic and security blocs. The other main cases – Sweden and Finland's membership of NATO, and Brexit are driven by core security concerns and, for the UK, exiting an economic bloc to reorientate foreign political and economic policies. Full reorientation is a high-risk option, which carries corresponding levels of uncertainty. Exiting an economic bloc is complex and lengthy. In withdrawal, the terms of exit are critical in affecting subsequent implementation and may be unworkable in practice.

Of the three forms of reorientation, sectoral reorientation is the most widely used. It has the benefit of flexibility and carries least political risk. Its use has become more extensive in response to issues such as market loss and international economic instability. The major limitations of sectoral reorientation are availability of options and timescales. A further common problem is drift caused by lack of success or political attention shifting to other areas. Lack of apparent success invariably leads to counter assessments in favour of giving agreements more time to achieve results.

The third category, mixed reorientation, is one which has received greater attention and has expanded. Mixed reorientation is distinguished from diversification in that it involves conducting relations between two or more opposing ideological or political blocs. Mixed actor states are neither tied to one or other bloc. Foreign policy is based on exploiting the gaps and opportunities in the diplomatic space between bloc relations, as moderators or service provides. It is a risky form of foreign policy orientation, providing economic and political profile benefits.

Mixed orientation has expanded in response to the decline in US power and international instability with states which have moved into this category on a provisional or experimental basis, shifting from a longstanding or traditional ally or primary power. Its members include emerging powers and petroleum alliances, which have opened up exploratory membership of other blocs for hedging and creating long-term options in an uncertain landscape.

## Notes

1  On the breakdown of the WTO Ministerial Nairobi talks, see WT/MIN/15/DEC, para 30.
2  Fatoumata Jawara and Aileen Kwa, *Behind the Scenes at the WTO* (Zed Books, 2003) pp127–9.
3  K.J. Holsti, *Why Nations Realign* (George Allen and Unwin, 1982).
4  Holsti, ibid., p2.
5  Holsti, ibid., pp4–8.
6  Charles F. Hermann, "Changing Course: when governments redirect", International Studies Quarterly, vol. 34, 1 March 1990, pp3–21.
7  Hermann, ibid., p12.
8  See S. Jayakumar's assessment of nonalignment by the 1990s in *Diplomacy: A Singapore Experience* (Straits Times Press, 2011) p89.

9  Jerel A. Rosati, Joe D. Hagan, Martin W. Simpson, *How Governments Respond to Global Challenges* (University of South Carolina Press, 1994). Also Ryan K. Beasley, Juliet Kaarbo, Jeffrey S. Lantis and Michael T. Starr, *Foreign Policy in Comparative Perspective: Domestic and International Influences* (CQ Press, 2013). Bhagat Korany and Ali E. Hillal Dessouki updated their earlier breakthrough work in a second edition of *Foreign Policies of Arab States* (Westview Press, 1991).

10  Giampiero Giacomello and Bertjan Verbeek (eds), *Middle Powers in Asia and Europe in the 21st Century* (Lexington Books, 2020).

11  Nicholas Jepson, *In China's Wake: How the Commodity Boom Transformed Development Strategies in the Global South* (Columbia University Press, 2020).

12  Ralph S. Clem and Anthony P. Maingot (eds), *Venezuela's Petro-Diplomacy: Hugo Chavez's Foreign Policy* (University of Florida Press, 2015) esp. pp92–101.

13  See, for example, Thomas Tunstall Allcock's study of Thomas C. Mann's role in shaping the revision of US–Latin American policy during the Johnson administration in Thomas C. Mann: President Johnson, the Cold War, and the Restructuring of Latin American Foreign Policy (University Press of Kentucky, 2018). On the Kennedy period, Allcock argues that "while the new (Kennedy administration) planned its Latin American policy, the State Department had been largely sidelined...The State Department as a whole were struggling to make their voice heard in the early months of the Kennedy administration." pp38–9.

14  Gerhard Erasmus, "How AfCFTA fits into Africa's existing regional integration scheme" Tralac, 22 November 2022; EU–Africa summit.

15  See Alan Hardacre, *The Rise and Fall of Interregionalism in EU External Relations* (Dordrecht, 2009).

16  Jessica Byron, "Strategic Repositioning: Foreign Policy Shifts in Barbados and Trinidad and Tobago Foreign Policy 1990–2000", Social and Economic Studies, vol. 56, No 1/2. March 2002, pp209–31.

17  See Andrew F. Cooper and Timothy M. Shaw (eds), *The Diplomacies of Small States* (Palgrave Macmillan, 2009).

18  See Vangelis Vitalis on the dilemma of diminishing marginal returns from prioritising negotiation over implementation and promotion in New Zealand foreign policy, in Nicholas Bayne and Stephen Woolcock, *New Economic Diplomacy* (Routledge, 2017) pp200–1.

19  Holsti, op. cit., p57–8.

20  R.P. Barston, *Modern Diplomacy* 5th ed. (Routledge, 2019), on the shift in World Bank priorities to cities, pp258–60.

21  See chapter 3 on Australian revised bilateral diplomacy.

22  See chapter 12 for discussion of the role of secrecy in reorientation negotiations and provisions in agreements.

23  On Japanese sensitivities over bilateral or multilateral intelligence sharing with the US, Korea and others, see, for example, Richard J. Samuels, *Special Duty* (Cornell, 2019) pp194–203; 222. In the revised Japanese defence strategy discussed in the Japan–US 2+2 Joint Statement, Japan used the Joint Statement as part of its approach to setting out its position in a formal statement to reduce ambiguity, by including the phrase "Japan also reaffirms its determination to lead in its own defence."

24  See Nicolson on the correctness of not informing the domestic public about secret defence understandings, p78.

25  Shivshankar Menon, *Choices: Inside the Making of India's Foreign Policy* (Brookings Institution Press, 2016) esp. pp25–30, 40–53 and 73–81.

26  Menon, ibid., pp7–15, 40–53 and 73–81.

27  See Teddy Soobramanien, "The economic diplomacy of small and poor countries in the global trading system", in Bayne and Woolcock, op. cit., pp210–4.

28  The letter setting out the mandate for the newly created post of Canadian Minister of Trade Diversification is at Office of the Prime Minister, letter of 28 August 2018. www.pm.gc.ca/en/mandate-letters/2018/08/28/archived-minister-international-trade-diversification-mandate-letter.

29  See T. Hartzenberg, working paper, WTO assessment of regional integration in Africa, www.wto.org/english/res_e/reser_e/ersd201114_e.pdf. For African Development Bank, see www.afdb/Documents/Policy-Documents. See also UN Economic Commission for Africa, www.uneca.org.

30  Byron, op. cit., p222.

31  For example, Debbie A. Mohammed's assessment of Caribbean's EU–CARIFORUM EPA associative diplomacy in A.F. Cooper, op. cit., pp162–7.

32  Ministry of Foreign Affairs, Barbados, 30 May 2020.

33  Holsti, op. cit., trade diversification, pp4–5.

34  The EU–Korea FTA was signed on 6 October 2010 and entered into force provisionally on 1 July 2011. See official Journal of the European Union L127/6, 14 May 2011, p6. For Korean difficulties with other Free Trade Agreements see, for example, Yong-Shik Lee on the US–Korea agreement in Lester, op. cit., esp. pp30–5.

35  See Lester, op. cit., pp142–3.

36  See Communique 31 CARICOM Intersessional Meeting.

37  On split sites, see chapters 3 and 5.

38  For details of the shifts in trade emphasis and representation of the South Pacific Forum, see www.forumsec.org. The Forum was originally founded as the South Pacific Forum in 1971, essentially as a Commonwealth-linked body. It changed title and functions in 1991 to the Pacific Islands Forum with UNGA observer status. The evolving and contested nature of the Forum was evident in the introduction of dialogue partner agreements in 1989 with a diverse range of 18 mainly non-regional countries (Canada, PRC, Cuba, EU, France, Germany, India, Indonesia, Italy, Japan, ROK, Malaysia, Philippines, Spain, Thailand, Turkey, UK, US). Further loosening of the original Forum concept accelerated during the Doha Round in concurrent negotiations to restructure existing Forum trade agreements with neighbours (Australia, New Zealand) and bilateral trade redirection with Asia.

39  Barston, op. cit., pp130–1.

40  On risk and policy initiatives in financial crises, see Malaysian Prime Minister Mahathir's non-standard methods in the Asian financial crisis, in Dhillon, op. cit., pp55–6. On political risk and response in Indian foreign policy over border conflict, terrorist incidents and nuclear security, see Shivshankar Menon, *Choices: Inside the Making of India's Foreign Policy* (Brookings Institutions Press, 2016) pp25–30, 40–53 and 73–81.

41  For further discussion of the effect of linkage on other methods, see chapter 8.

42  See Richard Samuels, *Special Duty* (Cornell University Press, 2019) pp259–60.

43  William J. Burns, *The Back Channel* (Hurst, 2019) pp67, 112–45.

44  Paul Richter, *The Ambassadors* (Simon and Schuster, 2020) pp132–44.

45  Samuels, op. cit., pp194–203, 222.

46  Jonathan Holslag, *The Silk Road Trap* (Polity, 2019) pp100–9.

47  Yanus Varoufakis, *Adults in the Room* (Penguin, 2017) pp313–9.

48  Luuk van Middelaar, *Alarums and Excursions* (Agenda, 2020) pp107–8; Reuters 8 June 2023, 23 June 2023.

49  Paris Memorandum of Understanding (PMOU) 1982 Annual Report. https:// parismou.org/system/files/2024-07/Paris%20MOU%20Annual%20Rep ort%202023.pdf The European Maritime Safety Agency was founded in 2002 following the Erika and Prestige oil spill disasters, widening its functions as a parallel EU maritime regulation and ship inspection organisation in Europe. See www.emsa.eu.

50  Burns, op. cit., pp330–1; 356–77.

51  On the longstanding Jordan–Israeli relations see Nabil Fahmy, *Egypt's Diplomacy in War*, Peace and Transition (Palgrave Macmillan, 2022) pp80–1.

52  Maritime incidents included those targeted against exploratory operations in areas north of the Rosneft bloc, around the Vanguard Bank, off Danang (ExxonMobil, Repsol; UAE) see Petroleum Times, 13 March 2020.

53  Karminder Singh Dhillon, *Malaysian Foreign Policy in the Mahathir Era 1981– 2003* (NUS Press, 2009).

54  Dhillon, ibid., p7.

55  See Dessouki, in Korany and Dessouki, op. cit., pp182–3.

56  Clem and Maingot, op. cit., p2.

57  Dhillon, ibid., pp96–8.

58  Clem and Maingot, op. cit., pp7–8.

59  Sweden and Finland applied for NATO membership in simultaneous letters, 18 May 2022, becoming full members on 4 April 2023 and 7 March 2024, respectively.

60  See www.government.se/government-policy/migration-and-asylum. The European Commission and Swedish Council presidency hosted the International Donors Conference on relief support for Turkey, 20 March 2023.

61  See Prime Minister Boris Johnson's speech at the Munich Security Conference, 19 February 2021.

62  Compare with the UK Labour government's defence position in the Strategic Defence Review, 17 July 2024 on NATO first doctrine.

63  The UK signed an accession protocol to the CPTPP on 16 July 2023. For details of the conditions to be met by the UK and CPTPP members, see Section IV Final Provisions in Article 21.

64  See www.dfat.gov.au/trade/agreements/in-force/cptpp/comprehensive-and-progressive-agreement-for-trans-pacific-partnership.

65  UK–Australia–US Defence Cooperation Agreement 2022.

66  Trade and Cooperation Agreement (TCA) UK–EU 30 December 2020, TS No 8 (2021) 30 April 2021. Shortened forms of treaty title are used in this and subsequent references.

67  United Kingdom treaties are published in the treaty series which includes bilateral treaties (country series), treaties for which the United Kingdom is a depository, and multilateral treaties published in the miscellaneous series. The treaty series also publishes other technical documents such as mutual recognition agreements (marine equipment standards; veterinary standards; meat certification; plant disease control, (e.g. UK–USA Marine Equipment agreement (CS USA No 4 2019, 18 February 2019) and a general conformity assessments agreement (CS USA No 5 2019, 12 March 2019). Conformity assessment agreements were

not reached in a number of critical areas such as fisheries in the EU–UK Trade and Cooperation Agreement, December 2020), discussed in chapter 6. The texts of agreement and explanatory memorandum are published separately by a number of individual ministries and are a useful check on entry into force and locating some informal MOUs. Treaties laid before Parliament include new agreements as well as amendments to earlier instruments. For further discussion of MOUs see Anthony Aust, *Modern Treaty Law and Practice*, 3rd ed. (Cambridge University Press, 2013 ) esp. pp40–42 and 46.

68  UK–Japan Agreement for a Comprehensive Economic Partnership (CS Japan No 1 2020).

69  UK–Singapore Free Trade Agreement (CS Singapore No 1 2020).

70  UK–Ghana Interim Trade Partnership Agreement (CS Ghana No 1 2021). The EU treaty style of "stepping stone agreements", which indicate partial scope, was copied over into UK bilateral agreements because of time constraints, e.g. UK–Cote d'Ivoire Stepping Stone Economic Partnership Agreement (CS Cote d'Ivoire, No 1 2020) adding to the new UK mix of widely titled bilateral instruments in its bilateral portfolio.

71  Framework agreements have been used as stop gap measures particularly where negotiations are complex, linked to other issues or negotiations and are domestically sensitive. They are particularly weak forms of international instrument, with high risk and probability of being bypassed or failing to reach substantive later agreement, with longer term impact on bilateral relations. Framework agreements used in the UK reorientation included the UK–Faroes Framework Agreement on Fisheries (UK–Faroe Islands No 1 2020) and UK–Norway Framework Fisheries Agreement (CS Norway No 1 2020). In both instances the UK failed to reach bilateral mutual access agreements as a result of differences over access fees (UK EEZ access), species and quotas. An indirect effect of failed negotiations to implement framework agreements is to increase pressure on weaker or smaller parties to move to unilateral measures. Framework agreements tend to facilitate unilateralism.

72  The concept of ensuring trade continuity was carried over into the titles of several of the bilateral trade agreements, e.g. UK–Canada Agreement on Trade Continuity (CS Canada No 1 2020); UK–Mexico Continuity Agreement (CS Mexico No 1 2021).

73  Partial or interim arrangements, include the UK–Switzerland Temporary Agreement on Services Mobility (CS Switzerland No 2 2021); UK–Indonesia Voluntary Partnership Agreement on Forest Law Enforcement, Governance and Trade (CS Indonesia No 1 2019). The limitations of the Indonesian voluntary agreement were partly the result of restrictions on treaty-making in the transition period prior to formal departure from the EU. It is also notable that in some agreements, the technique of leaving gaps or incomplete provisions for future negotiation reflected, on the UK side, time pressures and lack of settled policy on issues such as fisheries import regulations and competition law. See, for example, UK–Egyptian Agreement establishing an association (CS Egypt No 1 2020) (Article 14 fisheries); Article 34 (2) competition law; Protocol 4 (rules of origin criteria).

74  For further details on UK free trade agreements concluded after Brexit, see UK trade agreements in effect at www.gov.uk/guidance/uk-trade-agreements-in-effect.

75  See chapter 4.

76 Windsor Framework, CP 806, 27 February 2023.
77 For example, the UK deposited an instrument of accession to become a party to the FAO agreement dealing with measures to counter illegal and unrecorded international fishing (Port State Measures Agreement, PSMA). See FAO COFI 34th Session on Fisheries for background on the parties to the agreement. The Russian Federation deposited an instrument of ratification of the PSMA on 24 February 2021 at a virtual meeting between the Russian Federation Permanent Representative to FAO and UN Agencies in Rome and the FAO Director General. See also www.fao.org/about/meetings/Council/documents.
78 The UK became the sixth contracting party to the North East Atlantic Fisheries Convention (NEAFC) on 7 October 2020 (NEAFC Press Release) and seventh contracting party to the North Atlantic Salmon Fisheries Organisation (NASCO).
79 International Sugar Agreement (1992) (MS No 30 2019); International Grains Agreement (1995) (MS No 31 2019).
80 Headquarters include International Maritime Organisation, North Atlantic Salmon Conservation Organisation and Northwest Atlantic Fisheries.
81 See WTO Trade Policy Review of Mexico, UK Statement by Ambassador Simon Manley, 5 October 2022. Further details on the WTO Review of Mexico are at www.wto.org/english/tratop_e/tpr_e/tp529_e.htm.
82 The problem of finding a means for delivering UK language training projects at ASEAN regional level, rather than bilaterally, was addressed provisionally in a British Council paper, not eventually followed up. See British Council Concept Note "UK-ASEAN Partnerships and Exchanges Baselines", 27 November 2020.
83 The US–ASEAN Smart Cities Partnership (USASCP) was launched in 2018 by the Department of State, a US multi-agency project involving the Departments of Transportation, Commerce, National Science Foundation, Center for Disease Control, universities and private sector, with ASEAN counterparts, to promote sustainable ASEAN city projects. The USASCP is also linked to the US Smart Cities Business Innovation Fund (BIF), providing finance at subnational level for projects such as bioseaweed packaging, solar panels and hydrologic monitoring. See www.state.gov/u-s-asean-smart-cities-partnership-usascp-sharing-expertise-between-cities-to-benefit-the-people-of-asean/. See PRC counter diplomacy via press release on Singapore and Shenzhen Drive Smart City Collaboration, Singapore Ministry of Communications and Information, 14 December 2023.

**Chapter 2**

# Time as method in diplomacy

## Introduction

Elements of time are found in most diplomatic action. Time features across a range of diplomacy from setting or adjusting goals, in the conduct of negotiations and breaking deadlock, through to the use of various forms of time-related methods in coercive action. It is a key element of statecraft which, other than perhaps the use of time as a method in crisis, is generally under-studied. The central purposes of time in diplomacy are the promotion and protection of interests. As part of statecraft, time can be distinguished as cooperative or coercive action. The precise mix within and between these categories will of course vary according to style and general level of cooperation or tension in the international system.

This chapter is concerned with the use of time in managing external relations, negotiation, time-related provisions in treaties, management of information and as strategic manoeuvre. The chapter will also introduce the idea of counter methods to show opposition or circumvention as part of parallel or counter diplomacy. The final parts of the chapter pick out some of the factors suggesting the greater use of time-related methods in diplomacy.

## Managing external relations

In managing external relations, time is used for a variety of purposes built around promoting and protecting interests. These involve questions of timing – the appointment of an ambassador, when to commence talks, reschedule inbound or external visits, extending technical assistance agreements or transport agreements, which are standard areas involving decisions on the most suitable or appropriate points at which to act. The timing of a visit or when to open talks for a bilateral trade agreement with a major ally may be convenient and necessary for one party but not for a

DOI: 10.4324/9781003204039-3

new administration reshaping and reworking multiple issues in its external policy. In most cases the window of decision opportunity decreases over time and the corresponding costs of delay increase, as other negotiations or issues compete to command attention.

In these instances, the task of diplomacy is to smooth the impact of rebuff or indications of going to the back of the queue in trade talks. In other cases, such as particularly sensitive issues with consequences of broader impact on bilateral or multilateral relations, difficult decisions may involve recalling a diplomatic representative or ambassador, deciding when to not attend events, rescheduling conferences and summits or, more fundamentally, severing diplomatic relations.

## *Wait-and-see strategies*

The scheduling of bilateral meetings, for example, at ministerial or summit level, can be used as a method of introducing uncertainty and increasing pressure on an adversary.[1] It can become an identifiable feature of diplomatic style as part of a wait-and-see strategy used extensively, for example, in Chinese diplomacy to maintain a superior bargaining position. Wait-and-see strategies give flexibility, making it possible for surprise moves and flanking diplomacy. Carefully timed inbound visits can be used by adversarial states to gradually weaken or erode an opposing alliance or coalition by visits, keyed into alliance or domestic disaffection. For the asymmetrical state, the inbound visit may have other purposes, such as normalising trade or political relations after a period of punitive sanctions. Difference in purpose opens the possibility for erosion strategies. Withholding bilateral meetings offers several interpretations over intentions and, for the withholding state, the possibility of bidding up the agenda.

## *Non-attendance, initiatives and timing*

Withholding confirmation of attendance at a multilateral conference has the effect at one level of turning the issue into a kind of speculative journalistic guessing game. At another, it is indicative of disengagement from bilateral or collective international relations and order, which has become a marked feature of contemporary diplomacy.

The underlying purpose behind non-attendance of head of state/government or other senior government representative is to focus attention on the absent delegate, elevating the significance of their decision to attend or not.[2] The increased use of non- or nominal attendance is now one of the important changes in diplomatic methods and has become a built-in feature of the approach of a number of states, regional organisations, international institutions, CEOs of corporate actors to regional and multilateral conference diplomacy.

Decisions at bilateral level over when to normalise relations with a longstanding adversary are especially domestically sensitive. These cases are generally infrequent. Dealing with sudden reversal, breakdown or failed initiatives is now increasingly common. It is necessary to respond in these circumstances with a face-saving formula, temporary measures or alternative deal to compensate for loss of face and to minimise damage or loss of prestige.[3] Set speeches are used not only to outline views on change but also to implicitly put time pressure on allies or opponents to change or revise policy. Obama's landmark Cairo speech outlining future middle east policy put considerable pressure on the Netanyahu government to respond.[4]

The use of initiatives is a further important area which contributes over time to a recognised role as conflict manager, drafting specialist or mediator. Mounting and promoting initiatives of these types is perhaps one of the more difficult methods in diplomatic practice. Finding the right moment at the margins of multilateral or plurilateral meetings to promote ideas or services requires opportunity.[5]

In other instances, mounting or reviving an initiative may run up against alternative proposals or domestic constraints in other regimes. Finding the appropriate timing for initiatives to revive a nuclear production control agreement or international weapons inspection access may have limited or no success for a considerable period.[6]

## Defensive diplomacy: when things go wrong

Defensive diplomacy has been a traditional method employed by foreign and other ministries to defend or limit damage. It may be used to buy time; put together a holding position, divert or distract. The underlying rationale is the protection of a particular action or policy and forestalling or limiting damage to the states' international image.

Defensive diplomacy essentially relies on four principles: repetition of counter narrative; speed and anticipation; replacement; and compensation. Replacement is used here in the sense of finding another deal or agreement to offset loss of contract or negotiations failure. Compensation strategies are lengthy and perhaps more opportunistic. Essentially these rely on dividing responsibility for conflict or spreading causality in order to influence settlement formula (e.g. the Ukraine grain deal and Russian co-deal on fertiliser exports).[7]

### The main uses of defensive diplomacy

Defensive diplomacy is used mainly in three areas: protection of national image, leader defence and damage limitation. In the first of these, management has become increasingly more difficult. The pace of diplomacy has altered with changes in communications, with the prospect of almost simultaneous critical political attacks from external sources, foreign media, disguised states and other actors. The expansion of potential sources of adverse data, such as economic forecasts, statistical projections, reports of UN bodies and investigations of international accidents adds to the threats to image and pressures of compliance reporting which have become standard instruments of multilateral organisations.

An early leader in widening compliance reporting beyond insurance and commercial risk, the International Maritime Organisation (IMO) introduced inspection of vessels for flag state compliance with maritime safety regulation, and extended inspection into marine accidents, environment and international maritime labour compliance with international conventions.[8] Management is complex in view of the volume of shipping registration, emphasis on quality compliance, charter parties and beneficial owners.

In some instances, the causes of accidents may take some time to determine or, in worst case scenarios, remain unresolved but political pressure for resolution, as in the loss of Malaysian airliner MH370 increase in relation to the pace of investigation.[9] Improving safety records is lengthy, during which states with bad compliance records remain members of regional or international institutions, finding it difficult in the short term to shake off adverse tags.[10]

In environmental diplomacy, categories of risk, for example, over high involvement in wildlife trafficking and poor enforcement have been developed to increase pressure and speed up compliance by threat of commercial sanctions for non-compliance. In response, states with poor records have resorted to protecting their image by building allies using definitional diplomacy to redefine categories to limit or avoid receiving adverse classification. Some have responded in varying degrees by improving data returns and giving declaratory commitments on domestic measures to strengthen measures to such curtail of illegal trades or smuggling. In other cases, a small number have not responded, reduced participation or withdrawn from a convention.[11]

## Leader defence

The use of defensive diplomacy to protect leaders or heads of agencies from adverse political attack remains a key part of defensive diplomacy, linking protection of national image and damage limitation. Support for a particular foreign leader might be politically controversial domestically but the best available to support a foreign policy or for economic access.[12] In other instances, linkage may sometimes be misjudged, as in whether to attend or not a high-level diplomatic event, the effect of non-action in crisis, and decision to prioritise a domestic issue or single foreign policy event over a wider set of initiatives. For example, the non-attendance of Xi at COP26 misjudged the short-term effect this would have on perceptions of Chinese leadership and linkage between the elements of national image and policy participation. The pre-COP26 offsetting actions by China, relying on participation in the Biodiversity convention and biodiversity aid package, were insufficient to allay some concern over non-participation.[13]

The case involving the IMF Managing Director over allegations of financial data manipulation whilst previously chief executive at the World Bank underlined the change in types of challenge.[14] The office of head of an international institution is one of the most difficult chief executive positions, vulnerable to political attack, having to appear to reach all sides and scrutiny of previous record. In addition to financial probity allegations, the IMF case underlines the issue of neutrality of international civil servants. At stake for the Bank and IMF was their reputation as multilateral institutions for independent and accurate international financial data. A further unusual feature of the case illustrating additional limits of the office, was the need for the IMF director to use of an international PR firm to act as part of the defence counsel.[15]

## Damage limitation

Damage limitation is concerned with minimising the implications or consequences of a particular event or policy. It is distinct from safeguarding or advancing the national diplomatic image in that its focus is narrower and directed generally to a particular statement, event or process. The range of methods is likely to be flexible or mixed, with the possibility in some instances of threat or coercive action, rather than quiet diplomacy or side event contacts. Loss of face from failure to secure a major agreement or arms deal needs to be offset immediately with an alternative.[16]

As part of counter action, damage limitation relies for success on fluidity and anticipation. The use of alternative conferences as arenas for publicity, setting new funds and soft power events, are intended to blunt or minimise criticism and maintain dynamism. Postponement or cancellation of an international conference or meeting is a major loss for event organiser states. As part of the response to reviving multilateral conferences post-COVID 19, the WTO switched the 12th ministerial meeting from Kazakhstan to Geneva. Kazakhstan was compensated with the chairmanship. Whilst illustrating flexibility as a principle, the case illustrates how a critical WTO ministerial meeting was chaired by a state with no significant substantive track record in current international trade negotiations.[17]

Damage limitation is used in a wide range of other foreign policy contexts such as minimising the impact of a breakdown in bilateral relations, discounting or denying secret negotiations, deflecting adverse publicity from the disclosure of sensitive commercial relations, glossing over concessions in negotiations in "bad" agreements and limiting the impact of failed policies.[18]

## Time in negotiation

In the following sections, time-based methods used in managing external relations are discussed in more detail through three areas: negotiation, implementation of agreements and coercion.

Time-based methods are evident particularly at three points in negotiations: the preface; changing momentum; and final phases.[19] The preface stage is critical for the overall shape and duration of negotiations. Decisions at this point involve the format for conducting negotiations and likely type of agreement.[20] The format may vary from relatively simple arrangements for a bilateral trade or cooperation agreement, negotiated by officials, cleared and signed off at ministerial level to complex multisector agreements.

Format issues can often be negotiated under time constraints, either to achieve a preferred negotiating format (e.g. single issues or concurrent negotiations) or to gain the upper hand over later process. Format influences the structure of talks in terms of the priorities, agenda and frequency of meetings. Securing early success at the initial technical stage on structure in negotiations facilitates the use of format for later advantage.

The loading of the agenda fundamentally affects the dynamic of negotiations and eventual outcomes. In complex bilateral negotiations formats using concurrent negotiations, the problem of maintenance of progress across all sectors arises. Therefore in concurrent negotiations it is critical, as far as possible, to minimise cross-leverage on issues in other sectors.[21] The problem is lessened for those states regularly using this method, so that elements of subheads are automatically drafted as part of an overarching commitment to undertake obligations in all sectors (trade, fisheries, electricity supply, banking services). Non-compliance or regulatory deviation in one or more sectors is compensated by provisions on immediate threat of loss of access to other sectors and provision as compensation for loss. These type of clauses have been termed "mirror clauses" in EU diplomatic practice and attempts to introduce them into inter-regional agreements (e.g. EU–MERCOSUR) have proved controversial and a cause of treaty delay.[22]

### *Changing momentum*

Momentum refers to the overall flow and pace of negotiation. Negotiations are seldom evenly distributed in terms of progress and congruence between the parties. They may be slowed or temporarily stalled on an issue or negotiation may be approaching critical points on concession. Momentum is shaped in some instances by schedules and other timetables, which set completion or renewal dates. For example, several concessionary trade and aid agreements concluded early in the new millennium between advanced states and developing countries had 20-year clauses expiring in the period 2020–5, postponing the entry effects of higher or full tariffs. Among these was the Cotonou agreement linking economically the EU and Afro Caribbean Pacific Group of States (ACP), which ran out in 2020.[23]

The start date for the renegotiation in the autumn of 2018 created considerable time pressure for the ACP in preparing a common position and having it approved at short notice to commence negotiations with a party well practised in trade agreements. Under time pressure, the ACP position departed quite substantially in the opening exchanges.[24] The ACP mandate was in fact conceded controversially by its lead negotiator, Robert Dussey (Togo, Minister of Foreign Affairs and African Integration) in preparatory exchanges with EU negotiator, Neven Mimica. Rather than the ACP mandate of one revised ACP institution, the EU format for a new agreement was framed as three separate protocols with Africa, Caribbean and Pacific rather than one single instrument covering a reformed ACP not broken into separate regional protocols.[25] The ACP mandate had been carefully prepared prior to the start of EU–ACP negotiations in extensive meetings chaired by Jamaican ambassador, Sheila Sealy Monteith but abandoned by ACP negotiators in closed negotiations in the opening meetings.

Issues of time frame occur in other cases of expiry dates such as tariff access schedules or mandates of international missions. They become focal points in negotiation around which talks may be stalled on issues such as length of data protection for exclusive ownership of pharmaceutical product license or duration of preferential treatment for particular products. Inability in a multilateral institution to agree termination of a mission may lead to the unsatisfactory situation of repeated short-term extensions, with those seeking continuation favouring short-term compromises to keep a project or mission functioning.[26]

## Multilateral negotiations: the differing role of time

In multilateral negotiations several methods are used to keep negotiations moving using standard time-based techniques for agenda management, including ensuring momentum through moving the order of items on an agenda to bring forward less controversial items. In preparatory or review phases, proposals to move an item may also be used to try and gain greater attention for an item.[27] Conversely, an agenda item can be moved in the course of negotiations to try and push it through by finding a gap in a working group agenda or plenary session to bring forward a difficult issue or lose it in detail of other discussions.

The effect is to push at the limits of multilateral consensus. Issues over which there is incomplete consensus may be opposed at a later stage or, if carried by vote or consensus, may be implemented only in a nominal manner. Opposition in final plenary is a high-risk, make-or-break move, used by China, for example, in the concluding session of COP26 to weaken language in the final draft text on the phase-out of coal.[28]

In bilateral concurrent negotiations, a time-based method relies on giving the appearance of making progress by switching to other, less difficult, areas such as promotion of bilateral cooperation and tourism.[29] This, for example, partly explains EU chief negotiator Barnier's comment during the later phases of the Brexit negotiations that he felt that, on a number of occasions, the talks were "going backwards"[30] as the EU attempted to find topics to progress the talks without making concession in too many other areas.

Momentum is frequently maintained in situations of unresolved issues by resorting to informal meetings between negotiators for "contact maintenance". The use of indirect video and Zoom-type methods has facilitated some negotiations by assisting frequency of meetings and avoiding lengthy travel. It has assisted archipelagic island states' access to remote locations or in conflicts in which diplomatic travel is difficult.[31] It removes, however, direct personal contact and changes the form of some negotiation more to that of plenary type statements. Enforced use of Zoom as a result of COVID-19 was used as an advantage by the EU to evade detailed negotiation, in order to eventually push through its contested application to the North Pacific Fisheries Commission.[32] Real-time alterations to drafting in working groups at bilateral and plurilateral level become more difficult, whilst personal exchanges within and between delegations or making real-time drafting amendments are also more difficult, with a tendency to defer items.

At a substantive level, moving talks along from structured exchanges to direct negotiation frequently involves a combination of time and procedural methods using, for example, a draft prepared by the chair. In the WTO discussions on the flagship investment agreement, Chile (as chair of the plurilateral Investment Facilitation Committee) presented a working draft of what the agreement might contain, as a basis for negotiation. This set a time frame of completing a revised text by the forthcoming WTO Ministerial Conference.[33]

Counter strategies to slow or halt negotiation of an item mainly involve time-related procedural methods to use repetitive blocking of an opposing measure by tabling contrary agenda items. The method has been used within international and other institutions by leading developing countries in debates within the WTO to protect continued provisions for, and discussion of, core LDC principles such as preferential access and special treatment for developing countries in statements, resolutions and agreements. It was particularly evident in the dispute over the post-Doha agenda in the WTO between those seeking to move the WTO into new areas such as e-commerce and investment as the lead WTO agenda, opposed by India and South Africa, supported by smaller states, who argued for keeping traditional multilateral procedures in the WTO and retaining concepts emphasising development and special treatment.[34]

Use of procedural methods described above tend to diminish in effectiveness unless supported by other methods. Indian and South African diplomacy needed greater backing, drawing on the G77 and G90 networks and Geneva-based LDC diplomatic representatives but this level of diplomatic coordination or sustained resolutions never commanded sufficient agreement or consensus as bloc G77/G90 diplomacy.

Without preparatory and ongoing networking to bring together backing, repetitive defensive diplomacy, based on defending principles and special provisions, runs the risk of attack from revisionists arguing that change is being blocked and that an organisation should adapt to rapidly changing requirements.[35] Here, weakening or splitting opposition levers a potentially major developing economy from its region or group by a combination of methods, including joint sponsorship of resolutions (e.g. EU–Nigeria, Philippines in WTO), promoting joint regional meetings and webinars and joint position papers. The last acts as an archival reference point in narratives to suggest planning, cooperation and helps to build up perceptions of role as a co-sponsor in the development of ideas.[36]

## Impasse and final phases of negotiation

The use of time-related methods is most widely seen in negotiations which are stalled, having reached apparent deadlock over several core issues. It is also a feature of negotiations which, after several rounds, are now in a make-or-break situation and are entering a final phase.

Apart from standard diplomatic techniques for breaking deadlock (drafting formula, definitions of illegal activity, traded concessions) three time-based techniques are common: deadlines; major agenda alteration (scaling back expectations); and coercive threats. First, deadlines are mainly used in bilateral negotiations between asymmetrical states (trade negotiation) or in relations in which there are high conflict of interests, risk and unpredictability. In the latter case (e.g. US–North Korea) time-based methods are principally for cover, delay or to create tension by ambiguity.

Second, in bilateral and multilateral negotiation, a common method for resuming or completing deadlocked negotiations is via substantial reduction of the agenda. For example, the classic multilateral conference on Law of the Sea dealt with two major areas holding up completion of a consensus-based package – rules for fish stocks straddling or moving between EEZs, and the regime for the deep seabed – by moving the items off the agenda for separate negotiation and later incorporation into the UNCLOS text.[37]

Third, the growing use of coercion over trade, or trade linked to political issues, is one of the important changes in contemporary diplomatic methods. It is reflected institutionally after the international financial crisis (2008–12) in assertive trade policies and resort to dispute settlement as part of intensive trade competition, trade restructuring and increasing geopolitical positioning. In EU practice it is termed trade defence. Emerging economies responded with counter action by setting up trade defence divisions within trade ministries as safeguards against trade coercion.[38]

Similar concerns are also reflected in the opposition to trade dispute provisions in bilateral and plurilateral trade or cooperation agreements. Rather than managing trade conflict through judicial procedures based on elaborate dispute settlement provisions – the rule of law approach – some trade and technical agreements simply require that disputes are handled through bilateral discussions, e.g. China, Australia, India, UAE.[39]

At a substantive level, illustrations of growing use of trade coercion are COVID 19-related vaccine supply disputes, trade access restrictions and supply chain disruption. The periodic linkage of trade through tariffs and coercive threats to non-trade disputes has become a notable aspect of changes in diplomatic methods and, above all, the functions of diplomacy. These changes suggest continued erosion of traditional notions and common understanding of the purposes and functions of diplomacy.

## The use of time in the implementation of agreements

Time-based methods feature extensively in various phases of implementation of agreements. Two in particular – delay and restructuring – are focused on in this section. The use of delay is pervasive in international relations. In this sense, time is used to protect interests rather than promote implementation.

Delay is used to block, defer criticism, contain and limit risk, buy time and convey strategic advantage.[40] Much of time-related diplomacy uses procedural and partial compliance-delaying methods to protect interests and deflect criticism of non-compliance. In multilateral and regional organisation diplomacy, criticism of non-compliance is closed down quickly by respondent states using defensive diplomacy which gives undertakings to investigate, seek information on pollution incidents or fisheries violations by vessels from the flag state, accompanied by commitments to report back on consultations with other states and organisations as appropriate. Other defensive closure techniques rely on suggesting doubts on identification, denying knowledge of a company or vessel, or non-registration in that state.

The use of time for delay and minimising demands to reopen an agreement are evident in EU–UK relations post-Brexit. EU strategy on the fisheries provisions in the TCA with the UK was based very much on using time to maximise the gains from the TCA negotiations by slowing down implementation.[41]

Establishment of joint Specialised Committees on Fisheries to decide future policy was delayed, annual catch levels were interim[42] and bilateral negotiations with the UK were made dependent on completion of other EU third-party access negotiations (Norway, Faroe Islands) instead of treating these negotiations as separate from those with the UK as the major coastal state. Talks with the UK were delayed to enable completion of the internal EU negotiations on financial support packages for member states for fleet renewal post-Brexit.[43]

On the UK side, the lack of prioritisation in securing bilateral access agreements with non-EU states immediately after Brexit, especially covering distant water Northern access for arctic cod for UK east coast vessels and blue whiting trade-offs with Norway and Faroes, was a critical strategic and bureaucratic failure. Lack of contingency planning and tendency for last-minute, short-term decision making within the UK fisheries bureaucracy and at ministerial level, resulted in loss of traditional UK distant water grounds. The failure to reach bilateral agreements with Norway and Faroes created a negotiating vacuum, which prompted further Norwegian and Faroes unilateral action on quotas.[44]

These examples offer a valuable insight into how time is used in implementation to protect interests but also show conversely how diplomatic space is lost through lack of policy, contingency planning and bureaucratic support. These cases also illustrate the need in access negotiations to handle concessions imaginatively, accepting some loss in order to cut a deal for longer-range benefit to retain a distant water capability, rather than a narrow rules-based species approach.[45]

In other aspects of the EU–UK TCA, EU strategy was again largely successful, with only marginal adjustments to the TCA. Central to not reopening the TCA with the UK was the deployment by the EU of various delaying methods (slow response to calls for revision, legal arguments to justify inaction – good faith, keeping commitments – and media leaks to project the third party as unreliable). The linking of European energy access and resource (fisheries) access based on compliance was an ever-present factor in clashes over resources.

EU strategy muted and deflected calls for change. Long-running deflection strategies tend to benefit from domestic factors in an opposing polity. In this instance, EU delaying strategy benefitted from disintegration within the UK government post-Johnson, change of government in the UK to Labour and piecemeal UK concessions, in response to an EU minimalist strategy of avoiding reopening withdrawal issues and safeguarding the gains of the BREXIT negotiations. Delay strategies benefit above all from competing agendas and the diversionary effects of regional and international instability and subsequent corresponding dilution of Brexit through the reorientation to improved bilateral relations with France and acceptance of Commission proposals for partial revision of the Northern Ireland Protocol.[46]

## Case example of multilateral negotiations: reforming climate and the UNFCCC

The following example – the UK presidency of the COP26 climate negotiations – shows four methods used by the UK to promote reform: parallel diplomacy, scheduling, media and agenda format, to bring greater pace and focus on climate implementation. The case is also used to show the methods used in the UNFCCC-led counter diplomacy to revert to traditional COP agendas.

Multilateral conference diplomacy is based on accommodating multiple agendas. The compressed nature of multilateral conferences, packing large agendas into limited time places considerable challenges on maintaining consensus. Issues over how best to present multiple national statements at plenary sessions and purpose of thematic side events, so that all interests are seen to be included are recurring problems. How to build into the decision-making leader positions and turns these into policy and commitments has presented similar challenges. The UNFCCC secretariat's basic approach to managing these issues used the standard UN high-level segment formula in which leaders are scheduled merely as an event on a crowded calendar, competing with other particular committees, side events and group meetings, rather than cutting back and positioning the leaders in a central policy role. The paradox of the all-in NGO-led approach is that it creates a large-scale event at the expense of engaging critical policy leaders.

The COP26 institutional reforms under the UK presidency moved multilateralism more towards an à la carte approach to managing complex environmental problems. This format in effect results in two agendas: the leaders' agenda and the UNFCCC bureaucratic agenda for the COP. The latter UNFCCC approach relies on stylised agenda items such as election of officers, receiving reports, definitions of damage, matters relating to finance and reviews.[47]

In contrast, the UK initiative attempted to transform the UNFCCC format in three respects: front loading COP26 with a substantive leaders' summit; the Breakthrough Agenda[48] based on a rolling list of critical sectors to achieve required climate reduction (e.g. phase out coal, energy, transportation fuels) which governments could select and make public commitments to, and additional financial support for selected climate "pioneers". Central to the reform was altering the scheduling and function of the COP summit as quickly as possible in response to the lack of leadership on climate. The summit would become the main executive agency in this strategy, brought to launch the conference and oversee the New Agenda.[49]

The aim of the Breakthrough Agenda was to speed up the process of securing actual commitments from key actors to achieve a reduction of 1.5°C. It was to be the fulcrum of climate change rather than the UNFCCC process. In this sense, reform was to be achieved by shifting institutional responsibility from the UNFCCC to a wider set of supporting organisations such as IAEA, IRENA and other institutions, which had direct responsibility for promoting change in their areas of responsibility and would report to the summit. These were bold and high-risk moves directed at major climate players, backed by financial project support to selective developing and emerging economy actors.[50]

At COP26 around 40 states signed up for the key sectors, making the approach, in effect, plurilateral rather than multilateral, built around a core founding group which was not dissimilar to the plurilateral small group, rather than the multilateral approach being developed in the battle within the WTO to create a new post-Doha agenda, which split advanced states and many less developed countries.

Overall, these three strands were conducted as parallel diplomacy to the UNFCCC secretariat-led official daily COP programme. Relations between the UK and UNFCCC secretariat during the COP26 were at best uneasy. The separate UK[51] and UNFCCC reports issued at the end of conference give a sense of the diplomatic tension between the two approaches.[52]

## *The importance of COP26 in the reform of the UNFCCC*

The COP26 case study is important as an example of the difficulty in implementing reform or major change in institutions established under multilateral conventions. Many of the ideas underlying the UK initiative under its COP presidency were not subsequently carried through.

The UK initiative responded to increasing national and international concern over the slow implementation of the Paris climate agreement. In the UN, the similar dissatisfaction of Secretary-General, António Guterres, is reflected in his rare public criticism of climate process commitments on climate reduction from member states. Guterres used his political capital independently of the UNFCCC to try and drive states to make greater commitments by creating separate Climate Action Summits.[53]

The reasons why the UK reform initiative was not carried over into subsequent UNFCCC COPs lie in three sets of factors. The first is the tendency for reversion to occur in response to gaps or failure of an agreement. In the case of the Paris climate agreement, the emphasis therein was creating a framework of obligations rather than address institutional aspects of implementation, which meant that the Paris structure quickly reverted on ratification to the existing UNFCCC institutions and processes, rather than enter into a further round of lengthy negotiations to build new institutions to implement the Paris agreement. Climate issues were pushed back into a framework which was heavily bureaucratic and compartmentalised and had very limited previous success, producing road map after road map in various negotiating rounds prior to Paris.

A second important factor relates to the impact of the rotating presidency on climate policy direction. In those organisations which use rotation, the effect frequently is to introduce into the conference orientation particular issues, arrangements and guests favoured by the incoming head of conference. Many of the fundamental ideas in the UK reform concentrated on a few critical issues and were radically altered in subsequent COPs, shifting the COP agenda to thematic groupings such as civil society, agriculture and the centrality of water. Each change of presidency brings in a new set of policy issues and priorities.

A third set of factors stem from what might be termed the institutional style of the UNFCCC process and secretariat. Style influences how an organisation is run and the selection of priorities and framing of policy. The style of the secretariat is heavily bureaucratic (reports, subsidiary bodies, plenary meetings, decentralised sub committees) rather than innovative or driving change. The role of Executive Secretary has receded from visible association with policy and promoting initiatives after the Copenhagen crisis, to coordination and reporting on individual COPs.

Following ratification of the Paris agreement, the UNFCCC framework quickly reverted to its pre-Paris meetings structure of individual negotiating committees and decentralised working groups, which characterise a technical organisation dealing with parts and detail, but which are being driven by charismatic climate leadership to push the boundaries of policy and change and to take on risk.

The UNFCCC secretariat drew on the UN drafting styles and many of the UN General Assembly procedures, emphasising the centrality of the secretariat as event manager, with a single agenda for the COP reasserted after the dual agenda of the UK COP26 presidency. The details of this type of approach were channelled by the secretariat through the liaison meetings with the new COP27 and subsequent presidency, to reassert the UNFCCC perspective in the climate diplomatic discourse.

At leader level, summits after COP26 were reintroduced not as policy summits but more as theatre events with short-timed speeches modelled on UN General Assembly and high-level event lines. No hard copies of leader statements were available during the plenary, except subsequently on the UNFCCC website. The effect of reducing leader input was to enhance the decentralisation of the COP process, made-up multiple subevents and agendas. The UNFCCC moved on from the Glasgow reform back to its standardised event format, coordinated and choreographed by the Secretariat. The event aspect attracting over 70,000 participants and 140 countries was further underlined by two features: the continued transformation of high level events at the UNFCCC, originally intended to facilitate contact and policy at head of government or senior level, into several hundred side events; and, related to that, the absence of key primary powers and other leaders at the COP, symbolising disengagement as a continuing feature of contemporary diplomacy. The absence of core leaders continues to weaken approach and outcome. The case for a new, narrowly defined climate treaty remains.

## Time as method in strategic manoeuvre

Strategic manoeuvre is the use of diplomacy and other instruments for the acquisition or denial of critical assets to increase diplomatic space and long-term strategic aims. Critical assets include ideas, personnel, resources, physical locations, institutions, ports and transportation systems. Critical strategic assets can be defined as assets which are obtained from a sole or limited sources essential for production or services not easily substituted or replaced, where absence would impair or prevent specific core operations. Strategic assets are essential for the continuation of key facilities and contribute to very significant advantages in economic and military capabilities.

Strategic manoeuvre has been a traditional element in diplomatic statecraft as part of defence diplomacy. In this context diplomacy is concerned with the development of alliance and military cooperation at bilateral or regional level through liaison with host counter parts, contact networking, negotiation and secret diplomacy.

As part of the changing scope of trade in economic diplomacy and geopolitics, strategic manoeuvre has become more extensively used as method in economic statecraft. Interesting aspects of this are changes in agency (e.g. the greater use of corporate infrastructure actors as diplomatic actors and port diplomacy in the BRI) and development of different genres of strategic manoeuvre.

Other related changes in methods include use by external actors of domestic expatriate entrepreneurs in strategic manoeuvre deals as go-betweens and lobbyists linked to host domestic political parties. The extension of linkage via expatriate business groups has also been used in counter diplomacy against a host government and to undermine domestic groups opposed to an adversarial actor.

Strategic manoeuvre is shaped by combinations of the following principles:

- Surprise
- Identification and exploitation of vulnerability
- Flexibility for asset acquisition with primacy for economic interests
- Incremental movement as necessary to gain operating control
- Short-term action for long-term strategic gain
- Flanking diplomacy for blocking or access advantage

- Active covert identification of opportunity gaps
- Acquisition and denial
- Adjust rapidly to adverse counter diplomacy

Examples of strategic manoeuvre diplomacy:

- US–UK–Australia nuclear submarine agreement (strategic advantage and counter-carrier denial)
- Nord Stream 2, Russia–Germany (energy crisis, western European vulnerability)
- White Nile Dam project, Ethiopia (counter diplomacy, asset denial)
- Norway–Russia Barents Sea Fisheries (flanking operation for strategic access, impacting on other allocation agreements)
- China's application for CPTPP membership (counter diplomacy and as denial operation)
- Ukraine conflict–Kursk expansion (counter diplomacy; escalation)

## Developments in time-based methods

Time and distance factors have come together to raise further concerns over the continued viability and utility of the concept of large single-subject UN conferences such as cities, habitat and information. The lessening of willingness to travel to long-distance or remote venues is a post-COVID 19 factor affecting some UN and other multilateral institutions practices such as the WTO switch of the delayed ministerial meeting from Kazakhstan to Geneva.

Important changes in time-related methods in negotiations have followed as a result of dissatisfaction over the failure of consensus-based multilateral diplomacy on subjects such as agreeing the post-Doha agenda and the urgency of an effective agenda for implementation of the Paris agreement.

The concept of consensus rule-making is being eroded by the switch to plurilateral procedures in some multilateral fora. Plurilateral approaches have been used, for example, in environmental diplomacy to push through action agendas on climate change as plurilateral initiatives through Paris, UNFCCC and COPs. Whether these are sustained by rotating presidencies limits the scope and effectiveness of non-consensus-based approaches.

Changes in economic diplomacy using time-based methods have been influenced by uncertainty over reorientation in economic and military alliance groupings and growth of primary power conflict. Strategic manoeuvre has developed as a more widely used method.

Greater trade conflict has been matched by rival competitive moves to conclude quickly bilateral and inter-regional agreements. Agreements have been marked out as in principle to stake claims and protect from competition.

Membership application is used for the strategic blocking of rivals and expansion of influence into large regional trade blocs. Overall, the growth of trade tension has probably been the most significant factor in introducing very significant changes to several core methods, contributing to further fractionalisation of international relations.

## Conclusion

The role of time as method in diplomacy has generally been addressed from the perspective of crisis. Relatively little attention has been given to how time is used in non-crisis contexts. Time, in fact, is used in a wide variety of non-crisis contexts which illuminate and give dimension to elements of diplomacy we often do not consider, giving a much richer understanding of the nuances of diplomacy. Many time-based methods tend to be used for negative purposes such as blocking or delay.

In this chapter, time has been discussed through four areas: managing external relations, negotiation, implementation and strategic manoeuvre. In the management of external relations, defensive briefing has become much more important. This is partly because of the expanding content of diplomacy involving different "domestic" agencies, secrecy and the diminishing ability of ministers to coordinate or fully oversee a constantly expanding range of international relations. The general scope of defensive diplomacy covers three areas: protection of national image, defensive communications to support the leader and damage limitation. The latter is a continuous function, concerned with mitigating or diverting attention from failure.

In negotiations, trade coercion features especially in disputes in which asymmetrical powers are put under time pressure to conclude an access agreement. Time is used to create market pressure (e.g. high tariffs) to achieve changes of attitude to favour external party proposals, or to dissuade another state to reconsider membership of current adversarial coalition.

In respect to implementation, time-related methods are used extensively by adversarial and external powers for delay, diversion and avoidance of multilateral commitments. The case study of COP26 illustrates the downside to rotating presidencies as agendas switch, reversion to earlier UNFCCC processes as a rejection of reform and counter diplomacy by the UNFCCC Secretariat to regain control over the format of annual UNFCCC Conferences of the Parties to the Climate Convention.

Finally, the chapter has highlighted important shifts in methods with the use of strategic manoeuvre. It is an established method, which is now more frequently part of diplomacy, relying on offensive action and surprise rather than delay, blocking action or damage limitation. For effectiveness, strategic manoeuvre is frequently linked to other offensive actions, including denial and flanking diplomacy, raising risk and marking shifts in the levels of conflict.

# Notes

1 www.Whitehouse.gov/21/09/21/remarks-b;  www.uk.usembassy.gov/readout-of 22 September 2021.

2 *Financial Times*, 5 October 2020.

3 https://greekreporter.com/greece/ 18 October 2021.

4 Following Obama's speech in early June 2009, the Israeli prime minister set out his conditional two-state policy re. Israel and Palestine in the Bar Ilan speech on 14 June 2009. See Barack Obama, *A Promised Land* (Viking, 2020) pp629–34; see also Nabil Fahmy, *Egypt's Diplomacy in Peace and War* (Palgrave Macmillan, 2020) pp186–7 on domestic Egyptian factors.

5 See Nabil Fahmy on the intense Egyptian diplomatic campaign to counter Ethiopia's Grand Renaissance Dam project, in *Egypt's Diplomacy in Peace and War* (Palgrave Macmillan, 2020) pp140–5.

6 On resumption of the Iran nuclear negotiations.

7 Russia withdrew from the grain deal on 17 July 2023. The UN Secretary-General attempted to keep the grain deal alive in proposals on 30 August 2023 https://news.un.org/en/story/2023/07/1138752.

8 R.P. Barston, *Port State Control: Evolving Concepts*, in Harry N. Scheiber (ed.) *Law of the Sea* (Brill Nijhoff, 2000).

9 See Australian Safety Transport Bureau Report AE-2014-054: Technical assistance to the Department of Civil Aviation Malaysia in support of missing Malaysia Airlines flight MH370 on 7 March 2014 for details of Australian search missions.

10 The IMO played a leading role in the introduction of procedures for assessing compliance with international maritime safety and environment codes and conventions. It set up the Flag State Committee and promoted regional port state control.

11 See, for example, the Convention on the Control of Endangered Species (CITES), 71st Meeting Standing Committee, 16 August 2019, para 9.

12 On the 2013–4 Sudan crisis and US Secretary Rice's support for Kiir, see Elizabeth Shackelford, *The Dissent Channel* (Public Affairs, 2020) pp183–4.

13 The WTO rescheduled the 12th ministerial meeting from Kazakhstan to Geneva. COP15 of the Convention on Biological Diversity was scheduled for October 2020 and was postponed twice. Rescheduling was affected by disputes over funding of sessions, format and the need to hold an emergency session on the CBD budget. An online meeting was eventually held 11–15 October 2022 from Kunming and an in-person, second-part meeting resumed in Montreal, at CBD HQ, 7–19 December 2022.

14 "Data scandal heightens IMF identity crisis". *Financial Times*, 27 October 2021.

15 *New York Times*, 1 October 2021.

16  www.ejiltalk.org/an-international-law-assessment-of-the-collective-self-defe nce-clause-of-the-2021-treaty-on-the-establishment-of-strategic-partnership-of-cooperation-in-matters-of-defence-and-security/. Nicholas Tsagourias and Constantine Antonopoulos, 28 October 2021.

17  www.wto.org/english/news_e/news21_e/news21e.

18  See Paul Sharp, *Diplomacy in the 21st century* (Routledge, 2019) pp49–53, 120–3.

19  R.P. Barston, *Modern Diplomacy* (Routledge, 2019) pp55–64, 66–9, 80–6 on the Brexit negotiations with the EU on early phases and framing the structure of the negotiations.

20  Michel Barnier, *My Secret Brexit Diary* (Polity, Cambridge, 2021) pp46–7.

21  Barnier, ibid., p60, stressing the need for his negotiating team to strictly adhere to the principle of parallelism (even progress in key sectors, no sector trade-off concessions).

22  Barnier, ibid., ruling out trade-offs on energy and fisheries, p345. The TCA reflects this position, by introducing concepts of balancing and judicial compensation for non-compliance, closely linking fisheries compliance to continued access to EU electricity networks.

23  For the text of the Cotonou agreement see Partnership Agreement 2000/483/EC, OJL 317.12.2000, pp3–53.

24  See ACP–EU initial exchanges on the agenda and format of the post-Cotonou agreement negotiations, at the margins of the UNGA. For the ACP mandate see ACP /00/011/18 FINAL, Lome 30 May 2018. The main elements of the ACP mandate agreed at the special ACP Council were: single instrument (section 18); industrialisation/integration into the world economy (section 19); cross-cutting themes, e.g. capacity building (section 27). The central aim as a single agreement with three pillars was trade and investment (Tier 1), development cooperation (Tier 2) and political dialogue (Tier 3) were conceded in the first session and the negotiations moved ahead on the mandate of the EU.

25  Information on the ACP process is limited. For a view of the EU position in the negotiations see www.kas.de/en/web/mned-bruessel/single-title/-/content/insights-into-the-eu-oacps-negotiations-2018-2021.

26  See Connie Peck, in Sebastian von Einsiedel, David M. Malone and Bruno Stagno Ugarte (eds) *The UN Security Council*, pp464–70.

27  See, for example, moving the order of an item as a procedural agenda method to maximise attention, Convention on International Trade in Endangered Species of Wild Fauna and Flora, 18th meeting of the Conference of the Parties, COP18, summary record, COP18 Plen.Rec.1, para 3 (adoption of the working programme).

28  For China–US coordination using personal diplomacy of Kerry and China envoy Xie Zhenhua see *Financial Times*, 11 November 2021 and *New York Times*, 9 November 2022.

29  See Alan Hardacre, *The Rise and Fall of Interregionalism in EU External Relations* (Dordrecht, 2010) on EU–MERCOSUR negotiations, and the concept of informal contact maintenance used by negotiators to keep relations ticking despite major differences or breakdown, pp198–9.

30  *The Times*, 22 August 2020.

31  On "Zoom fatigue" see Pacific Island Fisheries Agency Annual Report, 2020–1, p29.

32  See chapter 5 on EU application to join the NPFC.

33  www.wto.org/english/news_e/news_e.htm.

34 See WTO WT/GC/M/190. The joint text of the India and South Africa challenge to so called "flexible" plurilateral procedures at WTO is at WT/GC/W/819, 19 February 2021.

35 See WT/GC/M/190, paras 10.24 and 10.25 for the arguments in favour of plurilateral negotiation procedures within multilateralism.

36 WTO WT/MIN(17)59, para 5; WT/L/1072 (Rev.1), 22 November 2019.

37 See chapter 5 on the separate UNCLOS negotiations on straddling fish stocks.

38 For EU trade defence instruments see https://policy.trade.ec.europa.eu/ enforcement-and-protection/trade-defence_en. For further details of investigations, see Special Report, European Court of Auditors.

39 See, for example, Australia, where anti-dumping cases are dealt with by the Productivity Commission, reports of the Commission and procedures, in Commonwealth Gazette No GN 39, 5 October 2005, notified to the WTO Safeguards Committee, G/SG/NI/Aus/2/Supp. 1 (16 December 2005).

40 On blocking an agenda item, see Zimbabwe's attempt to limit further discussion of resolutions on the definition of the term "appropriate and acceptable destination" (with respect to the international trade in live elephants), COP18, ibid., Plen. 3 (Rev. 1) para 44.

41 EU–UK Trade and Cooperation agreement (TCA).

42 The EU–UK Trade and Cooperation Agreement entered into force formally on 1 May 2021.

43 EU fisheries support budget post-Brexit.

44 Norway failed to reach an access agreement with the UK for 2021–2. It resulted in the collapse of the last remaining distant water fisheries from Hull, leaving the Anglo-Dutch Kirkella with no northern cod quota. Norway and Faroes set unilateral catch levels and concluded agreements with Russia in 2020–1 and 2022–3. The landing agreement with Russia was considered by the UK and EU as a breach of international sanctions.

45 UK–French fisheries clashes.

46 Windsor Agreement CP/806/2023.

47 For the UNFCCC COP26 Agenda see FCCC/CP/2021/1.

48 For the Breakthrough Agenda, see www.gov.uk>government>publications>cop Statement on the Breakthrough Agenda, 2 November 2021.

49 https://unfccc.int/cop26/world-leaders-summit, 1–2 November 2021; see https://climatechampions.unfccc.int/cop26-world-leaders-summit-statement-on-the-breakthrough-agenda/ on the Glasgow Breakthroughs: power, road transport, steel, hydrogen.

50 COP26 Finance Ministers meeting, 3 November 2021, https://unfccc.int/news/global-finance-ministers-discuss-transition-to-net-zero.

51 See www.gov.uk/government/publications/cop26-presidency-outcomes/cop26-presidency-outcomes.

52 See https://unfccc.int/process-and-meetings/the-paris-agreement/the-glasgow-climate-pact-key-outcomes-from-cop26.

53 Remarks of the Secretary-General, Climate Action Summit, 21–3 September, 2019. www.un.org/sg/en/content/sg/speeches/2019-09-23/remarks-2019-climate-action-summit#:~:text=pollution%2C%20not%20people.-,Dear%20 friends%2C,need%20to%20accelerate%20financial%20support.

# Chapter 3

# Summit diplomacy

## Introduction

Summits have now entered into a wide range of diplomacy. They feature diplomatic and other transactions, differing significantly from earlier conceptions of high-level meetings on international order. In this chapter we will look at the development and use of summits in three areas: multilateral UN summits, regional organisations and bilateral summits. The fourth and final section discusses the growth of additional types of hybrid and commercial summits.

## Background

The term "summit" traditionally had the sense of special high-level meeting. Conducted at heads of state or government level, summits were intended to bring focus to critical policy issues. Part of the original conception placed considerable importance on summits as a means of facilitating personal contacts between heads of government. These ideas drew on the wartime conferences, including Cairo, Tehran, Yalta and Potsdam; early post-1945 institution-building conferences establishing the United Nations and post-war financial institutions.[1]

In looking at how the allies might continue wartime relations in the post-war world, Winston Churchill used the term "summit" to describe future high-level conferences. Growing post-war differences between the United Kingdom seeking periodic informal conferences of leaders, the United States with its preference for regular, choreographed agendas with regional responsibilities and the Soviet preference for narrow territorial and reparations agendas, differentiated the positions of the three powers.[2]

The breakdown of wartime cooperation, conflict over post-war policy for Germany and the shift to the cold war after 1947 heightened differences over the form and use of later conferences for handling

DOI: 10.4324/9781003204039-4

foreign and security relations between the main powers.[3] The Geneva summit conferences of 1954–5 were perhaps the closest to a classical model of summit conferences as high-level vehicles for resolving territorial and other conflicts.[4] These were based on preparatory meetings at foreign minister level at which particular issues were ironed out, proposals considered and areas of agreement (or disagreement) established, laying the basis for finalisation (or not) at head of state/government level.[5]

Four criteria distinguish the summit conferences of the early post-war period: special purpose, level of participants, decision capacity, and non-routine nature. Much of the underlying sense behind the meaning and use of summits has remained.

Changes in the use of the term "summit" have been to the title, in some instances to find terms to describe bilateral or other meetings, level of participants, scope or content, and the parties involved. Some of the other changes alter the purposes of summits more towards regular meetings for managing bilateral and regional organisation relations, launching political or commercial initiatives, or business events. Other, mainly political, changes have moved summits away from earlier conceptions of resolving conflict, contributing to international stability over partial territorial or other agreements and furthering cooperative contacts, to using summits for competitive or coercive purposes.

## Categories of summits

Summits in contemporary diplomacy can be broadly broken down into four categories: diplomatic, hybrid, NGO and commercial. The latter include events which copy or imitate some of the features of diplomatic summits but are entirely commercial activities related to the sale or promotion of particular goods or services and, as such, fall outside the scope of this chapter.

Diplomatic summits, in which at least one of the parties is a state or international institution, represented at head of state or equivalent level, include bilateral, regional, plurilateral and multilateral international institutions forms. In the regional category, developments of note apart from the growth of continental sub-regional summits, are three new forms of bilateral summits – associative diplomacy between a regional organisation and single state, single state-continent and inter-regional summits.[6] Other types of diplomatic summits include unilateral host initiatives, emergency and crisis summits. The latter have been held, for example, on climate, drought, food security and marine pollution.[7]

In the diplomatic category, the definition of summit has been extended by the use of the concept of informal summit in some diplomatic practice to refer to meetings of heads of state without formality or specific agendas in order to portray and signal to closeness of relations. An example of this which reflects the pressure on heads of state/government is the now standard usage of leaders holding a "retreat".[8]

A further novel addition is holding short courtesy meetings which are termed "summits". A variation of this is the "breakfast summit", favoured in Indian, Japanese and Latin American diplomatic practice. These have expansive agendas and touch on areas of domestic and international interest.[9]

Other alterations in definition have involved avoiding use of the term "summit" by using the term "assembly" to refer to high-level meetings. A similar rationale of inclusiveness underlies UN diplomatic practice on representation, which extensively uses the term "high-level meeting" to refer to, not only heads of state/government, but a wide range of other actors such as eminent persons, senior private sector executives, NGOs and UN Champions as representatives in mixed actor meetings.[10] A variation of this is the use of the concept of a "high-level segment" in UN practice to refer to a short final section of a conference or summit which heads of state/government would attend, rather than be present during all proceedings, to make critical contributions or break deadlock.[11] A major weakness of this concept is that it detaches the leader from a clear appreciation of the framing and detailed aspects of a negotiation.

Hybrid categories of summits consist of meetings of partnerships between states, international institutions and commercial actors, or commercial actors and international institutions, to promote or develop projects and showcase commercial events.[12] The concept of hybrid summits is intended to depict the nature of the link up not as intergovernmental, or between government and international institution, but as involving ties with a commercial third party. The state component may be nominal. In this case the lead party may be an NGO linked to a state as a "disguised" state or international institution responsible for hosting an international event described as a summit.

## Purposes of summits

The traditional purposes associated with summits – governance are,[13] launching initiatives,[14] signalling,[15] security agreements,[16] and multilateral coordination.[17] The newer uses are suggested by the various forms of hybrid summit, linking states or international institutions with commercial actors in partnerships with the commercial as lead actor in the summit event. Hybrid summits also exist in essentially political form, sponsored by private actors, often linked to states, operating parallel club diplomacy by invitation, as free riders at the margins of existing international institutions and events. The rationale is off-radar private contact and alterative agendas or lobbying space. Examples include DAVOS,

Munich Security conference, Singapore conferences on regional security and Deep Seabed Mining conference events in parallel to meetings of the UNCLOS Seabed Mining authority.[18]

Commercial entities now widely use the term "summits" for commercial conferences and are included here only as a nominal category to reflect entities which imitate titles and styles of diplomatic summits but for entirely commercial purposes, further eroding the original concept of summit as a high-level political meeting conducted at leader level.[19]

Parallel diplomacy, counter diplomacy, diversion and tactical framing fall into the negative and coercive category. This category is intended to capture summits designed to track, undermine or bloc an initiative or secure narrative advantage, illustrated in the Ukraine conflict by moves to restrict western political and military support for the Ukraine. These restrictive policies reflect approaches to foreign policy which rely on counter moves (selective peace plans, reconstruction, heavy media), flanking diplomacy, coordinated media for image projection and strategies of erosion and use of flexibility to respond to political and security voids.[20]

Flexibility is essential with respect to summits in that they are particularly vulnerable to adverse domestic and external events and incidents. These can affect timing, participation or last-minute cancellation. One of the major lasting impacts of external events is from pandemics, which affect participation, scheduling and create backlogs of bilateral and multilateral conferences, which are very difficult to rearrange and may reoccur. The global diplomatic calendar is effectively blocked for considerable periods impacting on the ordering of international issues, bilateral and plurilateral meetings and more widely on multilateralism.

## UN collective governance summits

The following sections of the chapter now turn to focus on the first of the four areas, the use and development of summits within the UN system.

The UN has contributed to global governance through the evolution of ideas and regimes, the promotion of issues on the international agenda, highlighting food emergencies and, as critic, pushing for enhanced implementation of conventions in areas such as climate and sustainable development. Within the UN system, summit meetings in the narrower traditional sense are not widely used. Rather, summit meetings have been used as an auxiliary method to support the system of collective meetings based on the differentiated charter responsibilities between the Security Council, Assembly and other UN institutions and agencies.

The UN format has relied on collective meetings with wide participation at different levels and composition and various types of conferences, rather than summits. In those limited cases in which summit meetings have been used, summits have been used as a device to augment or supplement existing formats, but are not used regularly.

The authority for UN summits is normally the General Assembly and the subordinate Economic and Social Committee, through decisions and mandating resolutions. Summit meetings have occasionally been called by the UN Security Council at heads of state or government level.[21]

In addition, the Secretary-General has periodically played an indirect but important role in promoting the need for additional meetings in summit format in selected areas. That role has been enhanced by using implicitly or explicitly the reporting functions of the UN Charter which give the Secretary-General authority to garner support and promote ideas and issues.[22]

In UN diplomatic practice since 2000, five types of summits can be distinguished: single issue (e.g. food security),[23] review (e.g. UN Conference on Human Settlements Habitat II,[24] long-range goals (e.g. sustainable development goals),[25] multilateral implementation summits[26] and specialised agency summits.[27]

Single-issue UN summits are periodically held to try and refocus attention within the UN, e.g. by the FAO, on the question of widespread and acute food shortage crises affecting a large number of communities and the need for nutritional assistance. The FAO has generally operated through special conferences rather than summits but did use the summit format for the food security conference to try and shift focus and move the issue onto the international agenda rather than remain within the existing committee structure of debate.

The UN Secretary-General tried again to refocus attention on food security by calling for a food security summit during the COVID-19 crisis as part of his drive to implement the Millennium Sustainable Development Goals.[28] Initiatives such as these, whilst having some initial success, eventually decline in effectiveness as competing summits, other calls on the international agenda and domestic economic and political issues create alternative demands.

Other examples of issue summits are migration and the acute problems of Least Developed countries. They are difficult to gain collective support for and are only intermittent, with long gaps between summits. A special UN summit scheduled for 2001 on large-scale population movements was cancelled because of the 9/11 crisis. Migration was eventually elevated as a core agenda area in 2015 when the status of the International Organisation for Migration (IOM) vis-à-vis the UN was upgraded in an MOU concluded between the two organisations, giving the IOM cooperating status.[29]

UN review summits such as Habitat II face not-dissimilar difficulties. They must compete with other conferences and summits for diplomatic time and event space in the UN system and other diplomatic calendars. Conference meeting space and support language facilities for large-scale multilateral conferences is an ongoing major administrative and budget problem for international organisations, regional and other actors.

The expansion of the international community, larger non-state actor participation and the standard use of multiple sub-working groups of 50–100+ participants within multilateral conferences, in addition to plenary sessions, makes high demands on available facilities. Venue options have dwindled and become difficult to source in all formats on facility and cost grounds.

Review summits within the UN system, although important devices for refocusing on an issue and bringing together members of the international community, have declined on cost grounds and transformed into a forum format. Whilst virtual formats have been retained for some multilateral preparatory and plenary meetings to reduce costs, their effectiveness is limited by the tendency of such meetings to revert to transactional diplomacy, characterised by prepared speeches and rehashed statements of known positions. A further impact is the reduction of NGO participation and influence in virtual diplomatic meetings. NGOs are not able to mix, lobby or use interviews and media in the same way. Their virtual presence may be contested, and statements limited by procedural time restrictions.

The central difficulties of UN special issue and review summits, e.g. Habitat III[30] are securing attention and traction on reintroduced thematic issues and sustained follow up in the intervals between review summits.

A third category of UN summits is long-range goal-oriented summits. Since 2000, long-range UN goals have been set out in development summits beginning with the Millennium Development Goals (MDG)[31] and Monterrey Declaration on financing development.[32] These have formed a core agenda of successive UN Secretary-Generals. The MDG were revised in 2012 at the UN multilateral conference on sustainable development in Rio de Janeiro and reduced at the 2015 UN summit on SDG in response to concerns over the scale and complexity of the goals.[33]

A fourth form of summit, which may be termed an implementation summit, is used in the context of multilateral conventions to publicise lack of support and seek more commitments or reform coordination such as the global governance summit proposals.[34] It became a standard method used by UN Secretary-General, António Guterres, to try to improve implementation of environment and sustainable developments goals, and step up implementation of national commitments under the Paris climate convention and other agreements at special action summits. The common purposes are to obtain concrete, additional national financial and carbon reduction commitments. As Guterres put it prior to the 2019 special UN Climate Action summit in a rare public combative appeal questioning the multilateral process, "this is not a climate negotiation summit...this is a climate action summit...the ticket to entry is not a beautiful speech but concrete action."[35]

The Guterres Climate Action summit was actually made up of three summits (financial commitments, carbon initiatives and small island-state sustainable development targets) and ran at the same time as the annual UN General Assembly. The tripartite format was an interesting device, drawing on the Secretary-General's warning over the climate crisis and need to get further commitment at head of state and government level in order to put life into the stalled Paris Convention process. It made the point that the climate debate needed to narrow its scope and concentrate on a reduced core of topics if it was to make any further progress. The summit was an example of high-risk parallel diplomacy which required participation and climate commitments from all key players. It succeeded in extracting additional individual commitments but absence from the Assembly and varied participation in the separate summits continued to echo the Paris process of selective engagement.

The "Ticket to Entry" speech had perhaps a longer term impact on flagging up the limitations of the Paris Convention implementation format which had shifted back after entry into force into its pre-Convention gridlocked structures of specialist committees. Radical reform on climate required a new format and agenda to move it on from that of the annual multilateral COP event and rotating presidencies formats. At national level, the speech was used some three years later by Australian Prime Minister, Anthony Albanese, to signal Australia's shift of policy on climate.[36]

The action or implementation summit concept was curtailed by the COVID-19 pandemic, which led to the overall cancellation or suspension of in-person collective UN multilateral summits and other large-scale conferences. Meetings were instead conducted in virtual rather than in-person format, ruling out direct diplomacy. For example, the UN biodiversity summit involved some 11 hours of pre-recorded formal statements presented in video format. The use of digital formats weakened multilateral initiatives and momentum, made formal plenary proceedings lengthy and reduced the possibilities for diplomacy.[37]

Earlier forms of diplomacy are never easily regained. Rather, contemporary multilateral diplomacy is marked by conference rescheduling disputes, political use of multilateral hosting, contested agendas and location disputes. The 5th UN conference on the Least Developed Countries (LDC5) stalled because of the COVID-19 pandemic and difficulties over agenda, location and participation. The conference was mandated on the formula "at the highest level possible, including heads of state and government" and eventually split between New York and Doha.[38]

In the rescheduling of the Biodiversity convention meetings a split-site formula was used, similar to the LDC5 example, the first part in Kunming and the second in Montreal. However, a second high level segment was added to the Montreal meeting, chaired by the PRC, despite the detailed work and role of Canada during the preparatory and committee stages of negotiation and drafting. The two annual meetings of the Biodiversity convention were in effect treated as separate events, with the pandemic used by China to justify a second high level segment at the Montreal session, altering the declaration to Kunming-Montreal, rather than Montreal.[39]

The Guterres global governance reform package is an attempt to revive the role of the UN in a fragmented and contested multilateral setting using special summits, for example, on the reform of international financial architecture, and policy reform briefs.[40]

## Summits and UN specialised agencies

The use of summits in UN practice has been extended in a fifth area by UN specialised agencies, e.g. the World Bank, UNIDO[41] which have styled their meetings on specific sectors or programmes as summits. They are mixed in scope and level of participation, including governance summits on replenishment and use of World Bank IDA facilities, African economic diversification and youth summits.[42] These developments have brought variety to the idea of summits, whilst retaining the concept of special meetings to plan, coordinate and introduce innovation. They have also varied the level of participation, involving mixed groups of states, commercial actors, specialised agencies and individual actors. Youth summits continue the multilateral idea of wider involvement of young citizens in governance.[43]

## Summits and regional organisations

The continued expansion of regional and sub-regional organisations from 2000, together with splintering of blocs and regrouping, has been accompanied by increasing numbers of separate regional summits. However, the growth of summits has been uneven, with the dense web of summits developed by ASEAN contrasting with the limited summits of the Arab League and South Asian Association for Regional Cooperation.[44] Expanded agendas have raised major budgetary issues for nearly all regional organisations. Many face severe financial crisis (e.g. OAS) and serious ongoing financial short falls on budgets against assessed contributions.

The summit conferences of the Arab League have remained largely confined to meetings at high level on political issues rather than economic or financial policy, with limited subordinate support institutions. Individual members of the Arab League, however, have extensive cross-membership of African regional and sub-regional organisations, participating in summits as members or observers. Other links have been developed via bilateral trade cooperation and fisheries agreements with the EU and bilateral meetings and summits with other actors.[45]

### Setting long-range goals

Setting and driving long-range goals are two of the main functions of regional organisation summits. Major new initiatives such as the African Continental Free Trade Area and "The Africa We Want" are launched through summits.[46] The eventual signing of the African Continental Free Trade agreement took almost twenty years from the Arusha Declaration, via repeated revised road maps, target setting and eventually as a main agenda item on subsequent African Union summits.[47]

The slow path on goals and implementation reflects differing development status, opposing conceptions of integration (especially relations with external actors) and bilateral arrangements. Differences over purposes have become a recurring feature of many regional organisation, as within the EU, over such areas as ideas for closer integration based on a two-speed Europe, sanctions, arms sales to Ukraine, defence cooperation, the powers of national judiciaries and post-Brexit relations.[48]

In the African Union example noted above, cooperation through sub-regional organisations had been the principal mode of cooperation since independence, rather than at a continental level. Competing conceptions of integration in Africa were clearly reflected in the regional Tripartite Agreement and the signature of the rival African Union Continental Free Trade Agreement as a counter organisation, with a race for ratification. The Tripartite Free Trade Agreement initially led by Egypt, South Africa, Kenya and Uganda linked three of the eight regional communities – the East African Community (EAC), Southern African Development Community (SADC) and Common Market for East and Southern Africa (COMESA).[49]

### Summit agendas of regional organisations

The overall increase in volume of issues dealt with at summit level means that regional organisations are unable to complete key business at a single annual session, resulting in additional emergency or ad hoc meetings at ministerial or agency level. The European Council, for example, has more than doubled its four annual meetings, to include international summits, e.g. G7 and additional informal summits (e.g. migration, strategic planning). A further new type of summit – the Tripartite Social Summit – is a domestic summit on the EU carbon neutral economy directives, as part of Paris Climate Convention compliance run back-to-back with Council meetings, in the style of ASEAN[50].

Separate Eurozone summits for eurozone members only are also held back-to-back twice annually with Council meetings. Other short ad hoc EU Council summits are called, for example, over international incidents, sanctions extensions or Ukraine funding. The international summit category is continuously expanded by new regional grouping links such as CELAC, absorbed partly by alternating summits.[51]

Shifting from reliance on international peacekeeping for regional security and peacekeeping has led to an extensive shift in regional organisation agendas and institutions. The African Union, for example, established the AU Peace and Security Council at the inaugural Durban summit,[52] symbolising a significant enhancement of AU involvement in African regional security.

Various aspects of membership issues add to the agenda of regional organisations. Changes of membership often mean that regional organisations import security problems, shifting the agenda, defence and peacekeeping budgets. In other instances, new members may fundamentally alter the political balance of a regional organisation.

The expansion of summit agendas impacts on decision-making, moving decisions to foreign or other ministerial level, secretariat or specialist agency. Summits in this respect may become rubber stamps for deals negotiated by delegated agencies and lead members of a regional organisation. How to retain strategic control over core policy and reform institutions have been constant issues. In other areas, such as negotiations with external actors, keeping track of mandated negotiations becomes more difficult with expanded agendas and competing member interests.

The oversight function of summits relies on delegated agency and good channels of reporting between lead negotiators and mandated ambassadorial committees to foreign or other ministers on details, concessions and keeping to an organisation's agreed negotiating positions and red lines.

### ACP and the EU–Cotonou negotiations: failed oversight

The collapse of the Afro–Caribbean–Pacific position at the start of the Cotonou negotiations to revise the preferential agreement with the EU, and the failure of the ACP at ambassadorial, foreign minister and summit levels to review the opening exchanges fully, remains a classic case study in failed summit oversight.

The ACP mandate agreed at the ACP summit envisaged future links with the EU being based on the ACP as a single entity.[53] That position was, however, conceded by the ACP lead negotiator in the opening exchanges with the EU to favour the EU position of breaking up the ACP into three separate regional blocs, each with an individual protocol with the EU. The concession, in effect, meant the end of the old ACP model which linked the former colonies as a single entity, meeting at ACP ambassadorial and summit level.[54] The episode remains a controversial and largely closed area of ACP–EU relations, with limited public documents. For its part, the ACP was concerned to maintain the unity of the ACP and under its mandate retain a reformed but single entity despite differences within the group. Different considerations shaped the AU position, above all the need to keep quite separate their negotiations with the EU on a revised partnership, from the ACP–Cotonou negotiations.

The Cotonou negotiations nevertheless provided an opportunity to develop an African dimension, confirmed at the 11th Extraordinary Session of the AU Assembly, to ensure the break-up of the ACP through separate regional protocols. The African protocol would be the major piece in the future revised ACP. It left unanswered the question of how the AU would conduct relations with the African protocol members.[55]

## *Breakaway groups*

In regional organisations, accommodating different interests and mixed levels of development is an ongoing preoccupation. Shaping and securing an adequate representation of interests in summit agendas may not be sufficiently achieved to dampen dissatisfaction, separatist pressure or the search for other routes. Breakaway groups have included the OECS as a separate monetary authority in the Caribbean and the GCC as a separate grouping from the Arab League.[56]

At continental level, a common factor of concern to intermediate and larger developing members is loss of political freedom over domestic economic support policy to minimise the impact of larger trade groupings following membership of mega blocs, the balance of payments trading deficits with large external powers, and intracontinental fears of becoming swamped after tariff reduction with regional goods and cheap imports. These concerns lay behind Nigeria's ambivalent approach to the AfCFTA.[57] Similar concerns were held in ASEAN by Malaysia, Indonesia, the Philippines and Thailand over joining the CPTPP.[58] India eventually withdrew from final phase summit negotiations on the RCEP over failure to achieve adequate mechanisms on import and other safeguards in earlier negotiating rounds.

A common political concern of smaller powers in regional organisations is the feeling of being sidelined in the core summit debates on strategic priorities.[59] Dissatisfaction with the emphasis of traditional development models in the Pacific focused on a "Blue Ocean" model, revised with sustainability and environmental provisions preferred by multilateral agencies and resource powers, contributed to the splintering of Pacific states. Alternative strategies shifting to small-scale industrial promotion, moving the economies away from slogan diplomacy ("Blue Ocean") with its traditional dependence on fisheries to creating a diversified and permanent workforce favoured by Papua New Guinea and others, made little head way. The Solomon islands took the debate further and undertook a major revision of alignment.[60]


## *South–South summit diplomacy*

South–South diplomacy has mainly developed at regional and subregional levels. Regional organisations have taken on the role of promoting and developing responses to issues at regional level. At multilateral level, the axis for developing country collective development diplomacy has shifted to the G77, with the loss of *raison d'être* of the Non-Aligned Movement coinciding with the ending of the cold war.[61] The decline of the Non-Aligned Movement was accentuated by the loss of charismatic leaders from the South. However, outbreaks of severe international conflicts in Europe, Africa and the Middle East post-2000 provide contexts for regaining some of its previous relevance.

The G77 – the flagship collective institution for LDCs – has tended to become less effective for a number of reasons. Much of its focus is in New York and Geneva, based around UN agendas. G77 activity is closely tied to representation at UN committees and responding to the agendas of the UN Secretary-General in communique-style diplomacy, rather than being independently outward looking, bringing sustained strategies and coordinated programmes for LDCs. Frustration at the lack of G77 involvement in the South, energy and grain crises, and G77 rhetorical style drove India, as part of its rotating presidency in the G20, to organise the Voice of the South summit in virtual format as a matter of urgency. It found strong resonance but was only held as a single event by India.[62]

G77 institutions have remained largely unaltered since the establishment of the Group, with assembly-styled collective bodies and chapters.[63] Only one chapter is located in the developing world (Nairobi, UNEP liaison). Other chapters act as liaison offices located with UN agencies: Geneva (UNCTAD), Paris (UNESO), Rome (FAO) and Vienna (UNIDO). A G77 technical assistance committee has been added and representation in the IMF–World Bank Group meetings via the G24 established in Washington.

One of the major implications of the continuation of chapter format is that it encourages the splintering of the G77 and lack of core or integrated policies. However, the G24 financial link is the strongest technical structure within the G77 and has been important in creating technical capability, making it one of the strongest sectors within the G77's vast political and economic agendas. The establishment of summits by the World Bank on financing African industrialisation was an important reorientation by the Bank, which has facilitated greater African continental coordination and co-involvement of UNIDO.[64]

The fact that the G77 has not developed a greater international role has been influenced by several factors. One of the surprising aspects of the G77 is that it has held only three summits devoted to problems of the least developed countries.[65] Part of the reason for the limited approach lies in the absence of charismatic actors to drive ideas and policy, and chapter structures. Closely related to these factors is the continental rather than wider internationalist approach of the AU, the lead regional organisation within the G77. Finding an external role, other than inter-regional diplomacy, has remained largely unresolved for the AU.

The limitations on developing collective positions was evident in the long-running UN Doha Trade and Development Round, for an AU membership which preferred to protect interests in the detail of specialist trade product groups, rather than resolutions of the G90.[66] The inability of the AU to gain observer status at the WTO has been one of the significant factors which limited its role as an African coordinating voice on trade problems and standards issues in Geneva.[67] Admission to the G20 may not offer enough options.

A further group of factors affecting the G77 role in the South is suggested by the other forms of association in South–South diplomacy. Of these, inter-regional diplomacy post-2000 seemed to offer great potential for South–South cooperation but in practice, inter-regional link-ups such as between the Arab League and AU, and ASEAN–AU at head of state/government summit level, were intermittent.[68] Part of the reason in the League case was cross-membership of individual League members in African sub-regional organisations, which created separate lines of bilateral rather than inter-regional relations. ASEAN and the AU remained largely focused on their respective regions. Bandung was a different era and a different politics.

In terms of other South institutions which might have filled the institutional gaps in the G77 and promoted in-depth summit coordination, the ACP was broken up in the Cotonou trade preference negotiations. The successor grouping, the 79-member Organisation of African, Caribbean and Pacific (OACPS), meeting at ministerial and summit level, has found it difficult to define an international role. ACP–EU relations remain uncertain over of the status of the initialled Cotonou agreement, with ongoing differences over Caribbean offshore financial centres and immigration, and EU interest in the ACP model cooling.[69] Further EU division over trade with MERCOSUR and political relations with CELAC added to the limitations of inter-regional diplomacy as a form of diplomatic cooperation.

## Bilateral summits

Bilateral meetings and summits are the preferred method of many states for managing external relations. Bilateral summits are versatile and flexible over content, easily accommodating public as well as private agendas.

Bilateral summits are different from regional or multilateral methods in three main respects. Firstly, they have a strong personal element relying on direct face-to-face personal exchange between two heads of state generally over two or three days, without the participation of rivals or allies. This personal element is the key distinguishing feature which differentiates bilateral meetings from other methods such as meetings on the margins of events. Secondly, the level of risk is higher than in regional or multilateral formats. The focus is on the visiting leader, the agenda may not be known and the direction of the talks uncertain. Thirdly, outcomes may be significantly less than originally planned or intended in the short term, in part because of different perceptions and expectations of what the summit is intended to achieve. Bilateral summits too have a long and uncertain timeline for implementation.

Traditionally bilateral summits have been associated with meetings at head of state/government level, in areas such as security cooperation, crises, political consultation, economic agreements, normalisation and acting as a venue for direct and indirect signalling. Relations may have stalled or slipped into a backwater of cooperation. Summits are key methods used to revive dormant relations through official head of state or government visits backed by media and a raft of economic MOUs.

Saudi King Salman's visit to Indonesia in 2017, the first of its type since King Faisal bin Abdulaziz Al Saud met with President Suharto in Jakarta in 1970, was intended to rejuvenate relations in areas such as trade, tourism, pilgrimage education and SMEs.[70] No major investments followed, though there a number of subsequent smaller and intermediate projects in these areas together with Islamic religious cultural cooperation[71] confirming the implementation limits of high-level summit visits in matching cere-mony. Alterations in oil prices have been important in limiting the scope of Saudi–Indonesia relations.

## *Development of bilateral summits*

Bilateral summits have undergone development in several areas, four of which will be highlighted in this section. At primary power level, bilat-eral summits have decreased in importance following their central role in détente and arms control pre-2000. Increasing international tension post-Doha Round has affected the scope and frequency of bilateral primary power summits, changing the format to brittle direct exchanges, lengthy restatements of positions and intermittent telephone contact. Summits in reduced form have become an option in intermittently managing tri-lateral primary power relations rather than a prerequisite for successful governance. Limited bilateral meetings serve as ad hoc mechanisms for damping down political and trade tension or for mechanisms for eroding adversarial trade sanctions. The latter presents diplomacy with difficult choices over how to manage adversarial relations; whether and to what extent easing of strategic goods or other trade restrictions is likely to lead to improved cooperations or, conversely, limit transactions.

The changed nature of primary power relations is reflected in the shift to an international agenda dominated by extensive trade clashes, intensified territorial conflicts (Middle East, Taiwan, Korea, South China Sea, Ukraine) and the introduction of intractable geopolitical and commercial issues. The Ukraine war fundamentally altered the dynamics of summits, impacting on NATO and, at a global level, on other summits, conferences and commercial transactions following the imposition of sanctions on Russia.[72]

Many of these issues go beyond the scope of short heads of state summits. A Sino-America trade rebalancing agreement represented a rare albeit short-term success.[73] Most other Sino–American summits are brief meetings at the sidelines or specifically organised events which are devoted to statements of known positions, augmented by telephone calls to convey concern or dampen down incidents.

## Summits and regional organisations

Summits are used in regional organisations at bilateral and group level as methods to protect presence, competitiveness and diplomatic space. The method involves establishing and repeating annual summits, regardless of content, which become an entrenched pattern in bilateral or other relations. Established summits come to symbolise closeness of relations.

This type of approach has become a major feature of ASEAN bilateral dialogue partner diplomacy, built on the ASEAN centrality doctrine, which aims to contain potential threats posed by larger actors and ensure ASEAN has a lead role on southeast Asian geopolitics by a plethora of meetings and summits.[74] An underlying concern is fear of exclusion or irrelevance. Whether the summit as an institutional defence mechanism is sufficient for this purpose is ASEAN's greatest challenge.

Somewhat similar concerns are seen in the approaches to summit diplomacy in other of regional organisations. There are differences between the summit diplomacy of ASEAN and the EU in that the ASEAN approach to external agreements tends to be from the perspective of a fixed regional organisation, whilst the EU is outward looking, attempting to establish presence through outreach with a wide range of other regional organisations.[75]

EU shifts between regional and bilateral approaches are shaped by the progress of individual regional negotiations whilst its bilateral options are reverted to in the event of deadlock, as it attempts to expand its global regional network and presence. In cases of stalled or failed regional nego-tiations, the EU tends to face pressures to revert to bilateral trade links with individual regional powers to meet trade exigencies rather than await prolonged or uncertain outcomes.[76]

Other differences of approach to regional relations are seen with Singapore which is active in new large mega trade blocs (RCEP, CPTPP) but switches in and out of its regional base (ASEAN) into a plethora of bilateral and plurilateral arrangements to protect flexibility and promote innovation in areas such as digital trade norms, which are then fed back into regional organisation summits in a vast moving choreography of agreements.[77]

A significant change in methods is reflected in the increase in security-related summits. Driven by changes in international tension, traditional defence cooperation has been elevated to cover wider areas of cooper-ation and partners at bilateral levels beyond traditional equipment supply, bases and interoperability agreements to higher strategic and oper-ational planning and detailed cooperation. These changes have been incorporated along with other areas of cooperation as agenda items in annual bilateral and plurilateral summits, for example, India–Japan[78] and the Quad (US, Japan, India, Australia).[79] Russia–China naval cooperation has featured in carefully timed operations against adversarial summits.

The Quad has been augmented by secret agreements on the extension of UK–US bilateral nuclear submarine cooperation to include Australia.[80] The extension of US–UK nuclear submarine technology to Australia had a long-running diplomatic impact on Franco–US–UK relations. Bilateral and special summits between the US, France and EU have only somewhat mitigated the reversal.[81]

Additional aspects of security as a summit agenda item are questions relating to the scope of security items outside the traditional defence and threat categories and whether summits are a suitable framework for addressing these concerns. Traditional areas such as dual-use goods and services have been augmented by connectivity, supply chain disruption, effects of pandemics on logistics and a range of normative issues related to international trade competition. These constitute what might be termed the new security agenda, which have progressively filtered into summits separately or in large measure.[82]

Parallel diplomacy and counter diplomacy are diplomatic methods which use summits for essentially negative purposes rather than for cooperation. The intention is to use summits to block or undermine similar or other moves. Counter diplomacy is distinguished from parallel diplomacy by moving beyond parallel diplomacy to include actions which undermine or destroy an idea, organisation, policy or individual. Parallel diplomacy aims to imitate, offer an alternative or block a rival or adver-sary. It involves tracking the initiatives and visits by other actors so as to put on competitive visits back-to-back or closely afterwards. Its use is captured in the idea of echo diplomacy: in surface vessel and submarine operations the sonar operator is waiting for echo identification and instantaneous echo readings. The target state waits to see which aspects of its external policy are being tracked (diplomatic reporting) and which initiatives are being imitated or undercut (assessments).

### Some further considerations: keeping bilateral diplomacy bilateral

Keeping a bilateral relationship bilateral is a perennial problem. Bilateral relations are cultivated for confidence, security and acceptance. The main purpose of using bilateral relations is to try and push through ideas and positions within a framework which can be influenced and adjusted and have a large measure of success. Preferred positions are not lost in the wilderness of multilateralism.

Challenges to bilateral relations occur in several contexts. In trade negotiations, bilateral and other meetings are closely scrutinised by allies and opponents. The UK's bilateral trade continuity negotiations post-Brexit were carefully shadowed by EU members, Commission and other interested states, including Canada, Australia and New Zealand in parallel and counter diplomacy to undercut UK trade positions. Scrutiny of this kind often forces states into error – attempting to speed up or defend positions can lead to too many, or unnecessary, concessions.[83] A related error is over-responding with initiatives and negotiations in an attempt to demonstrate proactive involvement or get agreements concluded in a diminishing electoral or political time frame.

Special relations as a particular type of bilateral relations face additional problems. These may be formed in particular historical circumstances, which may have become less relevant, e.g. post-war Franco–German relations. The strands or elements which make up why two actors have a special relationship are frequently tested by external events and issues which pull the bilateral parties apart. In the UK–US special relationship, the strongest components are military and intelligence cooperation but the two frequently differ significantly over bilateral trade issues.

In trade negotiations with the US the UK definitely goes, in Obama's well-rehearsed phrase, "to the back of the queue", and is a non-summit agenda item. More generally, the UK has found it difficult to operate bilaterally with the US in a G7 summit context, other than via secret diplomacy on nuclear equipment deals. It faces constant alignment issues as partners seek to create special understandings with the US individually, bilaterally or in coalitions which exclude the UK. It overshadowed the UK G7 presidency. The G7 summit format is used as a platform for resetting EU relations with the US to launch initiatives such as new summit councils on supply chain cooperation, dual use technology and standards.[84]

The limits, however, of summits as methods for resetting or driving new European–US cooperation, are in the detail of implementation: over issues on dual use lists, conflicts between EU rules on subsidies and US economic support programmes to promote recovery and European DFI in adversarial states, which open up significant differences.[85]

A final aspect of bilateral summits which is relevant generally to special as well as bilateral relations concerns expectations. What does a state expect to achieve from a summit? What is it necessary to concede?

States seldom have common shared understandings of outcomes or benefits from negotiations or summits. Rather, summits will be viewed as providing different opportunities and benefits, with some common areas of agreement. The issue of benefit arises in an increasingly important area of summits relating to the concept of transfer value.

In transfer value calculations there is an expectation that agreements which significantly contribute, for example, to a states' security, such as advanced weapons supply or specialist communications not available on the open market, would be matched by reciprocal support in other areas as a recognition of support. It is not always reciprocated, raising doubts about the value of special high-level visits and more generally the substance of a bilateral relationship. US defence support for Saudi Arabia was not reciprocated as oil support for the US, for example, in the post-2023 energy crisis.

## Summits: commercialisation

UN specialised agencies have influenced the development of summits in several different ways, particularly link-ups with single states, commercial and other actors from differing sectors, using summits. It has largely been overlooked in literature on international institutions which has tended to focus on the UN Security Council or the development of the strategic ideas underlying UN programmes.

International institutions face two potentially conflicting areas in governance: questions of focus and issues relating to methods. Questions of focus centre on agenda and orientation. That is, what kinds of things should the organisation be tackling, and what proportion of organisational resources and finance should be directed to relevant areas?

The second question, methods, centres on issues such as responsibility for an issue, perceived exclusivity of role and loss of centrality through reduction in function or duplication by cooperating partners. Underlying these two areas are concerns over acquisition or loss of political capital. International institutions need and use up political capital, to maintain relevance or redirect programmes.

UN specialised agencies have used summits periodically to bring specialists together or raise the profile of an issue to speed up regulation or ratification. Examples include UNCTAD commodity summits or on scientific issues. The International Maritime Organisation (IMO) convened a rare summit in Greenland as a round table discussion with interested parties led by the IMO Secretary-General on problems of navigation in ice-covered areas. The main purpose was to raise awareness of the new IMO Polar Code and speed up ratification.[86]

In other instances, summits used by specialised agencies are more extensive as part of development initiatives, such as the World Bank coordinating summit with Africa on use of loans under the IDA.[87]

Summits are also used as part of major reorientation in the agenda and operations of a specialised agency. The World Bank, for example, moved away, at some risk, from its standard range of development agenda projects to shift focus to other areas such as cities by introducing biennial summits on cities with themes such as resilient cities, sustainability and urban development.

Other areas addressed through summits include finance for infrastructure (with Singapore). These have proved attractive events for shaping ideas, adding contacts and introducing new technologies but have raised concerns in agricultural-based national economies over loss of attention.

One of the problems which the World Bank and other agencies have with this form of summit is, having established a thematic area or niche position, maintaining authorship or influence over the ideas whilst cooperating with others with different or imitative agendas. In the cities example, the theme was picked up by the G20, which legitimised its involvement by bringing in the World Bank as a strategic cooperating partner in its version of the G20 Urban 20 initiative but duplicated, as argued earlier, the work of the World Bank.[88]

Similar duplication has occurred in other cases such as G20 involvement in anti-money laundering policies and financial fraud recovery (established areas of World Bank operations)[89] and related disputes with the OACPS.

### Commercialisation: "private" foreign policies

The term "commercialisation of summits" is used here to refer to the practice of international specialised agencies forming joint arrangements with states and other actors such as sub-regional organisations and commercial actors.

The growing involvement of specialised agencies with commercial actors in setting up or sponsoring summits is a relatively new development. Examples include bilateral links Germany and UNIDO, and UAE and UNIDO. Germany is also linked to UNIDO via a headquarters agreement and as a host for the revolving UNIDO Global Manufacturing and Industrial summit held around the theme of the Fourth Industrial

Revolution and application in industry or AI, robotics and supply chain management.

The method relied heavily on visit diplomacy linked to a city but was revised in the pandemics to digital format before resuming in city format. At trilateral level, Germany and UNIDO are linked with the East African Community on regional development projects. Summits are used by Germany and UAE in these illustrations as techniques to promote private foreign policies, conducted within a development or commercial remit and outside the remit of parent regional organisation or competitors.

Keeping bilateral or private initiatives bilateral is never easy. Initiatives are monitored by other organisations and agencies, keen to step in and establish presence. EU counter diplomacy has relied on displacing links created by other actors with UNIDO, by its own summit relations with UNIDO at Director General level.[90]

For UNIDO, hybrid diplomatic-commercial summits fit well with its revised charter, which moved the organisation away from traditional industrialisation-agricultural development. It has remained out of the spotlight and is able to function without extensive publicity. In contrast, the World Bank has placed its activities more directly in contested areas of attention. The space though for bilateral initiatives is closing as regional organisations and multilateral agencies compete to expand influence and secure funding in new and traditional development sectors.

## Conclusion

Summit conferences have gradually changed from wartime and postwar meetings for dealing with major political and security issues, to regular meetings for managing relations especially at bilateral and regional level. For the most part primary power summits post 2000 have been transformed into limited meetings for exchanges of views and damping down incidents or tension.

At regional level summits are now leading agencies for governance. They have become standardised as devices for political cooperation; settling budgets; long range goals and managing bloc external relations. Peace keeping and mediation have been increasingly added at regional level. Above all the volume of business of even small regional organisation is high, preoccupied with membership, adjudicating interests and cohesion.

Bilateralism retains its relevance, sense of importance and use of occasion with summits particularly for small and medium powers providing a mechanism for projecting leader image, exploring new orientation and reaffirming sovereignty.

The setting for summit conferences above all has changed considerably. Part of that change is influenced by the progressive decline post 2000 of multilateral diplomacy. Within the multilateral system, the gradual decline of large scale periodic UN summits such as habitat, cities and information society reflected loss of collective interest in large scale formats, competing events and cost. UN development related summits have struggled to gain financial and political traction, along with the format for the promotion of UN Sustainable Development Goals.

Three important factors affecting the management of multilateral summits are cost, finding hosts and the use of split sites. One of the legacies of covid on the management of diplomacy is the accelerating reluctance to mount large scale events partly on cost grounds but it also reflects reluctance to undertake diplomatic travel outside regions or central transport hubs. In order to try and overcome these difficulties the use of split sites (mandate meeting New York/Geneva) implementation conference (separate location) is unsatisfactory, contributing to fragmentation and decline of engagement in multilateral cooperation in favour of bilateralism or limited group arrangements.

## Notes

1 James F. Byrnes, *Speaking Frankly* (Heinemann, 1955). On the role of Keynes in the negotiations see John Morton Blum, *From the Morgenthau Diaries: Years of War 1941–1945* (Houghton Mifflin, 1967) pp273, *passim*. On the Bretton Woods conference see J. Keith Horsfield, *The International Monetary Fund 1945–1965* (IMF, 1969) vol. 1, chapter 5.

2 Byrnes, ibid., pp32–46, 69–79, 112; Anthony Eden, *Full Circle* (Cassell, 1960) p62.

3 F.S. Northedge, *Descent from Power* (Allen and Unwin, 1974) pp89–93.

4 See Eden, *Full Circle*, on differing ideas over the form and purposes of summits, p290.

5 Eden, ibid., p291.

6 Examples of the three types are EU–South Africa, China–Africa and Arab League–AU.

7 On the work of the International Maritime Organisation see www.imo.org for details of the three main working committees of representatives: Maritime Safety Committee, Environment (MEPC) and Facilitation Committee. For World Trade Organisation, see www.wto.org for details of Trade Negotiations committee, Committee on Regional Trade Agreements (CRTA) as examples of trade diplomacy at the operational level of officials and permanent representatives.

8 Retreats are regularly used a method for stepping back. Retreats of heads of government and agencies are widely held in the AU, regional African economic communities and ASEAN, as informal summits without records or procedures. See, for example, 5th Retreat of the Summit of Heads of State on Infrastructure Development, East African Community, 14 February 2023.

9  In Japanese diplomatic practice, short courtesy meetings are styled as summits. The practice is also extended to telephone summits, for example, between Canada and Japan following the assassination of former Prime Minister Abe, 27 September 2022.

10  UN eminent persons groups have been widely used by different UN office holders (e.g. UNSG, UNGA president) and Divisions (e.g. Division of Economic and Social Affairs) to focus attention and galvanise support for an issue using statements, evidence to committees and reports. The subject matter is varied, including Least Developed Countries, peacebuilding and the SDG Development Agenda goals.

11  For uses of high-level segment (HLS) in the United Nations Industrial Development Organisation (UNIDO), see www.unido.org/who-we-are/glo bal-manufacturing-and-industrialisation-summit-gmis. HLS was used in the Nairobi summit of the Landmines Convention www.nairobisummit.org/high-level-segment/overview/. The method is also widely used in international conferences, including annual meetings of the parties, special sessions and review meetings, e.g. Biodiversity convention, www.cbd.int/conferences/2018/cop-14-hls. For climate change practice, see e.g. Copenhagen, https://unfccc.int/conference/copenhagen-climate-change-conference-december-2009; cf. Madrid session UNFCCC COP25 https://unfccc.int/event/cop-25. The high-level meeting method has been used by various formal UN organs and agencies, e.g. ECOSOC, for policy dialogue by heads of financial and trade institutions, see https://ecosoc.un.org/en/meetings/ecosoc-sessions.

12  For discussion of the different categories of business membership and restrictions on political entourages to facilitate high-level personal meetings, see Elizabeth Friesen, *The World Economic Forum and Transnational Networking* (Emerald Points, 2020) pp28–31.

13  For example, North American Leaders summit; AU Assembly; high-level segment Biodiversity conference, 15–17 December 2022, Montreal.

14  For example, EAS summit (US) 2020.

15  EU–Ukraine Summit, 2023.

16  See Quadrilateral Security Dialogue (QSD) Japan–Australia–India–US Security Summit (annually from 2021).

17  Examples of multilateral coordination summits include the annual meeting of the World Bank and IMF, e.g. Marrakesh; UNFCCC COP; and the ad hoc South–South Summit (G77).

18  On hybrid conferences by UN agencies see, for example, UNIDO www.unido.org/our-focus/global-manufacturing-and-industrialisation-summit-gmis. For political hybrid summits see Friesen note 12 op. cit., and chapter 7 on parallel diplomacy.

19  For commercial use of the term, see the confusingly titled "South Summit Madrid". www.southsummit.io.

20  See chapters 7 and 8.

21  See, for example, UN leaders' summit on peacekeeping at https://peacekeep ing.un.org/en/leaders-summit-peaceekeeping.

22  Articles 98 and 99 UN Charter. See also Marrack Goulding, in *The UN Security Council: From the Cold War to the 21st Century*, D.M. Malone (ed.) (Lynne Rienner, 2004) pp268–9.

23  The UN FAO World Food Summit in Rome, 1996, closely followed UNGA procedures and resembled a multilateral conference: credential committee,

reservations, interpretive statements and alternative representation in working session, formal statements, subcommittees and final Declaration. Side issues included a credentials item over Pakistan's objections to the Head of the Afghanistan delegation, cross-referred to the UNGA. See WFS/ 96/ 2 Provisional Rules of procedure; participants 96/2 and Rome Declaration (96/3). Attendance was high, including 41 heads of state and 42 heads of government.

24  See www.un.org/en/conferences/habitat/istanbul1996 and https://unhabi tat.org/history-mandate-role-in-the-un-system.

25  www.un.org/sustainable%20development%20/sustainable-development-goal

26  www.un.org/en/climatechange/2019-climate-action-summit.

27  The 1996 UN FAO Rome summit on food security issued a declaration and plan of action. A second summit was not held until 16–18 November 2009, in Rome. See www.fao.org/4/w3613e/w3613e00.htm#:~:text=The%20 Rome%20Declaration%20on%20World,national%2C%20regional%20 and%20global%20levels.

28  See www.undp.org/sustainable-development-goals.

29  See www.un.org/pga/70/wp-content/uploads/sites/10/2015/08/Briefing-on-UN-IOM-relations-19-July-2016.pdf.

30  Habitat I took place in Vancouver, 1976; Habitat II in Istanbul 1996; Habitat III in Quito, 2016. A special session of the UNGA reviewed the international work of Habitat and created an additional forum on urbanisation.

31  See Millennium Declaration 55th session UNGA, A/RES/55/2, 18 September 2000; UN World Summit, A/RES/ 66/1, 24 October 2005.

32  See MDG Gap Task Force Report 2015, "Taking Stock of the Global Partnership for Development" www.un.org/en/development/desa/publications/mdg-gap-task-force-report-2015.html; www.un.org/en/development/desa/pop ulation/migration/generalassembly/docs/globalcompact/A_CONF.198_11.pdf

33  See https://sdgs.un.org/partnerships; also A/69/L85, Draft Outcome UN Summit on the adoption of the post-2015 development agenda. On the structure of the summit see A/69/L43, 16 December 2014, list of designated speakers and time limit on presentations.

34  See UN General Assembly Resolution A/RES/76307; www.un.org/en/com mon-agenda.

35  For the Secretary-General's criticism of the slow progress and commitments on climate see www.un.org/sg/en/content/sg/speeches/2019-09-23/rema rks-2019-climate-action-summit. Cf note 33 ibid., A/69/L43 paras 8 and 10, on the rules of procedure with respect to time and selection of plenary speakers, which underline the problem of conducting large collective plenary sessions and allowing as many as possible to speak, albeit for five minutes and selecting who would be allowed to speak, at a global summit.

36  Anthony Albanese, Australian Prime Minister, press conference, Thailand, 22 November 2019, www.pm.gov.au/media/press-conference-thailand.

37  For the texts of the 11 hours of statements, see www.cbd.int/article/2020-UN-Biodiversity-Summit/statements.

38  There were major difficulties over hosting, chair and finance of the 5th Least Developed Countries Conference. A split site formula was eventually adopted with the mandate session in New York on 17 March 2022. A second session was held in Doha on 5–9 March 2023. The Secretary-General of the conference was the High Representative for Least Developed Countries. Finance for the

conference was provided by Qatar, Turkey and Finland. See www.un.org/ldc5/; www.un.org/ldc5/about.

39 See guidance note on the delivery of national statements and statements by organisations 15–17 2022. A sense of the difficulties and duplication in the split method is conveyed in the procedures used by the high level segment Chair for statements at the second high level segment, to be given "during the plenary sessions of the second part of the high level segment of the second part of the 15 meeting of the Conference of the Parties" (para 3). www.cbd.int/doc/c/da3e/9576/55784204c3352ebcfaf7fa51/hls-cop15-guidance-en.docx

40 See    www.un.org/sites/un2.un.org/files/our-common-agenda-policy-brief-international-finance-architecture-en.pdf. International Financial Architecture (policy brief 6) recommended a new biennial summit comprising G20, ECOSOC, heads of specialised agencies and the Secretary-General. The brief identified areas such as representation in finance and development banks, short-term crises and the need long-term financing to support sustainable development. It did not include major factors such as country distribution of loans and liquidity. The top ten IBRD loans are to BRICS (except the Russian Federation and South Africa) plus Indonesia, Turkey, Egypt, Colombia, the Philippines and Argentina). IBRD/IDA includes, in the top ten, Bangladesh, Pakistan, Nigeria, India, Tanzania, Kenya, Mozambique and Ethiopia. See IBRD Annual Report 2023 www.worldbank.org/en/about/annual-report, Notes to Financial Statement p44; pp84–5 and for IDA Financial Statements, pp73–4.

41 World Bank, IDA for Africa: Heads of State Summit, Dakar, 7 July 2022. www.worldbank.org/en/events/2022/06/27/ida20-for-africa-heads-of-state-summit. The Dakar Call to Action was signed by Cabo Verde, Cameroon, DRC Congo, Egypt, Ethiopia, Guinea Bissau, Guinea Equatorial, Ivory Coast, Kenya, Liberia, Madagascar, Malawi, Mauritania, Nigeria, Republic of Congo, Rwanda, Senegal, Sierra Leone, Tanzania, the Gambia, Togo, Comoros and Zimbabwe. The IDA Heads of State Summit site has useful links to Joint Statements, participation and subsequent World Bank Africa IDA summits. See also https://documents.worldbank.org/en/publication/documents-reports/documentdetail/163861645554924417/ida20-building-back-better-from-the-crisis-toward-a-green-resilient-and-inclusive-future    documents-reports/documentdetail/163861645554924417/ida20-building-back-better-from-the-crisis-toward-a-green-resilient-and-inclusive-future. On UNIDO see UNIDO-IDDA3, 20–25 November 2022 and www.uneca.org/eca-events/idda3.

42 See, for example, UNIDO Global Manufacturing and Industrialisation Summit www.unido.org/our-focus/global-manufacturing-and-industrialisation-summit-gmis.

43 See    www.worldbank.org/en/events/2024/05/30/youth-summit-2024-powering-progress.

44 League of Arab States members of the AU: Algeria, Mauritius, Morocco, Tunisia, Libya, Somalia, Comoros, Djibouti, Sudan and Egypt.

45 https://policy.trade.ec.europa.eu/eu-trade-relationships-country-and-region_en.

46 The African Continental Free Trade Area was signed on 21 March 2018. There are 54 members of the AU of whom 43 have ratified the agreement, phase 1 of which entered into force for the original 24 ratifications on 30 May 2019.

47 The UNCTAD special study "The African Continental Free Trade Area: Policy and Negotiation Options" contains a chronology of key stages in the negotiations. See https://unctad.org/system/files/official-document/webditc20 16d7_en.pdf.

48 See, for example, the UK re-examination of global security threats in the defence and strategic policy review "New Era for Defence", at www.gov.uk/government/news/government-launches-root-and-branch-review-of-uk-armed-forces.

49 See www.comesa.int/new-deadline-set-for-ratification-of-tripartite-free-trade-area/ Fourteen ratifications are required to bring the TFTA into force. The agreement entered into force on 25 July 2024.

50 See chapter on the Paris Climate Convention negotiations, R.P. Barston, *Modern Diplomacy* 5th ed. (Routledge, 2019) pp494–503.

51 Short one-day summits were held, for example, on Ukraine on 15 December 2022. For details of Council summits see www.consilium.europa.eu/en/meetings/calendar/.

52 AU inaugural Durban summit 9–10 July 2002. https://au.int/sites/default/files/decisions/9549-assembly_en_9_10_july_2002_assembly_heads_state_government_first_ordinary_session_0.pdf.

53 See 107th Session of the ACP Council of Ministers, Lome, Togo, 30 May 2018. ACP/00/011/18 Final.

54 Negotiating Directives for a Partnership Agreement between the EU and ACP, Brussels 21 June 2018. 8094/18 Add 1. The negotiations were conducted by Neven Mimica (Commissioner for Development Cooperation) and Robert Dussey (Minister for Foreign Affairs and African Integration, Togo).

55 See AU Eleventh Extraordinary Session 17–18 November 2018. Ext/Assembly/AU/Dec.1-4(XI).

56 The OECS group (Antigua and Barbuda, Dominica, Grenada, Montserrat, Saint Kitts, Saint Lucia, Saint Vincent and the Grenadines), created under the treaty of Basseterre 18 June 1981, later joining CARICOM, but retaining separate currency unification. https://oecs.int/en/who-we-are/about-us.

57 See "Why is Nigeria foot-dragging on the AfCFTA?" at www.africannewspage.net/2020/10/analysis-why-is-nigeria-foot-dragging-on-the-afcfta/.

58 See chapter 4, Economic Statecraft.

59 "Blue Ocean" is a term used by Pacific states to refer to their chief resources (fisheries and artisanal fisheries) subsequently adopted by the World Bank in GEF projects and other multilateral institutions. For reorientation away from traditional approaches see https://rnz.co.nz/international/pacific-news/493 661/solomons-pm-signs-new-deals-with-china-on-beijing-trip.

60 For discussion of some of the difficulties for diplomacy caused by different understandings or interpretation of slogans like "Blue Ocean", see the valuable report of Kahlil Hassanali, "Marine Policy", 5 October 2020, pp104–37. www.sciencedirect.com/science/article/pii/ S0308597X20301123.

61 Nonaligned summits have been held at three-year intervals since the inception of the Non-Aligned Movement in 1961. The first summit was held in Havana.

62 Voice of the Global South Summit, 12–13 January 2023. Press Release, High Commission of India, Ghana. www.mea.gov.in/voice-of-global-summit.htm

63 www.g77.org/doc/.

64 www.unido.org; cf. note 40, op. cit.

65 G77 has held three South–South Summits: Havana 12–14 April 2000, Doha 12–16 June 2005 and Kampala 10–12 December 2023. An Extraordinary

Summit on national development and South–South cooperation was held at Santa Cruz 14–15 June 2014. South Bulletin, 81, 25 July 2014.

66  See Aileen Kwa, *Behind the Scenes at the WTO* (Bantam books, 2003).

67  WTO, WT/GC/W/759, 25 November 2019. The AU was admitted into the G20 summit in Delhi 2023.

68  Arab League–AU summits have been held irregularly at Cairo (1977), Libya (2010), Kuwait (2013) and Equatorial Guinea (2016). The fifth summit scheduled for 2023 in Saudi Arabia was postponed at the request of the AU to ensure better organisation. *North Africa Post*, 19 February 2023. In the ASEAN–AU case, the early foundation for Asia–African relations was set at the 1955 Bandung conference but never significantly developed. Diplomatic conferences such as the first Asian–African Sub-regional Organisation conference (AASROC) (2003) and New Asian African Strategic Partnership (NAASP) commemorative summit (2005) were not followed up with summits every two years as envisaged in the Summit Declaration. Apart from initiatives proposed by South Africa and Indonesia, there has been little follow up by other members, with methods limited to occasional visits (e.g. World Bank South–South visit project), the African Union Commission visit to Indonesia (2012) or sideline meetings in the annual UNGA, constituting the extent of inter-regional diplomacy. See also on Arab League–Africa Kuwait Declaration (AU Press Release, No 221/2013). On ASEAN–AU, South Bulletin 85, 15 May 2015. The 60th Commemorative Anniversary summit of Bandung included a Declaration on Reinvigorating the NAASP. See also Mark Edel V. Diaz, "ASEAN and the African Union: Time for Stronger Cooperation", Philippine Foreign Service Institute, FSI Insights, https://fsi.gov.ph/asean-and-the-african-union-time-for-a-stronger-cooperation/.

69  The partnership post-Cotonou agreement between the EU and OACPS was initialled by negotiators on 15 April 2020 and officially signed only on 5 November 2023 in Samoa. See M. Carbone (2019), "The calm after the storm…" https://eprints.gla.ac.uk/196335/7/196335.pdf. For President Macron's carefully worded statement implying a change in the French position on ACP following the European Council summit, at which Hungary indicated it would vote against the ACP agreement, and details of other divisions within the EU 27 and between Community institutions, see www.euractiv.com/section/africa/news/ "Holdouts cast shadow over new EU pact with Africa", 16 November 2023.

70  Robert Mason, *Saudi Arabia and the United Arab Emirates* (Manchester University Press, 2023) pp269–71.

71  Mason, ibid., p2.

72  NATO Vilnius summit 11–12 July 2023 www.nato.int/cps/en/natohq/ official_texts _217320.htm. See www.consilium.europa.eu/media/ 66739/g20-new-delhi-leaders-declaration.pdf for New Delhi Leaders Declaration.

73  US–China Phase 1 Deal, see https://crsreports.congress.gov/product/pdf/ IF/IF12125;"Biden's Dilemma: How to enforce Trump's Trade Deal", 15 December 2021, see www.nytimes.com/2021/12/15/business/economy/ china-trump-trade-deal-biden.html.

74  https://asean.org/our-communities/asean-political-security-community/ outward-looking-community/external-relations/overview/. See, for example, asean.org/asean-notional-calendar and contrast for switch to video conferencing in response to COVID-19. ASEAN has Development Partnerships

with Chile, France, Germany and Italy. The separate bilateral develop-ment partnerships with France, Germany and Italy preceded the EU, which concluded a Partnership agreement only in 2022. ASEAN also has two add-ition summit-level regional mechanisms – the ASEAN Plus 3 (Japan, Korea and China) and the East Asia Summit, which meet back-to-back with the ASEAN Summit.

75 See UNIDO 5<sup>th</sup> High Level Dialogue as part of its extension of relations with UNIDO, www.unido.org/news/fifth-unido-european-union-high-level-dialogue.

76 On Spanish trade policy with Latin America in the Ukraine war grain crisis, favouring bilateral arrangements with Latin America, temporary suspen-sion of EU agricultural environmental regulations and backing for EU Latin America–Caribbean summit, see Bloomberg, 28 April 2022 (supply chain latest Spain); Foreign Affairs Council, Press remarks High Representative, Euractiv, 18 July 2022.

77 See www.worldcitiessummit.com.sg/. World Cities Summit and US–ASEAN Smart Cities Partnership. Singapore extended its cooperation in the World Cities Summit project with an MOU with the World Bank on provision of spa-tial data technology in 2018.

78 See Japan–India relations archives www.in.emb-japan.go.jp/itpr_en/Japan _India_ Relations.html for details of bilateral and other meetings between Japan and India.

79 Joint Statement First Quad, 24 September 2021 www.mofa.go.jp/regions/asia/pacific-data.

80 UK–Australia–USA Agreement for the Exchange of Nuclear Propulsion Information (MS No 8 2021) and CP 575, 29 November 2021.

81 www.whitehouse.gov/briefing-room/statements-releases/2022/05/16/fact-sheet-u-s-eu-trade-and-technology-council-establishes-economic.

82 For US–EU trade and Technology Council agenda and perspectives on cooper-ation see https://ustr.gov/useuttc.

83 www.gov.scot/publications/public-procurement-australia-and-new-zealand-free-trade-agreements-sppn-1-2023/. See also former UK minister George Eustice on the Australia and New Zealand deals as bad deals, *Financial Times*, 14 November 2022 www.ft.com/content/a9ce4564-930f-439a-ac42-d9b05 5712ee6.

84 US–EU Trade and Technology Council, Joint US–EU Statement following 4 May 2024 meeting, see https://ustr.gov>useuttc.

85 The dispute revolved around US subsides and concession to attract for-eign capital and investment in the environment sectors in the US Inflation Reduction Act, which the EU sees as a trade threat area. The EU introduced restrictions on foreign firms operating in the EU through extensive financial data requirements on past subsidies, in EU regulation 2022/2560, entering into force 12 January 2023. See www.ft.com/content/0f8bf631-f24c-48da-905f-e37f8dc5d5f8 *Financial Times*, 26 February 2023.

86 IMO, International Code for Ships Operating in Polar Waters. See www.imo.org/en/ourwork/ safety/pages/polar-code.aspx.

87 World Bank, IDA for Africa: Heads of State Summit, Dakar 7 July 2022.

88 See www.urban20.org.

89 See https://star.worldbank.org/.

90 See www.unido.org/news/fifth-unido-european-union-high-level-dialogue.

# Chapter 4

# Economic statecraft

## Introduction

Trade is a core element of economic statecraft in foreign policy. Whilst traditionally an important, if separate, branch of external management, trade has moved to a central focus in policy making. In this chapter we will focus on trade agreements in different contexts to show what diplomatic methods are used to support strategies and policies on trade deals and why methods are changed or, in some instances, abandoned.

The initial background sections of the chapter outline key features of the international trade setting, trade presence and differing forms of trade agreements. Subsequent sections explore methods used in trade diplomacy through five areas: the problem of conflict trade and foreign policy interests, trade presence, growth of trade blocs and groupings, trade diplomacy and security.

## Background

The contemporary international trade setting is critically shaped by the impact of the breakdown of the Doha Trade Round and the international financial crisis (2008–12).[1] Both factors have accelerated the decline of multilateralism, as states and other actors move focus to regional and bilateral arrangements. Intensive international trade rivalry is seen in Asian-driven global logistics schemes, the intensification of geopolitics and the general failure to build on earlier collective international agreements.[2] The Doha Round, which finally broke down at the 2015 Nairobi Ministerial conference, is perhaps the last significant attempt to negotiate a revised consensus based comprehensive agreement on trade rules incorporating trade and development.[3] Subsequent trade agreements have been shaped and routed through plurilateral interest groups.[4]

DOI: 10.4324/9781003204039-5

Alongside these institutional developments, trade has altered in scope and actors. The content of trade has widened in the services sectors in traded areas such as international financial agreements, e-commerce, service agreements and regional agreements which were part of a contested WTO agenda post-Nairobi, which shifted the WTO from development perspectives on international trade.

The third major factor shaping the international trade setting – the residual impact on trade and international financial relations of the COVID-19 crisis, added supply chain issues and logistics to the international agenda and the wider issue areas of deglobalisation.[5]

Finally, resource competition has introduced new players in trade diplomacy, accelerated the more extensive use of bilateral agreements to secure supply access and contributed to the spread of geopolitical conflict.

## Trade, foreign and defence policy

Trade is linked to foreign policy, defence and other sectors most commonly through orientation, relations with major partners, trade promotion, diversification and negotiation. In this sense, trade is used to support foreign and defence policy through visit diplomacy, initiatives, trade conference events, defence sales and import-export controls. However, trade may depart from foreign policy in a number of situations. The traditional model of trade supporting foreign policy is now being countered by growing instances in which trade is a major ongoing source of tension or contradiction in a state's overall foreign policy.

Reorientation is one of the major sources of tension between foreign and defence policy. In open systems, tension over the impact of significant changes in foreign policy orientation on trade interests can become divisive as media, parliamentary or congressional committees conduct inquiries, investigate and produce reports. The involvement of external actors in seeking to slow down or prevent reorientation has become a more extensive problem in contemporary diplomacy, through the activities of trade lobbies linked to external actors. Other sources of tension are badly negotiated agreements which revive criticism over implementation and charges of failure, calling into question the original intentions and rationale for reorientation.

Negotiations on trade and foreign policy are seldom conducted by unitary actors. Policy on climate, energy company tax, whether to source loans through the rigours of a multilateral institution, renew an agreement or mount an initiative to reset relations may be incomplete or ambiguous, giving scope for many voices. In other contexts, such as mediation or normalisation initiatives, a lead negotiator may feel it necessary to keep negotiations bilateral rather than in a wider ad hoc alliance group, and conduct them in secret using trusted third-party venues to conduct exchanges and run over draft proposals.[6] In sensitive negotiations, secret exchanges have been augmented by bilateral negotiations using high-risk strategies of parallel diplomacy using the larger group negotiations as cover for secret exchanges. Bilateral secret negotiations are used primarily as the preferred device by lead powers to protect negotiating positions, control scope and minimise the use of trade-related concessions.[7]

Diplomatic methods in these and other instances may ultimately be a source of tension between trade and foreign policy ministries. The impact of the risk of premature disclosure or failure of secret negotiations[8] and the corresponding feeling of members of ad hoc larger groups of being excluded or used for other purposes is regarded by lead negotiator powers as an acceptable cost.[9]

A common and recurring source of tension between trade and foreign relations is found in inadequately prepared visit diplomacy. Visit diplomacy is often used to signal the importance of a bilateral visit and symbolise that a country or region is not being neglected or overlooked. This type of method can be ineffective because of different understandings of what the purposes of the visit are and what might be achieved. The agenda of the external party might be heavily framed around environmental or human rights issues, whereas the concerns of the receiving state are on securing a revised trade agreement.[10]

As a result, bilateral political relations remain ambivalent or unsatisfactory for a receiving state, with limited diplomatic space to raise or promote the idea of a revised trade agreement in a crowded diplomatic calendar of external actors.

Major sources of potential conflict between trade and foreign policy tend to occur in situations in which trade deals or arrangements are affected by changes government, at variance with emerging or new foreign policy reorientations or pose national security threats.[11] External actors may create separate agreements with sub-national agencies which generate ambiguity about threat or undermine national policy towards an adversary. In the context of intra-allied relations, making choices over who receives defence contracts or transfers of strategic weapons are difficult and highly sensitive decisions.[12]

## Dealing with conflicts between trade and foreign policy

Diplomatic methods which are used to deflect criticism of possible conflict between trade and foreign policy rely on denial and diversion. Denial is time limited. It is a stock technique used to buy time using official statements or leaks to indicate lack of information about an event or suggest it is not the present policy of an administration.

A related method relies on the time gained by denial to create a narrative which acts as a diversion. It may be on an unrelated issue, counter allegation or a false flag operation. Diversion aims to shift attention away from one issue so as to move discussion onto others. International institutions and foreign media are used for formal statements or briefings to keep diversionary issues running whilst counter policies are formulated.[13]

These standard or traditional techniques have been augmented by modern methods which rely more on strategies of disguise and blending adversarial and target interests. For example, disguised commercial operations are used to minimise or deflect questions over ownership and nationality, especially in the context of multilateral sanctions. Trade is reflagged to third party vessels; petroleum and goods exports rerouted via allies. Recurrent regional conflicts in the Middle East and Europe have been used by small contiguous powers in these and other regions including central Asia, to build up service roles as cargo transit hubs, export zones and trade diversion.[14]

In transport logistics, notable developments are the use of agreements to open up new international cargo services by regional powers (e.g. Turkey–US)[15] which in practice operate and manage vessels of other actors (e.g. COSCO Shipping) fronted by regional powers to reduce potential hostility to the use of adversarial carriers in shipping.[16]

Blending strategies which mix competitors in consortia trade deals have now tended to replace traditional diplomacy which relied on the standard formula of heads of state/government visit diplomacy, showcase tours to foreign port or infrastructure projects, MOU signing ceremonies and return visits.[17] Rather, SOEs manage consortia deals with counterpart agencies in host states on a private basis, with formal signings by CEOs at inbound ceremonies at SOE headquarters. These methods represent a major shift in strategies and how relations are advanced. The overlying strategy of mixed deals aims to mesh competing economic interests in multiple deals which tie adversarial powers into a host economy. As a result, blending makes it increasingly difficult for western powers to implement sanctions or other coercive action against an adversarial power because of the economic connections embedded in port, shipping and infrastructure agreements.

## Trade presence: improving diplomatic space

Trade presence is made up of the symbols, images, ideas and representatives associated with commercial and diplomatic operations of a country. The main components of presence are:

- representation, offices, media
- agreements
- international role
- individual representative or envoy

Presence is not constant or automatic; it can be won or lost. It may be lost through lack of attention, neglect, overfamiliarity, trade challenges from other actors or financial restrictions. It may be won via new backers, appointment of special envoys, active trade diplomacy, rapprochement with adversaries or normalisation.

In the post-Brexit international setting, for example, UK diplomatic space for trade reorientation was heavily reduced by EU counter moves which sought to contest UK attempts to create new bilateral trade networks.[18] Longstanding neglect of the Commonwealth limited the UK's capacity to resist moves into its traditional African agricultural import markets, in contrast to the high-level Franco–German political attention to West and Southern Africa in bilateral, EU and UN agency projects post-Doha.[19] The US neglect of trade and in particular CPTPP membership under President Biden was a major strategic error but perhaps domestically unavoidable in view of the competing US COVID-19 economic recovery legislation.

The importance of individual physical components of trade presence have changed considerably. with emphasis shifting to other forms of representation and wider use of envoys and representatives from companies, commercial lobby groups and NGOs. Budget limitations, too, place increasing restrictions on embassy-consular trade diplomacy.

Presence has traditionally been associated with diplomatic roles in international institutions. The diplomatic representatives of small powers play major roles in ad hoc and standing conferences, as chairs of working groups, sub-committees, facilitators and rapporteurs. These roles are also particularly important in UN technical specialised agencies such as IMO, WTO, FAO, UNCTAD and UNIDO, together with hosting events, conferences and major annual or special meetings.[20]

## Trade agreements – developments in methods

Bilateral diplomacy has traditionally been the preferred form for managing external relations. Despite the growth of regional and other arrangements, bilateral diplomacy has developed and expanded in scope and use. Its main advantages are ease, speed and flexibility. A long-term energy supply deal can be quickly and unobtrusively concluded. Alternatively, an agreement may be presented with great publicity as part of signalling regional intent and presence. In most instances though, sensitive trade and security relations are generally conducted as closed transactions.

Three main forms of agreements can be differentiated by the extent of institutions created in the agreement and drafting of obligations. These categories are approximations and will vary according to type of agreement or parties. They are nevertheless useful for helping to understand why some forms of agreements are chosen, and why some are successful or others run into difficulties. The categories also help in getting a sense of emerging structures in international order.

In category 1 are agreements with elaborate institutions and deep obligations (e.g. EU bilateral and inter-regional)[21]; category 2 are intermediate agreements (e.g. Australia bilateral)[22] and category 3 are institutionally light agreements in framework form, standardised or soft obligations (e.g. US, China, developing states).[23]

One of the main changes in design is preferencing relatively simple agreements which can be concluded speedily. These meet the need of establishing presence quickly in geoeconomic contexts. Most bilateral trade agreements are generally in category 3 in the form of a cooperation agreement or MOU and benefit from simplicity, scope and ease of implementation. In response to pressure to speed up agreements and circumvent slow entry into force, typified by category 1 agreements, intermediate trade cooperation agreements have been imaginatively developed as basic framework or standard clause agreements, by moving issues which may delay entry into force or cause implementation difficulties to a series of side letters for separate administrative clearance (e.g. India–Australia).[24] Trade cooperation or MOUs were concluded rapidly, for example, by the PRC as framework instruments with over 100 countries in an 18-month period as the method for laying the basis for the Belt and Road Initiative (BRI).[25]

Although other bilateral instrument have been used by China – the 2008 bilateral agreement with New Zealand was one of the first experimental training negotiations for China in more complex cooperation agreements with western-aligned powers – the MOU became the standard model for the PRC. New Zealand became a long-term hub for future PRC presence in the Pacific. For this, the bilateral category 2 agreement was a showcase cooperation instrument. It is interesting to note that the 2008 agreement was subsequently updated by Protocol to include additional provisions including environmental sections, perhaps with compliance with the CPTPP in mind.[26]

An unusual feature in PRC practice is that, unlike a lot of other state practice, MOUs are not informal interdepartmental or soft law instruments but are multipurpose instruments for high-level forward financial commitments or binding arrangements on foreign entities. The flexibility of MOUs is used by the PRC to signify change and endorse a partner with new status, with packets of project MOUs signed as part of visit diplomacy.

In US practice, bilateral trade agreements are generally relatively low key, short or framework instruments, with key strategic partners, modified periodically by protocols to update or correct. They are handled as routine functional instruments rather than high politics, with trade cooperation discussions conducted at embassy level through joint committees at ambassadorial or visiting senior official level and Congress representatives, rather than elaborate permanent committees and high-level personal visit diplomacy.[27]

Two further important changes are revision of some economic cooperation agreements to strategic cooperation agreements, and creation of sectoral coalitions to negotiate specific plurilateral agreements, e.g. on investment or standard entry conditions for environmental goods. Changes in the title of an existing agreement to strategic cooperation may be made to reflect greater and closer cooperation over common goals and objectives, trade and security cooperation and political solidarity. Underlying the changes are a variety of other possible factors such as the failure of arrangements governing current bilateral trade relations. The EU's switch to the use of strategic cooperation agreements is influenced particularly by the failure of its inter-regionalism negotiations with Africa, Latin America and the Pacific to conclude trade-based agreements at inter-regional level.

The effect of changing a title is to move existing agreements from a conventional inter-party trade format to a general multisector cooperation agreement, covering political cooperation, rule of law provisions (labour, level playing field, environment, trade) and miscellaneous cooperation proposals.[28]

In category 3, agreements have increased as a result of states seeking to restructure trade relations across sectors such as rare mineral supply agreements in response to supply instability associated with post-pandemic supply chains, international decoupling and trade conflict in Asia-Pacific.[29]

A second significant change in methods is the use and development of ad hoc coalitions both within and outside the WTO. Coalition-driven agreements include investment services and environmental goods (WTO); Indo-Pacific Economic Framework (IPEF–US).[30] The use of small group coalition agreements raises two issues: the first concerns the impact of coalition agreements on collective multilateral processes; secondly, whether normative based framework agreements are an adequate substitute or counterweight to compensate for non-membership of CPTPP. That is, whether the Quad plus normative agreements are sufficient to counter and limit PRC influence and expansion.

### Bilateral agreements: projecting presence and strategic influence

Bilateral agreements are central to building up trade interests and strategic projection. Projecting presence has benefitted from identifying opportunities and dormant relations as platforms for establishing both political and trade relations. The cumulative use of visit diplomacy adds to political visibility. Turkey, for example, built up a geopolitical presence in Africa over a decade using all opportunities for establishing contacts, as part of its wider international projection built around acceptability by differing blocs. An African reorientation was symbolised in Erdogan's high-level multi-delegation visit to Algeria, previously neglected, to launch trade and connectivity agreements, framed against his symbolic call at the Martyr's Memorial on first arrival.[31]

The effectiveness of visit diplomacy as part of building strategic presence is dependent on timing and political context. Finding the right moment to follow on a competitors' visit is indicative of effectiveness and is a mark of diplomatic reputation. In Sino–American relations, US foreign visits are carefully monitored by the PRC, which has developed echo diplomacy as an established part of its watching-and-waiting diplomatic style.[32]

Other changes in methods include the growing importance of side diplomacy. Side diplomacy at meetings such as G7, G20, APEC, EAS and BRICS is now extensively used as a major method for exchanging views, signing off bilateral agreements and being seen (or not). A head of state is able to hold court privately, hold courtesy meetings and decline requests to meet other representatives.

A related development in side diplomacy is the changing use of venues such as G7, BRICS and OPEC, enlarged by associate and visiting members, which has contributed to the widening functions of these institutions, altering them into hubs for the exchange of information, intelligence, defence as well as dark trade deals.[33]

### Bilateral agreements: identity

Bilateral agreements have been increasingly used for other areas of political cooperation notably as part of external policy on partnerships to strengthen organisational identity and by states to develop separate international roles from the parent institution. ASEAN, for example, was alert enough to see the value of offering something external actors different from a traditional bilateral trade agreement.

The creation of several types of "offshore" membership of ASEAN was a startling and innovative initiative, much more flexible but nevertheless valuable, than counterpart arrangements. Germany, for example, has Development Partner status.[34] The ASEAN style is very much one of multiple links, regular but brief back-to-back meetings with members and associates, to project the doctrine of ASEAN centrality, presence and reduce political risk to its survival.[35]

### Limits of presence and strategic influence

Trade presence is a contested area, increasingly subject to trade rivalry and competition which limit or negate presence.

Exploratory trade initiatives to open up new areas are high risk, in that visits to states with whom there has been no previous contacts, or where agreements have lapsed, may appear politically successful but difficult to match with two-way trade.[36] The timescales of each party to an agreement may differ considerably and attention declines. After signature, agreements in this category are also vulnerable to delay or changes of government in the initiating party. Changes of government affect the future priorities of which countries or institutions are visited, as visits and agreements are adjusted as part of initial assessments on the direction of external policy, leading to interruptions in negotiations and often shelving of agreements.

An additional difficulty which has emerged in trade development is the problem smaller regional organisations made up of members with different trade and development profiles have in mounting external trade initiatives as a single regional organisation. For example, the Caribbean regional organisation CARICOM's bilateral trade summit with Colombia was unsuccessful partly because very few of CARICOM's members had any significant trade with Colombia, other than Trinidad and Tobago (petroleum products); those that wished to explore trade opportunities preferred to do so bilaterally.[37]

The format of the meeting – ministerial summit – was unsuited to an exploratory mission. As Elizabeth Morgan argues, foreign trade policy and strategy need to be carefully worked out in collaboration with the private sector as part of pre-summit assessments in order to avoid empty ceremonial summits and generate greater effectiveness by targeting specific sectors.[38] In contrast, the 8th CARICOM–Cuba meeting provided an example of a model summit, focused on agriculture, with subsequent Cuban participation in CARICOM agricultural projects.[39]

## *Safeguarding presence: negotiations*

The limits to presence are primarily affected by the structure and content of trade negotiations. In response to international trade rivalry and maintaining bloc cohesion, three changes in methods are particularly significant for safeguarding presence: the use of advance notification, sequencing and linked clauses. Linked clauses, which cross-link benefits to successful compliance of others substantive clauses, have been resisted in asymmetrical negotiations and are generally unpopular as devices for extracting more concessions.

Advance notification is used for two main purposes: either to stake out a claim or to signal active and forward commitment. Differing formats include unilateral publication of main negotiating objectives and positions, red lines, joint statements on intentions to start or speed up negotiations and detailed pre-negotiation draft texts. Examples are the EU–Kenya joint statement on future negotiations, which was used by the EU, and the

Taiwan–US joint statement on future negotiations.[40] The EU document is also of interest for its detailed statement of binding legal commitments and the level playing field doctrine prior to resumed negotiations:

> The EU and Kenya agree to negotiate as an integral part of their Economic Partnership Agreement, binding provisions on trade and sustainable development-building on the ACP–EU partnership acquis-which will be subject to an appropriate dispute settlement mechanism. The implementation of their Agreement will be backed and supported by the EU's development and cooperation tools.
>
> (17 February 2022)[41]

The EU–Kenya agreement was concluded on 18 December 2023, in a multisector, sustainable economic governance format, framed as an economic partnership agreement between the EU and Kenya.

Michel Barnier, EU chief negotiator in the UK–Brexit negotiations, provides in his *Secret Diary* an unusual and valuable account of his approach to diplomatic methods and interpretation of sequencing as conditional progress in the withdrawal negotiations with the UK. A strict line was essential since withdrawal had become an important issue in the growing fragmentation in the bloc.

For Barnier, sequencing was not the usual idea of moving from issue to issue, step-by-step negotiation and trade-offs within and between sectors, typical of traditional diplomacy. Rather, the withdrawal negotiations were seen as progression: moving through stages, setting conditions for assessing progress and acceptance of core concepts and principles before any progression.

In an illuminating insight he recounts an exchange with UK chief negotiator David Davis,[42] in which Barnier agrees not to use the term "sequencing" in progress reports in response to UK concerns but makes it clear that the first part of the agenda would not be dealt with in a loose or disaggregated manner: "we will not move onto the second step without having reached an agreement on the first one."[43] That agenda listed priorities as residual institutions, the Ireland border regulations and financial settlement, rather than the UK's trade-first withdrawal agenda, which put resolving financial payments and Ireland very much as lower order questions.[44]

In the opening phases, the UK conceded the format and agenda which had a fundamental impact on later phases and overall outcome of the negotiations. It was high personal statecraft and an EU diplomatic victory but at the cost of workability.

## *Contested presence: geopolitical shifts and trade blocs*

The geopolitical shift of attention to Africa and Pacific island states introduced challenges to traditional European areas of bilateral influence. In Africa, in addition to PRC port and infrastructure initiatives, other actors who have shifted focus include Saudi Arabia, UAE, Qatar and Turkey (as noted above), operating against traditional European bilateral agreements. Michael Tanchum has argued that in the absence of a coherent EU policy:

> Leading EU member states will partner with actors outside the Union to create Africa-to-Europe corridors...any space left by the European Union in the development of trans-Mediterranean connectivity will be filled by China, Russia, Turkey and GCC states.[45]

In the Pacific, China's strategy relied on focusing on the Solomon Islands using visit diplomacy, trade, education scholarships and a pre-drafted internal security training pact. In response, Australia used emergency counter diplomacy with a media campaign prior to, and during, the visit of the Chinese Foreign Minister to stress the value of traditional links and the dangers of external dependence.

Bilateral trade agreements were also used by Australia as part of emergency counter diplomacy to shore up relations with the Solomon Islands and Micronesian states in response to China's step-by-step strategy of splitting groups, using multilateral contract funding projects and building strategic presence.[46] It was just about sufficient in the short run but not in the long term.

## Mega trade blocs and groupings

The decline of multilateralism following the breakdown of the WTO Doha Round was underlined by the acceleration of negotiations of mega trade blocs and various forms of inter-regional and bilateral trade diplomacy.

The creation of two mega free trade blocs with overlapping membership shifted the process of trade regulation from collective multilateral rulemaking into bloc regulation. The Regional Comprehensive Partnership (RCEP)[47] and the Comprehensive and Progressive Agreement for Trans-Pacific Partnership (CPTPP)[48] contributed to the spread of geopolitics in the management of international trade.

The RCEP was a major long-term PRC project to link key Asia-Pacific economies with ASEAN economies in a single organisation as a mega bloc, replacing the existing network of partnership agreements negotiated by ASEAN. The political objectives of positioning the RCEP as a new trade actor outweighed any economic trading facilitation. The RCEP comprising 15 members accounts for an estimated 25% of world trade.[49]

It interesting to note that in negotiating the RCEP, China was acutely aware of the need to distance itself from the public political negotiating process and remain in the background to avoid publicity regarding its presence and sensitivity over future RCEP relations with ASEAN. Distance was achieved by low media coverage and avoiding hosting RCEP negotiating rounds. In over 13 rounds, only one was held at an early stage in China. In the later phases, additional secret talks were held with India to try and secure its participation in the RCEP.

The RCEP came into force on 1 January 2022, after nearly eight years of negotiation, for ten of the original parties: Australia, New Zealand, Brunei, Cambodia, China, Japan, Laos, Singapore, Thailand and Vietnam. Ratification was subsequently completed by the Republic of Korea, Malaysia and Indonesia.[50]

India, a member of the RCEP drafting committee, withdrew from the negotiations in November 2019, in part over continued concerns about the draft texts on agriculture, the adequacy of trade safeguard provisions and import effects of RCEP, given its burgeoning trade deficit with the PRC. The loss of India was acknowledged in an RCEP Ministerial Declaration[51] which left later accession open and created the option of an interim association pending renegotiation. Of the ASEAN members, Philippines ratification was withheld because of Senate objections and opposition from domestic sectors concerned over the impact of RCEP on agriculture.[52]

The CPTPP was signed in Santiago, Chile on 8 March 2018 by 11 countries. It entered into force on 30 December 2018 for Australia, Canada, Japan, Mexico, New Zealand and Singapore; for Vietnam on 14 January 2019, Peru on 19 September 2021 and Malaysia on 30 September 2022. The ratification by the final three countries was critical for the overall political authority of the CPTPP, after the earlier withdrawal by the United States, leaving Brunei and Chile as the outstanding signatories not ratifying. Ratification by Chile extended the geographic coverage of the CPTPP in line with its title, differentiating it as a Trans-Pacific Partnership, rather than an Asia-Pacific orientation.[53]

## The CPTPP

The CPTPP is significantly different from the RCEP in terms of membership, geographic coverage and structure. It has become a counter organisation to RCEP, although interestingly its origins were bilateral in the Singapore–New Zealand Closer Economic Partnership (ANZSCEP).[54]

The RCEP differs from the CPTPP in that it is essentially a basic tariff-reduction agreement built around individual tariff-commitment schedules and reservations, headed with voluntary general commitments covering different sectors. In contrast, the tariff regime in the CPTPP is integrated and progressive. Other differences are the more extensive scope on labour and environmental rules and the use of obligatory rather than voluntary language. Some changes to the scope of the agreement followed the US withdrawal[55] but the remaining provisions in the CPTPP[56] are incorporated from the TPP.[57] The overall scope and level of coordination in the CPTPP remains considerably wider than RCEP. Other distinctive provisions on capacity training for members and reviews of implementation reflect its progressive approach.[58]

One of the major implications of the withdrawal of the US was the creation of a strategic gap in membership. The withdrawal of the US reduced the strategic economic impact of the CPTPP but it also created a significant strategic gap through the absence of a primary power.

Additional membership of the CPTPP was not initially a major issue, with the UK, although "out of area", applying for CPTPP membership largely for economic reasons as part of Brexit reorientation. It did, however, underline the question of open accession clauses in agreements and the implications of additional membership on the functions, objectives and compliance standards of organisations. Whether to permit new or associate membership has become a difficult and divisive issue.

It is seen, for example, in the growth of flags of convenience being used in international fisheries for transfer loading and supply services in and outside EEZs. This has now become a general problem, discussed further in chapter 5, affecting trade and many other forms of related agreements covering fisheries and regional organisation states (e.g. Panama, Liberia, PRC, Korea, EU). Other entities use extant or long-forgotten provisions in agreements and other methods to gain membership or participation rights some considerable time after the original agreement entered into force in order to find new resources, which may have restrictions on fishing effort.[59]

The PRC application to join the CPTPP introduced an additional geopolitical dimension to membership issues made as a counter diplomacy move almost immediately following the public announcement of the AUKUS nuclear submarine deal.[60]

Different membership issues are posed for the RCEP. Apart from the question of Indian withdrawal, a continuing broader issue concerns the long-term relationship between ASEAN and the RCEP. Whether the RCEP will develop parallel functions to ASEAN, eventually absorbing it and ending the "ASEAN centrality" doctrine is unclear, though possible. The ring of bilateral partnership and dialogue agreements around ASEAN (e.g. ASEAN–Australia) may reduce or delay that possibility.[61]

Individual ASEAN members have become important entry hubs into the RCEP, as is likely with the CPTPP, acting as trade platforms for export redirection and local production to ASEAN states taking advantage of limited rules of origin. Malaysia has expanded its diplomatic and trade space by means of a bilateral agreement with Turkey, to act as hub into the RCEP. As part of the deal, Malaysia used the side exchanges to try and secure commitments from Turkey to meet bilateral trade levels with Malaysia set in the existing bilateral agreement which were substantially under-utilised by Turkey.[62]

## Inter-regionalism: EU–Africa and Latin America

The idea of inter-regionalism is based on the concept of developing institutional-based trade relations which go beyond the scope of basic trade agreements. It is associated with initiatives by regional organisations, and especially linked to EU diplomacy in this area. Inter-regionalism envisaged cooperation meetings at foreign and other ministerial levels and was an intermittent feature of experimental diplomacy from the end of the cold war as the international system began to open up and new forms of relations were being considered. It has had mixed success.

The EU's failed inter-regional diplomacy in Latin America, Africa and Asia left four significant legacies for diplomatic methods. First, the inconclusive negotiations with MERCOSUR over two decades[63] left EU relations with Latin America in an indeterminate and unsatisfactory form which prevented wider development of relations. At an internal EU level, the terms on agricultural access for MERCOSUR products were a source of ongoing domestic tension for France, Ireland and other EU agriculture producers.[64]

Second, the failed African negotiations impacted on African regional integration, leading to differing African trade links and tariffs with external actors and split sub-regional organisations. The institutional legacy left behind shells of EPA agreements, such as EU–Cote d'Ivoire and Ghana with incomplete agreements in West Africa,[65] the East African Community (EAC)[66] and other East African states.[67]

Different African continental and external tariff negotiations added to the problems of the African Continental Free Trade Agreement (AfCFTA).[68]

At regional level, the EAC was divided over the Tripartite Free Trade agreement, negotiated as an east-southern Africa grouping prior to the continental rival organisation the African Continental Free Area.[69] Bilateral issues included Kenya–UK relations[70] tracked by media outlet Politico in EU counter diplomacy against the UK. AU economic relations with the EU,[71] US[72] and China[73] each presented complex bilateral and regional difficulties. The question of the nature and extent of relations with external powers became one of the enduring sources of division within the EAC.

In contrast the acceptance of the Democratic Republic of the Congo (DRC) as a member of the EAC provoked perhaps less controversy, although the long-term political and economic implications were, in some respects (particularly membership balance and security), no less daunting.[74]

Third, inter-regional failure impacted on the future of the Afro-Caribbean Pacific Community (ACP)[75] linked to the EU under the Cotonou preference agreement. The EU effectively abandoned its traditional links with the ACP in order to secure a cooperation partnership agreement instead with the AU, in parallel negotiations with ACP and

EU.[76] It meant the loss of an old style, semi-nonaligned approach of a tricontinental body set up over 50 years earlier, loosely grouped around trade, development, cultural and parliamentary cooperation but which now seemed dated in a very different international system.

Opinion within the EU over budgetary support costs and political relevance of future links with a reformed ACP was divided[77] as it was in the AU[78] and ACP.[79] Breaking up the ACP[80] into three regions nullified its founding ideas.[81] There was also the separate issue that the proposed reform of the ACP created institutions which duplicated AU bodies and CARICOM. Disconnected from the membership, the replacement institution – the Organisation of Africa, Pacific and Caribbean countries (OACPS) – was a new international organisation representing the ACP, which had no obvious role or adequate finance to function internationally.

Doubts on these points are reflected in the decision of South Africa to withdraw from the OACPS.[82] Its relations with the ACP had at best been ambiguous. That decision nevertheless was to a large extent a consequence of EU methods used to negotiate inter-regionalism. These relied on switching to bilateral agreements with individual states or seeking special relations with others when progress in inter-regional or sub-regional negotiations was limited.

It can be argued that this approach contributed to the splintering of African regional groups and added to tendencies to break away or seek other sources, rather than contributing to the building blocks of continental integration, used to justify EPAs.

South Africa justified its decision to withdraw from the OACPS on the basis that its bilateral agreement with the EU now made membership of the Group unnecessary. The withdrawal decision was an important loss for the OACPS, removing a key continental and international player from its membership and ability to lobby. The issues OACPS faced remained: EU blacklisting on financial governance, trade access and diversification, and financial support for effective, rather than selective, development made its survival more difficult.

Fourth, the EU switched from trade based inter-regionalism to using strategic cooperation agreements as the basic template for cooperation agreements. The EU had limited diplomatic space in terms of options for maintaining an African presence in view of internal doubts about ACP and budgetary competition. The failed shell agreements with East and West Africa offered little scope for further revision. Residual negotiations were kept going with the small East African island states (EAS5) through multiple rounds, essentially to retain a political presence. The AU has found it difficult to develop an international role beyond it continental focus, and its relations with the EU at inter-regional level have lacked coherence.

These concerns were at the basis of critical commentaries drawing on concern within the AU at the third EU–AU summit, questioning its purpose and lack of a joint agenda.[83] Underlying these views was the ongoing debate within regional organisations over the role and involvement of external actors.

Rebadging inter-regionalism as strategic cooperation constituted a major shift in diplomatic methods, in view of the impact on style and substance of cooperation. It moved away from a trade-based focus into a framework for general cooperation.[84]

Titles matter in terms of how an agreement is interpreted and, above all, implemented. In strategic cooperation agreements, the content tends to become more segmented, diffuse and implemented by revised plans, road maps or vision-oriented goals. Projects may not be linked or set in a strategic plan, as in the classic case of the EU-funded Cameroon–Nigeria road bridge project. The style of leader summits in strategic cooperation tends to become communiqué-dominated, reminiscent of the East Asia Sumit or G20.

EU strategic cooperation agreements with the AU, ASEAN and GCC are similarly constructed around a preferred list of topics identified by the EU as challenges (green transition, energy, climate, digitalisation, trade and investment). In the GCC case, the agreement is not adjusted to a Middle Eastern context or the interests of petroleum powers but repeats the same formula used in the AU and ASEAN agreements. Repetition limits innovation and influences the tendency for communiqué form rather than substance.

## Trade, security and conflicts: changing methods

In armed conflicts there is often limited scope or interest for mediation involving trade flows. The grain deal in the Ukraine war is an illustration of a relative rare agreement to maintain exports of grain and agricultural goods from parties in war. It was brokered by Turkey, the UN Secretary-General and officials from two specialised UN agencies – the International Maritime Organisation and UNCTAD. It eventually broke down the following year.[85] The brittle nature of mediation in armed conflict was similarly illustrated in the Israeli–Gaza war, with Qatar-brokered, temporary ceasefire prisoner and humanitarian access breaking down.[86] Even though short term, the mediation did indirectly assist other conflict reduction initiatives for the Lebanese border and on exploratory proposals for post-war arrangements. The risk of escalation over freedom of navigation through the Red Sea[87] and global trade routes impacted by attacks on shipping in regional conflicts have periodically underlined the vulnerability of supply chains and global reach of shipping.[88]

## Trade diplomacy and security: development of agreements

In bilateral and plurilateral relations, the widening of the content of the international trade agenda is reflected in the greater use of informal group meetings and bilateral dialogues, as well as more formal devices such as leader summits on issues such as supply chain security, technology cooperation and diversification of supply sources. Supply chain issues have moved onto the WTO agenda but have not been multilateralised into collective trade agreements.[89] Rather, mega trade blocs have become focal arenas for trade security.

It is noticeable, in the absence of multilateral supply chain agreements, that an additional form of bilateral relations, rather than collective multilateral diplomacy, has developed. These have been augmented by third states (bilateral plus) as part of pre-emptive geo-economic diplomacy on e-commerce cooperation, to block out an international institution, competitor or adversary. Bilateral plus agreements are open membership. In other similar cases, agreements which were originally sub-agreements between CPTPP partners have now become mixed plurilateral hubs, reinforcing the move away from multilateral collective processes and agreements.

Second, risk reduction in trade is an area of increased attention. In conflicts, the boundaries of risk are altered in order to maintain positions. Creating new EU–Taiwan business formats for semiconductor trade exhibitions and missions on joint manufacturing push at the risk boundary.

In other instances, mechanisms are created to reduce trade vulnerability by innovating new trade roles, for example, by using a bilateral agreement with a member of a mega trade bloc for joint or rebadged trade to other bloc members or external markets. In these and similar examples, decisions are taken to redraw lines on what is possible by challenging the conditionality of risk (meetings, visits, conferences, statements).

Third, in terms of ideas and institutions, values-based approaches (principles, norms rule of law and selective engagement) contrast with realpolitik methods (drawing lines around allies, recognition of zones of influence, tariffs, trade rebalancing and sanctions), reflecting different approaches to international trade security.[90] The landscape of institutions has altered to take in a growing range of plurilateral, coalitions, clubs and bilateral deals covering supply chains and raw material agreements, along with the expanding the role of the G7. Common to these routes, however, is the scope and depth of engagement with adversaries. What to put into engagement and how far to delineate no-go areas remain enduring dilemmas for whatever orientation is chosen on the paradox of conflict and cooperation.

## Conclusion

Trade questions have come to occupy a central position in the management of external policy. That change has been influenced by increasing post-Doha trade rivalry, supply vulnerability and recognition of trade dependence, blurring the lines between trade and security. A greater range of security issues has moved onto the trade agenda, related to market access, commodities supply, trade classification, vulnerability of supply chains, and the impact of regional conflicts on commodity exports and inbound trade.

Tension between trade and foreign policy at a bureaucratic and policy level has been heightened by the above issues, along with other factors such as badly negotiated or ineffective trade agreements and commercial interests running ahead or being conducted independently of foreign policy.

Trade vulnerability has correspondingly led to wider domestic debate over methods for reducing supply dependency, how to recover from loss of market access, how best to create other trade and cooperation arrangements, and appropriate strategies and methods for dealing with adversarial states.

The growth of international trade rivalry and geopolitical competition has led to several important changes in trade methods. Greater emphasis has been given to bilateral trade diplomacy as part of trade security.

Bilateral methods have been used to create new alliance institutions, extend side diplomacy and innovation. The extension of side diplomacy into a wider range of plurilateral agreements has facilitated greater and more frequent contact. Bilateral sector cooperation has become widely used as interim device to back a membership application to a grouping or bloc. It relies on repetition and using additional traditional methods such as ring-fencing a contentious area, dispute or issue to smooth over sector cooperation.

At regional organisation level, contrasting methods have been used to deal with issues of organisational identity and limit the rival regional influence of mega trade blocs. Proliferating bilateral links with external actors and summits may provide a sense of identity and have diplomatic value for regional organisations, though in the longer term the possibility of absorption by a mega trade bloc may become unavoidable.

Limited diplomatic space may force regional organisations into acceptance of other routes, built on multiple levels – inter-organisation (intercontinental), inter-regional and bilateral cooperation, which prove eventually too complex or of limited development value.

Failure in inter-organisation diplomacy has influenced a new diplomatic vocabulary: paused negotiations, high ambition, steppingstone agreements, and the unusual term "variable geometry" to describe the development of parties to negotiations.

In addition to these developments in methods at bilateral and regional level, a significant feature of trade diplomacy is the use of methods at the margins of diplomacy and coercion, such as counter diplomacy and parallel diplomacy, to block or undermine a competing application or trade initiative.

Trade negotiations and new groupings are monitored, initiatives blocked and warnings given on trade realignment, adding to the politicisation of trade and conflicts between trade and foreign policy.

## Notes

1 The WTO was created by the Marrakesh Agreement, establishing the WTO on 15 April 1994, entering into force on 1 January 1995. ("The WTO Agreement") For the text of the agreement see www.wto.org/english/docs_e/legal_e/legal-e_htm. For discussion of the functions of the WTO, see Michael J. Trebilcock, *Advanced Introduction to International Trade Law* (Edward Elgar, 2015) chapter 3; also Peter Van den Bossche and Werner Zdouc, *The Law and Policy of the World Trade Organisation* (Cambridge University Press, 2016).

2 Most of the substantive WTO law is contained in Annex 1 of the Agreement, in three parts. Annex 1A contains 13 multilateral agreements on trade in goods (GATT 1994); 1B, the General Agreement on trade in Services (GATS); 1C, the agreement on Intellectual Property Rights (TRIPS).

3 See on the breakdown of the Doha Round the assessment of competing positions in the impasse at the Nairobi Ministerial Meeting, at WTO, WT MIN(15) DEC, part 111, paras 28–30. For discussion of the main factors for the breakdown, see R.P. Barston, *Modern Diplomacy* (Routledge, 2019) 5th ed., pp212–6.

4 For further discussion, see chapter 6.

5 The defence of globalisation was put by the WTO Director-General, Ngozi Okonjo-Iweala, in "We must push for re-globalization…" at www.wto.org/english/news_e/news23_e/igo_21jun23_e.htm.

6 See, for example, Catherine Ashton, *And Then What?* (Elliot and Thompson, 2022) p145.

7 On the P5+1, see Burns' note to Secretary Rice in William J. Burns, *The Back Channel* (Hurst and Co., 2019) p341.

8 See the debate over when to inform the P5 of US–Iran bilateral discussions, in Burns, ibid., pp 346–7.

9 Celso Amorim, *Acting Globally* (Hamilton Books, 2017) pp34–5.

10 On the political and environmental focus of Secretary Blinken's visit to Kenya in November 2021, see https://ke.usembassy.gov/secretary-blinken-travel-to-kenya-nigeria-and-senegal-november-15-20-2021/

11 For example, German–China trade and EU policy in the Ukraine conflict.

12 *Sydney Morning Herald,* 18 November 2022 for account of the Australia–US–UK negotiations on AUKUS defence upgrading for submarines.

13 For the narrative link between the Ukraine war and global food security see G20, Indonesia, Bali Leader's Declaration, para 8, 16 November 2022. www.whitehouse.gov/briefing-room/statements-releases/2022/11/16/g20-bali-leaders-declaration/.

14 See www.swp-berlin.org/10.18449/2022C64/.

15 See chapter 10 on Turkey's shipping role.

16 See https://port.today/apm-terminals-expands-chinese-partnerships-in-italy/.

17  See www.lloydslist.com/LL1146607/US-targets-Turkish-shipping-support-and-Arctic-ambitions-in-latest-Russian-sanctions.

18  See Michel Barnier, *My Secret Brexit Diary* (Polity Press, 2021) pp332–3 on the importance for the EU of the concept of the level playing field in negotiations.

19  See www.bmz.de/news/press-releases/, 29 October 2022; www.bmz.de/en/ministry/working-approach; www.bmz.de/resources/blog/, 1 July 2022.

20  Examples of small states with multilateral roles include Singapore (UNCLOS, BBNJ agreement) and New Zealand (WTO agriculture, Doha Round).

21  Joint Statement, "CETA at Five Years: the cornerstone of Canada–EU economic relations", Government of Canada, 2 December 2022; especially penultimate paragraph which briefly touches on market access issues. See https://policy.trade.ec.europa.eu/news/joint-statement-ceta-five-years-cornerstone-canadaeu-economic-relations-2022-12-02_en.

22  *Financial Times*, 30 October 2023.

23  See US–Common Market for Eastern and Southern Africa (COMESA) TIFA, https://ustr.gov/trade-agreements/free-trade-agreements/oman-fta

24  India–Australia exchange of letters on the Economic and Trade Cooperation Agreement of 2 April 2022 along with side agreements at www.commerce.gov.in/international-trade/trade-agreements/ind-aus-ecta/.

25  Disaggregating participation in China's Belt and Road Initiative, see www.brookings.edu/articles/signing-up-or-s.

26  www.mfat.nz/trade/nz/china-free-trade.

27  A workshop format was used for the US–Japan–Vietnam initiative on promoting LNG trade options.

28  *Financial Times*, 6 June 2023 and 11 July 2023, "Australia-EU trade deal stalls over meat quotas"; also *Financial Times*, 30 October 2023.

29  Indonesia–US request for minerals agreement similar to US–Japan.

30  "United States and Indo-Pacific Economic Framework Partners Announce Negotiating Objectives", USTR 9 September 2022; *IPEF* (Trade Pillar), USTR 23 September 2022.

31  www.morrocoworldnews.com/2020/05/tab b.

32  Xi visited Saudi Arabia 5–7 December 2022, some five months after President Biden; see "A New Order in the Middle East", Foreign Affairs, March 2023 www.foreignaffairs.com/china/iran-saudi-arabia-middle-east-relations.

33  On the dark trade in Ukraine grain see *FT* investigation, 29 June 2022, www.ft.com/content/86d2be80-d69c-4b93-b448-dd006b070854.

34  https://asean.org/asean-external-relations/Germany. Development status for Germany was agreed at the 49th ASEAN foreign ministers meeting, Vientiane, 24 August 2016.

35  The ASEAN doctrine on its centrality to the management of ASEAN relations is restated in official documents such as communiques following ministerial meetings.

36  The Malaysia–Chile free trade agreement was the first agreement for Malaysia with South America. Negotiations opened in 2007 and concluded in May 2010; the deal was signed on 13 November 2010 in Yokohama. It entered into force on 25 February 2012 and was a showpiece for a short but carefully thought out South–South agreement. Nevertheless, the agreement highlighted the limits of exploratory trade, especially between states with limited regular political contact and difficult transportation links. Within four years of entry into force,

total trade with Chile had decreased by 29.3% (exports declined by 20.5%). See https://fta.miti.gov.my/index.php/pages/view/Malaysia-Chile?mid+43.

37 See      https://caricom.org/declaration-of-barranquilla-ii-caricom-colombia-ministerial-summit/.

38 Elizabeth Morgan "CARICOM-Colombia trade relations", https://jamaica-gleaner.com, 16 February 2022.

39 Bridgetown Declaration Eighth CARICOM–Cuba summit 6 December 2022. https://caricom.org/final-declaration-eighth-caricom-cuba-summit-bridget own-barbados-6-december-2022/.

40 US–Taiwan Initiative on 21st-century trade: negotiating mandate, 17 August 2022.

41 EU–Kenya joint statement on intensifying negotiations for an interim revised trade cooperation agreement. See https://policy.trade.ec.europa.eu/ news/eu-and-kenya-advance-talks-interim-economic-partnership-agreement-sustainability-provisions-2022-02-17_en.

42 Harold Nicolson, *The Evolution of Diplomatic Method* (Cassell, London, 1954) p70.

43 Michel Barnier, *My Secret Brexit Diary* (Polity Press, 2021) p59.

44 EU–Northern Ireland Protocol. Article 5(6) prohibits quantitative restrictions; article 9 electricity market linkage, state aid; article 10(1) restrictions on exemptions; article 10(3) unlawful measures; article 16 (safeguards); countered by proportionate rebalancing. See also Barnier, op. cit., pp364–5 re. the Brexit negotiations on the EU position that tariff-free access had to be matched by equivalent measures on fisheries, linking electrical interconnection to Europe, for example, with fisheries quotas.

45 Michael Tanchum, "Europe–Mediterranean Africa Commercial Connectivity: Geopolitical Opportunities and Challenges" Med Dialogue Series, 2020.

46 The Solomon Islands awarded its main port development to a PRC company in a project funded by the Asian Development Bank. See visits by Australia, Japan and US envoys as counter diplomacy and US–Pacific summit, 25–26 September 2023. The Solomon Islands did not attend the summit.

47 www.dfat.gov.au/trade/agreements/in-force/cptpp/comprehensive-and-progressive-agreement-for-trans-pacific-partnership.

48 www.mfat.govt.nz/en/about-us/who-we-are/treaties;      www.international.gc. ca/trade-commerce/trade-agreements-accords-commerciaux/agr-acc/cptpp-ptpgp/index.aspx?lang=eng.

49 25% world trade RCEP data.

50 Republic of Korea, 1 February 2022; Malaysia, 14 March 2022; Indonesia, 3 November 2022. Effective 60 days after ratification.

51 RCEP Joint Leaders Statement and attached Ministerial Declaration on India's Participation in the Regional Economic Partnership, 11 November 2022.

52 *Manila Bulletin*, 8 September 2022.

53 https://en.mercopress.com?2022/10/12/chile-s-senate-greenlights-cptpp-agreement. The agreement had been approved by the Lower House in April 2019 but held up in the Senate and elections. Although approved by the Chile Senate, implementation has made conditional by the Chilean President, Gabriel Boric Font, on bilateral side letters to confirm the withdrawal of investment protection dispute provisions by Mexico, New Zealand, Australia, Brunei and Thailand before final implementation. See

https://aftinet.org.au/aftinet.org.au/latest-news/Chile-CPTPP-side-lett
ers-stop-ISDS.

54 Timothy Barnes, *A Naked View of the Trans-Pacific Partnership* (Dog Ear
Publishing, 2016) p24.

55 Press release, Office of the United States Trade Representative, 1 January 2017.

56 The CPTPP agreed by consensus to suspend nine articles following US withdrawal. These provisions remain part of the CPTPP but there has been no
application under international law. For details of the suspended parts of articles (customs, investment (ISDS), cross border services, financial services,
government procurement, intellectual property, environment, transparency
and anti-corruption. See www.dfat.gov.au/sites/default/files/cptpp-suspensi
ons-explained.pdf.

57 For the full texts of the CPTPP, see www.mfat.gov.nz>free-trade-agreements/
cpttp.

58 See CPTPP especially chapter 20 (environment) and chapter 21 (cooperation
and capacity building). www.dfat.gov.au/trade/agreements/in-force/cptpp/
comprehensive-and-progressive-agreement-for-trans-pacific-partnership.

59 See chapter 5, notes 95, 106.

60 China applied for accession to CPTPP though the depository power of New
Zealand by letter on 16 September 2021, the day following the announcement
of the AUKUS security agreement.

61 Chairman's Statement 2nd annual ASEAN–Australia summit, Phnom Penh, 12
November 2022.

62 Bernama, 7 July 2022.

63 Hardacre, op. cit., *The Rise and Fall of Interregionalism*, pp193–210; German
Council on Foreign Relations, https://dgap.org/en/research/publications/
last-chance-at-eu-mercosur-agreement.

64 Cote d'Ivoire EPA, Ghana EPA. L287(21/10/16); L340 (15/12/16), signed 28
July 2016. Provisional application 15 December 2016 but modified to Interim
EPA (iEPA) effective 1 July 2021. See https://policy.trade.ec.europa.eu/eu-
trade-relationships-country-and-region/countries-and-regions/west-africa_en.

65 See https://policy.trade.ec.europa.eu/eu-trade-relationships-country-and-reg
ion/countries-and-regions/west-africa_en.

66 Negotiations for a regional EPA between the EU and East African Community
(EAC – Burundi, Kenya, Rwanda, Tanzania and Uganda) were completed in
2014. Kenya and Rwanda signed in September 2016 but only Kenya ratified the
EPA. South Sudan and Democratic Republic of the Congo joined the EAC in
2016 and 2022 respectively. The EPA is only in force for Kenya. Further negotiations with Kenya on a revised agreement were announced in an EU Joint
Statement, 17 February 2022.

67 Report of the ninth round of negotiations between the EU and ESA 5, 19–
23 September 2022 in Antananarivo, Madagascar. The group comprises EU,
Comoros, Madagascar, Mauritius, Seychelles and Zimbabwe, as a separate
group from the EAC, AfCFTA or other negotiations. The integration of these
into other agreements is indicative of the problem of splintered negotiations.

68 For text of the AfCFTA, see https://au.int/en/treaties/agreement-establish
ing-african-continental-free-trade-area. On the tariff and related issues of continental and sub-regional alignment see Gerhard Erasmus, "How the AfCFTA
fits into Africa's existing regional integration scheme", Tralac, 23 November

2022 at www.tralac.org/blog/article/15813-how-the-afcfta-fits-into-africa-s-existing-regional-integration-scheme.html.

69 The TFTA was signed 10 June 2015. The initial summit meeting on linking the Common Market for East and Southern Africa, Southern African Development Community and East African Community was held 22 October 2008. Negotiations for the TFTA were opened on 12 June 2011. The draft text was presented for signature at the third summit on 10 June 2015. See www.eac.int/trade/international-trade/trade-agreements/comesa-eac-sadc-tripartite-free-trade-area-tfta-agreement.

70 See United Kingdom–Kenya agreement, Misc. No 9 (2020), 8 December 2020.

71 The EAC Heads of State Summit, was held via video conference on 27 February 2021 which curtailed discussion. It was attended by Rwanda, Kenya, Burundi, South Sudan, Uganda, and Tanzania (HE Samia Suluhu Hassan for President Magafuli). The summit was unable to reach consensus on an EPA with the EU and referred the issue to members for individual decision.

72 Standard (Kenya) 29 October 2022. "*32 Agri farmers jet into Kenya as part of a US delegation.*"

73 On significance of China in the Kenya elections, see Financial Times, 2 April 2022. On the death of President Magafuli, see The Guardian, 17 March 2021.

74 DRC joined as a 7th member the EAC on 29 March 2022.

75 Georgetown Agreement, 6 June 1975, creating the ACP. The ACP was linked to the EU through the Cotonou Agreement, which expired on 29 February 2020.

76 www.consilium.europa.eu./press/2018/06/22.

77 For President Macron's comments on the ACP and OACP, see www.devex.com/news/macron-puts-eu-deal-with-africa-caribbean-pacific-on-death-watch-104934.

78 AU Executive Council Decision on the African Common Position for a New Cooperation Agreement with the EU. AU Doc. Ext/EX.CL/2(XVIII).

79 See remarks by Jamaican Foreign and Trade Minister, Kamina Johnson Smith as tribute to Ambassador Sheila Sealy Monteith and diplomatic staff for their work on the ACP mandate, based on an all-ACP approach as a single entity, https://mfaft.gov.jm/jamaica-closes-successful-presidency-of-acp-council-of-ministers-group-now-ready-to-negotiate-post-cotonou-agreement. Ambassador Monteith later served as head of the Ministry of Foreign and Trade Affairs.

80 Press Release Ministry of Foreign Affairs and Tourism, Foreign Affairs Department, Republic of the Seychelles, 17 September 2018 on the discussions of the ACP negotiating mandate at the 19th Extraordinary Session of the AU Executive Council.

81 See https://www.com>news>eu-rebukes-african-cari-19June 2024; Euroactiv, 16 November 2023, "Hold Outs cast shadow".

82 "The EU wants to be Africa's friend…", Africa Renewal magazine EU–AU Summit 2022.

83 See report by President Paul Kagame on the institutional reform of the AU, 37th AU summit, 17 February 2024, at www.paulkagame.com>report-by-the-president-pau.

84 See AU Reform Advisory Committee https://au.int/en/AUReforms/advisory and progress report.

85 Russia withdrew from the grain deal on 17 July 2023. The UN Secretary-General attempted to keep the grain deal alive in proposals on 30 August 2023. https://news.un.story/2023/07/1138752.

86 Qatar initiative, www.reuters.com/world/middle-east/how-qatar-swayed-israel-hamas-make-truce-work-2023-11-30/.

87 An MSC container ship was attacked 26 December 2023, two days after the 2M Alliance partner announced it would consider resume transits through the Red Sea and Suez Canal following the decision to set up an international naval task force to protect shipping in the region. See www.joc.com/article/msc-ship-becomes-latest-targeted-red-sea-attack_20231226.html.

88 Global Supply Chains Forum Dialogue Report "Easing supply chain bottlenecks for a sustainable future". See www.wto.org/english/news_e/ events_e/ gscforum 2022_e.htm.

89 Digital Economy Partnership Agreement, www.mfat.govt.nz/en/trade/free-trade-agreements/free-trade-agreements-in-force/digital-economy-partnership-agreement-depa.

90 Charlie Laderman and Brendan Simms, *Donald Trump: The Making of a World View* (I.B. Tauris, 2017) pp111–12.

Chapter 5

# Environmental diplomacy

## Introduction

Environmental diplomacy is probably the most diverse and challenging of the various forms of diplomacy. It is distinctive in terms of its scope, impact on other sectors, technical requirements and timescales of negotiation and compliance. The problem of securing the universality of agreements is reflected in the use of declaratory goals, codes, guidelines and other informal instruments to achieve some measure of common acceptance of measures. Other limits arise from factors such as national capacity, economic cost, threats to established interests or opposition to the creation of amended or new international regulations.

In environmental diplomacy, several methods have been developed to fill regulatory gaps, develop new areas and limit constraints. The process, nevertheless, is slow and uneven and constraints on creating workable multilateral agreements in this sector are greater than in other forms of diplomacy. Multilateral environmental diplomacy is a constant pulling and hauling between those who seek to create and develop regulatory regimes and those who seek to evade or minimise collective rules and cooperation.

In this chapter, two areas of environmental regulation are explored: the development of regulations and institutions for marine fisheries resources beyond 200nm as a follow up to Law of the Sea Convention, and international negotiations to combat pollution from the disposal of plastics.

## Background

The Law of the Sea negotiations (1973–82) undertook a major reform of an extensive range of maritime, resource and environment issues within one overarching convention.[1] The UNCLOS convention codified existing practice but also innovated with new regimes including 200nm EEZs,[2]

DOI: 10.4324/9781003204039-6

living and non-living resource regimes,[3] the concept of archipelagic states,[4] new regulatory norms and provisions with respect to the prevention, reduction and control of marine pollution in the EEZ, and new concepts such as port state control with respect pollution and safety and pollution offences.[5]

The concept of 200nm EEZs extended sovereign rights and jurisdiction beyond traditional territorial sea limits with significant implications for fisheries and other resource management, and enforcement potentially over large areas of sea, previously designated as high seas.

The emphasis in the UNCLOS negotiations on the regimes for the territorial sea, EEZs and new normative issues relating to institutionalising rights to the deep seabed mineral resources beyond 200nm as the common heritage of mankind, meant that management and conservation of fisheries in high seas areas received relatively little attention in the Convention. Provisions were limited to general requirements to cooperate either directly or through a regional or sub-regional organisation overfishing and conservation for the same or associated stock in high seas areas adjacent to an EEZ,[6] or in other areas of the high seas where identical stock is being fished.[7]

The extension of maritime limits to 200nm had the effect of shifting responsibility for marine resource management to states for large ocean areas which, in many cases, had limited national maritime administration and token naval or coastguard enforcement assets. The Marshall Islands is a classic example of the modern maritime micro state: very large sea space, low population, governance issues and a resource-dependent economy. Under the Law of the Sea Convention, the Marshall Islands is an archipelagic state comprising over 1,500 low lying islands and atolls linked by archipelagic baselines, which enclose as internal waters or EEZs an area of 180,000 square miles of former high seas in the central Pacific.

Responsibility for maritime environmental policy at multilateral level is dispersed through a number of multilateral institutions, principally the IMO (shipping, special areas), FAO (conservation, management, institutional development), UNEP (habitat, protected areas) and, to a more limited extent, ILO (vessel safety, working conditions).

Progress on new international maritime institutions from the 1970s was geographically uneven. These included attempts by developing countries to set up short-lived wider littoral state functional organisations as in the Indian ocean case.[8] International institutions including FAO and UNEP promoted environmental cooperation through sub-regional cooperation,[9] guidelines and codes of conduct on environment and special areas.[10] Negotiation of framework agreements became a widely used method for structuring environmental cooperation and commitments.[11] The prevalence of codes as methods underlined the limits and scope of international political cooperation balancing flag, shipping and coastal interests.

New regulatory areas tend to be taken up periodically and incorporated into the corpus of regulations on a piecemeal basis. For example, IMO shipping-based special areas under the MARPOL convention, e.g. North Sea, Great Barrier Reef, were progressively added over some twenty years. Some remained incomplete owing to failure to meet the entry into force requirements for sufficient oil and waste reception facilities. Other special areas were eventually added under the UNEP regional and sub-regional seas programmes. But interagency cooperation between IMO, UNEP and FAO remained limited, as each institution protected responsibility for its own sectors of activity.[12]

With respect to fisheries, progress on conservation and regulation has been much more fragmented. Early international agreements on fisheries institutions were limited to bilateral or dealt with by single species or advisory bodies, set up as part of loose regional cooperation, such as the Inter-American Tropical Tuna Commission or through institutions set up under FAO auspices, including the General Fisheries Commission for the Mediterranean and the International Commission for the Conservation of Atlantic Tuna (ICCAT).[13,14]

By the 1990s it had become increasingly apparent that major fish stocks were under substantial strain or overexploited as a result of overfishing, including in high seas areas.[15] In response to growing pressure within multilateral institutions including warnings by the FAO Fisheries Committee,[16] the UNCED Rio conference[17] and calls within the UN General Assembly for a moratorium on high seas drift net fishing,[18] international conferences began to address the need to negotiate new codes and additional regulations on overfishing, flags of convenience and stock conservation.

FAO initiatives include strengthening flag state responsibility (Compliance Agreement) and a code of conduct for responsible fisheries.[19] The Agreement, however, did not enter into force until 2003 with 25 states, largely made up of the then regulatory drivers (Canada, Iceland, Australia, New Zealand, US), states with strong regional fisheries interests (Norway, Sweden, Chile, Peru) and a cluster of smaller states, ratifying or acceding to the agreement.[20] Fishing and support service flag of convenience registry states[21] and long-range fleet operators remained largely outside or only nominally involved in the multilateral regulatory framework.[22]

## High seas: closing the gap

The high seas fisheries gap in the UNCLOS convention was subsequently addressed by an ad hoc UN diplomatic conference on straddling and highly migratory fish stocks. The conference, modelled on UNCLOS methods: consensus procedure,[23] conference documentation,[24] working groups,[25] alternative draft texts[26] and chairman's consolidated texts,[27] reached consensus on the High Seas Fisheries Agreement relatively quickly. This was largely due to the fact that many of the major concepts and areas of difficulty had already been established and problem areas resolved in over a decade of previous negotiations of UNCLOS. In particular, relevant principles and ideas such as duty to cooperate, criteria for "clear grounds" for investigation of offences and enforcement procedures were already a feature of the 1982 Law of the Sea Convention.[28]

The UN High Seas Fisheries Agreement dealing with straddling and highly migratory fish stocks, known somewhat misleadingly by its abbreviated title as the UN Fish Stocks agreement (UNFSA), entered into force in 2001, some six years after signature. Several important provisions, not in the 1982 convention, were added in the UNFSA, for example, on the precautionary principle as a factor in stock assessment, in addition to maximum sustainable yield, and detailed provisions on flag and coastal state enforcement.

A further major change is in the detailed provisions introduced on regional cooperation and access to resource regimes beyond 200nm. These go beyond the 1982 convention in the extent to which there is provision for fishing access for external states, without corresponding rights or different rights for existing members of regional organisations for conservation or competences to manage stocks. The revised part of the 1982 convention is heavily weighted in favour of long-range fisheries operations. It failed to incorporate explicit provisions enabling coastal states in RFMOs to deal with changing technology or developments such as industrial fishing. These particular regulatory changes were to have significant future ramifications with changes in long-range fishing vessel design fuelling an expansion of distant water operations, and the spread of geopolitical conflict to RFMOs.[29]

Controversy over the real interest provisions was temporarily shelved, awaiting entry into force of RFMOs.[30] Whilst the UN Fisheries agreement, along with earlier agreements and codes, plugged gaps in the LOS convention, the central problem had intensified. The issues centred on overfishing in and outside EEZs, illegal and unauthorised fishing in high seas areas, evasion of regulation, non-acceptance of agreements, reflagging of fishing vessels and transshipment. Additional problems involved competing national claims over stock arising from biomass movements of species such as cod, mackerel and blue whiting between EEZs[31] or stock movement into high seas areas.[32]

## Closing the GAP: development of multilateral and regional fisheries management post–2000

### *Shift from multilateralism to regionalism*

In the period before 2000, the FAO had been the lead agency on agriculture, resources, technical assistance on crops and emergencies. Its role was in four parts: facilitation (rules, agreements, conferences), reform, technical assistance/emergencies and information (registry, reports, warning/brake and data). That role after 2000 was progressively challenged by other multilateral institutions, including the IMO on fishing vessel safety and pollution.[33]

The Law of the Sea agency (DOALOS)[34] has a special coordinating role on a wide range of maritime matters.[35] Multilateral agencies have boundaries like other counterpart organisations which inevitably leads to difficulties over territory[36] and mandate.[37] External factors affecting FAO were related directly to the weakening of multilateralism which led to the fall in the number of major conferences, leaving a gap in FAO functions. Above all, the slow entry into force of FAO conventions, and non-ratification by key actors (e.g. long-range fleets states – China, Taiwan, Korea, Thailand, Japan) and growth of flags of convenience used by long-range fleets, plus European and other operators) contributed to the uncertain role and limited influence of the FAO on the multilateral policy dimension of resource management and wider debate on conservation.

The FAO efforts to recover its former role offer an interesting illustration of the scope and limitations on an international institution. FAO strategy was based on reorientating from central to secondary or local roles based on residual areas of its expertise, e.g. reform of existing regional fisheries organisations in developing countries, periodic conferences based around its flagship annual report on the state of world fisheries, and trilateral project diplomacy on commercial fish development (e.g. Marshall Islands).[38] Recognising the trend to regionalism, the FAO shifted to a new administrative role promoting coordination between the emerging RFMOs.[39] In addition, considerable diplomatic attention was devoted to sector resource management issues, particularly the campaign to eradicate illegal fishing (IUU) backed by the EU and reformist states, predominantly associated with creating RFMOs.[40]

The loss of its treaty and conference roles moved the FAO away from developing implementation initiatives, promoting international agreement on questions such as overfishing, catch reduction and conservation, as it had in the pre-2000 period to sector, report and data roles.

## Multilateralism: the search for alternative solutions

Five regional fisheries management organisations were established post-2000 in the south-east Atlantic, western and central Pacific, southern Indian Ocean and South Pacific, which meant that geographically most significant high seas fisheries were now at least formally covered. The new organisations were independent and mainly outside the FAO administrative or institutional framework.[41]

As new agencies, with responsibilities which included fisheries operations outside 200nm, covered by UNCLOS and UNFSA, they inherited a batch of new and outstanding issues including major issues of external membership and transshipment, as well as the inherited issues of overfishing, catch reduction and stock rebuilding as part of conservation.

## Membership issues in RFMOs

The emphasis in the UN straddling and highly migratory stocks agreement on regionalism inevitably raised the issues of membership in RFMOs and how to deal with external fishing states (distant water fishing or DWF).[42] Ensuring limits on the number of regional organisations and entry for distant water fleets was favoured in the UNFSA negotiations by some in the coastal states group, whilst in contrast ensuring continued access was of key concern to DWF fleets.

Negotiations on access centred around the concept of "real interest" as a vehicle for building consensus.[43] The UNFSA contains restrictive language on membership, defining it in terms of "real interest". The drafting of this section of Article 8 of the UNFSA is based on a Chilean proposal which attempted to narrowly interpret Article 118 of UNCLOS in order to prevent the proliferation of regional organisations and restrict entry of DWF states. The Chilean amendment proposed the inclusion of "real interest" in the text and a cross-reference to Article 118 of UNCLOS.[44] Whilst the term "real interest" was subsequently added to the draft text of the UNFSA, consensus could not be reached on the cross-reference to Article 118, hence substantially weakening the article.

The give-and-take aspects of international conference drafting are also illustrated in the final section of Article 8(3) which is heavily qualified in favour of distant water fishing states.[45] It is achieved by an offsetting clause in the final part of Article 8(3) to the effect that (decisions) on applications to a regional organisation should not be applied in a discriminatory manner against any state or group of states with a "real interest" in the fisheries concerned.

**Table 5.1** Post-2000 RFMOs

| | |
|---|---|
| South Pacific Regional Fisheries Management Organisation | (SPRFMO) |
| Western and Central Pacific Fisheries Commission | (WCPFC) |
| South East Atlantic Fisheries Organisation | (SEAFO) |
| Southern Indian Ocean Fisheries Agreement | (SIOFA) |
| North Pacific Fisheries Commission | (NPFC) |

Table 5.1 lists those regional fisheries management organisations (RFMOs) set up post-2000 to manage high seas fisheries resources, including straddling and other stocks, on the margins of 200nm EEZs. They are largely independent international institutions, separate from FAO authority and have limited links to FAO processes.

It is one of the ironies of drafting in diplomacy but it also underlines the longevity of agreements. In this instance the drafting of the language on discrimination in Article 8 was used some thirty years later by the EU to attack opponents following initial rejection of its application for membership of the NPFC discussed below.[46]

## Membership: approaches to the non-party question

In response to the membership problem, a special category of membership has been used in some RFMOs to cover those states with limited or no direct fisheries interest but whose vessels are involved in a convention area either to some degree or in active in-service roles (e.g. flag registry, charter, cargo transshipment, freezer cargo vessels) and who claim benefits under the convention.[47]

Continued concern over non-contracting party status (NCP), is reflected in initiatives to encouraging full membership rather than special categories of non-member. For example, cooperating members in the South Pacific Regional Fisheries Management organisation are Belize, Curacao and Liberia, which are FOCs used as transshipment flags.[48] Panama is a member of the SPRFMO.[49] To circumvent these objections, several major open registry states have started to routinely accede to nearly all contemporary maritime and environmental agreements as a way of demonstrating "real interest". In other instances, the NCP limited membership category has been withdrawn by some organisations.[50]

The Law of the Sea Convention provides that every state shall set conditions for the grant of its nationality to ships, for the registration of ships in its territory and for the right to fly its flag. The final sentence in Article 91(1) adds the requirement (that) "there must exist a genuine link between the state and the ship."[51] Further, the state shall "effectively exercise its jurisdiction and control in administrative, technical and social matters over ships flying its flag".[52]

The term "genuine link" has been the subject of extensive and continuing debate as to what "genuine" means. At a multilateral level, IMO has avoided the detail of negotiating overarching criteria to establish whether a link is "genuine" or not, relying instead on bypassing the issue, leaving it unresolved, and using in response an open or closed registry distinction with general rules for all states.[53]

As part of defensive diplomatic methods, active FOCs (e.g. Panama, Liberia, Vanuatu) have developed strong defensive institutional positions within IMO. This is backed by polished PR and presentations on the performance of their flags, active participation in IMO plenary meetings and committees, and arranged seminar participation along with considerable off-radar quiet diplomacy.[54]

## Conservation and management

### *Freezer trawlers, transshipment and containerisation*

Transshipment has posed significant problems of regulation and enforcement of fishing effort in EEZs and transboundary areas for small coastal and regional powers. The process involves the transfer of cargo at sea to a receiving vessel without the receiving vessel necessarily having to go into port for cargo. It has now become a key part of China's revised DWF strategy which has moved the focus of its operations increasingly outside EEZs without landing, thus avoiding port inspections and catch reporting. The fleet moves (in darkness, with AIS off) in and around the boundaries of EEZs to adjacent high seas areas beyond. As a result, high seas fishing has now become a contentious issue over straddling stocks and unreported high seas operations. It has turned the focus from EEZs to RFMOs and away from the central issue of stock conservation.

Transshipment is one of the important technical developments in trawlers and support vessels. A related development is the growth of larger long-range combination trawlers and freezer support vessels. The modern multifunctional super trawler is in the 14,000GRT range, equivalent to a WW2 SD14 cargo ship, plying between the US and UK with wartime supplies.[55] Freezer ships may be on charter, part of a fleet or service a small pack of vessels. They can generally stay on station for anything up to three or four months at a time with no need to enter port, transshipment enabling them to stay longer in a selected area and conduct cargo transfer operations.

China, as part of a changed strategy on high seas DWF, has eight freezer vessels operating in the North Pacific convention area. Most are second generation refrigerated vessels of 5,000–6,000GRT, built in China and coming into service from 2019, replacing the earlier smaller freezers built in Japan.[56]

A major advantage is that freezer carriers give fleet groups or individual vessels more mobility, making possible easier and more cost-effective moves within and between RFMO convention areas. Large fleet groups are able to form and move in and around the boundaries of EEZs or shift location from off, for example, the Galapagos Islands to Peru.[57]

The development of very large trawler freezer vessels has also enabled smaller specialist companies in Europe and North America to operate with a limited number of large vessels. It has also influenced the use of very large vessels for commercial exploratory purposes or for staying on location for a period to test or extract newly arriving stock before shifting to remote or other distant locations.

Short-operation tactics are favoured by large industrial vessels to minimise domestic political opposition. The diplomatic aspects for states involve defensive diplomacy over fishing operations, supporting and furthering fishing company interests in access agreements. Defensive diplomacy is backed by specialist distant water vessel lobby groups.[58]

## Case study 1

### Micro states and EEZs: transboundary fisheries management challenges – the Marshall Islands

In this section, the first case study shows the problems of managing large archipelagic sea areas, as illustrated by the Marshall Islands. The issues covered include finding appropriate partners, donor agendas, role of international institutions and wider implications of project-switching for international fisheries agendas. The second case study – EU application to join the NPFC – shows the reintroduction of "real interest" issues over purposes and conservation effects of new long-range fishing, and the diplomatic methods used to secure admission to a regional fisheries organisation.

The Marshall Islands case offers insights into the challenges and compromises micro states make in managing extensive sea areas provided under the Law of the Sea Convention with minimal administrative and maritime enforcement assets. Micro states are heavily dependent on licensing or similar sources of revenue; they are also economically vulnerable to shifts in core income from incidents, climatic factors and rival competitors. Options are generally limited and often come with high political cost. Study of the challenges faced by the Marshall Islands is uniquely aided by an FAO video "Making More Out of Tuna", prepared as part of the FAO–ACO FISH4ACP project. It contains valuable footage on location, transshipment and port operations in Maduro harbour, which give a rare insight into a remote area.

### *Background*

The Marshall Islands has an area of 180,000 square miles stretching over 1,150 islands, averaging only two metres above sea level. The small population of 68,000 is spread over 29 atolls.[59] The western and central Pacific region produces over 60% of the world's tuna.[60]

Since WW2, the Marshall Islands have been under US administration as a UN Trust territory.[61] The economy is almost entirely dependent on bilateral US assistance, multilateral agency project finance and licensing revenue traditionally supplemented with revenue from tourism. It has enjoyed geographic and strategic isolation for much of the twentieth

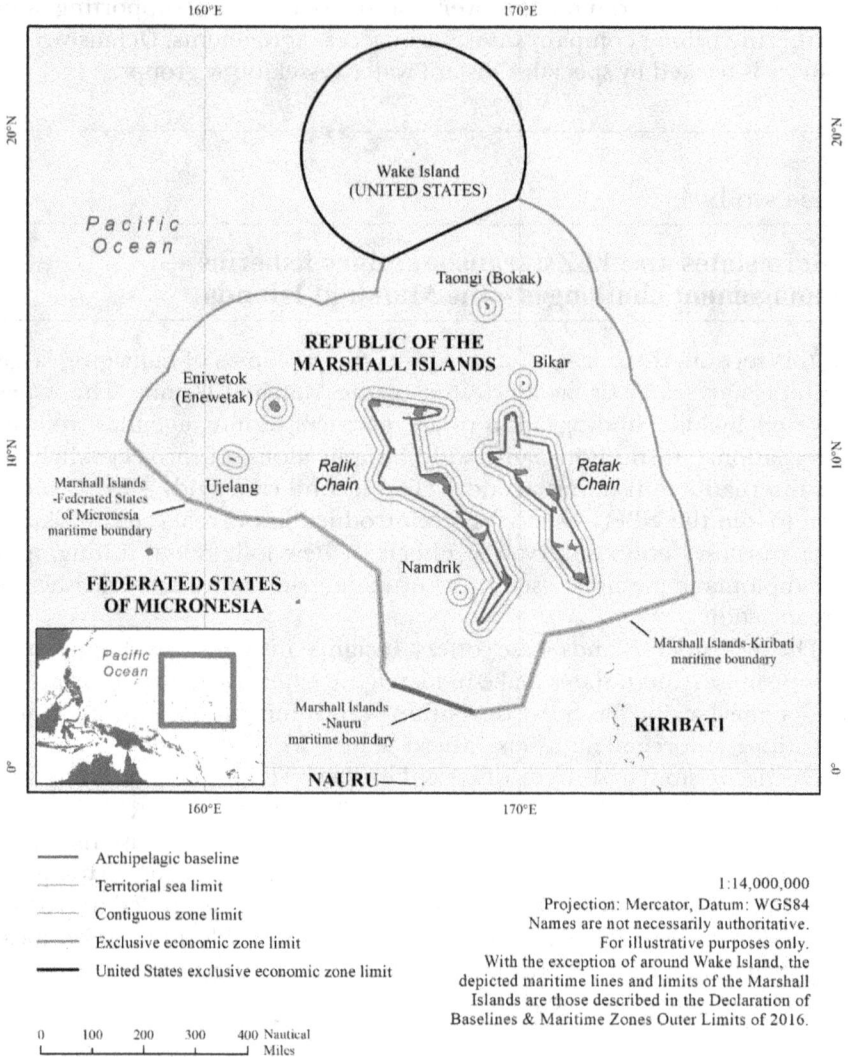

**Figure 5.1** Marshall Islands

Legend:
- Archipelagic baseline
- Territorial sea limit
- Contiguous zone limit
- Exclusive economic zone limit
- United States exclusive economic zone limit

1:14,000,000
Projection: Mercator, Datum: WGS84
Names are not necessarily authoritative.
For illustrative purposes only.
With the exception of around Wake Island, the
depicted maritime lines and limits of the Marshall
Islands are those described in the Declaration of
Baselines & Maritime Zones Outer Limits of 2016.

0   100   200   300   400 Nautical
                              Miles

century. Remoteness is reflected in its early post-war use as a nuclear test site. Its economic and strategic importance has dramatically changed post-2000 in line with resource demands, climate change and primary power geopolitical factors. Taiwan, Japan, Korea, and China have traditionally fished in the Marshall Islands and adjoining areas.[62]

The Marshall Islands has struggled to cope with governance of an international fishery (administration, enforcement, lack of coastguard)[63] and an economy dependent pre-2000 on bilateral and multilateral loans. After independence in 1986, the maritime development model moved through a series of failed externally funded fisheries projects (national fleet, nautical college to train Marshallese seafarers, local fleet schemes, artisanal fisheries support projects).[64]

Post-2000, the approach shifted to projecting the Marshall Islands as a high-end international ship registry (tankers, gas carriers, bulk carriers),[65] fisheries transshipment Pacific hub and active IMO registry and environmental member. By 2020 some 300,000 tons of fish, most of it transshipped were from Maduro.[66]

The Marshall Islands' position as a leading transshipment hub has been challenged by competition for transshipment and the introduction of containerisation for the shipment of frozen tuna.[67] Frozen containerisation offered transshipment hub states the chance to achieve some diversification but raised issues of control of the process and value-added issues, captured in the video-debate on "Making more out of tuna".[68]

What foreign joint ventures should be concluded? How would these affect existing transshipment operations? Would new projects displace existing containerised operations? How would another competitor, such as Nauru, Palau, Kiribati and Vanuatu react?[69]

## New projects and new partners: bilateral or trilateral diplomacy?

The longer-term implications of finding partnerships and problems of political trade influence were illustrated by the Marshall Islands' involvement in the FAO FISH4ACP initiative.[70] This was presented by FAO–EU as an ACP project to bring the ACP countries much more into the fisheries value chain through greater involvement in fish processing and production.[71]

In practice, however, the ACP had little connection with the project. The scheme was structured as a set of bilateral fishery resource projects between the EU and 12 individual ACP members, of which the Marshall Islands was the Pacific segment.[72] The overall aim for the EU was to secure a market and trade presence in strategic developing economies, using relations with regional actors, RFMOs and multilateral institutions.[73] The method uses link ups with a multilateral institution and project partner in so-called triangular diplomacy, which acts as a formal framework for the conclusion of bilateral arrangements. The involvement of the FAO internationalised the project and reduced the political exposure of the EU. It is one of a suite of methods in EU diplomacy, which includes visit diplomacy, bilateral negotiations, membership applications, promotion of regional conferences and funding projects, all which distinguish EU diplomatic style.[74]

In the Pacific component of the EU–ACP FISH4ACP programme, the selected partner was not a developing Pacific country with artisanal fisheries problems but the leading Pacific transshipment tuna actor, i.e. the Marshall Islands.

In the north Pacific, the EU had also applied to join the North Pacific Fisheries Commission for quota access for EU vessels as an additional part of its overall strategy of using membership to establish a presence in all RFMOs to project itself as a global political environment actor, though it had few vessels or DWF operations.[75]

The ACP project offered the EU the opportunity in that part of its external relations, as a trader organisation, to establish a trade foothold in a Pacific hub (canning, refrigeration technology and SPS certification). Trilateralism provided the diplomatic cover.[76] The EU shift from trade agreements to sustainable economic cooperation partnership agreements, symbolised in the new generation EU–Kenya agreement, with fisheries provisions, provided additional platforms for the new goals of long-range EU fisheries operations.

One aspect, however, was lacking – a development label. The ACP–EU–FAO project was almost the last of the development projects funded under the EU voluntary European Development Fund (EDF) before the ACP ceased to exist, becoming the OACPS. EDF itself was absorbed into the EU International Partnerships division. An interesting solution was found which solved two problems. It involved creating a development dimension by not only adding the German Development Agency to the trilateral agreement as a development project partner, but turning the agreement into a quadrilateral agreement.[77] It set a precedent as a model for EU–German cooperation and brought in separate German development initiatives, at least in this case, under one European label.

Variations of the EU–German format have been used in other areas to give the EU more diplomatic flexibility and soften the agreed bloc positions aspects of the EUs external presence, such as in the preparatory consultations to the resumed UNEP diplomatic conference on an international plastics agreement. Fisheries provisions within the new generation of EU governance-styled sustainable trade agreements similarly increased diplomatic flexibility.[78]

For the ACP, the ACP–EU–FAO project diplomacy was a well-established feature in its diplomatic relations. The involvement of the FAO provided diversity, finance and multilateral links for the ACP, which had become more important with the ACP changing to an International organisation (OACPS) from a loose interregional grouping of 79 countries. For Germany, the addition of the GIZ as a development partner in the Fish 4 ACP project gave it political credit in its future relations with the European Commission.[79]

In the FISH4ACP case, the GIZ project was not directly related to fisheries management but on transitioning to small, low-cost inter-island cargo sailing vessels.[80]

## Case study 2

## Geopolitics and regional organisations: membership – NPFC and EU

Regional fisheries management organisations have become zones of conflict not only over the scale and type of resource access but as contested areas of political influence. The initial resource focus has now widened so that RFMOs are zones of regional political and strategic value. They have become platforms for promoting political environment issues, regional influence and international legal enforcer roles.

The EU application for accession to the North Pacific Fisheries Commission (NPFC) caused a major crisis for the organisation.[81] The NPFC had been originally created as a new closed management organisation set up by those principally fishing in the region. The EU application threatened those arrangements, potentially introducing a competitor and, for some members, a normative and regulative opponent. The case study offers a number of interesting insights into the evolution of EU diplomatic methods and, for the NPFC, the methods used by individual members to protect individual positions in a consensus-based system.

### *Background*

The NPFC supplemented the existing single-species anadromous stocks agreement NPAFC, which dealt largely with migratory salmon fisheries, with a new additional all-species agreement covering all other high seas species. It entered into force in 2015 between the Russian Federation, China, Japan, Taiwan, US and Canada.[82]

The primary fishing members are Japan, Russia, China and Taiwan, though the fishing effort of Russia and Japan prior to the creation of the NPFC had been conducted mainly within their respective 200nm EEZs. However, part of the Japanese mackerel stock biomass straddled the EEZ and was vulnerable to high seas fishing operations east of 150 degrees.[83]

The EU–Japan fisheries dispute in the North Pacific Fisheries Commission over access to Pacific chub mackerel found around Japan. Fish stocks never keep to international boundaries but face increasing pressure on conservation from long-range vessels of outside actors. The EU application for accession to the NPFC was unexpected since the EU was not party to the original negotiations and had no current fisheries involvement in the convention area. It coincided, too, at a time of declining catch levels and uncertainty over the future prospects for the NPFC convention area.[84] The application significantly divided the members of the convention, which operated on the basis of consensus through a central committee and two scientific subcommittees (see Figure 5.2).[85]

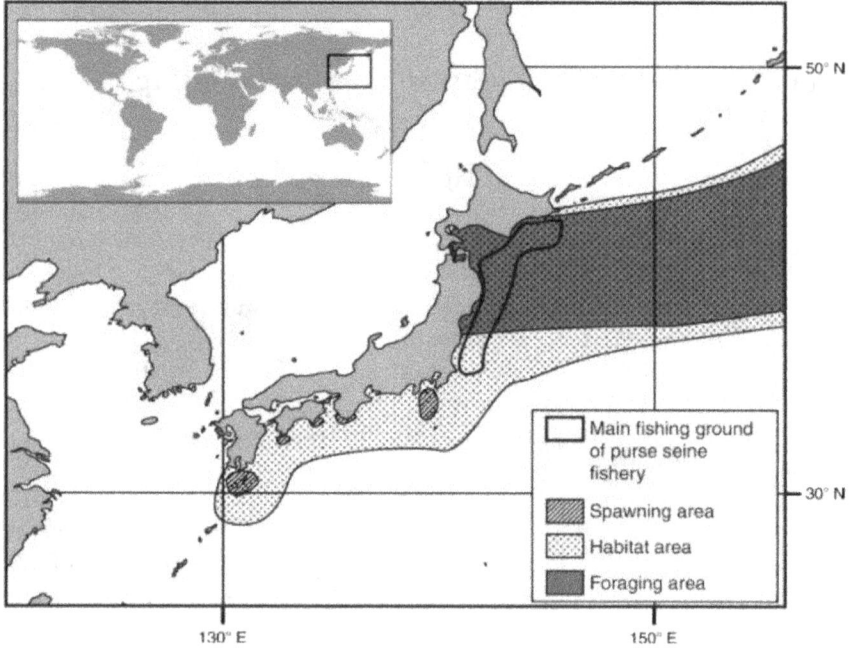

**Figure 5.2** Spatial distribution of North West chub mackerel stock

Source: Ichinokawa et al. (2015).

The primary purpose of the application was to secure additional area access for the EU fleet in a period of uncertainty over access, and criticism on environmental and political grounds of its larger all-function long-distance vessels. A related set of secondary, presentational objectives set out environmental and scientific aims such as improving stock knowledge, conservation and reducing fisheries related pollution (plastics, net loss, or by catch dumping).

The third set of longer-term political objectives were to gain access to a regional organisation as part of the build-up of an EU trans-regional presence. These aims were set out in a general document on EU–Regional Fisheries Organisation relations:

> The EU, represented by the Commission, plays an active role in 5 tuna-RFMOs and 12 non-tuna RFMOs. This makes the EU one of the most prominent actors in RFMO worldwide.[86]

In addition to characteristic EU diplomatic methods, there were a number of unusual additional features in the methods used to support the EU application. One particularly striking feature was the annual repetition of the application after the first rejection. Another was the effort to disguise, in the drafting, the purposes of the application by seeming to minimise the fishing effort and depict its primary purpose as an expedition to

explore the potential for fishing the chub mackerel, previously not extensively fished in the proposed area. The NPFA scientific committee, however, drew attention to the wider intentions indicated in the drafting in the
EU letter of application, which referred to "mackerel and other pelagic
species".[87] Similar difficulties arose over the ambiguity in the application as
to whether the application was for a single vessel or several.[88]

There was considerable concern over the size of the vessel which would
be used. What was referred to in the application was not a relatively small
fishing trawler, epitomised in WW2 or modern disaster movies, but a
14,000 ton super trawler nearly treble the size of exiting freezer vessels.[89]

The EU application was handled by the NPFA as a negotiation by
letter,[90] with modifications by the EU in response to issues raised at NPFC
committee level. The major concerns of the Russian Federation, Japan
and China were tabled as formal statements either individually or bilaterally as express support. Their main concerns were over vessel size,
impact on other stocks and on their own operations, particularly in view
not only of declared declining stocks but also, for Japan, the movement of
the stock biomass outside the Japanese EEZ into high seas areas to the east
of Japan. How to secure this position was difficult in a small, consensus-
based, organisation.

On the applicant side, the EU aim was to maintain momentum in the
presentation of its case, show it was complying with information requests
aimed to slow it down or undermine the EU position, and find a decisive
move which would weaken its opponents (Japan and China). The latter – a
gamechanger – was found by the EU through the discovery from commercial intelligence in Japanese on fisheries sources of scientific research which
seemed to allow for a three-month catch window for chub, but the data was
uncertain on possibilities of future exploitation. It demonstrated the depth
of EU commercial intelligence used to back up the application and efforts
made to secure the EU proposal.[91] Although not decisive, the move made
it more difficult for Japan and China to resist the EU application.

The diplomatic methods used by the EU relied on drawing up tailor-
made arguments to suit each of its constituencies. Internal arguments
referenced, for example, the opportunities operationally for the EU fleet
to shift between regions, or were directed to the agenda of the EU as an
environmental regulator in regional organisations and guardian of the
"level playing field". The EU-NPFC narrative stressed science, limited
vessel activity and benefits of environmental cooperation over by catch
and plastics.

The environmental advantages listed in the EU application drew almost
verbatim on the Rwandan cosponsored draft texts, drafted in consultation
with the EU, to the UNEA 5th assembly negotiations on a multilateral
plastics treaty, discussed below.[92]

The EU application was eventually agreed at the 6th NPFC Commission,
held as a virtual meeting 23–25 February 2022, following a succession
of annual EU applications. The virtual format of the meeting probably

worked in favour of admission of the EU, in that it is difficult to sustain technical discussions in a small group virtual format.

For their part, the NPFC had not developed considered defensive positions at a political level on why accession could not be accepted. Nor did it have an agreed position challenging the EU argument. In the final exchanges before the 6th Commission, the EU ratcheted up the pressure on the NPFC prior to the meeting in coercive diplomatic correspondence, which contained an implicit allegation of possible discrimination: "(in view of the above) I hope the Commission accept our request."[93]

Although the EU was admitted to the NPFC, Japan, to protect its position, placed reservations on EU operations. This was supported by China, in a statement attached to EU admission (annex D), which limited the EU to one super trawler, operating as a midwater trawler east of 150 degrees east, with limitations on catch.[94]

The future dynamics of a consensus based RFMO had been fundamentally altered. The case illustrates the need to prepare counter positions in consensus and other organisations to Article 8-type challenges, to affirm the rights of RFMO on conservation. Diplomacy is essential for the protection of RFMO member rights in disputes over external access.

## Multilateral regulations: competing strategies and methods

The fourth section of this chapter returns to the place of multilateral issues, raised in the opening part, which dealt with closing the Law of the Sea gaps and the shift from multilateralism to regionalism. This section returns to the general argument over the limitations of multilateral processes in order to cover current multilateral developments.

The development of fisheries conservation and management has centred on issues such as conservation versus management, voluntary or mandatory rules, catch levels and enforcement (reporting, observers, standardising rules and vessel inspection). Progress at international and regional levels in these areas has for the most part been limited, both with respect to EEZs but also in framing and implementing workable solutions to regulating traditional high seas fishing operations beyond 200nm. The growing pressure to incorporate formally ecosystem and environmental considerations into fisheries management has brought additional areas of dispute at national level and within regional organisations evidenced in debated over widening special areas.

In order to put brakes or limitations on the extension of fisheries regulations, traditional distant water and regional fisheries powers have drawn from a suite of standard methods used in conflicts to limit reform initiatives or proposals.[95] These include diplomatic moves such as publicly appearing cooperative and working for solutions, whilst in practice seeking narrower or covert interests; negotiations to secure qualifications by amendment or alternative drafts or language to cover particular exceptions; delay (e.g. requests for further clarification, more scientific data or postpone consideration to the next meeting) and procedural devices (agenda, extend consultation process, challenge consensus, voting).[96]

## *Apparent commitments*

Review conferences are one of several platforms for the use of apparent commitments. That is, commitments which appear to support a policy but which, when examined, are so qualified to make them of limited value. The review conference of the UN Fish Stocks Agreement contained extensive examples. Part of the debate on the state of fish stocks was reported by the Secretariat as follows:

> Many delegations stated they were committed to reducing capacity commensurate with the state of the stocks....

The addition of the drafting qualification "commensurate with the state of the stocks" renders the commitment of limited value since lack of precise data on the state of stocks is a longstanding problem which has constrained fisheries management.[97]

Examples of restrictive or minimalist methods include widespread failure to secure reduction of total catches by RFMOs,[98] opposition to stock rebuilding proposals, e.g. Indian objections to the IOTC yellowfin tuna stock rebuilding plan, opposition to mandatory observer and AIS regulations.[99] Rules on transshipment differ between regional organisations with some RFMOs opting for lax arrangements, whilst development at collective international level has similarly been constrained by lack of consensus.[100] Rules may eventually be agreed in these areas but only after extensive delay.

One of the main sources for delay or blocking is the use of available scientific information on the state of fisheries stocks within regions or at a global level.[101] Sources of scientific assessment vary from an autonomous institution (e.g. International Council for the Exploration of the Sea), multilateral collated data (e.g. FAO), collaborative regional research institutions and national research.[102]

Elements of national research on stock mass and location may be considered as commercially sensitive. Against that view, regional and external actors favouring the opening up of regional organisation processes and extending regulations have developed the so-called transparency doctrine to promote more clarity in decision-making.[103] The post-2000 RFMOs and international institutions have the added task of building up a high seas database, complicated by inability of separating EEZ and high seas catch beyond 200nm.

Uncertainty over data and lengthy timescales facilitate conflicting use of data by differing interests. A recurring complaint of the FAO is the lack of up-to-date and comprehensive fish stock and catch data, resulting from inadequate or partial returns by member states.[104]

Two further negative or non-cooperative methods can be distinguished. These are direct attacks to undermine a proposal or report and methods used in circumvention strategies.

Direct attack is used to question the judgement or conclusions of a report and its main assumptions, with the aim of halting possible constraints or a moratorium. It is used against annual or other specific reports of regional and multilateral agencies, to question critically the scientific assumptions and raise counter arguments favouring continuation of similar levels of operations.[105]

Circumvention strategies are an established feature of non-cooperative state practice. Circumvention involves active acceptance of various aspects of non-compliance, including the use and growth of dark fleets, switching off AIS-locating systems on vessels, fraudulent identity and unreported or inaccurate transshipment.[106] Mandatory AIS was initially seen as a major addition to enforcement tools, though its subsequent widespread breach in the fisheries sector has underlined the limitations of this technique especially for vessels operating in remote areas and making limited or no port calls. The use of transshipment at sea has added to the gaps.

Diplomatic methods to support circumvention rely particularly on various forms of defensive denial (disputed location, identity challenges, apologetic explanations for administrative error in not removing vessels, or failure to observe closed areas). Other moves include unilateral moratorium of fleet operations in sensitive areas to ease international pressure.[107] Separate unilateral quota declarations and bilateral deals have also been a feature of fisheries management in northern Europe (Norway–Russian Federation).[108]

Counter strategies by regulatory powers have attempted to address various aspects of circumvention at multilateral level through FAO-IUU campaigns, visit diplomacy to promote wider FAO agreement ratification, periodic IMO (Maritime Safety Committee) debate and regulatory initiatives on maritime fraud.[109] Whilst port and state control on merchant ship regulatory compliance has been one of the major multilateral achievements for IMO, as an enforcement tool it has had limited success because of the type of vessel, areas of operation, minimum port calls and difficulties in identifying beneficial ownership in cases against shadow companies.[110]

In recognition of the limitation of methods at multilateral level, separate initiatives have periodically emerged, and have been taken by individual states and ad hoc groupings. In the case of fisheries and other sectors, these have included the EU's attempt to link trade access and fisheries regulatory compliance – so-called market measures – with pressure on smaller developing flags of convenience to tighten registry and operation of companies.[111]

The United States has linked counter flags of convenience initiatives to wider security issues, creating an ad hoc working group on flags of convenience and shadow companies, comprising South Korea, Taiwan, Thailand, EU, US, to counter Russian and Chinese commercial and military activity.[112]

Of note is the switch in orientation of members of the group from previously being in the distant water fishing lobby in the early years of UNCLOS, to shift to a regulatory powers group. A transformation from poacher to gamekeeper, as fleets either decline and pull back to closer waters, or defensive interests, drives moves to international regulatory routes.

The third phase of environmental treaty accession is notable for ASEAN members acceding to the UNFSA agreements, as opting for the use of treaty membership for added security and possible leverage in conflict become the methods of first choice in the revised operating styles of ASEAN members.[113]

## International negotiations over plastics pollution

The remaining part of the chapter turns from resources management to examine the diplomatic methods used in creating an international agreement to tackle plastics pollution, including marine debris. Moreso than other areas of environmental diplomacy, how to deal with critical environmental pollution caused by various forms of plastic use has led to deep division within the international community.

The pervasive use of plastics in social, industrial, trade and other uses makes substitution or shift to alternatives high cost. At a diplomatic level, in polarised issues, traditional concepts of accommodation, compromise, splitting the difference or simplistic notions of win-win are either unworkable or inappropriate in contexts of complex, deep-seated interests. Limits to consensus in environmental diplomacy are reflected in the use of codes, guidelines, voluntary provisions and limited enforcement.

The plastics case is of value in that it illustrates the contrasting methods states and international institutions use to push consensus solutions, shift momentum, control agendas, slow negotiations and advance interests in contested areas.

### *Background*

Plastics pollution entering into the land and marine environment is a major and neglected area of environmental diplomacy and regulation.

The focus of environmental diplomacy in the golden era of environmentalism (1973–92) was a mix of periodic major multilateral conferences (UNCLOS, Earth Summit) and ongoing specialised technical diplomacy, conducted at multilateral level in UN specialised agencies.

At regional level, agreements included the Stockholm Convention (chemical pollutants), Barcelona conventions and the UNEP regional seas programme.[114] Ad hoc agreements were added on specific areas, such as oil pollution from ships (MARPOL) and prohibition of dumping (London Convention) rather than wider sources of pollution, including litter and plastics.[115] The transportation of hazardous and other waste was the subject of the Basel Convention.[116]

At specialised agency level, multilateral diplomacy developed professional and technical consensus-based regulations. These tended to be focused around specific areas such as oil pollution and safety aspects of vessel construction (e.g. double hulls for oil tankers, inspection for compliance with international conventions). The diplomatic methods developed involved consensus meetings, close secretariat agenda liaison, technical committees, correspondence groups between sessions and constant draft revision of regulations. Regulatory maritime and normative powers used these processes to create an epistemic process welding maritime owners and service providers, building a complex architecture of regulatory debate, review, agreements and codes of practice.

For revisionist and minimalist states (e.g. flag of convenience) standard methods relied on slowing down the regulatory process, negotiating opt-outs or phasing in new regulatory requirements. For less developed countries, the agenda was principally on capacity building framed as technical assistance, training academies and technical missions, rather than negotiating the detail of common but differentiated responsibilities (CBDR) epitomised in UN climate negotiations.[117]

The issues of marine litter and plastics pollution began to receive increased attention from a variety of states, institutions, NGOs and national governments, moving the issue area onto the international agenda of several multilateral institutions other than IMO, including UNSD, UNEP and WTO.

The growing recognition of the critical impact of plastic and associated marine debris was reflected in the revision of the of the Basel Convention to include the Plastic Waste amendments. This covered the global trade and transportation of hazardous and other waste, along with commitments on waste management and disposal.[118] A global campaign to tackle plastic and marine debris became an associated dimension of the COP climate debate, as periodic environmental events brought sharper and continuous focus in G7, G20 and in the Ocean Plastics Charter. The IMO Action Plan was extended as a Marine Plastics strategy.[119]

## *The response: approaches to the regulation of marine litter and plastics pollution*

The issue of plastics pollution has proved to be one of the more obdurate issues in environmental diplomacy in efforts to reach multilateral consensus. Whilst there is general agreement on the need for some form of international response – whether that should be voluntary or enforceable – remains a major source of contention.

The methods used by states and international institutions are a mix of traditional approaches but also indicate the introduction of several changes in methods. Some of these were necessarily context driven, such as the form of COVID-influenced meetings; others reflect an operational shift to exploit negotiating openings and use different procedures and groupings.

The case is interesting in this latter respect for the introduction of new groupings. Whilst these constituted innovation, they were nevertheless at the expense of multilateralism, in that outcomes tended to be plurilateral rather than multilateral. Key actors were missing from the list of those critical for effective implementation.

## UNEP: holding the line or innovation?

The methods used in UNEP were essentially traditional approaches using resolutions, expert working groups and reports. This approach was not varied by the UNEP Director-General to a more proactive response to promote negotiations for a new international agreement on plastics reduction, relying on presenting options to the next meeting from the Ad Hoc Working Group of Experts (AHWGE).[120]

Concern over the apparent lack of international consensus was undoubtedly a major consideration in limiting the scope of inquiry and recommendations. Expert Working Groups were a means of delay and postponing decisions on difficult issues in the absence of agreed policy.

## Momentum: filling the gap

In bilateral and multilateral contexts, impasse and gaps in negotiations present opportunities for initiatives. These might be filled by stop gap proposals, amendments or, more extensively, by new substantive proposals or initiatives. Initiatives can include special missions, bilateral meetings or, at multilateral level, informal exchanges to discuss how to break impasse or advance a stalled or blocked meeting.

There are a number of potential difficulties with some elements in this type of method. In particular, the impact of an initiative on existing talks, the risk of the initiative being perceived as an alternative negotiation or breakaway challenge to the role of existing institutions and processes, perceptions of exclusion, or contributing to the collapse of multilateral consensus in favour of limited or plurilateral deals can each be a source potential progress but also sow the seeds of disaffection and exclusion. What links these methods is the common idea of trying to find ways to advance discussions or meetings which have entered a standstill or void created by uncertain direction, though the risks are high and potential for uncertainty and misperception considerable.

In the UNEP plastics case, the UNEP Special Assembly had discussed the various options recommended by the AHEG and had deferred further discussion until UNEA 5.2 in 2021. COVID travel restrictions meant that the UNEA 5.2 was further postponed until 2022, leaving a gap of 12 months.

The use of split meetings by international institutions and standing conferences has now developed as a mechanism for delay, agenda changes and avoiding difficult substantive issues. In this context the EU made a surprise initiative using co-sponsors for a ministerial conference on marine litter and plastic pollution. The ostensible aim was to maintain momentum prior to UNEA 5.2, though the wider aims of promoting a binding agreement became apparent in the external public relations of the EU depicting its lead role in promoting new binding rules on plastic pollution.[121]

## Ministerial conference: parallel diplomacy

The move was highly controversial in view of substantial divisions on the issue and absence of a UNEP mandate for an interim conference.[122] It used several new diplomatic methods. The formal co-sponsors of the conference were Ecuador, Germany, Ghana and Vietnam. The EU was able to distance itself by using Germany as a lead co-sponsor and decoupling the EU membership, who were present as individual actors. The method of distancing and co-sponsorship has been developed as part of EU diplomatic style, used, as discussed earlier, in so-called trilateral diplomatic initiatives linking the EU, ACP and FAO, and a quadrilateral variant used in development projects diplomacy with Germany added to the EU, ACP, FAO link up. The initiative was, in effect, parallel diplomacy to create an alternative arrangement to steer the UNEP into negotiating a legally binding agreement, something opposed by a substantial number of UNEP members.

The protocol of the meeting described it as a "ministerial conference", to give added weight. Its subtitle, however, added some uncertainty over legitimacy by referring to its status and proceedings as "informal consultations". The initiative in effect created a conference within a conference, raising doubts about holding this type of meeting in advance of the second session of the UNEA5. It is an example of parallel diplomacy.

Consultations would normally have been used for informal meetings between the Director-General or chair and individual delegations, bilateral exchanges, regional group level discussions or between like-minded states, with some measure of participation by secretariat representatives from the responsible organisation in most of the formats.

Such methods might not have suited the narrower purpose of setting up processes to create a legally binding and enforceable agreement, the focus of the Ministerial conference and a common objective of EU style and methods. That aim was to be realised by inviting participants to sign up at the end of conference to a statement which called upon the UNEP to set up as an international negotiating committee to coordinate negotiations for a legally binding agreement on plastics.

The draft resolutions used at the later UNEA 5.2 were substantially drawn on in the environmental documents used to support the EU application to join the NPFC.

An unusual feature of the initiative was its status as a hybrid meeting held in person at WTO headquarters in Geneva and also with online participation. The meeting location at WTO added to the uncertainty over the status and purposes of the proposed ministerial conference, given other initiatives, including that of WTO's dialogue on trade and plastics.

How the proposed ministerial conference would relate to that in future was unclear. The question of the status of the conference was raised in statements by a number of delegations (Malawi, Russian Federation), which expressed concern that the appropriate forum for discussions on the form and nature of an agreement was at UNEP and not the current meeting.

The eventual conference statement was an unusual document calling on UNEP to set up an INC, suggesting that meeting was a conference rather than informal consultations. The statement was signed by 25 states, although 100 were represented in some form online. The mixed level of representation, typically found in UN environmental conferences, inevitably limited its success.

Above all, the general involvement of the primary powers was limited. Japan, for example, in recognising this point, did use a carefully crafted reference in its main statement on the importance of having all primary powers and major users present and fully engaged (US, China, Japan, India, EU) for an agreement to be both agreed and fully implemented. India, for example, was not present, nor were major agricultural polluters such as Spain.

The concluding conference statement was not signed by the United States. Brazil, although present, also refused to sign the statement, on different grounds – principally that the document did not incorporate or refer to the doctrine of "Common but Differentiated Responsibilities" (CBDR).

In an attempt to raise the number of signatures, the date for signature was left open until October 21 though, in practice, the use of this particular method had very little success. No official record of the meeting exists, limiting public scrutiny, both being features of this type of diplomatic method.

The resumed UNEA 5.2 underlined the continued polarised positions on the form and binding or voluntary nature of an international agreement on marine litter and plastic pollution. The gulf was reflected in the documents submitted by the four main groups: India (voluntary agreement, informal expert groups, reporting); Japan (narrow focus on marine pollution); EU (regulatory reform/legally binding); Less Developed (informal/CBDR, financial assistance). All four positions remained unresolved and were put as documents to the INC.[123] These positions remained largely unresolved in the subsequent rounds of intergovernmental negotiation committee after Uruguay, in Nairobi (INC-3), Ottawa (INC-4) and Busan (INC-5). The fundamental differences are reflected in the draft texts[124] which are heavily bracketed, or contain compilations of multiple options,[125] which are indicative of the weak state of multilateralism, heavily qualified obligations and defective or "bad" international agreements. Whilst some form of plastics agreement may be reached, resistance to implementation increases and the precise impact on a critical global issue remains uncertain.

The initial UNEP negotiations on plastics provide an interesting and quite rare insight into the preparatory phases of a multilateral negotiation. In the case of plastics, the difficulties of creating even minimum consensus were substantially greater than those on filling the gaps in UNCLOS relating to highly migratory and straddling stocks, in that many of the core ideas on revised maritime regulations had been worked through during nearly ten years of previous negotiations on different aspects of the draft convention. The plastics negotiations are interesting in terms of the development of diplomatic methods in several respects. In particular, the reform group of states developed new methods to maintain momentum and driving influence on the agenda to circumvent delay and divisive counter strategies. These included building up a new co-sponsor group with Germany, Ecuador, Ghana and Vietnam, and parallel diplomacy to the UNEP process, to create an ad hoc conference between UNEP sessions to push for a legally binding agreement. The EU also continued its revised approach of disguising its involvement by distancing itself from its exposed apparent high-level role and moving nominally offstage through decoupling individual members and facilitating co-sponsor with single members of the EU. The decoupling method has now become a standard feature of EU diplomatic methods. The major difficulty is that it creates dualism in EU diplomacy between the role of the Commission, as a lead EU driver, and initiatives of individual members. Other examples of institutional and policy dualism are in the UN BBNJ negotiations for an agreement on biological diversity in areas beyond national jurisdiction and in the One Ocean conference, led by France, with the Commission also involved, leading to divided authority and policy conflict, including inconsistencies with the Common Fisheries with its emphasis on maximising access in the North Sea and Atlantic and resumed long range fishing operations in the Pacific through membership of the NPFC.

## Conclusion

This chapter has explored diplomatic methods used to develop agreements on high seas fisheries and plastics pollution. High seas and EEZ straddling fish stocks and deep seabed mining were two areas which had been taken off the UNCLOS agenda in order to maintain the consensus on the bulk of the remaining text.

Recognition of overfishing, combined with acceptance of the limited impact of codes and partial agreements to strengthen flag state responsibilities influenced bringing the question onto the international agenda to negotiate a new agreement. The question of a multilateral agreement on plastics pollution gained traction from related work in IMO on vessel pollution, specialist plastics agreements and integration into the climate debate.

It differed, however, in so far as the UN fisheries agreement negotiations greatly benefitted from the previous diplomatic work done over a decade on the Law of the Sea Convention, providing a framework and agreed concepts. Negotiations for a plastics agreement, however, did not have the benefit of a prior general or overarching framework. Substantial differences existed over the content and whether, or the extent to which, an agreement should be voluntary or binding.

In the fisheries negotiations, methods were developed in three main areas: new regional organisations largely separate from the multilateral FAO institutions, membership and trilateral diplomacy. The introduction of increased geopolitics into new groupings triggered the search for new fisheries access and mixtures of bargaining and implicit threats in trade and access negotiations.

On membership, the question of "real interest" as grounds for access to fish resources was inevitably revived in article 8 with the conclusion of the UNFSA on straddling and highly migratory fish stocks, though the problem of defining appropriate criteria was masked by the delay in entry into force of the convention and the new fisheries management regional organisations foreshadowed under the agreement. It has remained an unresolved and contentious issue.

The chapter underlines the weak role of multilateral processes in developing and enforcing collective rules in environmental diplomacy on marine resource management. The limited links between collective multilateral processes and decision-making and RFMOs weakens global progress on core conservation and management issues. It also contributes to the fragmentation and patchwork of global governance, moving problems into regional, subregional and national boxes. Management of marine resources is increasingly pushed down to a national level, where capabilities and interests diverge greatly.

The case study on micro states highlights the little known area of plurilateral diplomacy and the weakness of this type of donor-institution model. Micro states and international institutions are heavily controlled by, and dependent on, donor agendas. UN specialised agencies are often unable to redirect failed or non-operational projects. All UN agencies are acutely aware of funding issues and trying to maintain regular budgetary funding and secure voluntary financial backing.

A second important theme is the introduction of external actors and geopolitics into RFMOs. RFMOs have become arenas for geopolitics and expansion of influence. As a consequence larger strategic issues become displaced for national projects or other coalition agendas.

Finding regulatory and cooperative multilateral solutions to marine resource and plastics pollution remains one of the most difficult areas of diplomacy.

## Notes

1 United Nations Convention on the Law of the Sea (UN, New York, 1983).
Documentation, Official publications: General UNSG reports to GA on world fisheries; the FAO review on state of world fisheries; DOALAS; UN Specialised agencies; IMO Committee structure; MEPC documentation; UNFSA. Useful secondary sources on the Law of the Sea from an IR perspective include Clyde Sanger, *Ordering the Oceans* (University of Toronto Press, 1986) and R. Churchill, V. Lowe and A. Sander, *The Law of the Sea* 4th ed. (MUP, 2022). See also, on the changes introduced by the UNCLOS Convention, R.P. Barston and P. Birnie (eds), *The Maritime Dimension* (Routledge, 2024).

2 See inter alia UNCLOS, Part V, articles 55–75; Churchill, Lowe and Sander, ibid.; Barston and Birnie, ibid., chapters 1, 5 and 8.

3 UNCLOS, article 56 (1) (a) (sovereign rights in the EEZ for exploring, and exploiting, conserving and managing living and non-living resource; articles 61–68 (conservation and utilisation); article 76 (continental shelf); article 116–120 (rights and duties with respect to living resources of the of the high seas); part XI (sea bed resources for the common heritage of mankind in the area beyond the EEZ including solid, liquid and gaseous mineral resources, and polymetallic nodules).

4  For the concept and regime for archipelagic states see UNCLOS, Part V, articles 46–54.

5  R.P. Barston, "Port State Control: Evolving Concepts", in Harry H. Scheiber (ed.) *Law of the Sea: The Common Heritage and Emerging Issues* (Brill Nijhoff, 2000) chapter 4, pp87–102. See also articles 56 (1) (b) iii; articles 218–20 UNCLOS.

6  On high seas rights, see UNCLOS articles 116–9. The right to fish on the high seas is cross-referenced inter alia with the EEZ provisions (articles 64–7) to cover straddling or migratory stocks.

7  The term "straddling stocks" is not used in UNCLOS; the problem is regulated as "same stock or stocks of associated species (which) occur in and area beyond and adjacent to the zone (EEZ)" article 63 (2). Provisions on highly migratory stocks are inter alia in article 64. A major gap in UNCLOS is the absence of regulations relating to geographic shifts over time of stock and associated biomass from one zone to another (stock "ownership") due to factors such as global warming and loss or reduction of feeding grounds due to deep or mid-water fishing gear, density of trawling and climatic factors.

8  See Indian Ocean Rim Association (IORA), 7 March 1997.

9  See index of IMO environmental agreements relating to oil and chemical pollution and guidelines and index to MEPC resolutions. For environmental pressure to reduce carbon emissions related to shipping, see IMO, MEPC.1/ Circ. 897, 1 November 2022.

10  Special areas were negotiated by UNEP under the Regional Seas Programme over a lengthy period of over twenty-five years via framework action plans, resetting objectives, protocols and revised agreements. UNEP attempted to facilitate visionary goals and coordination, but was constrained by geographic scale, financial resources, differing national capacities and regional political differences. Special areas included the Mediterranean (Barcelona Convention, 1976; revised 1995 and Protocols); the Wider Caribbean (Action Plan, Cartagena Convention, 11 October 1986); West and Central Africa (Abidjan Convention, 1984); the North West Pacific (China, Japan, Republic of Korea, Russian Federation Action Plan, 1994 and Joint UNEP–IMO agreement for oil and chemical spill coordination, 2003 and 2008); East Asian Seas; East Africa and the Caspian Sea.

11  R.P. Barston, *Modern Diplomacy* 5th ed. (Routledge, 2019) pp251–8 and pp498–500 (Paris Agreement).

12  Incomplete oil or other waste (Annex V) reception facilities for MARPOL compliance.

13  For the IMO–UNEP joint oil pollution project under the Northwest Pacific Regional Oil and Hazardous Substances Spill Contingency Plan (PRC, Japan, Korea, Russian Federation) and Spill Centre under the UNEP regional seas programme, see www.unep.org/topics/ocean-seas-and-coasts/regional-seas-programme.

14  See R.P. Barston, "Regional Fisheries Management" International Journal of Marine and Coastal Law, 14, 3 (1999) pp235–56.

15  Report of the 14th Session of the FAO Committee on Fisheries, No 459 (Rome, 1991).

16  FAO report on the Technical Fisheries Consultations on High Seas Fishing, Rome, 7–15 September 1992.

17  Earth Summit, UNCED, Rio 1992; Agenda 21 Section C, 17.45, 17.49.

18 UN General Assembly Resolution 46/215, 20 December 1990, calling for a moratorium on pelagic drift net fishing.

19 Agreement to Promote Compliance with International Conservation and Management Measures by Fishing Vessels on the High Seas (FAO, 24 November 1993) Code of Conduct for Responsible Fisheries (FAO, 1995).

20 States not party to the Compliance Agreement include China, Russia, Thailand and Taiwan.

21 Japan deposited an instrument of acceptance on 20 July 2000 and Republic of Korea on the entry into force of the Compliance agreement on 24 April 2003.

22 UN Fish Stocks Agreement A/CONF/164/37, 8 September 1995.

23 On the simplified consensus procedure, see A/CONF/164/5, 26 April 1993; A/ CONF/164/6, 3 May 1993; A/CONF/164/2/ Rev. 1, 21 August 1993. Rule 33 provides for the conference being conducted on the basis of general agreement. Article 35 has further detail on procedures for dealing with breakdown, except that voting is to take place only after all efforts to achieve general agreement have been exhausted.

24 At UNCLOS, diplomatic documentation methods included working documents by individual or several states (L papers), working group reports, reports of specialised agencies and secretariat information and technical documents. L papers deal with a variety of subjects such as key principles, aspects of what a draft agreement should include, drafting provisions on particular topics, special interests or compromise proposals, facilitator reports and draft provisions. L papers may be issued by a single state or facilitator, bilaterally or through several co-sponsors. L papers in the UNFSA negotiations included Ecuador (L 44), special requirements of developing countries (Australia plus co-sponsors New Zealand and Pacific Island states (L24). A core documentary method in multilateral and other types of conference diplomacy is the use of chair's revised and consolidated texts. At UNCLOS these formed the basis of the consensus-based so-called "package deal final text". For details of the structure and documentation at UNCLOS, see Final Act of the Third United Nations Conference on the Law of the Sea (United Nations, New York, 1983) pp158–69.

25 Working Group documents at UNFSA included an expert group on the principle of the precautionary approach in straddling and highly migratory regulation (L41).

26 The use of alternative draft texts prepared by the chair on parts of the text (sections 1V, V, V1, V11 UNFSA) is well illustrated in A/CONF/164/13, 23 November 1993.

27 The revised UNFSA negotiating text prepared by the conference chair in the UNFSA negotiations is at A/CONF/164/13/CRP 3, 28 March 1994.

28 The concept of "clear grounds" is used as a basis for undertaking inspection and enforcement action against vessels suspected of not complying with international regulations relating to construction, seaworthiness, navigation and pollution (see UNCLOS Articles 218 and 220). The concept has become an established principle in merchant shipping regulatory compliance, assisting its extension to fishing vessels.

29 See www.un.org/oceancapacity/unfsa#:~:text=The%20United%20Nations%20Agreement%20for,that%20regulates%20key%20fisheries%20that%2C.

30 See UN Conference on Straddling Fish Stocks and Highly Migratory Fish Stocks, guide to the issues before the conference, prepared by the chairman; A/CONF.164/10, 24 June 1993. Further post-conference assessment is in

the report of the Secretary-General to the resumed review conference of the UNFSA, A/CONF/210/2016/1.

31  See Peter Gullestad, Svein Sundby, Olav Sigurd Kjesbu, "Management of transboundary and straddling fish stocks in the Northeast Atlantic in view of climate-induced shifts in spatial distribution", Fish and Fisheries, vol. 20, No 6, September 2020, pp1008–26. Examples of stock shifting from zones are blue whiting, mackerel (north west Europe) and chub mackerel (Japan).

32  On the UK failure to frame the negotiations with the EU on the basis of zonal attachment see "Negotiation Outcomes", NFFO, 26 December 2020; *The Guardian*, 29 December 2020; *Fishing News*, 26 December 2021.

33  The Torremolinos Convention was the only major fisheries agreement for which the IMO did not receive sufficient ratifications or acceptances to enter into force. The FAO has issued various informal guidelines on conduct of fishing operations. The ILO is involved through labour standards (safety, welfare, crew food, repatriation) with Convention 147. This was subsequently accepted by the IMO as one of the international conventions which come under national and regional port state control inspection of vessels.

34  UN Secretary-General, Bulletin, ST/SGB/2021/1.

35  The briefing on the Law of the Sea Convention twenty years on was conducted at UN Headquarters 25–6 September 2002 jointly by DOALOS and UNITAR, rather than with FAO. See www.un.org/depts/los/convention_ agreements/convention_20years/Information%20Note.pdf.

36  See letter 6 February 2019, Executive Secretary Commission for the Conservation of Antarctic Living Resources (CCAMLR) to the Under-Secretary-General for Legal Affairs, UN Division for Ocean Affairs and Law of the Sea (DOALOS). In the letter, the Executive Secretary tersely observes as follows: "The Under-Secretary-General is invited to recall that CCAMLR is a distinct organisation and not a Regional Fisheries Management Organisation. Article 11 of the CCAMLR Convention states that 'the Objective of this Convention is the conservation of Antarctic marine living resources…'. Therefore these comments are offered to DOALOS from CCAMLR as a *relevant organisation* in the terms of the letter of invitation."

37  See FAO's defence of its mandate and critical reaction to involvement of DOALOS in its "territory", in Report Concerning UN General Assembly Resolution 52/29 (Large Scale Drift Net Fishing, unauthorised fishing in zones of national jurisdiction and the high seas, fisheries bycatch) June 1998, p1.

38  For the modernisation of the Western Central Atlantic Fishery Commission (WECAFC) see WECAFC/SAG/X1/2022/16. WECAFC was originally established as an advisory regional body, which includes the Wider Caribbean, mandated under Article VI of the FAO constitution. It also includes sub-regional aquaculture organisations, There are six similar regional bodies (CECAF, CIFAA, COPESCAALC, EIFAA and, SWIOFC, WECAFC). Apart from these, there are five regional fisheries bodies established under Article XIV (APFIC; GFCM; IOTC; RECOFI and CACFish), with greater degrees of administrative and financial autonomy. Of this group, the IOTC was part of the optimism of the second wave of institution-building in the 1990s, entering into force on 27 March 1996. Most regional fisheries bodies established after 2000 (Table 1) are outside the FAO framework. On formation of regional organisations, see R.P. Barston, "Regional Fisheries Management" Note 14.

39 On the membership of the Regional Fishery Body Secretariat's Network, see www.un.org/Depts/los/convention_agreements/ICSP14/Presentations/n/ GUILLERMOCOMPEAN.pdf. FAO was heavily involved in the negotiation and subsequent adoption of the Agreement on Port State Measures to Prevent, Deter and Eliminate Illegal, Unreported and Unregulated Fishing, approved following intense and protracted negotiations in 2008–9 at the FAO conference on 22 November 2009. See Agreement on Port State Measures, FAO, 2010, piii.

40 Interview with Stefán Ásmundsson, Secretary Northeast Atlantic Commission. Further details on regional fisheries bodies are in FAO Technical Paper 651, 2020.

41 See wwwcdn.imo.org › IMLIWMUSYMPOSIUM-in.

42 See Chairman's statement closing the 5th session of the UN highly migratory and straddling fish stocks convention, 12 April 1995. A/Conf/165/28, 1 May 1995, para 16.

43 FAO Constitution, article XIV uses the term "real contribution". See FAO basic texts (Rome, 1994).

44 Chilean amendment, 24 July 1995 proposed the inclusion of "real interest" in paragraph 1, A/Conf / 162/22, 11 April 1995 and a cross-reference to article 118 UNCLOS (regional cooperation), but consensus could not be reached on the cross reference. "Real interest" doctrine has now become a standard formula for distant water fleet operators and governments, articulated on all available diplomatic platforms as a right of access; See 12th review conference UNFSA, para 44, ICSP/UNFSA/INF 3, 20 May 2016, para 44.

45 UNFSA, article 8 (3).

46 See North Pacific Fisheries Commission (NPFC) Circular 006/2020, 7 February 2020, for the EU Letter, Veronika Veits to Dr Vladimir A. Belyaev, Chair of the NPFC, on the EU's application to accede to the NPFC. The letter used the term "request membership" rather than "application for".

47 See, for example, the practice of the CCSBT at https://ccsbt.org/en/cont ent/origins-convention.

48 Status of cooperating non-member withdrawn by CCSBT on 12 October 2017. See https://ccsbt.org/en/content/origins-convention.

49 For Panamanian application for renewal of non-contracting status, see NPFC 5th Technical and Compliance meeting, agenda item 7.4, NPFC-2021-TCC05-WP02; and 6th Technical and Compliance meeting 16 March 2022, NPFC-22-TCC06-WP01. Meeting postponed as a result of the Ukraine war.

50 SPFMO non-contracting parties are Belize, Curacao and Liberia. Open registries with membership are Cook Islands, Ecuador, Panama and Vanuatu. See www.sprfmo.int.

51 See David H. Anderson, Negotiating History of Article 91 of UNCLOS. Paper to IMLI/WMU Symposium on flag state responsibilities and the future of article 91 of UNCLOS, co-hosted by IMO and ITLOS, IMO headquarters, 5 March 2020. www.imo.org/en/OurWork/Legal/Pages/Registration-of-ships-and-fraudulent-registration-matters.aspx.

52 UNCLOS, article 94.

53 IMO measures to enhance flag and port state jurisdiction and enforcement include IMO member audit scheme, ship identification (company and registered owner, mandatory under SOLAS XI-1/3 and SOLAS XI-1/3-1) and continuous synopsis record.

54  See presentations by the Marshall Islands and Liberian registries at the IMLI/WMU Symposium on Flag State Responsibilities, IMO HQ, London, 5 March 2020.

55  See the valuable study on China's fleet operations by Tabitha Mallory and Ian Ralby at https://ipdefenseforum.com/2021/09/evolution-of-the-fleet/#:~:text=A%20Closer%20Look%20at%20the%20Chinese%20Fishing%20Vessels%20Off%20the%20Galapagos&text=A%20flurry%20of%20news%20stories,October%20to%20fish%20farther%20south.Of the other large vessels one of the largest fish factory vessels, is the Vladivostok 2000 (ex LaFayette), a converted former oil tanker, previously flagged Belize.

56  See WCPFC vessel list, www.wcpfc.int/vessels.

57  See https://odi.cdn.ngo/media/documents/chinesedistantwaterfishing_ web.pdf.

58  For super trawlers, see the *Margiris*, banned from Australia for two years and purchased by Dutch Company Parlevliet & van der Plas, registered Lithuania. "Fishers Fears as Supertrawlers Appear off Sussex Coast", www.theargus.co.uk/news/17949145.fishers-fears-super-trawlers-appear-off-sussex-coast/.

59  FAO Status of Worlds Fisheries and Aquaculture 2020, pp12–14.

60  https://rmiparliament.org/cms/. Marshall Islands. Illustrative Map of claimed Maritime Limits and Boundaries of the Marshall Islands. Source Department of State Bureau of Oceans and International Environmental and Scientific Affairs, Office of Ocean and Polar Affairs, and Office of the Legal Advisor Limits in the Seas, No 145.

61  Limits in the Seas, No 14 "Republic of the Marshall Islands: Archipelagic and other Maritime Claims and Boundaries", United States Department of State Bureau of Oceans and International Environmental and Scientific Affairs, 14 February 2020. See www.state.gov/wp-content/uploads/2020/02/LIS-145-Marshall-Islands.pdf. See also https://cnmilaw.org.

62  MIMRA, Annual Report 2020, p33, Annual Report, 2023, pp16 and 20–1.

63  UNCLOS Part IV, article 46–54.

64  See Marshall Islands Climate Risk Country Profile: 15817-WB_Marshall Islands Country Profile-WEB_0.pdf.

65  See "The Structure and Operation of the Marshall Islands Registry" wwwcdn.imo.org/localresources/en/OurWork/Legal/Documents/IMLIWMUSYMPOSIUM/8%20Panel%203_Bouchard.pdf; "The Marshall Islands Ship Registry Passes 200mgt" at www.seatrade-maritime.com/regulations/the-marshall-islands-ship-registry-passes-200-million-gt.

66  See MIMRA, Annual Report 2020, p34 for discussion on the transshipment hub aims and 2023 on limited landings for freezer containerisation.

67  See www.rnz.co.nz/international/pacific-news/444414/tuna-transshipment-in-majuro-shows-first-sign-of-rebound#:~:text=Majuro%20%2D%20In%20the% 20wake%20of,of%20the%20previous%20four%20months on COVID impact and competition from reduced port charges by smaller regional hubs.

68  See YouTube, Jo Jo Kramer, Making More Out of Tuna, 12 July 2021. The video includes footage on the Marshall Islands lagoon transshipment area.

69  MIMRA, Annual Report 2020, pp34–6.

70  www.fao.org/in-action/fish-4-acp/en/.

71  www.oacps.org/news/oacps-ministers-endorse-new-oacps-eu-partnership-agreement-proposals-on-fisheries-and-the-eu-blacklist-at-111th-session-of-the-council-of-ministers/.

72 "FISH4ACP. Unlocking the potential of sustainable fisheries and aquaculture in Africa, the Caribbean, and the Pacific. 12 value chains in 12 ACP countries" www.fao.org/in-action/fish-4-acp/where-we-work/en/.

73 www.fao.org/in-action/fish-4-acp/where-we-work/en/.

74 See www.oacps.org/uncategorized/accelerating-progress-on-food-security-and-nutrition-in-small-island-developing-states/, 17 July 2019.

75 NPFC Circular 006/2020, 7 February 2020.

76 See "Launching ceremony for GIZ Pacific Island supply vessel", www.giz.de/en/worldwide/135847.html.

77 The GIZ Transitioning to Low Carbon Sea Transport project was already in place, running from 2017–23. See www.giz.de/en/worldwide/59626.html.

78 Ministerial Conference on Marine Litter and Plastic Pollution, 1–2 September 2021, Geneva. See https://ministerialconferenceonmarinelitter.com/.

79 For details of the EU(GIZ)–ACP–RMI Low Carbon Sea Transport project, see www.giz.de/en/worldwide/59626.html.

80 For the change in the EU–Marshall Islands FISH4ACP project from diversification in the fish value chain (more local fish processing factories) to an EU low carbon sea transport project under the German Federal Ministry for Economic Affairs and Climate Action (BMWK) which also linked the Marshall Islands to the High Ambition Coalition, see www.giz.de/en/worldwide/59626.html.

81 NPFC Circular 006/2020, 7 February 2020.

82 See www.npfc.int.

83 M. Ichinokawa, H. Okamura, C. Watanabe, A. Kawabata, Y. Oozeki. "Effective time closures: quantifying the conservation benefits of input control for the Pacific chub mackerel fishery" https://pubmed.ncbi.nlm.nih.gov/26552265/.

84 On decline in catches of Japan, Russia and China, and stock movement, see NPFC Year Book 2018–9.

85 See NPFC Year Book 2018–9 for Russian statement on EU application for accession. For Japanese concerns see Annex D of 6th Commission Report.

86 https://ec.europa.eu/oceans-and-fisheries/fisheries/international-agreements/regional-fisheries-management-organisations-rfmos_en

87 See NPFC, SC05 report 2019, section 4.3.2 para 22.

88 EU letter of 19 March 2019, discussed at 5th Commission meeting, 16–18 July 2019.

89 EU Fisheries Operation Plan, 20 November 2020. The plan indicated the intention was to undertake fisheries other than chub mackerel. See NPFC-2021-TCC05-OP1 and 6th Session annual meeting 23–25 February 2021 agenda item 2.2 (EU Application).

90 The EU application was conducted by diplomatic correspondence which dealt with revisions to the Operations Plan made in response to the NPFC Scientific Committee evaluation and points raised at the 5th Commission meeting. The meetings of the Commission in 2020–1 were postponed because of Covid restrictions, whist the 6th meeting was held as a virtual meeting via Webex. The March 2022 session of the Commission was postponed in response to the Ukraine conflict.

91 On the discussion of the Japanese research on chub mackerel see NPFC, Report SC 05, 2019, agenda item 4.3.2, paras 21–22.

92 For the Rwanda–Peru draft resolution (Cluster 1) to UNEA 5, 28 February 2022, backed by the EU, see https://wedocs.unep.org/handle/20.500. 11822/37808?show=full.

93  NPFC, Circular 006/2020, 7 February 2020.

94  North Pacific Fisheries Commission, 2021, 6th Meeting Report. NPFC-2021-COM06 Final Report Rev.01 pp43–7pp, Annex D for the Japanese conditions attached to the EU admission, para 10 and annex D, NPFC Circular 006/2020.

95  See R.P. Barston, *Modern Diplomacy*, op. cit., pp35–52.

96  On the use of relevant institutions in debate to limit discussion see para 49 of the 12th Informal Consultation on the UNFSA, with efforts to limit the discussion on capacity by reference to the UN 2030 agenda and the role of the high level body as the competent institution for discussing the issue. Formal objection was used to put on record opposition to the inclusion of any language on "indicators of sustainable development"; the UNSDG committees were considered as the relevant channel.

97  See the report of the 12th round of informal consultations of states party to the UNFSA, ICPS/UNFSA/INF 3, 20 May 2016, para 29. For illustration of the concept of apparent commitments overlooked or not recalled, see commitments to reduce overcapacity of vessels made in the general debate on the UN Secretary-General's report to the UN Fish Stocks Agreement, which highlighted commitments made in various fora, such as the UN Sustainable Development Commitment, and failure to implement. One delegation reminded the meeting that calls for specific commitments were already covered in commitments made in an earlier agreement. Using reminder as diplomatic method indicates technical "memory" but may not be popular. For summary of the general debate see A/CONF/210/2016/.

98  See report of the Secretary-General, ICSP/UNFSA/INF3, 20 May 2016, pursuant to UNGA Resolution 70/75, 8 December 2015.

99  On the Indian objection to the IOTC stock recovery plan for yellowfin tuna because of its impact on Indian artisanal fishing, blaming the stock decline fault not on artisanal fishing but industrial fishing by external fleets. The dispute highlighted the classic artisanal versus industrial fishing access controversy which has remained a dominant and unresolved issue in international fisheries management see www.seafoodsource.com/news/environment-sustainability/india-objects-to-iotc-yellowfin-tuna-stock-rebuilding-plan.

100 Global Fishing Watch, "A Comparative Analysis of AIS data with ICCAT Reported Transshipment Activity" 2020. See https://globalfishingwatch.org/wp-content/uploads/ICCAT-2019-Report_final.pdf.

101 See A/CONF/210/2016/1.

102 See, for example, on cod fisheries Ices.dknews>pages>NScod23.

103 On the transparency doctrine, see ICSP12/UNFSA/INF 3 para 31 and report of the Secretary-General, review UNFSA 2016, ibid., para 183. It is a key feature of EU diplomatic doctrine (access, dispute settlement, level playing field, joint institutions) and echoed by resource focused NGOs.

104 See ICSP12, UNFSA/INF 3 ibid., para 35.

105 For example, see ICSP 12, UNFSA para 21 on the controversy over the discrepancy between the assessment for skipjack tuna in the Western Pacific in the advance and unedited report of the UN Secretary-General to the meeting, which tentatively suggested some reopening, whilst the interim target reference point adopted by the WCPFC indicated that the stock was fully exploited. See 2016 review ICSP12/UNFSA/INF3 para 21 (debate on disputed assessment if WCPFC between UNSG's report and WCFPFC on tuna stock).

106 Fisheries Committee for the West Central Gulf of Guinea, "How Europe's Dark Fishing Fleet Threatens West Africa". See www.iuuwatch.eu/2021/03/how-europes-dark-fishing-fleets-threaten-west-africa/.

107 See note 55.

108 For examples, see https://fiskerforum.com/norway-and-russia-strike-2024-fisheries-agreement/ and the Faroe exemption for Russian fishing vessels, *Fishing News*, 19 May 2022.

109 IMO initiatives included the Ship Identification Number (SOLAS reg. X1-1/3; X1-1/3-1; Assembly Resolution A1142(31) on verification of registration. For other measures see IMO "Registration of ships and fraudulent registration matters", www.imo.org.

110 Miren Gutierrez, Guy Jobbins, "*China's Distant water fishing fleet*" See https://odi.org/en/publications/chinas-distant-water-fishing-fleet-scale-impact-and-governance/.

111 The UNFSA was adopted on 4 August 1995 and entered into force on 11 December 2001, in accordance with article 40(1) (30 ratifications or acceptances). Ghana acceded 27 June 2017, Benin on 2 November 2017.

112 www.seafoodsource.com/news/environment-sustainability/working-group-of-nations-go-after-china-s-flags-of-convenience#:~:text=South.%20Korea%2C%20Taiwan%2C%20and%20Thailand,not%20part%20of%20the%20group.

113 In the third phase of accession to UNFSA, Asian states acceding to the UNFSA included Philippines, 24 September 2014; Thailand, 28 April 2017; Vietnam, 18 December 2018; Pacific Vanuatu, 15 March 2018.

114 Barcelona Convention, 14 August 1978, UNTS vol. 1102, 1-16908; Stockholm Convention on Persistent Organic Pollutants, 22–23 May 2001; UNTS, vol. 2256, p119.

115 MARPOL (1973, as amended) 1978 Protocol, 1997 Protocol (Annex VI (sulphur emissions/fuel oil). Prevention of Marine Pollution by dumping of wastes and other matter (London Dumping Convention, 23 June 1997), UNTS, vol. 1046, p120.

116 Basel Convention (Transboundary Movement of Hazardous Waste), UNTS, vol. 1673, p57.

117 R.P. Barston, *Modern Diplomacy*, pp492–505 (Paris Climate Agreement).

118 The 14th meeting of Parties to the Basel Convention (29 April–10 May) adopted amendments to Annex II, VIII and IX of the Convention to enhance the control of transboundary movements of plastic waste by clarifying the scope of hazardous plastic waste and transportation requirements.

119 IMO Strategy to address marine plastic litter from ships (zero plastic waste discharges to sea from ships by 2025).

120 UNEP Ad Hoc Working Group.

121 See https://ec.europa.eu/commission/presscorner/detil/en/IP-22_1466.

122 See enb.iisd.org/unep/unep5/summary-report-22-23february-2021.

123 For the Chairs summary of options for future work on plastics see www.unep.org/environmentassembly/chairs-summary-aheg-4.

124 See revised draft text, 28 December 2023, UNE/PP/NC 4/3. For the treaty methodology of constructing composite multilateral agreements for the plastics negotiations, see Chairman's Explanatory Note UNEP /PP/INC.3/4.

125 See compilation of draft text, UNEP/PP/INC.5/4, 1 July 2024.

# Chapter 6

# Treaties
## Second thoughts, revision and withdrawal

## Introduction

Treaties are one of the principal means for ordering relations between states, as well as with other actors. As such, treaties contribute to the structure and continuity of the international system. Compliance with treaties of a universal or other kind provides and promotes stability through bilateral and multilateral agreed norms and rules.

Traditional concerns regarding the effectiveness of treaties have tended to centre on issues relating to universality, reservations and the binding nature (or not) of consent to a treaty. The more recent widening of the debate to additional areas such as bad agreements, revision, withdrawal and compliance, reflect changes generally in contemporary treaty practice, as well as increased dissatisfaction for some states and international institutions with ineffective bilateral, plurilateral and multilateral agreements.

Diplomatic practice regarding treaties has been influenced since the conclusion of the 1969 Vienna Convention,[1] by the diversification in the content and sheer volume of agreements, increasing diplomacy at bilateral and conference level by a range of actors, and the erosion of multilateralism post-2000. One of the critical features of contemporary diplomatic practice, has been especially shaped by two factors: the absence or selective involvement in collective multilateral diplomacy of one or more of the three primary powers across political, environmental and other sectors; and the fragmentation of the international legal setting. The contemporary legal setting above all is a patchwork mirror of bilateral, regional and secondary technical and functional cooperation (transport, maritime, selected environmental rules e.g. oil pollution) and regional integration, contrasting with the deep multilateralism of the classic pre-2000 period associated with the UN Law of the Sea and subsequent conventions.[2]

The focus of this chapter is on the revision of treaties and withdrawal in contemporary diplomatic practice. Modifying and updating treaties has become increasingly difficult in view of the enormous volume and scope

DOI: 10.4324/9781003204039-7

of issues covered post-2000, increasing membership of the international community and rapid pace of change.

Diplomatic practice nevertheless would suggest that a number of methods have been successfully developed in multilateral and other institutions to facilitate revision, speed up approval of amendments and use traditional methods of diplomatic communication. Diplomatic notes have been used flexibly to bring bilateral and other instruments speedily into force or work round restrictions, rather than wait for formal high-level ceremonies. Informal guidelines and detailed Codes of Practice have been used to avoid the slow entry into force of formal agreements.[3]

Dissatisfaction with treaties has nevertheless remained for a number of reasons. It is reflected in treaty competition as large powers and regional organisations seek to form new groupings or expand relations through additional bilateral or plurilateral cooperation agreements. Dissatisfaction also takes the form of action against particular agreements or organisations, including denunciation and withdrawal from agreements. The reasons are several, including various legal grounds, but political factors linked to the politicisation of UN specialised agencies have also led to withdrawal.[4]

Withdrawal, though, has not always been permanent with some states reconsidering and returning after a few years. In these instances, being able to influence an organisation from inside rather than outside is seen as likely to be of greater benefit than a position outside an agency. Withdrawal often leads to loss of regional involvement and informal personal links. Regaining lost ground in cultural and other functional diplomacy become elements in revised approaches to countering an adversary in periods of international tension.[5]

A further development of note over treaties is the debate over "bad" leaders in diplomacy[6] and so called "bad" agreements. Bad agreements are defined by criteria such as error, poor technical drafting, balance of concessions and whose terms are inherently unacceptable. A further common reason for dissatisfaction is somewhat different, relying instead on arguments relating to implementation: that implementation of an agreement has proved administratively and economically impossible to carry out. That is, the agreement is unworkable in practice in its current form because of drafting, changing context and opposing interpretations, which combine to support the case for major revision or termination/withdrawal. These latter arguments have been countered by rule of law treaty advocates, arguing that agreements must be kept and obligations honoured in good faith.[7]

The above issues are explored through diplomatic methods used in four areas:

- revision of agreements
- dissatisfaction and second thoughts
- unworkable agreements
- withdrawal

These four areas are preceded by a short discussion of developments in the linguistic aspects of treaties, vulnerable points in treaties and the implications of changes in the international legal setting for treaty practice.

## Language: changing treaty descriptors

One of the interesting aspects of recent treaty development is the introduction of a variety of new terms to describe treaty related discussions, objectives and types of agreement. These have added to diplomatic treaty vocabulary, though usage and meaning may not always be commonly understood and can lead to dissatisfaction with objectives not reached or detail of the agreement. Examples include the introduction of the expression "to commit" instead of "agree". The term "commit" is used in several different senses, including reference to agreement to take certain action in future bilateral and multilateral agreements. The term is traditionally found in WTO usage, linking agreements to trade tariff and other so-called trade disciplines, used to describe WTO rules and regulations.[8]

The term has also entered into resolutions or ministerial communiques of multilateral institutions and conferences, to describe involvement in plurilateral or multilateral discussions, though the actual impact on improving compliance is unclear in either of these uses.[9]

The term "commit" is used in a further sense, to give an advance indication of intentions, to stake out claims or to establish lead positions in situations of treaty competition with other actors.[10] In this usage precise details of the commitment or draft provisions are not indicated, perhaps to divert domestic opposition or scrutiny but which nevertheless stake out an area of cooperation or convey action. Similar issues arise with the greater use of the expression "reached agreement in principle". Exactly how much, if anything, has been agreed is frequently not disclosed, continuing the tradition of closed or secret negotiation, despite the veneer of domestic consultation with NGOs and other public transparency devices. It is commonly used in EU diplomatic practice to mark out treaty "territory" and convey dynamism.[11] The difficult or outstanding parts of a negotiation have yet to be resolved, and may take some considerable time.

Associated language is found in agreements described as "high end"; "high ambition" or "ambitious", referring to scope and standards. In a bilateral negotiation or joint press conference, the usage may very well not be commonly understood by other leaders or officials, storing up later problems of interpreting and implementing provisions in an agreement. The method too makes it difficult to walk away from a negotiation.[12]

Other language used for diplomatic treaty descriptions includes stepping stone agreements,[13] triangulation and the similarly unusual term "horizontal agreements."[14] The latter is used to describe common procedures or provisions in multisector agreements.[15]

Other changes in titles are reflected in the proliferation of various forms of cooperation agreements. Many have lost much of their traditional meaning, such as "strategic partnership", through general application rather than being an instrument originally intended to elevate or convey special significance.

Recalibrating the title of an inherited agreement may not be so easy diplomatically. Post-Brexit, the UK inherited a number of EU strategic partnership agreements after leaving the EU with Balkan and other micro states, which created dissonance with its revised orientation of tilting to the East. The continuation of inappropriate titles to agreements contributes to the weakening of the purposes of using treaties as cooperation instruments.[16]

## Dissatisfaction and breakdown of treaties

Treaties vary enormously in terms of scope and complexity. In order to ensure continuity and effectiveness, the process of revision and amendment has become a well-established feature of diplomatic practice.

The main reasons for the breakdown of treaties and later withdrawal lie in three areas: treaty structure and terms, changing contexts and norms and the impact of unexpected events or crises. The chapter focuses on the first of these sets of factors relating to the provisions and construction of a treaty. A number of critical or vulnerable points can be distinguished which contribute to fragility. It is helpful in assessing a treaty to identify points of weakness as suggested in Table 6.1.

The format of a treaty frames obligations, which will influence whether it is in MOU or other format; uses declarations, side agreements and annexes; or is a relatively simple "bare bones" agreement. Concession points contain the critical elements for identifying and assessing the extent of vulnerability. An indication of the degree of vulnerability can be gained from the distribution of concessions made in the various chapters or sections of the agreement. Most agreements are not "win-win", as suggested at signing ceremonies or in explanatory website literature, especially in agreements between asymmetrical powers. It is only likely to be found in simplified formats, establishing general intentions to cooperate, or in an informal MOU agreeing to jointly discuss in the future specific areas such as artificial intelligence or pandemic cooperation.

Time-related provisions are particularly important in debt repayment, duration of access and trade access agreements. They become critical points in an agreement which is close to phase out or the end of concessionary trade access. Indeed, revised agreements may trigger payment or crisis negotiations over contracted cargo and, more generally,

**Table 6.1** Treaty checklist

| | |
|---|---|
| **Structure** | complexity, omissions, review |
| **Drafting** | language, obligations, clarity, ambiguity |
| **Concessions** | win-lose calculation, balance, loading compromises |
| **Omitted areas** | gaps, outstanding items, controversial issues |
| **Hidden detail** | interpretations "lost", treatment of controversial issues |
| **Notes** | what's in the footnotes, what's in the annexes |
| **Side letters** | private bilateral arrangements; interpretations, secret understandings |
| **Workability** | aims, purposes, deficiencies of the overall agreement, of key parts |
| **Implementation** | trade facilitation, certification, mutual recognition certificates, rules of origin, run out dates |
| **Modernisation** | safeguards, updating, review |

continuation of similar preferential access. Less obvious areas of treaty vulnerability are the hidden items in an agreement.

## Hidden items

Included in this category are explanatory footnotes, annexes and linkage or "crossover" provisions, creating connected obligations by making one area dependent on another separate area, with coercive counter action if it is not implemented (e.g. linked provisions on trade and fuel supply). Frequently ignored at leader level, with technical negotiations being delegated to officials, they have nevertheless now become critical ongoing sources of serious dispute at bilateral and inter-regional level.

Another critical area is silent items. These are the issues which have been omitted from the final agreement, generally from concern that they might risk or preclude agreement. They are based on a common end-run consideration in negotiations: the principle that some agreement is better than no agreement.

In the final element of vulnerability are issues concerning the likely workability of the agreement. That an agreement is or has become unworkable has now become an important part of the defence of withdrawal, whether by consent or unilaterally.

## The international legal setting

Treaties are invariably shaped within a setting which may, to a greater or lesser extent, affect the scope and effectiveness of bilateral or multilateral instruments. In periods of high multilateralism (e.g. 1972–1990), the launching and implementation of a wide range of environmental initiatives and agreements are distinctive features of the collective multilateral emphasis of that period.

In contrast, the international legal setting post-2000 is distinguished by the increasing fragmentation and dispersal of rules. The issue of fragmentation of international law was recognised by the International Law Commission eventually in a set of reports (2007–13) as it moved cautiously away from its traditional areas of concern such as succession and state responsibility. The ILC's report highlighted the causes and some of the implications of legal fragmentation for treaty practice.[17]

The major areas identified include first, the splitting of international law into separate boxes (Law of the Sea, transport, environment), weakening of universality, regionalism and issues of hierarchy arising from different sources of law. The acceptance of separate sub-areas at regional or bilateral level tends to contribute to international legal fragmentation.

Second, the growth of specialised law would in the long run contribute to undermining universality and universal norms, as rules and exceptions to universality were developed in specialised instruments at regional level in areas such as pollution, regulations on the transportation of dangerous goods and classification of chemical products used in agriculture.

Third, the ILC report underlined the problem of regionalism, in terms of distinctive rule-making having internal and also external effect as a standards barrier to those with lower so-called standards.

Fourth, the growth of conventions and regional organisation has introduced issues of rule hierarchy. The ensuing debate has put the claim of higher regional standards versus different national standards at the centre of negotiations between large regional organisations and third parties.[18]

## Treaties: revision, amendment and review

The rapid increase in the volume of treaty activity, changing content and complexity of issues has underlined the need to develop new ways of bringing instruments speedily into force and keeping them up to date.

In the main, treaties have been revised through negotiation between the parties, amendment and review, rather than through the often elaborate procedures for dispute settlement or arbitration envisaged in some treaties. Two additional principles – reciprocal recognition of the need for flexibility in methods used to bring agreements into force, and commitment to forward looking innovation – have further influenced diplomatic practice bilaterally and within international institutions.

## Amendment and review

With respect to bilateral agreements, there is considerable variation in type and complexity. Relatively brief agreements comprising one or two pages have continued to be widely used to create short, basic cooperation documents. A number are drawn up as shell-type arrangements to promote economic and trade cooperation. The details are left to further discussion and implementation by agencies and private sector, backed unprompted by occasional external visits and side letters. There are very little institutional arrangements, with the exception of an annual overview conference at HOG level.[19]

As regards the other provisions section, most agreements contain drafting on duration, amendment, review and general category. The general provision section has tended to expand beyond traditional areas such as security or goods safeguards to include a wider range of new issues for which special treatment or safeguards is sought. Examples include health care, land access, plants and environment. The inclusion of undertakings on these helps to strengthen the reasons for, and acceptability of, those and other elements of an agreement.

Duration is often left unspecified to indicate the importance attached to an agreement. In some instances, in order to reflect the significance of an agreement between parties with perhaps limited formal exchanges in that area, a lengthy period is specified, reinforced by a requirement in the review clauses for an extension of similar length.[20]

Amendment procedures are used less in bilateral treaties than multilateral, with the exception perhaps of trade. Much bilateral amendment is of a routine administrative nature involving extension of agreements or service arrangements. However, the use of amendment and review provisions can be particularly important in agreements between relatively symmetrical powers with complimentary interests, as a means of promoting common interests and proactively introducing new areas of cooperation to expand an agreement.

For example, the Australia–Singapore free trade agreement (SAFTA) has been reviewed every five or six years since entry into force. Amendments have been made to the agreement in areas such as trade facilitation and opening up new categories of trade.[21]

Bilateral investment treaties (BITS) are specialist single issue treaties, in which emphasis is placed on the sections dealing with amendment provisions. These act as an indicator of the quality or standards of an agreement. One agreement contains provisions indicating that "the treaty will stand automatically amended at all times, provided the Parties agree".[22]

## Procedural and substantive innovation

Amendment and review processes have introduced into treaty methods both procedural and substantive innovations. Innovative alterations to the structure of treaty packages have used combinations of formal instruments linked to a large group or cluster of informal MOUs. The MOUs are parts of a modular package, each dealing with a particular area such as artificial intelligence or digital trade. They are in effect standalone instruments, each envisaged as running for two years. There is an implicit assumption that new MOUs will be added and others replaced as part of ongoing process of developing the modular structure, as a progressive part of developing bilateral relations.[23]

A further area of note is that some agreements specifically exclude provisions on dispute settlement, as a reaction to the expansion in the use of these as instruments in trade conflict, or as part of more aggressive level playing field/rule of law-type trade policies used by large actors and groupings.[24] The non-use of dispute settlement also signals the desire for close working relations. Any issues which come up are encouraged to be resolved through discussion and quiet diplomacy.[25]

Substantive innovation has been used to expand on the subject matter of diplomacy in a much more comprehensive and informal manner, covering areas such as supply chains, medical equipment supply, cooperation and digital trade procedures. Section 9 of the Australia–Singapore agreement discussed above places emphasis on resolving issues through discussion and quiet diplomacy, excluding recourse to courts or arbitration.[26]

Substantive innovation in plurilateral and in dialogue agreements has broadened the content and mix of actors involved in moving into areas such as supply chains; medical equipment supply cooperation and digital trade procedures agreements.[27]

Overall, the above methods have contributed to the continued relevance and effectiveness of a wide body of international agreements. They have helped to keep treaties in most cases "ticking over", preventing them from falling into disuse. And, in a number of cases they have made important innovations to procedures in treaty practice and the substance of diplomacy.

## Multilateral treaties revision: improving effectiveness

The revision of multilateral treaties is particularly difficult for UN and other multilateral regulatory agencies such as UPU, IMO, ITU, WMO which face a variety of rapid technical changes in communications, maritime safety, new hazardous cargoes, environmental pressures or safety design, and routing issues with large passenger vessels or deep ocean exploration vessels operating in remote or adverse areas.

Rather, the continuity, acceptability and effectiveness of multilateral treaties has been achieved through the use of several methods to facilitate updating and revision, including amendment, review, supplementary agreements and various informal and nonbinding instruments. Other instruments used include frequent use of resolutions drawn up by technical committees, e.g. IMO Maritime Safety Committee or assemblies, ad hoc conferences and informal methods for revision and updating.

Amendments have varied from relatively small changes to individual articles which have tightened documentary requirements for compliance, introduced individual regulations for new modes of cargo or transport, and drafted new chapters in existing regulations.[28] The committee structure of the World Intellectual Property Organisation (WIPO) was overhauled by resolution to speed up its regulatory response time to rapid changes in ideas, technology and intellectual property rights.[29]

In contrast, the WTO has been divided over reform and informal measures to speed up agreements and entry into force but has moved to a mixed system of amendment to the Marrakesh agreement, a variety of plurilateral instruments and declarations. Additional treaty instruments such as protocol, conventions and codes have also been used to supplement rather than amend existing agreements, dealing with subjects not previously covered in detail.[30] The use of codes and guidelines has been one of the main areas of criticism of multilateral diplomacy efforts to speed up entry into force of agreements. The main arguments against codes are the effect on standards and the introduction of a patchwork of maritime safety and trade regulations.

In order to speed up entry into force of revised multilateral regulations a tacit amendment procedure has been introduced, for example, by the IMO.[31]

In addition, ad hoc conferences have become a well-established method of updating and revising treaties. They may be mandated in response to serious accidents (e.g. oil pollution),[32] part of more general assessments made in periodic reviews, revised standards[33] or in response to global incidents (e.g. terrorist attack on international transport and infrastructure).[34]

## Treaties: dissatisfaction and second thoughts

In the previous sections of this chapter, the focus has been on the methods used to deal with updating and ensuring the continued relevance of various types of bilateral and multilateral agreements. In contrast, the remaining parts of the chapter discuss sources of dissatisfaction with treaties. Finally, the chapter considers those instances in which states decide to denounce or withdraw from an agreement.

Dissatisfaction here is understood as referring to situations in which states have substantial concerns which are not met or interests not accommodated in the existing framework or provisions of a treaty. Other causes of dissatisfaction are procedural, perhaps over delay in addressing issues or the need to speed up internal procedures. Dissatisfaction with lack of results under consensus formula in collective multilateral negotiation has led to efforts to move to plurilateral methods and sectoral negotiations on sub-areas for those with direct interest.

## Multilateral institutions and reform

Reform has shifted from changing central UN institutions such as the Security Council and General Assembly to the methods and agendas of UN specialised agencies and associated UN bodies. Building new institutions outside, or with varying residual links to collective institutions in the current multilateral system, has also become another route in the approaches to reform.[35]

International organisations and agencies have become arenas to contest diplomatic space, with acute differences over agendas or strategic direction. Such differences have led to varying levels of fragmentation in multilateral institutions and specialised agencies. Dissatisfaction is reflected in disputes over elections for officeholders, creation of separate institutions, shift to plurilateral rather than multilateral processes and emergence of excluded states.

Within the WTO, for example, fragmentation is reflected in the disputes over rival candidates for the office of Director-General,[36] the contested post-Doha trade agenda, procedural disputes over breaches of consensus and special provisions for developing countries in trade regulation.[37] Institutional disputes occur, for example, over whether the WTO Trade and Development Committee or the upgraded Committee on Regional Trade Agreements (favoured by the EU, US and Japan as the newly formed WTO vehicle to promote transparency and review all regional agreements) have significantly undermined the WTO as a collective lead multilateral agency.[38]

## UNIDO specialised agency: contested mission and finance

The United Nations Industrial Development Organisation (UNIDO) provides a classic illustration of the impact of alterations of mission through major programme shifts rather than formal constitutional amendment, largely as a result of chronic funding crises and politicisation.

UNIDO had an eclectic remit since it became a UN specialised agency in 1985. This has varied from environment, promoting business links, industrial development, before returning to promote the UN sustainable development agenda, reflecting changes in funding sponsors and directors. Its geographic focus on Africa, however, has remained largely unchanged. UNIDO came close to financial collapse in 1994–7 following the withdrawal of Canada, then one of the largest contributors.[39] Canada was replaced much later, at least politically, by China as part of a shift in strategy to acquire footholds at Director-General level in several off-the-radar, less fashionable multilateral agencies. As a preferred method, it benefitted from low political and financial cost and accordingly risked breaking the longstanding customary tradition that heads of specialised multilateral agencies, with the exception of finance, would not be bid for by primary powers but left open for smaller states, to enable them to become more involved in the international system. Success in UNIDO and similar smaller agencies would bring political benefit, whilst failure would not have lasting damage on individual or national diplomatic reputation.[40]

## Parallel and alternative institutions

At a broader institutional level, dissatisfaction is also reflected in general funding crises for specialised agencies, selective voluntary donor funding by hosts for ad hoc meetings and plenaries (e.g. Biodiversity Convention) and withdrawal or selective participation. Another important indicator of dissatisfaction is the establishment of separate and alternative sub-institutions within or outside a parent international institution. In these instances, separate organisations exist in parallel with the parent institutions but have a high degree of institutional autonomy and financial independence. An example is the World Food Programme, which is loosely associated with FAO but is largely financed by western powers (US, Germany, UK, Japan and others, including Saudi Arabia). The geographic spread and ability to respond to emergencies, easier administrative response and preference of donor projects outside the political framework of the parent institution, were central arguments underpinning the WFP model as it sought separate status.[41]

## Plurilateral agreements

The use of plurilateral agreements in international trade has accelerated the growth of mechanisms other than consensus in treaty making. Plurilateral agreements are negotiated by limited membership groups, either independently from other related international discussions and exchanges, or created through separate negotiations within a regional or multilateral organisation. Obligations are binding only the parties to the agreement. Within multilateral organisations, plurilateral agreements were initially accommodated as specialist or additional agreements, e.g. WTO civil aviation procurement contracts. The practice has been increasingly extended in response to continued dissatisfaction within multilateral institutions over aims and new agendas created in consensus decision-making processes.

In plurilateral negotiations, the parties create in effect a sub- or separate agreement, to which at a later point others may join. A plurilateral negotiation uses the opposite process to multilateral consensus decision-making, which is based on the principle of "nothing is agreed until all parts are agreed", e.g. Law of the Sea package as a collective negotiated action. In some respects, consensus processes appear similar to plurilateral approaches with the use of inner groups, invited core members and working groups. However, the starting point is quite different. In plurilateral processes, those outside the group are not involved in agenda setting, drafting or compromise processes. Those involved in driving plurilateral processes are more limited with a higher compromise denominator and are correspondingly less diverse in terms of willingness to incorporate LDC blocs and least-developed interests driven by large or established economies.

Plurilateral negotiations tend to use closed processes more than consensus-based multilateral negotiations, are more closed than the latter and have contributed to the growth of secrecy, despite nominal transparency. Other differences stem from the incremental aspects of the process, with states joining at a late stage, thus encouraging free riders.

Plurilateral agreements can exist in three forms vis-à-vis multilateral institutions: as special additional provisions collectively negotiated as part of a multilateral agreement; in a second form in which there is doubt over the institutional and legal status of a possible plurilateral agreement; and where a plurilateral agreement negotiated outside a multilateral institution is transferred into it for "multilateralisation". The idea of "multilateralisation" is defended by proponents of plurilateral agreements because, when transferred into the framework of a multilateral institution, a plurilateral agreement may gain greater legitimacy and a wider number of members may be eventually added. Advocates of plurilateral agreements also argue that some elements of the procedures and rules of the multilateral organisation may be transferred or absorbed into the plurilateral agreement as it is negotiated in preparation for ultimate endorsement.

Prior to the Doha Round, the use of plurilateral agreements as special additional provisions was relatively limited. The WTO Agreement,[42] for example, contained an annex with two plurilateral agreements on Trade in Civil Aircraft (of interest to the US, Canada, Brazil and European Communities)[43] and Agreement on Government Procurement (domestic products, services and service suppliers).[44]

Greater use of plurilateral agreements was linked to perceptions that the deadlocked Doha Round (2012–15), based on consensus, was unlikely to make significant progress. In parallel diplomacy to the Doha negoti-ations, a number of states negotiated bilateral agreements as a safeguard against Doha failure. A limited group of WTO members undertook sep-arate intensive negotiations outside the WTO over a four-year period on a Trade in Services Agreement, one of the deadlocked areas in the Doha Round.[45]

Negotiating in the Doha Round format was seen by major western econ-omies as unlikely to produce any significant results, especially in relation to rapidly changing issues such as e-commerce, trade communications and the corresponding need for reform of the WTO process. Not all shared this view,[46] with an opposing group led by India and South Africa defending the need to retain the consensus principle, as embodied in the WTO Agreement and other instruments – reflecting their longstanding positions of protecting developing country interests and above all ensuring issues such as agriculture remained high on the WTO agenda.[47]

## WTO: shift to plurilateral agreements – the Buenos Aires package moving from multilateral approaches

As part of the shift to informal methods within the WTO, experimental plurilateral agreements had been concluded prior to the four major plurilateral initiatives reached at the 2017 Buenos Aires WTO Ministerial Conference.[48] These included the Environmental Goods Agreement, launched initially by the EU and 13 WTO members at Davos[49] and an agreement on tariff abolition on Information Technology goods, revived and expanded for the Nairobi Ministerial WTO Ministerial Conference.[50]

The Buenos Aires package (investment facilitation for development, e-commerce, domestic services regulation and joint statement on medium and small enterprises) marked an important shift in agenda and working methods of the WTO away from the consensus-based principles used as the basis for amending the WTO Agreement to one of informal arrangements based on plurilateral agreements and joint statements. A core idea was that smaller groups could initiate and move forward ideas on particular sectors.

The Buenos Airies package was promoted largely by a grouping based on EU–Latin America–Asia, the core of which had participated in earlier Trade and Investment (TISA) talks.[51] Included in the group were Latin American states with a longstanding interest in customs reform and MME (e.g. Argentina, Uruguay, Guatemala), with China added. Central and Latin American states were strongly represented in the institu-tional structure established for chairing groups set up under the Buenos Aires initiatives: Costa Rica (Services Domestic Regulation), Uruguay (MSMEs) and Chile (Investment Facilitation for Development).[52] In other plurilateral negotiating groups, technical innovation states were strongly involved in the e-commerce group chaired by Australia, Japan and Singapore, with substantial bilateral experience in e-commerce and innovative digital agreements.

Whilst some aspects of plurilateral discussions resemble the consensus process, i.e. coordinators, facilitators, structured discussion, moving to unified texts and statements, major differences include participation and procedures for review and channels for objections. Similar to consensus, records of proceedings of negotiating groups, lists of group participants and working papers are very limited, despite nominal claims in WTO narratives to transparency and being "member driven".[53] The format probably also encourages more free riders to a greater extent than consensus. That is, the plurilateral agenda is selected and negotiated by a limited group and, at a later date, after most of the substance is decided, these attach themselves to the process through the periodic reporting statements on progress.[54]

Those states opposing the Joint Initiative were from Africa, Caribbean, Pacific and Middle East. Absent, for example, were Egypt, Morocco, Algeria, Tunisia, Mauritania, Jamaica, Cuba, Tanzania and South Africa. Efforts to attract African participation had some success, pushed through using the EU's West African links, following the joint Nigeria–ECOWAS high-level leader meeting on investment facilitation and other events.[55]

Nevertheless, absence of developing and least developing countries reflected continued concern over negotiations on an investment agreement linked to development.[56] It is partly because of the issue of balance in participation that primary or large powers (China, EU), whilst key drivers, have remained largely out of front line press and public information activities.

Related to the problem of imbalance of participants in plurilateral negotiations conducted within a multilateral organisation is that of dealing with objection and serious differences. Informal procedures in plurilateral negotiations generally have limited means for dealing with objections in principle or major substantive differences. On the question of the status and content of new plurilateral negotiations within the WTO, for example, India, South Africa, and others found it difficult to find an appropriate forum to challenge the legal and substantive basis, since the talks were not conducted within the established committee framework of WTO. One of the few avenues was to question the legality of the reform initiatives by seeking a debate within the General Council of the WTO.[57]

## Multilateral institutions: breaking up consensus

Excluded states have received relatively little discussion in the diplomatic studies literature as a source of dissatisfaction with treaties. Areas which have received attention are sanctions, recognition and crises involving recognition and relations with breakaway states.[58]

Excluded states can, however, have a significant impact on treaties and treaty practice in several other contexts. The most common involve participation in negotiations. In multilateral negotiations, especially under consensus, exclusion commonly occurs as a result of the formation of small "closed" working groups, or the general operating practice of using limited membership meetings (e.g. WTO "Green Room" meetings,[59] called frequently to advance negotiation through an agreed text or clear other initiatives. Such meetings are looked upon adversely by excluded states. Exclusion affects implementation in that it is one of the factors which account for indifferent implementation or differences in later interpretation of an agreement.

An unusual example from environmental diplomacy illustrates how lead coordinators and UN Secretary-General, frustrated at impasse in climate talks, used future climate (carbon) reduction commitments as a basis for excluding or deciding which states qualify to participate in a leaders' commitment conference.[60] One of the consequences of this type of strategy is the danger that excluded states seek to organise competing leader summits, or agree private deals on climate positions at the expense of wider obligations in advance of forthcoming multilateral meetings.

Other sources of exclusion arise from states and other actors frequently failing to get items onto an international agenda or secure adequate consideration of an item in multilateral conferences such as the Paris Climate COPs. The plight of small island Pacific states, highlighted in efforts to put their difficulties onto the international agenda, is a classic illustration of exclusion. Intensive diplomacy as part of counter exclusion strategies to raise their international conference profile and secure special provisions on financial aid for vulnerable islands has necessitated a long and difficult diplomatic campaign based on lobbying, resolutions and legal routes.[61] Limited progress in implementing financial commitments forced island states to turn to exploratory bilateral diplomacy to find an economic patron. In turn, commodity powers acquire new roles as event states and environment project promoters.

In other contexts, expansionist actors may use division as part of strategies to persuade particular marginalised states to leave a grouping or join an alliance. Dissatisfaction at lack of international acceptance and looking for alternative allies are also major factors shaping efforts to create new sets of relations or partners.[62] Saudi Arabian dissatisfaction with its relations in the G20 influenced reorientation to extended relations with China and the Shanghai Cooperation Organisation (SCO).[63] The EU worked to bring Nigeria into its orbit, aware of its interest in diversifying for the AU.

Another problem is illustrated by failed or suspended applications for membership of an organisation. In this type of case, one of the issues is the effect of opening up a plurilateral agreement or limited membership organisation to additional members. Keeping membership of an organisation limited in size is an inherent problem for smaller actors involved in specialist trade or financial cooperation agreements with other regional partners. The main argument used by smaller members to try and limit expansion is the potential impact of a larger economy on the economic balance of the organisation. For example, the tentative contacts between the UK and Norway over possible membership of EFTA were turned down over concern about the impact of UK membership on the smaller EFTA.[64] With that unlikely option, the UK had to turn to other routes beyond Europe.

Limited membership resource organisations (e.g. North Pacific Fisheries Commission) face similar dilemmas over external actors impacting on decision-making, allocation of resources and turning regional organisations into geopolitical platforms.

## Unworkable agreements

Agreements can be classified as unworkable on the basis of error, drafting, imbalance of concessions, unworkable provisions or non-compliance. Each, or combinations of these, can become major sources of dissatisfaction with an agreement and contribute to it becoming unworkable.[65] These factors can be grouped into five categories: resistance to holding talks on revision, concessions, omissions, hidden items in an agreement, implementation difficulties and inadequate remedies for adjustment or change.

Delay or resistance to revision is one of the common causes of difficulties over dealing with modifying an agreement. Resistance to holding talks or making commitments may be part of delaying strategies to put off alterations, diversion or create a basis for minimum change. It tends make change more difficult or lead to partial or unsatisfactory revision. It is stronger in more complex agreements and seen in resistance to reopening negotiations.[66] Reopening is opposed using arguments pointing up the delicate balance of compromise which would be damaged by any attempt to renegotiate concessions.[67] These and similar arguments were used by Egypt in the Nile Waters dispute over the Ethiopian Grand Renaissance dam project to divert the Nile river[68] as part of a blocking strategy retain its historic treaty concessions.[69] Similar arguments underpinned the resistance of the EU to reopening any significant negotiations on the Brexit agreements to reopen the Northern Ireland Protocol in the Withdrawal Agreement[70] or Trade and Cooperation Agreement (TCA).[71]

The basis for unworkable agreements varies but includes concessions which, when scrutinised or re-evaluated, are seen as problematic. Concessions made in the final phase of negotiations may significantly alter the balance of an agreement, as in the EU–UK TCA negotiations on fisheries access favouring EU vessels.[72] Proposals may cross red lines, which would fundamentally change existing arrangements, as in the EU–Swiss negotiations to move away from bilateral arrangements;[73] they may be made in the final phases of negotiations and affect the balance of concession with additional demands or new clauses;[74] or they may be included as hidden items, in footnotes or in the dense text of annexes.[75] The issue remains a major potential hurdle in UK–EU relations, as an unsatisfactory residual area of negotiation, and both a complex constraint in reopening UK–EU withdrawal issues and resetting wider UK–European relations post-Brexit.

Omissions in an agreement lead to loop holes, ambiguity and compliance issues. A major omission in the Trade and Cooperation Agreement is the lack of adequate trade facilitation provisions to speed up entry of goods and services.[76] Omissions inevitably become a longstanding source of implementation grievances and calls for substantial change. The institutions and procedures in an agreement may be inadequate, not jointly understood or overly elaborate for the kinds of issues which cause agreements to become unworkable.

## The Windsor Framework case study

The case study is used to show how reluctance to hold negotiations between the EU and UK on resolving issues of trade flows to Northern Ireland and Britain and Ireland is resolved through procedural methods, technical substantive concessions and policy revision. The respective concessions raise questions about the scale and implications of concessions necessary to reach an agreement.

EU–UK negotiations on the Northern Ireland Protocol over trade flows from Britain into Northern Ireland were eventually resumed at Windsor.[77] They provide an unusual insight into the various factors shaping the contrasting approaches to the talks. Both parties had to appear not to be making concessions and, for the EU, not seem to be reopening the Protocol. The contradiction in positions was resolved partly by the UK's changes of approach, policy and methods. Part of the change in methods involved soft power; to use location – Windsor – to suggest high-level intent, historic context and a shift in UK foreign policy orientation to a less strident Brexit. An agreement, however modest, offered prospects of Anglo–European accords on international issues.

For the UK, the focus was to be seen to have improved the trade flows into Northern Ireland from Britain.[78] For the Commission, how that might be achieved, without appearing to reopen the Protocol was critical: the outcome was termed "Windsor Framework" rather than agreement, and the administration of the joint decisions from the meeting was to be undertaken by the Joint Committee, with the EU passing additional legislation to give the Committee legal capacity.

To achieve progress on improving the flow of goods to Ireland, the UK made four concessions: new special goods categories with joint oversight, new stakeholder groups, commitment to address problems of regulatory divergence and EU monitoring of the agreement.[79]

In appearance, the changes to achieve less goods inspection were apparently of technical detail and not the subject of parliamentary or other scrutiny. The concessions appeared nominal, small or in obscure areas. An alternative view suggests that combining the concessions might overall have been secured at the cost of enhanced EU oversight of Northern Ireland, eroding the latter's links in the long term with the United Kingdom. How these and other reset issues are handled will continue to pose major dilemmas for diplomatic methods in EU–UK relations.

## International agreements: withdrawal and termination

First, withdrawal generally signals a major shift in foreign policy, as in withdrawal from the Paris Climate agreement[80] or Joint Plan of Action on Iran.[81] Withdrawal from an arms control agreement may be more than nominal readjustment to an agreement from another era, and instead intended to foreshadow a change of direction and new political boundaries.

In the second example, the withdrawal of South Africa from the ICC is used to illustrate the issue of conflicting obligations between universal and regional institutions, fragmentation and domestic reversal. In its denunciation statement on withdrawal from the Rome Statute of the International Criminal Court (ICC), South Africa set out the conflicting obligation to arrest former President Omar al-Bashir of Sudan under the Rome Statute, and the obligation to the AU to grant immunity in terms of the Host Agreement and the General Convention on Privileges and Immunities of the Organisation of African Unity.[82] South Africa, along with Burundi and The Gambia were strongly backed by the AU, as the "new pioneers" of the competing narrative of the "Voice of Africa". A further interesting feature of the case is the reversal of the instrument of withdrawal in a High Court judgement brought by the Democratic Alliance, on the grounds of it being unconstitutional and invalid, not having been put before Parliament. Nevertheless, the conflict between AU obligations and those of the ICC are indicative of fragmentation of rules and processes within the international legal system.

Third, jurisdiction issues over withdrawal of recognition have increased as states, international organisations and other actors seek to create or establish new relations with different institutions outside the traditional institutions initially established for advisory opinions, dispute settlement and other tribunals. Withdrawal in these contexts has wide implications influencing continued international legal fragmentation, impact on universality and triggering similar action. An explanation of the reasons for withdrawal is not necessarily required but it is becoming practice for some states and organisations to use withdrawal as a platform for explaining and promoting positions on issues.[83]

An unusual example of international organisation withdrawal of recognition is seen in the ILO–IFAD case. In this example, the International Fund for Agricultural Development (IFAD) withdrew its recognition of the jurisdiction of the ILO Administrative Tribunal, which deals with personnel complaints from staff in international organisations. IFAD concerns included the standard of proof applied by the Tribunal and appropriateness of these for investigations conducted by international organisations. The IFAD withdrawal of recognition was likely to have been influenced by the discontinuation of ILO Tribunal recognition by four international organisations in the preceding three years. The ILO subsequently prepared draft amendments to the Statute of the Tribunal to provide procedures for discontinuing recognition of the Tribunal.

Fourth, in environmental diplomacy, states may find it necessary to take the extreme step of withdrawal from regional cooperation agreements, in circumstances of high levels of conflict and dispute between members over persistent breakdown of cooperation and charges of administrative failure. For example, Uganda withdrew from the Lusaka Agreement on Cooperative Enforcement Operations in 2020. The seven-member body was originally set up to improve regional cooperation in support of the CITES Convention.[84]

## Termination of agreements

Provision of termination is provided for in most international agreements. In most cases it is not a routine act, but has wider implications. At stake in termination are links with that actor or organisation, affecting bilateral and multilateral relations. Termination symbolises the break. There are a number of wider implications, particularly from being outside an organisation, on external perceptions of treaty reliability, loss of capacity to influence decisions in particular areas and reduction of choice. Termination may also have implications for the continued viability of related international organisations.

At bilateral level, commercial disputes between primary powers and developing countries over commercial contract cancellation can add to the latter's complex debt arrangements and affect other aspects of bilateral relations. Cancellation of contracts is also relatively common in defence sales agreements, often with adverse effects on bilateral relations. The Australian decision to cancel the conventional submarine contract with France, in preference for US-supplied nuclear powered submarines as part of the UK–AU–US security agreement, caused considerable short-term political damage to bilateral France–US relations and in the longer term added to the latent unease in bilateral security relations.[85]

### Reversal of withdrawal from agreements

Reversal of withdrawal from an agreement occurs mainly in multilateral rather than bilateral agreements. Withdrawal almost inevitably reduces contacts and means of influence derived from multilateral level transactions and eventually leads to long-term concerns over adverse effects on image.

Changes of policy on withdrawal are generally shaped by incoming governments, as in the instance of the US rejoining the Paris Agreement, or seeking to revive exchanges with Iran initially via private envoys and intelligence services. Both reversals also underline the argument that reversal does not necessarily fundamentally alter approaches or substance. Continuity of interests limits change.

Rejoining an international organisation is one of the common examples of reversal. Reversal is particularly important for small and medium powers with concerns over influence and loss of access to contacts and resources. Australia, for example, withdrew from IFAD in 2004, on the grounds of lack of focus on south-east Asia and the Pacific. Loss of international contacts and regional participation were major factors in the decision to rejoin IFAD in 2012.[86]

### Conclusion

The development of treaties in contemporary diplomacy has been shaped by four issues: fragmentation of the international system, modifying and keeping up to date agreements, the growth of plurilateralism and increasing dissatisfaction over compliance and review. Fragmentation in the international system is reflected in the international legal setting, which has become splintered and divided as a result of expansion of membership, and the changing scope and volume of transactions.

Dissatisfaction with treaties has become more extensive and the causes of dispute over them wider. In order to contain and limit dissatisfaction, several methods have been developed at bilateral and multilateral level, including review, speeding up entry into force of amendments, codes and guidelines. In multilateral technical diplomacy such as IMO, ICAO, ITU, regular amendment has kept international agreements up to date, raised standards and become one of the critical elements in the functional "glue" of basic international order. The overall volume of amendment has resulted in some states falling behind and the informal codes resulting in the development of compliance gaps.

The causes of dissatisfaction are extensive, though often hidden in failing agreements, obscured under titles such as strategic cooperation or deferred through reluctance to enter into renegotiation which might expose further weaknesses. Lengthy rounds of bilateral and inter-regional negotiations leave unresolved issues or, conversely, leave little time to complete new or revised preferential agreements with weaker parties.

A further major source of dissatisfaction stems from unworkable international agreements, the reasons for which go beyond narrow traditional grounds for revision or change. So-called "bad" or unworkable agreements are a result of technical error, unbalanced concessions or failure to take into account probable difficulties of implementation, or deferring these to later joint committees, which progressively accumulate unresolved differences or difficulties.

The future workability of an agreement is also shaped by hidden clauses, postponed tariff phase-ins, or silence on contested issues, which continue in the political background, intermittently surfacing as focal points in wider debate. Hidden clauses have become controversial and destructive features of bilateral and multilateral agreements, in the form of obscurely located clauses or amendments, footnotes to clauses, as late drafting revision or added protocol. New methods include compliance clauses linking performance to access and compensation from unrelated sectors (e.g. energy, fish access). Taken together, these contribute to the likelihood of making an agreement technically and politically unworkable or unacceptable.

At multilateral level, attention periodically shifts from reform of the UN Security Council and General Assembly to the workings of the Specialised and associated UN agencies. Debate on reform within the UN Specialised Agencies has become divisive over future agendas and how proposals or initiatives are advanced. It has divided those favouring multilateral approaches against the reform group advocating plurilateral approaches. In plurilateral approaches, initiatives and draft texts are crafted to advance small inner-group trade and finance agenda issues, generating the new plurilateral agenda. The shift to plurilateral methods has weakened the concept of multilateralism, intensified secrecy and disengagement. There are few options for developing and other states to advance counter proposals.

# Notes

1 See Vienna Convention on the Law of Treaties, 23 May 1969 (VLCT), UNTS, vol. 1155, p331. Entered into force 27 January 1980; Signatories 45, Parties 116.

2 R.P. Barston, *Modern Diplomacy* 4th ed. (Pearson, 2013) pp183–91; *Modern Diplomacy* 5th ed. (Routledge, 2019) chapter 20 (Paris Climate Agreement) pp492–505. The Paris Agreement was probably one of the last classic UN multilateral consensus-based agreements.

3 The United States and Russian Federation used an exchange of notes to extend for a further five years the Prague Treaty (8 April 2010) on Further Reduction and Limitation of Strategic Arms, rather than a high-level signing ceremony or as an item at a bilateral leader summit. TIAS 21–201, 3 February 2021.

4 See Houshang Ameri, *Politics and Process in the Specialized Agencies of the United Nations* (Gower, 1982) esp. pp215–60 for background; Douglas E. Williams, *The Specialized Agencies and the United Nations: The System in Crisis* (Hurst, 1987) pp50–1, 55–73 on politicisation of specialised agencies. Williams was a Deputy Secretary at the UK Ministry of Overseas Development in the International Division (IBRD, FAO, UNIDO and UNDP). His account is interesting both from the technical perspective of a senior official but also as part of the extensive literature of the 1980s and 1990s devoted to international organisations and functional cooperation. See also Mark F. Imber, *The USA, ILO, UNESCO and IAEA: Politicization and Withdrawal in the Specialized Agencies* (Macmillan, 1989).

5 The United States decided to rejoin ILO on 15 February 1980. The Kissinger letter of 5 November 1975 to the ILO Director-General, which gave the two-year notice of intention to withdraw from the ILO, sets out four areas of major concern: erosion of tripartite representation (i.e. the unique ILO delegation system of separate representation for workers, employers and governments); disregard for due process; selective concern for human rights; and increasing politicisation of the organisation. For the text, see "International Legal Materials", vol. 14 1582–84 (1975).

6 See Paul Sharp, *Diplomacy in the 21st Century* (Routledge, 2019) pp49–53, 120–3.

7 Article 26, VLCT 1969 (*pacta sunt servanda*). As an example of treaties repeating this formula, see, for example, UK–EU Trade and Cooperation Agreement, heading 5: Fisheries, Article FISH 8(3) in the provisions relating to annual access negotiations: "…(conduct) in good faith, and with the objective of securing a mutually satisfactory balance between the interests of both Parties." UK–EU Trade and Cooperation agreement, 24 December 2020.

8 See Anthony Aust, *Modern Treaty Law and Practice* (CUP, 2013) pp160–1.

9 See WTO, Ministerial Declaration, 13 December 2017, WT/MIN/17 64: "Members recommit to implementation of existing reporting obligations."

10 UK–Australia FTA Negotiations: agreement in principle, 17 June 2021, para 4.7; para 4.10

11 See, for example, EU–Mexico trade relations https://policy trade.ec.europa. eu>mexico_eu.

12 Ceta plus 5, 20 September 2022. https://ec.europa.eu/commission/presscorner/ detail.

13 For stepping stone agreements see Cote d'Ivoire EPA. Provisionally applied 2016, OJ L540; EC–Ghana, OJ L287, 21 October 2016.

14 See www.unsouthsouth.org/wp-content/uploads/2021/04/United-Nations-system-wide-strategy-on-South-South-and-triangular-cooperation-for-sustaina ble-development-2020%E2%80%932024.pdf.

15 See UK–EU Trade and Cooperation Agreement. 24 December 2020, p383.

16 UK Strategic Partnership update list 2022. See, for example, UK–Moldova Strategic Partnership, Trade and Cooperation Agreement, Moldova No 1 (2021).

17 "Fragmentation of International Law: Difficulties arising from the diversification and expansion of international law". Report of the Study Group of the International Law Commission by Martti Koskenniemi. A/CN.4 L.682, 13 April 2006.

18 See Michel Barnier, *My Secret Diary*, op. cit., pp332–3 on the level playing field concept. Notice, too, the introduction and use in the EU team of allied concepts such as sustainable trade as a core idea, p321.

19 Brazil–India Bilateral Investment Treaty, 25 January 2020, Article 28.3.

20 See US–Japan Protocol amending the Status of Forces Agreement, 22 January 2016, TIAS 21-331.1. The Protocol renewed the dates of the agreement for a further five years.

21 Australia–Singapore FTA, 17 February 2003, chapter 17, article 7.

22 Brazil–India, ibid., article 27.

23 Australia–Singapore Digital Economy Agreement, 6 August 2020. The Singapore–Australia agreement includes seven MOUs: Artificial Intelligence; electronic invoicing; digital identity; personal data protection; data innovation; electronic certification and trade facilitation.

24 On EU trade defence, see https://policy.trade.ec.europa.eu/enforcement-and-protection/trade-defence_en; www.euractiv.com/topics/trade-defence-instruments/.

25 Singapore–Australia MOU on Artificial Intelligence, 23 March 2020, para X, Dispute Resolution.

26 See, for example, UK–Canada agreement to boost green technology supply chain, 6 March 2023; US–Japan Critical Minerals, 28 March 2023.

27 See "Securing Medical Supply Chains Will Take Binding Trade Agreements" www.csis.org/analysis/securing-medical-supply-chains-will-take-binding-trade-agreements.

28 See www.imo.org/en/About/Conventions/Pages/Amendments-to-IMO-instruments.aspx for amendments expected to enter into force. The range of technical diplomacy is immense, ranging from ongoing problem of cargo liquefaction (MSC 105) to obligations to keep ports operating in pandemics (FAL 46, January 2024) to Polar Navigation rules.

29 See PCT Reform, www.wipo.int/pct-reform/en/>?>.

30 The ship focus of the SOLAS (1974) Convention was altered quite fundamentally with the amendments to include the responsibilities of companies, creating a new chapter of SOLAS (International Safety Management Code, chapter IX). The amendment brought in IMO mandatory regulations relating to shipping companies and their responsibilities for maritime safety. The ISM Code entered into force on 1 July 1998. The Code has been regularly updated since by resolutions of the IMO Maritime Safety Committee and the Assembly.

31 Under the tacit amendment procedure, subject to being deemed accepted under the provisions of Article VIII of the SOLAS (1974) Convention, amendments enter into force on a specified date unless more than one third of contracting governments or, using tonnage criteria, contracting governments with at least 50% of gross tonnage of the world's merchant fleet notify their objections to the IMO Secretary-General (by a specified date). If no objections are received, the amendment will be deemed to have effect.

32  Major shipping accidents included the Exxon Valdez, 24 March 1985, Prince William Sound, Alaska, which spilled some 10m (US) gallons. In response to the severity of shipping and related oil pollution incidents, the Assembly of the IMO in resolution A.674 (16) convened a diplomatic conference on oil pollution preparedness and response which adopted a pioneer convention on response (OPRC, 1990).

33  See, for example, International Convention for Safe Containers (as amended, IMO 1992).

34  See International Ship and Port Facility Security Code (ISPS Code). The ISPS Code was adopted in 2002 by resolution at the IMO Conference of Contracting Governments to the International Convention for the Safety of Life at Sea (London, 9–13 December 2002).

35  The UN Charter has been amended three times to date. Each has involved the size of membership of principal institutions (the Security Council expanded from 11 to 15 members, and the Economic and Social Council (ECOSOC) expanded from 18 to 27 then, in a major shift, doubled to 54.

36  The rules of procedure for election of Director-General of the WTO are at WT/L/509. The WTO Director-General, Roberto Azevêdo, announced his resignation on 14 May 2020 virtually, with effect 1 August 2020 – a year early, against the background of the disputed post-Doha agenda, impasse on direction of the WTO and the dispute over filling the judicial appointment to the Appellate division. For details of the candidates, see www.wto.org /english/ thewto_e/dg_e/dgsel20_e/dgsel20_e.htm. The WTO General Council eventually agreed the following year to select Dr Ngozi Okonjo-Iweala (Nigeria) on 15 February 2021 as Director-General.

37  See R.P. Barston, *Modern Diplomacy* 5th ed. (Routledge, 2019) pp214–6. For the dispute over the WTO work programme see WT/MIN(15) DEC part III paras 28–30; Buenos Aires Ministerial meeting WT/MIN(17)/60 13 December 2017; and the Indian and South African legal challenge to the WTO services and e-commerce agenda, WT/GC/W /819, 19 February 2021.

38  Barston, *Modern Diplomacy* 5th ed., p218.

39  For a rare account of a less well-known UN specialised agency see, Intellectual History of UNIDO at www.unido.org/sites/default/files/2016-11/UNIDO_50 y_0.pdf.

40  See https://open.unido.org/projects/M0/donors/.

41  See www.wfp.org/history.

42  The Marrakesh Agreement Establishing the World Trade Organisation 1994 entered into force on 1 January 1995. legal texts-Marrakesh agreement https://wto.or>docs_e>legal_e>04wto_e> (WTO Agreement).

43  Annex 4, WTO Agreement. The Trade in Civil Aircraft agreement covers duty-free trade in civil aircraft, prohibits quotas and other trade restrictions on civil aircraft and government support for aircraft manufacture.

44  In the Agreement on Government Procurement, the parties have agreed to accord national treatment in 2011, entering into force 2 April 2012. The revision extended the coverage and lowered thresholds, opening up more market access, improved transparency and included non-discrimination provisions. See WTO, GPA/112, 15 December 2011; GPA/113, 2 April 2012. National schedules are at GPA/W/315. See, for example, Korea, GPA/W/315 Add 2; GPA/W/315 Add 3. A key part of the document is Annex 7(g) dealing with

General Provisions for each national schedule and is an essential source of information relating to exceptions in national schedules.

45 See, for example, the EU Report of the 20<sup>th</sup> round of talks on the TISA, https://policy.trade.ec.europa.eu/help-exporters-and-importers/accessing-markets/goods-and-services_en.

46 See WTO, WT/GC/W/820, 19 February 2021.

47 See wto.org>minist_e>mc10_>e>mc10_e.

48 www.wto.org/english/thewto_e/minist_e/mc11_e/mc11_e.htm; "Plurilateral initiatives and their interaction with WTO rules" https://twn.mt>title2>tnd44.

49 Environmental Goods Agreement (EGA) "Liberalising trade in environmental goods and services", EC DG Trade, 8 September 2015.

50 www.wto.org/english/thewto_e/minist_e/mc10_e/mc10_docs_e.htm.

51 For background to the TiSA negotiations see Patricia M Goff, "The Trade in Services Agreements", CIGI papers no 53, January 2015.

52 "New initiatives on electronic commerce, investment facilitation and MSMEs" at www.wto.org/english/news_e/news17_e/minis_13dec17_e.htm.

53 WTO Joint Statement on e-commerce, 18 December 2020 at www.wto.org/english/news_e/news20_e/ecom_14dec20_e.pdf.

54 There are no public records listing which states participate in the Joint Initiative working groups, or in the "small groups" format used at the margins of inter-sessional meetings. For example, Israel actively participated in the e-commerce and domestic regulations Joint Initiative group but it is a non-signatory to the Joint Ministerial statements. On Israeli participation in e-commerce group meetings, see the debate on India and South Africa's legal challenge to the validity of the Joint Initiative in WTO, N43 ibid., at para 10.76.

55 WTO, WT/MIN (17)/59; WT/L/1072/rev1.

56 See WTO News "Steady progress in negotiations", 9 March 2021, on out-reach activities. For details of the plurilateral agreements on Domestic Service Regulations (2021) see www.wto.org>tratop_e>serv_ejsdomreg_e; and for Investment Facilitation for Development (IFD) see WTO, WT/MIN(24)/W5, 16 February 2024. Also the Joint Statement Initiative on e-commerce agreement, INF/ECOM/87, 26 July 2024.

57 WTO, WT/GC/M/19.

58 See Nina Casperson, *Unrecognized States* (Polity, 2012) for discussion of the special category of de facto or unrecognised states. In the WTO context, the sense here is of exclusion: some states may not be consulted by lead group facilitators nor invited to inner groups, despite nominal claims of transpar-ency. The result tends to be a core inner group around an initiative, bulked by the EU27, and joined by free riders and a range of developing and larger states favouring a multilateral process.

59 On the concept of the "Green Room" and its use in negotiations, see R.P. Barston, *Modern Diplomacy* 4<sup>th</sup> ed. (Routledge, 2014) pp164–7.

60 UN Secretary-General climate-limited invitations linked to carbon reduc-tion plans.

61 On the diplomatic methods used for the inclusion of provisions on loss and damage, see Margaretha Wewerinke-Singh and Diana H. Salili "Between nego-tiations and litigation: Vanuatu's perspective on loss and damage from climate change", *Climate Policy*, vol. 20, no 6, 2020, pp681–92.

62 On Nigeria–EU cooperation, see www.eeas.europa.eu/eeas/seventh-nigeria-eu-ministerial-dialogue-joint-communiqu%C3%A9_en.

63 On Saudi–China relations see Robert Mason, *Saudi Arabia and the UAE* (Manchester University Press, 2023) pp146–70.

64 See, *The Times*, 31 October 2018. The main concerns of the smaller members of EFTSA were that UK membership would alter the balance of the grouping and that their economies might increasingly become marginalised under the pressure of the UK economy.

65 See Trade and Cooperation Agreement between the EU and UK (TCA), 20 December 2020, heading 5: Fisheries.

66 See chapter 2 on the use of timing in negotiations. See also the tariff concessions and timescale conceded by Pakistan in the Protocol to the China–Pakistan Free Trade Agreement, Phase II, FTA, article 3. www.commerce.gov.pk/protocol-on-phase-ii-china-pakistan-fta/#:~:text=A%20Protocol%20on%20the%20Phase, China%2DPakistan%20Free%20Trade%20Agreement.

67 www.euractiv.com/section/economy-jobs/news/algeria-chafes-against-eu-trade-deal-as-deadline-looms/; Yahia Mohamed Lamine Mestek, "Algerian–European relations: between partnership and servitude", Manara, 16 March 2021. See https://manaramagazine.org/2021/03/algerian-european-relati ons-between-partnership-and-servitude/

68 Anglo–Egyptian Treaty 1929 and the Egyptian–Sudan Agreement 1959 (The Nile Waters Agreements). The 1929 treaty allocated 48bn cubic metres to Egypt (increased to 55bn in 1959) and 4bn increased to 18.5bn in the1959 agreement. The 1929 treaty also granted Egypt veto power over construction projects on the Nile river and its tributaries.

69 Trilateral mediation initiatives over the Blue Nile were under taken from 2015 as quiet diplomacy by the United States and World Bank.

70 See https://assets.publishing.service.gov.uk/media/5da863ab40f0b659847e0184/ Revised_Protocol_to_the_Withdrawal_Agreement.pdf.https://commonslibrary. parliament.uk/research-briefings/cbp-9548/; www.consilium.europa.eu/en/polic ies/eu-relations-with-the-united-kingdom/the-eu-uk-withdrawal-agreement/the-protocol-on-ireland-and-northern-ireland-explained/.

71 "New Withdrawal agreement and Political Declaration", 19 October 2019; entered into force 1 February 2020. See www.gov.uk/government/publicati ons/new-withdrawal-agreement-and-political-declaration.

72 UK–EU Trade and Cooperation Agreement, TS No 8/2021.

73 Swiss Federal Council, "No Signing of Swiss–EU Institutional Agreement", 26 May 2021.

74 EU–UK Trade and Cooperation Agreement, ibid., Heading 5: Fisheries, 9.2 (b).

75 Hidden clauses in TCA included the linkage of sectors (e.g. fisheries access linked to other unrelated parts of the agreement, e.g. electricity supply. For details of the dispute see *The Guardian*, 8 May 2021 and *Fishing News*, 19 May 2021. The French Maritime Minister's remarks on cutting power were widely reported in the UK press: "UK blasts unacceptable threats by France", *Independent*, 6 May 2021. For details of late additions on the structure and access for EU fishing vessels see TCA Annex Fish 4, Protocol on Access to Waters, Preamble, Article 1 and TCA Part 2, Heading 5: Fisheries, Section 8 (access).

76 The trade facilitation issues to speed up entry included documentation, veter- inary certification and grouping of common items for single documentation.

77 See The Northern Ireland Protocol: The Way Forward. CP502 (July 2021).

78 Windsor Framework CP 806 (2023).

79 Windsor Framework, UK Legal Statement.

80 Paris Agreement, note 4, August 2017. CN575.2019.Treaties-XXVII, 7.d (Depositary Notification.). The US rejoined the Paris Agreement via a letter of acceptance on 20 January 2021 which entered into force on 19 February. CN10.2021. Treaties-XXV11.7.d (Depositary Notification).

81 For US–Iran, see S/2020/821, 26 April 2020; S/2020/497, 4 June 2020. See also Stephen P. Mulligan, "Withdrawal from International Agreements: The Paris Agreement and the Iran Nuclear Agreement", https://sgp.fas.org/crs/ row/R44761.pdf 4 May 2018.

82 See Declaratory Statement by the Republic of South Africa on the decision to withdraw from the Rome Statute of the International Criminal Court, 19 October 2016. CN786.2016. Treaties XV111.10 (Depositary Notification).

83 GB.337/PFA/13/1, para 4.

84 CN391, 10 September 2020, Treaties XXVII–II (Depositary Notification).

85 "Defence Minister will not apologise to France for 'backstab'…" *Financial Times*, 16 September 2021. See www.abc.net.au/news/2021-09-17/france-says- australia-has-stabbed-it-in-the-back-/100469308 "France recalls ambassadors to US and Australia…" *The Guardian*, 17 September 2021. See www.theguard ian.com/world/2021/sep/17/france-recalls-ambassadors-to-us-and-austra lia-after-aukus-pact.

86 AUSAID Proposal for Australia to rejoin IFAD, February 2012. See also www.aph.gov.au/Parliamentary_Business/Bills_Legislation/bd/    bd1213a/ 13bd030.(91).

## Chapter 7

# Parallel diplomacy

## Geneva, 5 January 2017

*AFTERNOON PRESS BRIEFING BY STAFFAN DE MISTURA, UN SPECIAL
ENVOY FOR SYRIA (MEDIATOR)[1] AND JAN EGELAND UN SENIOR ADVISOR
(HUMANITARIAN AFFAIRS).[2]*

What would otherwise have been a routine press briefing had in this instance two added special features. First, that it perhaps might be an opportunity for journalists to ask for additional details about the aims and emphasis of the new UN Secretary-General António Guterres in his third day of office, to augment the standardised fare of UN news bulletins. Second, the UN Security Council passed against the run two unanimous resolutions on Aleppo (demanding UN access to monitor evacuations from Aleppo)[3] and a second (UNSC 2336) on a new format for ceasefire talks sponsored by Russia and Turkey, to be held in Astana, separate from UN Geneva mediation.

Staffan de Mistura, veteran Italian-Swedish diplomat and special UN envoy for Syria, responded with a positive but nuanced reply to the second aspect:

> Our stand is that any such initiative as this one (2336)[4] needs to be supported, and we hope it will succeed and is definitely welcomed. We will continue contributing, at the request of Turkey and the Russian Federation, and the US co -chair,[5] with some type of statistical information until they set up their own monitoring system. That means, however, anyway that guarantors of the cessation of hostilities are going to be, and remain to be, and we want them to succeed of course, the Russian Federation and Turkey, who have been announcing the ceasefire.[6] (sic)

The press conference was important as a further indicator that the Geneva mediation process was beginning to splinter as a result of competing initiatives. The Astana talks illustrate the use of parallel diplomacy by the Russian Federation and Turkey. These, along with other later

DOI: 10.4324/9781003204039-8

initiatives designed to include Iran, aimed at shifting authority for mediation in the Syrian conflict away from the UN Geneva format by dividing ceasefire issues from political settlement questions and putting political issues to other Russian influenced mechanisms.

## Introduction

In this chapter we will discuss parallel diplomacy in terms of its use and relation to other diplomatic methods. Parallel diplomacy is very much an important part of diplomatic craft, closely linked to negotiation, quiet and secret diplomacy. The range and use of parallel diplomacy is a neglected area of diplomatic studies. The chapter will identify the main types of parallel diplomacy, how each is used and some of the main issues or problems associated with parallel diplomacy.

Parallel diplomacy is conducted within, or in proximity to, existing negotiations, discussions and exchanges to create alternative or competing agreements, institutions or arrangements.

In diplomatic practice four main forms of parallel diplomacy can be distinguished. These are parallel diplomacy directed at: (1) creating or defending alternative agendas; (2) competitive institution building; (3) protecting or promoting separate bilateral or group positions; (4) secret exchanges.

Parallel diplomacy is used to move to different approaches in conflict resolution based on other formats which are separate or outside existing multilateral or regional institution approaches. The purpose is to open up freedom of action and diplomatic space for initiating states, whilst retaining some links with the existing framework. Retention of links has the benefit of providing residual institutional legitimacy.

In other areas, parallel diplomacy is used extensively in various aspects of negotiation to protect bilateral or limited group agendas, or to develop specialist plurilateral sub-agreements on civil aircraft trade, electronic commerce and financial market access.

In multilateral consensus-based negotiations, parallel diplomacy is used by primary powers for bilateral coordination to block unacceptable provisions. In multilateral climate negotiations, US–China parallel bilateral coordination is a feature of annual COP climate conferences, in which each agree red line areas or some possible concessions.[7]

A significant area is in revision or restructuring agreements involving politically sensitive issues such as financial services access, trade dependence and labour provisions. In view of the sensitivity of economic issues and frequent unsatisfactory terms, media features prominently in this form of parallel diplomacy via leaked documents and interviews to highlight benefits rather than downsides.[8]

A further use of parallel diplomacy is in secret agreements. In this category, parallel diplomacy provides a cover for the main secret negotiations. The concept of parallel diplomacy as cover is highlighted in, for example, Japanese diplomacy prior to Pearl Harbor.[9] Like a number of forms of parallel diplomacy, it is high risk,[10] vulnerable to leaking, political opposition and dissatisfaction with exclusion.

A variety of channels have been developed to handle parallel diplomacy. Traditional channels have been augmented for sensitive, private meetings and secret parallel talks by back channels using third-party embassies, neutral host country and low-profile locations.[11]

In diplomatic practice four main forms of parallel diplomacy can be distinguished. These are parallel diplomacy directed at:

- creating or defending alternative agendas
- competitive institution building
- protecting or promoting separate bilateral or group positions
- secret exchanges

## Parallel diplomacy in practice

### Managing an agenda

In ad hoc plurilateral conferences, the responsibility for the agenda generally lies with the incoming or elected presidency. Particular themes or special interests can be reviewed via discussions with the previous host, lead actors and allies to determine the main focus and gain endorsement of the forthcoming agenda. The summit host also has the opportunity to design the schedule of the conference in such a way as to use soft power to showcase the country through side visits, exhibitions, environmental and other projects.

The use of invited non-members is an important area in the development of parallel diplomacy. As competitive types of governance arrangements have developed increasingly post-2000 at grouping and plurilateral levels such as G20 or BRICS, the issues connected with widening or altering membership have correspondingly assumed far greater significance. In addition to the state members of the group and designated international institutions, each host may invite a limited number of other states, international or regional institutions. The G20 normally has a limit of around six additional guests for the host.

In some instances, invited guests, such as Spain, have become de facto permanent members of the G20.[12] Singapore, for example, eventually became frequently invited to the G20 as a result of shifting political support for its inclusion and other pressures in favour of a revised G20 agenda to address the promotion of international financial transparency issues.[13]

In most cases, the list of invited states and organisations changes with the rotating presidency. Invitation to participate may be related to a theme or specific agenda item of the conference. Increasingly states and regional organisations are selected by the host for their economic and political value in promoting initiatives or international projects. For example, the promotion of German–African relations was an important element in German strategy of building up its international role under the Merkel administration. The Hamburg G20 summit was a valuable platform as host around which a mix of methods was used including bilateral German loan initiatives for Africa, project agreements with UN specialised agencies and parallel agenda diplomacy as a G20 host.[14]

Two other issues arising from the participation of non-members are of interest for the light they shed on the development of diplomatic methods. The first reflects concern over the impact of importing outside non-members on the identity and integrity of the organisation. Smaller groups like the G7 flourished in their early days partly through limited agendas but also through restricting membership and keeping the group as a narrow, high-level consultative and coordinating group. Concerns over whether these principles were being contravened were raised at the Cornwall G7 summit by Japan.[15] The Japanese concern principally lay with the UK's intention to invite to the summit India, South Korea and Australia, as a way of boosting the Asia reach of the G7.[16]

### *Host: new agendas*

At multilateral level, a rare example of the host fundamentally creating at the pre-conference stage an agenda linked to new initiatives is seen in the UK approach to the UNFCCC COP26 environment conference as co-host.

## The UK COP26 initiative

Three major changes were made to the traditional UNFCCC format which had stalled over implementing the 2015 Paris Climate agreement.

First, the UK initiative bypassed the UNFCCC bureaucracy-driven model (multiple committee meetings on reporting, implementation, the meaning of "environmental damage", finance and adaptation) which had dragged on since the conclusion of the Paris agreement.[17] Second, the UNFCCC agenda was refocused by the UK on collective action on major environmental threats (power, transport, steel) and the need for private finance. Third, the format for the first part of the COP26 was altered to create a parallel agenda; the first was Summit of World Leaders on core threats to the environment and new measures.[18] The second part continued with the traditional agenda UNFCCC agenda.

The UK initiative shifted the focus of COP26 away from the previous conference style of UNFCCC committees endlessly debating topics such as the meaning of environmental damage, adaptation and finance without significant progress.[19] The initiative was a major diplomatic advance in moving on from the existing UNFCCC approach to climate negotiations. It was resisted by the UNFCCC Secretariat which subsequently reverted to re-establishing its traditional role and format with the next rotating COP presidency.

The UK approach was based on a strategy of building up support for a revisionist approach pre-COP26. It echoed the initiatives of UN Secretary-General Guterres' action summits, which were parallel diplomacy summits in aimed at by passing the UNFCCC process in order to inject dynamism into environmental diplomacy.[20]

## Parallel agenda diplomacy: defensive action or counter diplomacy

Apart for the above uses, parallel diplomacy is used by external powers for tactical damage limitation. The rise of human rights, labour and social issues and linkage of these to other political, trade and sports events has widened the necessity for defensive diplomatic action.[21] One of the methods developed involves the tactical use of parallel diplomacy to influence the wording of communiques of an institution in order to secure the inclusion of favourable reference to an issue or interpretation of a forthcoming event. The communique in effect is used to endorse the host country holding the sporting event. Agenda and communique diplomacy are generally used in conjunction with information methods as part of defensive briefing.

It is a high-risk method in that the initiative could be opposed or fail to receive sufficient support. There are other potential limitations including the binding nature or otherwise of a communique. If released too far from the opening of a summit, it may leave the sporting event or issue overtaken by competing summit items and still open to attack. The European visit by the Chinese foreign minister[22] immediately prior to the G20 Rome summit[23] and the related controversy over China hosting the Winter Olympics illustrates tactical use of agendas in parallel defensive diplomacy. The visit came at a time of sharp deterioration in western relations with China and controversy surrounding its hosting of the Winter Olympics, over issues such as treatment of the Uighurs in the Xinjiang region,[24] internal security laws in Hong Kong[25] and the growth in Chinese military and economic power. One of the principal aims of the foreign minister's visit was to defuse the Olympics issue as part of China's strategy of damage limitation to secure its showpiece event, by including a welcoming reference to the Winter Olympics in the G20 Rome Leaders Declaration. A reference was subsequently added to the end of the Declaration.[26]

The case raises several issues with respect to diplomatic methods. The visit of the Foreign Minister to Europe was a late call visit on the eve of the G20. Late call methods are based on leaving a request or demand until almost the very last moment. It leaves little or no time for consideration, raises the level of tension and puts the host almost in a take it or leave it position. The Foreign Minister did not remain for the G20 meeting. The timing of the visit was parallel diplomacy, creating a back-to-back meeting with Italy, the G20 host.

The back-to-back style was reminiscent of ASEAN styled meetings, which cram as many events as possible into a short time frame. It also added to the clogged international calendar, straining under the build-up of rescheduled conferences, created as a result of COVID-19-related cancellations. A further point of note concerning the protocol of the parallel diplomacy initiative is that the G20 generally did not have sporting events on its agenda, making the purpose and request unusual.

## *Parallel institutions: extending influence*

Institutions are used as diplomatic methods in parallel diplomacy to establish presence, facilitate contact, promote interests and create alternative architecture. Parallel diplomacy is one of the key methods in strategies for creating a more visible presence or alternative agencies. Part of the process of establishing presence may involve gradually developing a dominant position within an existing regional or international institution and active committee engagement prior to setting up an alternative institution. The process of creating a lead position can be conceptualised as one of "hollowing out" an organisation.[27] It is used particularly in standards setting bodies, environmental institutions, resource and regional organisations. In the field of international shipping safety standards, for example, the original driving agency for additional maritime safety coordination was the Paris Memorandum,[28] set up in 1982 by 15 European and North American countries to coordinate, on an intergovernmental basis, IMO rule-derived ship inspection.[29] The Paris MOU was used as a platform by the EU as it hollowed out the MOU, eventually to create the European Maritime Safety Agency (EMSA).[30]

In development diplomacy, maintaining the exclusivity of bilateral initiatives and retaining diplomatic space, in the face of counter moves by regional organisations or international institutions, is a constant source of difficulty. Parallel diplomacy has been used by states as a method to lessen the difficulty, by creating separate specialist representative offices for special services such as promotion of financial investment opportunities in the sponsoring country. Representative offices provide symbolic presence and act as additional channels of communication.

For example, Germany concluded a bilateral agreement with the UN Industrial Development Organisation (UNIDO) for the establishment of a separate UNIDO Investment and Technology Support Office in Bonn.[31] The agreement was an important strategic element in maintaining German diplomatic space for its UNIDO/West African development diplomacy.[32] Bilateral relations with West Africa, particularly through ECOWAS, were major priority areas for the German Development Agency (BMZ)[33] since bilateral space had become progressively reduced by competing initiatives of the EU and G20.[34]

In African integration, parallel diplomacy has been used to project and develop a competitive model of continental African trade integration based on an African continental free trade agreement (AfCFTA), rather than the existing arrangements of separate regional economic communities such as ECOWAS or the Common Market for East and Southern Africa (COMESA).[35] The drive for further sub-regional integration was led initially by an initiative to create a development-based agreement – the Tripartite Free Trade Agreement, linking three regions – COMESA, the East African Community (EAC) and the Southern African Development Community (SADC).[36] The AU counter response for a continental trade agreement led to competitive parallel diplomacy to bring two rival parallel institutions into force and persuading TFTA members to switch to ratify the AfCFTA.[37]

## Parallel negotiations: protection and promotion of interests

In this following section of the chapter we will look at three aspects of protection and promotion of interests: channels; bilateral agenda diplomacy; and running separate sets of different negotiations.

## Opening up channels

Successful diplomacy relies on the establishment and development of multiple channels to cover all relevant areas for that country's bilateral and regional relations and at multilateral level, promotion of national and, as applicable, wider interests. The significance of individual channels will vary but will include at the formal level ministerial, ambassadorial, special and ad hoc representatives as well as informal envoys and other commercial and individual links. Some regimes particularly prone to political and transnational security instability depend heavily on informal channels.

In negotiations, parallel diplomacy is used mainly for three purposes: to expand channels, for defensive narratives and protection of initiatives. In initial phases, defensive and approach issues will come into play as a result of concessions on the construction of agendas.[38] The order or sequencing of issues at the start of talks are used as a part of strategies to limit an opponent's leverage or parallel counter moves to split coalitions or lobby individual states. The method relies on splitting up issues into small or micro packets in order to limit macro trade-offs on access for differing sectors (e.g. car production v. fish access provisions), control process and link negotiations to deadlines.

EU standard methods have relied on this approach, developing it with emphasis on establishing overarching legal obligations and principles (e.g. infringement, level playing field, settling accounts and outstanding financial obligations) before moving onto trade or other matters.[39] Future political or security cooperation are parcelled into separate blocs of negotiation, which may also be used as additional methods to give the appearance of progress or value in the event of overall impasse in other sectors.[40]

On agenda construction, for example, in the first phase of the Brexit negotiations, the UK conceded the EU proposals on the structure of the withdrawal negotiations: "the presidency remains vigilant to head off the parallel negotiations the British are trying to open up through every door and window in Europe".[41] To concede the structure of the overall agenda was a strategic error which put the UK on the back foot in subsequent exchanges, marked by responding to a standard EU negotiations style and format.[42] The UK subsequently tried to break out of the EU agenda and broaden its case within Europe through bilateral links and informal functional exchanges on banking and other European institutions. In one instance, an incident occurred as a result of an ECB scheduling error over a study group meeting with the Bank of England, which was due to meet on the same day as the European Council. An alarmed Mario Draghi, Central Bank president, contacted Michel Barnier, EU Brexit chief negotiator, the evening before, urgently seeking "to meet anywhere in Brussels" to minimise the political damage. Efforts to diversify channels often in sensitive political contexts, meet with counter action to limit or prevent diversification of exchanges.[43]

The development of diplomatic channels fundamentally relies on building up confidence and trust in the channel. The channel is a credible source and one in which diplomats and others can work within and through. It is at the core of multilateral diplomacy, as well as the conduct of diplomacy at bilateral and regional levels. In the lead up to the 2003 Iraq War, UK diplomacy within the UN relied upon the careful diplomacy of Ambassador Greenstock using channels of contacts to try and keep cohesion within the UN Security Council around Resolution 1441.[44] The Council was split over the Franco–Russian approach of giving more time for the UN inspection team under Hans Blix to ascertain the extent or not of WMD or other weapons and the alternative US and more qualified UK position on full compliance with Resolution 1441, before moving to a second resolution to approve use of force. The UK's qualified position became increasingly untenable, underlining not only the essential criteria for channels of trust and confidence in the source, but acceptance of an allies' supporting arguments.[45]

### Negotiation: bilateral and small group coordinating on agenda "red lines"

In multilateral and plurilateral negotiation, a key feature is the use of small groups to coordinate and manage drafting, promote compromise texts and agenda items. Separate from that, parallel diplomacy is used to track and monitor details on the progress of initiatives, working groups and strategic developments and to promote group or bilateral interests.

The use of parallel diplomacy by adversarial primary powers to coordinate the boundaries of their commitments and any blocking action as joint action in a multilateral conference tends to occur in cases where there is limited cooperation in certain sectors of relations. An example of bilateral format is the Chinese–US bilateral coordination at the UNFCCC COP26 conference.[46] US–Chinese coordination acted as a block or veto on text, fundamentally altering the core COP objectives, transforming Paris agreement commitments into à la carte environmental diplomacy: pick and mix, supported by interpretations of the Paris agreement.[47]

The Chinese approach to COP26 was shaped by the decision of President Xi Jinping not to attend. For the US, COP26 provided some opportunity for the Biden administration to engage and re-establish, within limits, an international role. In line with cutting back commitments, China used an indirect strategy, low key involvement at COP26 aimed at avoidance of new commitments and minimising adverse criticism. The methods were used by China to offset leader non-attendance at COP26 and support its indirect strategy were soft power, environmental loans to LDCs immediately prior to COP26 and media to build up the UN Biodiversity Conference in Kunming in order to embellish China's environmental credibility.[48] The main method involved bilateral technical and strategic coordination with the US over minimising commitments and ensuring both retained overall control of Paris implementation provisions on "red line" issues at COP26. The earlier coordinating meetings between US special envoy John Kerry and Chinese lead negotiator Xie Zhenhua in Shanghai, and the unusual setting of the port city of Tianjin on the Chinese east coast, had established respective red lines and preferred outcomes.[49] China tacitly accepted that Xi's absence would be criticised by the US, but chose not to oppose directly the UK–US list of major polluting sectors (transportation, coal, vehicles) showcased at the leader summit by the UK and US in week one. China merely signed the title cover sheet rather than commit to the projects.[50]

An unexpected joint China–US statement in the final phase of the conference carefully set out areas of future joint cooperation on a parallel alternative agenda, allowing flexibility over, for example, national schedules in interpreting and implementing the Paris Agreement.[51] The statement particularly highlighted future cooperation over methane but was silent on coal, using the formula of "phasing down" coal production, rather than "phase out."

Parallel diplomacy as above was backed up during the conference by a media strategy which used "drip feed" methods to release small packets of information. These took the form of wide-ranging musings about climate issues, interspersed with some brief clarification or comment on specific issues. Another purpose of the media strategy was to deflect criticism with intermittent, carefully crafted, defensive narratives for COP26, including the evocative "Five Lost Years", diverting attention to the Trump withdrawal from the Paris agreement. It was a simple slogan, into which many issues could be fitted – the mark of high innovation, and much more resonant than the tired and now dated "common but differentiated" responsibilities doctrine of earlier COPS.

An important method backing up the parallel diplomacy was the use of carefully timed coercive threats. Early in the second week of COP26, a veiled threat was very briefly introduced in a media interview to issue a warning which marked out the boundaries of participation: efforts to raise or speed up commitment levels risked reopening the Paris Agreement. In that event, it would be unclear if any future agreement on climate could be reached. As Xie put it,

> If we are to only focus on 1.5°C, it means we are destroying this consensus between all parties. And maybe countries will demand a reopening of negotiations if we are to change the target to only 1.5°C, and that will be a long process.[52]

The extent of US–China joint coordination on the environment was dramatically illustrated in the final plenary of COP26, with the US backing China's rejection in the concluding moments sections of the summary text which proposed, after discussions with nearly all delegations, retained the wording on coal ("phase out"). The threat of blocking the text potentially put the whole summary document at risk. A brokered climbdown by the secretariat and states seeking tougher wording reinstated the vague phrase "phasing down". It substantially weakened the text, highlighting primary power bilateral parallel diplomacy which, on issues like coal and financial commitments, endorsed the shift to à la carte environmentalism.[53]

## *Parallel diplomacy: packaging and running separate strands in negotiations*

Parallel diplomacy is an additional method used in negotiations which involves giving one area greater or more sustained attention than another to achieve alternative arrangements, whilst appearing to favour the first as the main framework for discussion and agreement.

Parallel diplomacy in negotiation tends to be used in situations in which a revised agreement may be sensitive in view of a poor previous record of an agreement, or there might potentially be loss of group identity as a result of restructuring proposals under discussion. In this method, media is particularly important in delivering a credible narrative as to why, for example, a new treaty should be necessary in that form. It is also frequently used in competitive international trade negotiations by lead powers to stagger or delay negotiations with third states ranking. In response, third states have resorted to signalling interim trade agreements to demarcate trade agreement territory.[54]

Parallel diplomacy in negotiations involves breaking down issues and running two (or more) sets of negotiations in separate strands. In a trade cooperation renewal or updating negotiation, for example, the division may be based on negotiating blocs around how future political and security cooperation might be managed, whilst a separate strand examines detailed technical, trade or financial relations. The main area of interest in this example, at least for the lead or dominant state, is the second set of negotiations on particular economic or other substantive issues.

That position may be concealed to obscure intentions by appearing to give attention to both strands of negotiation in order to minimise any potential domestic or external opposition. It can be augmented by time-based methods to maintain the track and momentum of the negotiation to avoid or minimise opposition.

## ACP–EU renewal of the Cotonou Agreement

The following example is used to illustrate packaging and running several strands of preferred outcomes in the renegotiation of the ACP–EU Cotonou agreement as a two-area negotiation covering general principles and ideas governing future ACP–EU relations and the separate negotiations on institutional arrangements.[55]

In the ACP–EU institutional negotiations, the EU pushed through its regionalisation agenda by insisting on three separate regional protocols with the ACP group rather than a single treaty.[56]

In contrast, the ACP negotiating mandate approved at its 107th special ministerial summit prior to the opening of the talks, envisaged a unitary ACP model based upon strengthened pillars of cooperation with the EU.[57] The revised agreement was intended to focus on the issue of greater industrial development, neglected under the Cotonou trade agreement.[58] The negotiations were justified in a narrative which pictured a solid constitutional foundation for the new arrangements and the prize of a new international organisation. However, the creation and construction of regional protocols dominated discussion from the outset under the joint chair of

Neven Mimica (EU Commissioner for International Cooperation and Development) and Robert Dussey (Togo Minister of Foreign Affairs and African Integration) who formed a negotiating partnership and a shared African integration vision which dominated the first phases.[59]

In this context, keeping constitutional issues under discussion using parallel diplomacy facilitated the principal EU aims of splitting the African and Caribbean components of the ACP as part of the "Africa One" strategy and ultimately bringing North African states into the revised Cotonou agreement.[60]

EU strategy used wedge and parallel diplomacy to split the ACP, dividing African from Caribbean–Pacific member states, to obtain sufficient approval for breaking up the ACP.[61] ACP links had become increasingly tenuous by the Cotonou run-out date, weakened by separate trade agreements with the EU and other external actors, loss of a shared ideology and a shift in the axis of political power within the ACP to Africa. The push to create regional protocols left the ACP political cooperation arrangements unfinished, postponed further by the COVID-19 pandemic until 2021. The EU–ACPS agreement was officially signed on 15 November 2023 and provisionally applied from 1 January 2024. The Cotonou agreement was initialled virtually in April 2021, though subsequently the terms were frozen at EU treaty approval stage.[62]

## Implications of parallel diplomacy for other diplomatic methods

The widespread use of parallel diplomacy has had considerable impact on other methods. For the most part, parallel diplomacy serves particular or narrow interests at the expense of wider consensus or cooperative methods. Frequently it undermines multilateral mediation efforts.

In conflicts, coalitions of states, organised to bring about ceasefires or seek political solutions, may be temporary and vulnerable to competing interests, outside incidents and clashes. Agreements are often not brought into force or are short lived parallel agreements as alternative vehicles for managing conflicts.

In terms of other impacts, parallel diplomacy contributes to the splintering of international institutions and duplication. Duplication of programmes and projects using parallel diplomacy has become extensively employed by multilateral institutions in the IBRD group. It has been extended through G20 operations and other plurilateral institutions, including the Asian Infrastructure Investment Bank (AIIB), which mirror and copy each other in areas such as sustainable development of cities, vaccine supply initiatives, financial loan facilities and international health conferences.

The widening use of parallel plurilateral negotiations and agreements in the WTO has raised issues about the consensus base of its proceedings. The contrary view is put that the WTO needs reform and new agendas. On the other hand, no satisfactory way forward has yet been found within the WTO on how to safeguard the interests of those states which disagree with plurilateral based initiatives.

Consensus procedures in multilateral institutions have also been eroded by parallel bilateralism in multilateral conferences as seen in US–China joint action to block text on phase out of coal and other non-renewable resources, and minimum or selective engagement on developing-country finance. Small states have been less able to benefit from multilateral processes. Some have used parallel diplomacy at the margins of summits to create new alliances and coalitions, such as the Ocean Alliance or coalitions on Ending Fossil Fuel, but nevertheless remain vulnerable.

## Conclusion

Parallel diplomacy has developed from its traditional uses to become an important extension for more assertive or coercive diplomatic methods. Traditionally, parallel diplomacy was associated with diplomacy directed to modifying agendas, side diplomacy and "guest diplomacy" used by rotating heads of plurilateral and regional organisation conferences. Parallel diplomacy has now expanded considerably in competitive and coercive areas to become a significant method used for negative or coercive purposes in conjunction with counter diplomacy.

The chapter is primarily concerned with discussing the various forms of parallel diplomacy which have been developed to create separate or alternative mechanisms to weaken or displace existing institutions or actors. Examples used in the chapter include the alternative initiatives on Syria, establishment of a rival European maritime safety administration and bilateral US–China cooperation to weaken conference drafting on fossil fuels ("phasing down"). The EU–ACP negotiations on a new ACP agreement are a classic study in EU parallel and counter diplomacy to break up the ACP. The success of these examples of parallel diplomacy owes much to narrow focus, lack of options and, in bilateral primary power selective cooperation, a joint willingness to use high risk and take the issues to the wire in the closing plenary. Parallel diplomacy is generally more successful with narrow bilateral focus, or when combined with other methods, including media and counter diplomacy. In competing integration, parallel diplomacy may be more successful for sub-regional actors in the longer run, as the complex continental integration diplomacy of competitors falters on trade integration, as in the AfCFTA. Parallel diplomacy nevertheless is a significant addition for a variety of contexts to the hard power elements of diplomacy.

# Notes

1 Staffan de Mistura, UN Special Envoy for Syria (2014–18). Previously UN special representative in Afghanistan, Iraq and Southern Lebanon. Deputy Foreign Minister, Italy. He was brought back as a UN special envoy post-COVID as the UN Secretary-General's personal envoy for Western Sahara.
2 Jan Egeland, Secretary-General Norwegian Refugee Council. Special advisor (humanitarian affairs) for Syria (2014–18). Previously State Secretary Norwegian Ministry of Foreign Affairs, UN Under Secretary-General Humanitarian Affairs, UN emergency relief coordinator. See Jan Egeland, *A Billion Lives* (Simon and Schuster, 2008) for an account of his UN humanitarian role.
3 S/RES/2328, 19 December 2016; SC/12367, 19 December 2016.
4 S/RES/2336/, 31 December 2016.
5 For details of the Russia–Turkey agreement see s/2016/1133, letter of 29 December 2016 to the UN Secretary-General and President of the Security Council and annexes.
6 See Note to Correspondents: Transcript of joint stakeout by UN Special Envoy for Syria, Staffan de Mistura, and Senior Advisor, Jan Egeland, Geneva, 5 January 2017.
7 US–China Joint Glasgow Declaration on Enhancing Climate Action in the 2020s. Para 9 (c).
8 Opening remarks, Carla Montesi, Director EC DG DEVCO, EU–ACP Knowledge Sharing 2 Conference on Trade and Investment, 12 February 2020.
9 See Richard J. Samuels, *Special Duty* (Cornell University Press, 2019 ) pp53–55.
10 Jeremy Greenstock, *Iraq: The Cost of War* (Arrow, 2016) esp. pp118–38; 187.
11 William J. Burns, *The Back Channel* (Hurst & Co. 2021) esp. pp359–61 and 376. For closure of the Iran back channel, see p381.
12 www.g20.org/en/about-the-g20.
13 www.g20germany.de/Webs/G20/EN/G20/Participants/participants_n ode.html.
14 Germany hosted a separate conference with African leaders prior to the summit on the Compact with Africa and had further bilateral meetings with individual African leaders both during the summit and subsequently on the German loan initiative. A special Germany–Africa summit was held on 27–8 June 2021 to commemorate the initiative at the end of the Merkel chancellorship with direct and virtual participation.
15 "Japan pushes back at UK plan to boost G7 Asia reach". www.japantimes.co.jp/news/2021/01/28/national/politics-diplomacy/uk-g7-japan-pushback/, 28 January 2021.
16 On Japanese strategic options, see Richard J. Samuels, *Special Duty* (Cornell University Press, 2019) pp257–62.
17 R.P. Barston, *Modern Diplomacy* 5th ed. (Routledge, 2019) pp 492–506.
18 For the Breakthrough Agenda for COP26 at the World Summit, see www.gov.uk/government/publications/cop26-world-leaders-summit-statement-on-the-breakthrough-agenda-2-november-2021/cop26-world-leaders-summit-statem ent-on-the-breakthrough-agenda, 2 November 2021.
19 For the UNFCCC secretariat account see "The Glasgow Climate Pact" at https://unfccc.int/process-and-meetings/the-paris-agreement/the-glasgow-climate-pact-key-outcomes-from-cop26.

20 UNFCCC COP26 Outcomes: Transparency and Reporting, see https://unf ccc.int/process-and-meetings/the-paris-agreement/the-glasgow-climate-pact/ cop26-outcomes-transparency-and-reporting#:~:text=The%20new%20trans parency%20system%20represents,in%20turn%20help%20build%20trust.

21 See on sport diplomacy in US–Russian relations Ambassador Burns' comment to Putin on the Sochi Winter Olympics, in William J. Burns, *The Back Channel* (Hurst and Co. 2021) p238.

22 The visit included Greece, Serbia, Albania and was preceded by meetings with the Taliban in Qatar.

23 See www.g20italy.org/rome-summit.html.

24 See *The Guardian* 27 March 2021; *New York Times*, 27 July 2021.

25 On revision of US legislation relating to Hong Kong, see www.state.gov/2021-hong-kong-policy-act-report/.

26 See Leaders Declaration G20 Rome summit, para 60, www.governo.it/sites/ governo.it/files/G20ROMELEADERSDECLARATION.pdf.

27 See Knud Erik Jørgensen and Ramses A. Wessel, "The position of the European Union in (other) international organisations", in Panos Koutrakos (ed.) *European Foreign Policy* (Elgar, 2011) pp276–7.

28 The Paris Memorandum of Understanding (PMOU) was initially signed in 1978 by Belgium, Denmark, France, Federal Republic of Germany, Netherlands, Norway, Sweden and the UK, later joined by the US, Canada and Russia. It was an example of intergovernmental administrative cooperation, based on International Maritime Organisation (IMO) shipping and pollution control regulations, which was part of the large increase in multilateral environmental diplomacy which accelerated after the UN Law of the Sea negotiations (1972–82). For summary data on the PMOUs vessel inspections see annual report.

29 See further on the diplomacy of the regional expansion of port state control regimes, R.P. Barston, "Port State Control: Evolving Concepts", in Harry N. Scheiber (ed.) *Law of the Sea* (Brill Nijhoff, 2000) pp87–101.

30 The creation of a separate European maritime safety agency (EMSA) created a parallel institution to the PMOU but also was a challenge to the central role of the IMO as the lead multilateral agency responsible of maritime safety and marine pollution regulation, contributing to the fragmentation of international law. See also Jørgensen and Wessel, note 27.

31 The United Nations Industrial Development Organisation (UNIDO) was established originally as an autonomous organisation, later specialised agency, by UN General Assembly resolution 2152 in 1966, headquartered in Vienna, at the International Conference Centre. UNIDO established sub-offices in New York and Brussels.

32 A German Investment and Technology Promotion Office (ITPO) was set up in 2017 in Bonn. See www.unido.org/itpo-germany.

33 www.giz.de/en/worldwide/africa.html. The members of ECOWAS are Benin, Burkina Faso, Cabo Verde, Cote d'Ivoire, The Gambia, Ghana, Guinea Bissau, Liberia, Mali, Niger, Nigeria, Senegal, Sierra Leone and Togo. Morocco applied to upgrade its membership from observer status to full membership in 2017. The application was subsequently stalled for political and economic reasons.

34 The EU and G20 initiatives include the AU–Africa summit, business, cultural and parliamentary links and the G20 Compact with Africa, launched during the German G20 presidency in 2017. See also Africa–EU summit,

www.un.org/africarenewal/magazine/eu-au-summit-2022-eu-wants-be-afr
ica%E2%80%99s-friend-need%E2%80%94and-indeed. For a different
assessment, see open letter from UNICEF on unequal vaccine supply to the
developing world during the COVID-19 pandemic at www.unicef.org/ corona-
virus/covid-19-vaccine-dose-donations-g7-letter.

35 COMESA has 21 members: Burundi, Comoros, Congo (DRC), Djibouti, Egypt,
Eswatini, Ethiopia, Libya, Madagascar, Mauritius, Rwanda, Seychelles, Somalia,
Sudan, Tunisia, Zambia, Zimbabwe, see www.comesa.int/.

36 The Tripartite agreement was launched at Sharm El-Sheikh, Egypt, 10 June
2015. www.comesa.int/comesa-eac-sadc-tripartite-free-trade-area-to-come-into-
force-on-25th-july-2024/#:~:text=The%20Tripartite%20framework %20is%20
based,reducing%20business%20costs%3B%20and%20Industrial.

37 Under article 23 of the AfCFTA, 22 ratifications are required for entry into
force. The agreement entered into force on 30 May 2019 for the 24 countries
which had deposited instruments of ratification with the Chairperson of the
AU Commission (AUC) by that date. South Africa was one of the TFTA, along
with Rwanda, Uganda and Kenya, which switched to dual ratification.
The TFTA, linking COMESA, EAC and SADC came into force on 25 July 2024,
following ratification of 14 of the 29 members. The members of the TFTA are
Angola, Botswana, Burundi, Djibouti, Egypt, Eswatini, Kenya, Lesotho, Malawi,
Namibia, Rwanda, South Africa, Uganda, Zambia and Zimbabwe. See www.
comesa.int/.

38 Barnier, *My Secret Brexit Diary*, op. cit., p57 on UK conceding agenda sequencing.

39 Barnier, ibid., pp131 and the doctrine of infringements, p147.

40 See Alan Hardacre, *The Rise and Fall of Interregionalism in EU External Relations*
(Dordrecht, 2009) p197.

41 Barnier, ibid., pp47, 150.

42 R.P. Barston, *Modern Diplomacy* 5th ed. (Routledge, 2019) pp80–5.

43 Barnier, op. cit., pp130–1, 150.

44 Jeremy Greenstock, *Iraq the Cost of War* (Arrow Books, 2016) pp154–5, 162,
171–86.

45 Ibid., pp130–4, 184.

46 See FCCC/CP/2015/10/Add.1, and supplementary provisions in FCCC/CP/
2015/L.9 Rev1, 12 December 2015.

47 For analysis of the Paris Climate negotiations and key provisions of
the agreement, see R.P. Barston, *Modern Diplomacy* 5th ed. (Routledge,
2019) pp492–504.

48 See www.state.gov/u-s-china-joint-glasgow-declaration-on-enhancing-climate-
action-in-the-2020s/; www.carbonbrief.org/wp-content/uploads/2021/05/
website-masthead-new-1550x804.png;
www.carbonbrief.org/debriefed-19-january-2024-john-kerry-retires-uncertai
nty-over-uk-labours-pledge-chinas-new-climate-envoy-profiled/.

49 *New York Times*, 16 November 2021.

50 See the cover statement on the Breakthrough Agenda with attached list of
endorsements at www.gov.uk/government/publications/cop26-world-lead
ers-summit-statement-on-the-breakthrough-agenda-2-november-2021/cop26-
world-leaders-summit-statement-on-the-breakthrough-agenda.

51 See US–China Glasgow COP Joint Statement www.state.gov/u-s-china-joint-
glasgow-declaration-on-enhancing-climate-action-in-the-2020s/ 10 November
2021. "Phase down" was replaced by weaker language ("transitioning to") at
COP 28 in Dubai.

52  See "Remove final Paris issues envoy urges", *China Daily*, 4 November 2021.

53  Glasgow Summit Final Summary, November 2021.

54  See, for example, UK–New Zealand FTA negotiations agreement in principle, 20 October, 2021; and UK–Australia 17 June 2021. Both agreements in principle contain without prejudice disclaimers with respect to the content of the document at that point and that it does not create legal or treaty obligations.

55  See text of the 2019 revised Georgetown Agreement www.oacps.org/wp-cont ent/uploads/2022/05/ACP-Brochure-Revised-Georgetown-Agreement-UK-def.pdf.

56  Commission general mandate for the ACP negotiations is set out in COM(2017) 763, 12 December 2017, www.consilium.europa.eu/en/policies/cotonou-agreement/.

57  See    www.oacps.org/wp-content/uploads/2018/06/Decision-2-of-the-107th-Session-of-ACP-Council-of-Ministers-English.pdf for the May 2018 ACP mandate approved at the 107th session of the Ministerial Council; ACP Aide Memoire Basic Principles for ACP–EU relations post 2020, 3 April 2017.

58  COM (2017) 763 Final, 12 December 2017.

59  For EU negotiating aims, see www.consilium.europa.eu/en/press/press-relea ses/2018/06/22/eu-african-caribbean-and-pacific-countries-future-partners hip-council-adopts-negotiating-mandate/. For ACP priorities, see www.oacps.org/uncategorized/107-acp-eu-countries-walk-the-talk-on-global-governance/; www.bilaterals.org/?acp-negotiating-mandate-for-the; https://au.int/sites/default/files/decisions/34054-ext_ex_cl_dec_1-2xviii_e2 6_march.pdf. The Eswatini press statement is a rare document on the regional negotiations with the EU in the period 2019–21. See https://eswatini-embassy.eu/2019/06/06/the-kingdom-of-eswatini-hosts-high-level-africa-eu-protocol-regional-consultation-as-part-of-the-negotiation-process-of-the-new-acp-eu-partnership-agreement-post-2020/#:~:text=The%20 Kingdom%20of%20Eswatini%20was,in%20Ezulwini%2C%20Kingdom%20 of%20Eswatini.

60  COM (2017) 763 Final, 12 December 2017.

61  Parallel meetings to the ACP–EU main negotiations were held to lay the basis for the three regional protocols in February 2019, Brussels (Pacific Protocol): Chad (African CNG meeting), 4 April 2019; Caribbean, 15 April 2019 and Eswatini, 3 May 2019 (African Protocol).

62  The OACPS–EU agreement was approved by the European Parliament in April 2024 and enters into force after internal EU member procedures for treaties.

# Chapter 8

# Counter diplomacy

## Introduction

Counter diplomacy is opposing action aimed at weakening, under-mining or destroying a policy, proposal, organisation or individual. It is distinguished from other forms of diplomacy by its competitive or coercive purposes and methods. These methods contrast with those other types of diplomacy which, in varying degrees, are based on constructive or cooperative processes aimed at reaching compromise, reducing differences over time and building cooperative relations. Counter diplomacy creates rival institutions, is used to dominate blocs or remove opposition, freeze a problem or undermine an agreement or opponent.

Counter diplomacy is generally associated with using cost, denial and other coercive methods, depending on purposes. Situated in the grey or border areas between diplomacy and force, it includes actions which block, deny, undermine, or are allied to coercion and force. It may be used within war and armed conflict for offensive or defensive purposes.

The values and assumptions of counter diplomacy are not always those of traditional diplomacy. In pursuit of short-term objectives or contracts, longstanding relations may be easily discarded, and apparent commitments to support a position are disguised or easily reversed. Time-based deadlines feature as additional methods backing up threats of implicit cost of non-compliance. Other indirect communication methods such as carefully timed statements, articles or think tank reports in selected press or other media are used to warn of potential political cost or loss of trade access unless policies are changed.

In relation to other methods, parallel diplomacy is often used in conjunction with counter diplomacy. In negotiation, parallel diplomacy may offer lines of potential solution which provide cover for the primary intentions of counter diplomacy. In other instances, such as long-running institutional competition, parallel diplomacy is transformed into counter diplomacy, as the "parallel" body moves from nominal cooperation to dominate or seek control of the functions of the existing institution.

DOI: 10.4324/9781003204039-9

## Counter diplomacy: strategies and principles

Four strategies are commonly used in counter diplomacy: time-based, division of opponents, rapid exploitation of events and defensive recovery. These strategies may be used as part of blocking action to delay or buy time for later action or in negotiation to divide negotiators. Counter diplomacy is commonly used to exploit options in a wide range of circumstances, from trade deals, international project tenders, and change of government to military advances. Counter diplomacy, too, has become a feature of defensive diplomacy as a method used to recover from diplomatic reversals.

Counter diplomacy is based first on the principle of maintaining flexibility so that if one initiative fails, another can be developed to continue the momentum. Second is the importance of recovering quickly from reversal. Reversal must not be allowed to damage diplomatic reputation, or weaken initiatives and accordingly should be countered by diversionary action. Third, counter diplomacy should utilise as wide a range of methods as possible to exploit leverage. Fourth, media back up is essential for effective counter diplomacy, not only as a part of standard explanation but also in those contexts in which it may be necessary to shield or distance the originator.

In diplomacy, the intentions of another party are frequently unclear. There may be ambiguity in statements or uncertainty surrounding adversarial actions, or limited time for evaluation. The situation might be novel with few, if any, relevant comparisons. Nor are analogies always a good guide to future action in view of changing contexts and personnel, but there may be little else. In these contexts counter diplomacy profits from uncertainties. Initiatives and proposals to resolve issues may appear cooperative and supported as ways forward but in practice are intended to hide or mask primary intentions.

In essence, counter diplomacy is high-risk diplomacy which depends on altering the dynamics of conflict processes and raising the stakes. Counter diplomacy moves to pose questions, draw lines, create presence in new or unexpected areas and elevate risk, either covertly or through open demands.

## Counter diplomacy: blocking and denial

In counter diplomacy, two main forms of blocking action can be distinguished: procedural and tacit. The purpose is to render a programme or institution ineffective by bypassing or blocking moves, often framed by a narrative demanding reform. Procedural counter diplomacy essentially relies on institutional and administrative provisions to promote, check or block initiatives. Formal or informal procedural devices may be used to shape the agenda, hold up or ultimately block proposals. Knowledge of how a multilateral institution functions is probably one of the more important factors contributing to national diplomatic success in collective fora. It can even out elements of hard power, at least in the short run. Indeed, skill in this area contributes to diplomatic reputation.

Tacit counter diplomacy methods use denial of access to ideas, personnel, institutions and non-attendance at diplomatic fora. Cancellation of meetings, withholding access for international inspection officials or withdrawal of working-level arrangements for lowering border tension add elements of uncertainty to the psychological dimensions of conflict. Central to tacit counter diplomacy is raising the level of uncertainty and associated risk. It might be a single action or part of a coordinated longer term set of methods to convey warnings.

Within the UN system blocking action has been perhaps most associated with Security Council resolutions. The UN Charter does not formally use the term "veto" as such by the permanent members. Much of the thinking of the early founders of the UN at the end of the second world war in 1945 was based on shaping post-war order on some measure of cooperation and unanimity. As Claude argues: "the arrangement (Articles 23 and 27 of the Charter) constitutes an important segment of the Charter's progress toward institutionalisation of the special role of the great powers in international organisation."[1] Nevertheless, those aspirations had largely been qualified or questioned within two years of the San Francisco conference.[2] Subsequently, the practice of the Security Council has developed to find ways of minimising primary power conflict and keep some elements of the multilateral ideal alive, through informal sessions, testing and clearing draft resolutions and closed meetings.

Within the Security Council, counter diplomacy in the Iraq conflict included the long-running effort of France and the Russian Federation to keep inspection channels for WMD open in Iraq as long as possible to stave off moves to a so-called second resolution authorising the use of force.[3] In the drafting of resolution 1441, one of the sticking points for France was that the trigger for further action against Iraq in para 4 should be both a false account by Iraq of WMD and (italics added) failure to comply in some other way, rather than the either/or formula in the draft, which would have made non-compliance easier to establish. The French amendment was initially accepted by Washington: para 4 reads:

> Decides that false statements or omissions in the declarations submitted by Iraq pursuant to this resolution and failure by Iraq at any time to comply with and cooperate fully in the implementation of this resolution shall constitute a further material breach of Iraq's obligations....[4]

For its part, the UK had a difficult middle role in the early stages of the debates, to which Ambassador Greenstock, despite intensive diplomatic efforts, found it hard to hold.[5] However, the France–Russian counter diplomatic position was eventually abandoned, conceding the issue under US pressure, though the reasoning for the change remains unclear.[6]

In the Iran conflict, the tacit use of the issue of international verification of the nuclear programme has been one of the central elements in either limiting diplomatic progress or in reaching a revised agreement to replace the JPOA.[7] Expulsion or readmission of UN inspectors has been used as a method for several different purposes, including influencing the dynamics of the conflict by variously raising the level of tension for domestic purposes or signalling a possible shift in position. The admission of UN inspectors has also featured as a secondary but related public information method to cultivate international opinion to create a favourable image of Iran as a cooperative power.

### Other uses of counter diplomacy: building alternatives to collective multilateral action

Counter diplomacy has also been used to put in place alternative groupings for managing a conflict, whilst retaining a nominal UN multilateral link. In the dispute, for example, over the terms of mediation in the Syrian conflict, the Russian Federation shifted to counter diplomacy because of concern over loss of influence and the need to regain a greater say over the outcomes of negotiations on Syria. Altering the format to a smaller group of principal interests outside the UN framework improved the chances of successfully directing efforts to resolve or stabilise the conflict within acceptable limits to some of the group, rather than allowing mediation to drag on inconclusively at multilateral level.

Russian strategy was based on creating an alternative regional grouping to the UN mediation effort, which retained a link to UN efforts.[8] That link, initially at least, was considered important as a source of legitimacy for the Russian initiative. Paradoxically, however, the longer the link was retained the more problematic it became as UN mediation was increasingly perceived by Russia as unnecessary as territorial control in Syria was slowly regained.

The Russian initiative was crafted on splitting the Syrian conflict into ceasefire and political resolution issues. The latter were left for the UN. It was high-risk counter diplomacy, dependent on drawing together conflicting Turkish and Iranian interests and factoring in uncertain, shifting battlefield developments in and immediately around Syria.[9] It raised the bar by pointing up the new Russian role and put into question the residual part for UN mediation. The humanitarian relief effort also became deadlocked at Security Council level over relief agency admission to Syria and convoy access in areas like Idlib.[10] Within the UN, Russian counter diplomacy was directed at defending its mediatory ceasefire role, ensuring control over the Syrian issues as chief architect within the Security

Council and blocking resolutions favouring wide relief access in and out of Syria. Russian blocking actions through vetoes or opposition within the informal permanent member (P5) meetings were sustained and selectively acerbic,[11] underlining, in this form of counter diplomacy, the importance of technical command of UN Security Council procedures and mastery of the content and drafting nuances of past UNSC resolutions.

The case illustrates how counter diplomacy is closely linked to the state of civil conflict, battlefield developments, humanitarian flash points and continuously fending off adverse criticism. In effect, counter diplomacy is an integral part of the use of force and coercive strategy.[12]

## Counter diplomacy through denial

Denial is used in counter diplomacy mainly in international conflicts involving resources, land and by sanctioned states as sanctions avoidance.

Additional areas are moves in cooperation with others involving limiting the access of transnational militants, NGOs and internet access (control of ideas).[13] Counter diplomacy traditionally has been used against rebel or opposition groups (denial of travel, security).[14] In these instances, extraterritorial action has extended to abduction and assassination.[15] The content of counter diplomacy shifts by design to the use of coercion and violence. The diplomatic aspects are confined to denial or defensive briefing and administrative operational support. It is a grey area which takes diplomacy outside what is regarded as appropriate in traditional concepts of the purposes of diplomatic activity.

The nature of diplomacy has also been affected as a result of the growth of counter diplomacy against individuals on political and security grounds. The distinction between action against an individual at a national level and its extension by association to other external actors (havens, political and financial support) has become blurred. Human rights, sports and civil issues, alongside trade, have substantially broadened the content and linkages shaping what constitutes diplomacy. In this respect the sources and potential for dispute and incidents have significantly widened.

Less obvious and indirect methods are found to criticise or attack individual representatives in negotiation. These rely on indirect methods such as delay or persistent failure to schedule talks or receive an inbound visit by a head of government/state or other representative. The lack of bilateral visit scheduling and non-attendance at multilateral fora periodically causes serious friction and tension in relations between the US, China and Russia in periods of strained or unstable relations.

Regimes which use dual systems of national security advisors and ministers or multiple envoys are particularly susceptible to divide-and-rule moves of this type by adversarial states or other actors seeking to create uncertainty, exert pressure for delay or foster divisions over policy.[16]

Other indirect methods include the use of press conferences for comments on the level and success of long-running talks to signal satisfaction with the approach of particular officials, rather than ministers. The main purpose of this method is to affect the way issues are prioritised as well as the substance of negotiations to favour the initiator, shifting emphasis and areas of possible compromise. It may also eventually serve to undermine relations between the opposing party's envoy and minister.[17]

### *Land and resources: counter diplomacy restrictions*

Land has featured increasingly as a dimension of contemporary international relations. It has become a sensitive issue for several reasons other than traditional factors related to naval and maritime bases. These include foreign port and terminal acquisition, competition over the development of new land and seaborne Asia–Middle East–Europe routes, supply chain connectivity and disruption caused by climate factors and growth in vessel size. Climate factors have affected water levels in strategic canals, particularly Suez and Panama which, combined with the impact on shipping and regional armed conflicts, has intensified concerns over routes and the importance of land acquisition on the margins of blocs (Mexico, North Africa) and joint DFI projects.[18] Overall, these factors have drawn attention to the changed content of diplomacy, with its emphasis on geo-economic competition, infrastructure and economic security and differences in maritime assets held by lead players.

In response to concerns over land acquisition, a number of countries including Singapore have restricted or prohibited the sale of land or passed legislation to restrict DFI. For example, Iceland blocked the sale of business land to Chinese interests but allowed the construction of a scientific research station as part of a joint project.[19] Wider restrictions on land use and sale are part of the qualifications made by several states in reservations to the RCEP trade agreement. The US has tightened offshore DFI coming into the US bilaterally or through regional organisations.[20]

In contrast, the development of western counter diplomacy strategies in response to foreign geopolitical port acquisition has been slow, with limited coordination. Several reasons can be suggested, which are reflected in the debate over whether port acquisition represents a security threat arising from loss of control over infrastructure or should be tolerated as part of market development.[21]

Differences in maritime assets have also strongly influenced perspectives. A striking feature of the leading container vessel operators is the role of small powers with large fleets (Singapore, Denmark, Israel) with joint slot deals linked to Asian carriers, which are now expanding into terminal and logistics operations. The United States is outside the group, as a continental rather than commercial maritime power, with limited US-flagged vessels or extensive global maritime logistics assets, which tends to narrow US perceptions and approach. The Indo-Pacific Economic Framework (IPEF) initiative, for example, was a late final piece in the revision of US foreign policy in response to global geoeconomic competition and supply chain security.[22]

## Resource conflicts: denial

The use of denial-based counter diplomacy in resource conflicts aims to prevent or freeze oil, gas or other exploration and drilling work in disputed zones. The strategy of the denial state relies on raising perceptions of risk, creating uncertainty using warnings and threats to maritime states and companies, and conducting coercive naval manoeuvres in the vicinity of drilling operations. The level of risk is raised to the point that no oil major would be prepared to risk initial or follow up operations, leaving assessments to smaller or independent operators.

The affected areas include the Mediterranean and large parts of south-east Asia. In the latter region, significant exploration has not been possible in sites in the EEZs of Malaysia, Philippines, Indonesia and Vietnam which are intersected by the China's so-called Nine-Dash Line claim. In Vietnam, for example, exploration by a Spanish and UAE consortia was eventually abandoned under intensive Chinese pressure.[23]

The Vietnam case is interesting in that it contains elements of a counter strategy, albeit unsuccessful, which was noted by a coalition of other powers in Asia. Vietnam tried a strategy of increasing the internationalisation of exploration operators by including the Russian operator Rosneft.[24] It was aimed at breaking out of the exploration stranglehold though ultimately blocked.[25] However, the concept of internationalisation was later returned to by south-east Asian maritime states in the form of asymmetrical counter diplomacy against China.

Denial strategies tend to freeze areas, which are subsequently opened up as a result of pressures to switch strategies because of resource supply issues. Reopening strategies depends on convincing oil majors or packets of smaller operators to run the gauntlet. By contrast, maritime resource powers have resorted to asymmetrical diplomacy as part of the long game in counter diplomacy. States bordering the South China Sea – notably Malaysia, Indonesia, Philippines and Vietnam – have begun to reassess how to deal with China's Nine-Dash claims, which are inconsistent with the UN Law of the Sea Convention. As part of the reorientation, greater attention has been directed to resisting China's maritime claims by coordinated protests registered through UN Law of the Sea channels and other legal methods, including accession to straddling stock and other UNLCOS fisheries conventions in order to remain, for dispute purposes, fully compliant and up to date with international regulations. Quiet diplomacy has also been used with erstwhile allies to revisit longstanding security agreements.[26]

South China Sea Islands

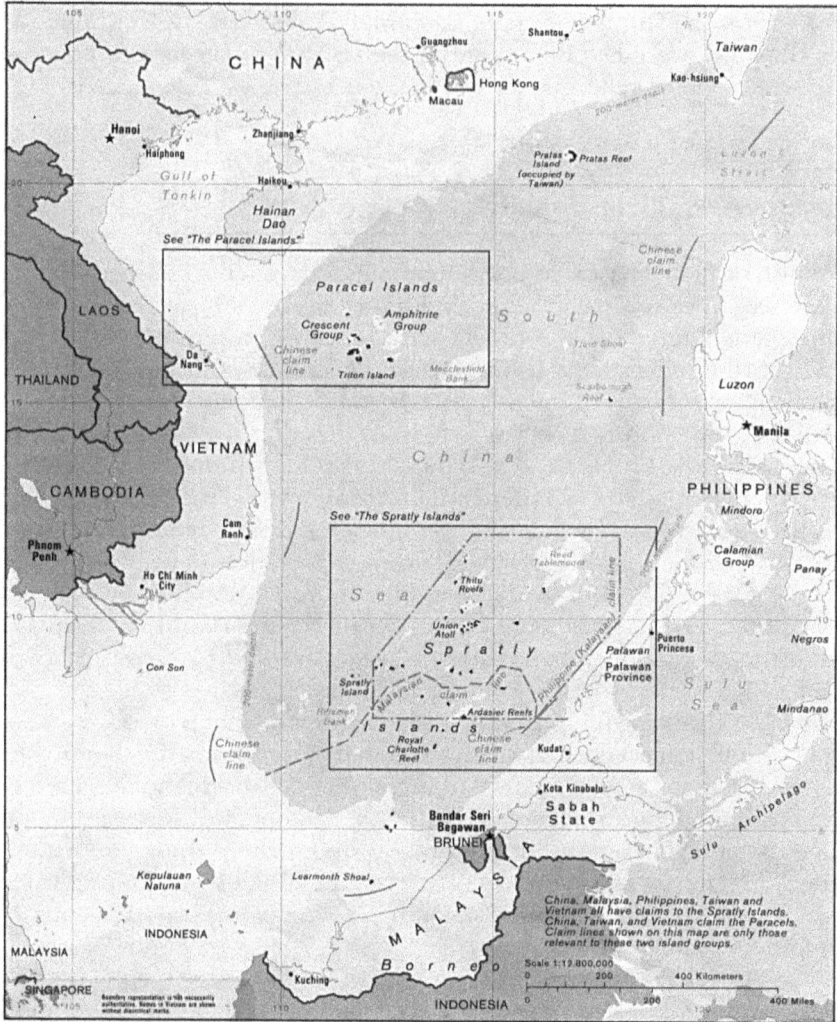

**Figure 8.1** South China Seas – disputed islands

Source: University of Texas Libraries. See note 23.

## Scope and limits of economic counter diplomacy

### *Institutions*

In counter diplomacy involving competition between an existing and newly formed organisation with similar areas of operation, the process of working out relations is invariably lengthy and tense. Conflict over regulatory responsibility is often long running and may never be finally resolved, as in the case of the relations between the International Maritime

Organisation (IMO) and European Maritime Safety Agency (EMSA).[27] Competing institutions tend to use step-by-step progressive approaches to build up a portfolio and solidify their position. The process involves hollowing out the established institution by adapting its data base and regulatory agendas.[28]

In conflicts involving new rival institutions, shifts to counter a competitor sub-regional economic organisation reach a decisive point as entry into force approaches for each of the rivals. The diplomatic effort of each party then shifts from parallel diplomacy to counter diplomacy to ensuring key states switch allegiance.[29] In cases involving new institution building, questions concerning the residual authority of sub-regions' regulatory relations with international or continental institutions can remain unresolved and contentious, e.g. relations between the African Continental Free Trade agreement and the regional Tripartite Free Trade Agreement.[30]

Another important outstanding issue is the impact on the options of those states who lose the race for ratification or whose separate interests are blocked or nullified. There are several examples in contemporary diplomacy of integration disputes of this type (AfCFTA Tripartite Agreement, OACPS–EU, CARICOM–OECS) which have left the weaker party in a difficult and indeterminate position over future integration. In the Tripartite agreement case, successive deadlines were revised and extended in a bid to achieve entry into force and to halt the switch to AfCFTA. The future position of the EAC–COMESA–SADC grouping, distinguished by its early coordinated development focus, was strengthened by the entry into force of the TFTA. Other factors were the active role of the TFTA Secretariat in promoting regional coordination between COMESA-SADC and EAC as a distinctive and successful model, more cohesive than the AfCFTA, and the maintenance of the momentum of technical and regulatory coordination prior to entry into force of the TFTA. EU counter diplomacy with Indian Ocean EPA negotiations in the EAS5 lost much of its relevance after entry into force of the TFTA though remains problematical. It faced difficult relations with its larger continental rival and political instability associated with its admission of new members in conflict zones. A major deficit was the diversionary effects of the long-running EU parallel trade diplomacy with four of the Indian Ocean islands in the EAS5, who would have been sufficient to bring the Tripartite agreement into force but were locked into endless EAS5 negotiations at the expense of the regional Tripartite agreement.[31]

## Geopolitics, projects and contracts

The changing nature of diplomacy, particularly connected with geopolitics and the diversification of economic actors, has introduced greater competition and conflict over project contracts. Dissatisfaction has correspondingly increased, leaving those dropped or rejected feeling uncertain

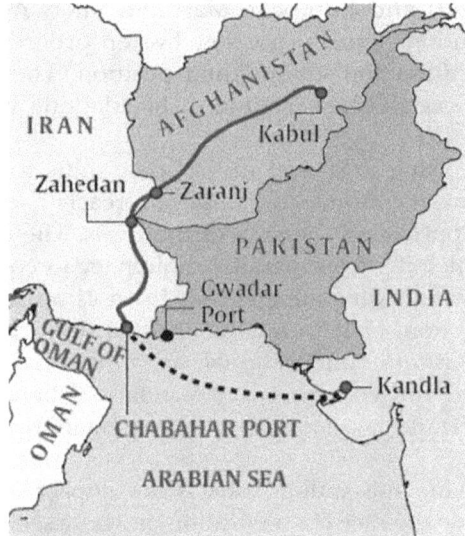

**Figure 8.2** Gwadar and Chabahar

or seeking to offset or find new partners. End-of-summit photo opportunities acquire a hollow sense of strained unity as tenuous links are tested.[32]

In the India–Iran contract negotiations, for example, over development of strategic rail port links from Chabahar to Iran, Afghanistan and Central Asia, China countered Indian proposals with a $400 billion multisector deal. The counter offers included free port and oil development facilities on the Makran coast.[33]

The Indian proposal built around Chabahar and a rail link for connectivity with Central Asia were also subject to counter proposals by Pakistan, promoting links via the China–Pakistan Economic Corridor (CPEC) from Gwadar to Uzbekistan.[34]

India was vulnerable to counter diplomacy, partly because of its internal style of decision-making over the time taken on implementation decisions. Common membership of the BRICS and SCO seemed not to have any relevance in competing financial matters. Added uncertainty on relations with Iran was increased because of US and international sanctions, making sourcing heavy rail project equipment difficult after 2020.[35] India's equipment problem was exploited in the counter offer. India was able to retain a limited residual role as port operator at Chabahar, although its wider regional ambitions as a logistics and rail power were blocked. The broader project design scenario of mega infrastructure development suited very few players. The difficulties over Chabahar influenced India to intensify its search for other venues, although a ten-year deal to operate the Shahid Beheshti terminal at Chabahar was eventually concluded.[36]

Two important elements are underlined in the above case: the importance of flexibility for exploitation of opportunities, and the capability to potentially deploy complex project assets.

The ability to move flexibly and exploit options was classically illustrated in the French recovery and use of counter diplomacy following exclusion from the US–UK–Australia nuclear submarine cooperation agreement.[37] The French reply to the exclusion included immediate announcements of defence contracts with Greece and UAE and counter diplomacy against the UK in the dispute over the Northern Ireland Protocol and more generally post-Brexit relations. The US was drawn into the French position on the Ireland dispute by proposals to link transatlantic trade concessions to progress on the Northern Ireland Protocol, in a way similar to the conditions set for lifting the suspension of UK research cooperation with the EU.[38]

## Sanctions avoidance and covert trade

Continued growth in the use of sanctions has led to a more prominent role for counter diplomacy directed at minimising or avoiding sanctions.[39] Efforts to limit or undermine international sanctions have fallen into three categories: textual amendment of resolutions in multilateral institutions,[40] creation of covert arrangements for sanctions evasion[41] and growth in flags of convenience.[42]

The development of covert alternative arrangements has been one of the more striking aspects of the development of counter diplomacy. Alternative covert arrangements have moved on, though not replaced, the transit state concept (e.g. Dubai, Abu Dhabi), which typified the pre-2000 period. These arrangements have included, at bilateral level, use of multiple shadow charter companies (specialist vessels, e.g. chemical carriers[43] (North Korea) and new groupings, e.g. China–Iran–Venezuela for crude oil supply and transportation.[44]

At an administrative level, providing cover for alternative sanctions evasion link-ups has continued to evolve. Chinese exploratory links with Pacific island states using inbound visits, student scholarships, rebuilding airports and infrastructure as part of disaster relief, has brought the added advantage of offering remote sources of shipping registration, investment passports and financial flows. Samoa was added to the list for oil tanker registry in counter-sanctions trades. The creation of an alternative oil/chemical carrier network has weakened IMO multilateral marine safety regulation.[45]

## Linkage in trade disputes and avoiding action

The purpose of trade coercion is to force a change of policy or reverse a particular decision. It alters relations based on the expectation of resolving differences through discussion and adjustment to one in which change is being brought about by pressure and inflicting cost and damage to alter policy. In particular, trade coercion threatens or triggers losses which may be difficult to sustain or counteract. Trade coercion essentially relies on exploiting dependence and limited market options. It exploits through punitive tariffs or other restrictions the inability to readjust trade in the short term. Factors such as product seasonality and finding new markets at short notice are generally problematic for most non-commodity export states, limiting their options.

Trade coercion relies on the assumption that the longer a dispute continues, the more likely that the initiating state will succeed because of the emergence of domestic and international opinion arguing for a change of policy.[46] In counter diplomacy, NGOs, foreign press and disguised think tanks have come to be more extensively used as instruments of counter trade diplomacy.[47] Commercial lobbies have traditionally been closely involved in the protection of trade interests and lead lobbying to prioritise trade over foreign policy.[48]

### *Trade coercion: limits of linkage*

Trade coercion is used in linked disputes to target vulnerable or specialist trade sectors for political or economic reasons.[49]

Linkage is a high-risk strategy for the initiating state because of unknown counter action or possible loss of external support. Targeted states have resorted to several methods to ride out linkage pressures, including switching production and finding other markets[50] until sanctions or other restrictions are lifted.[51] Internationalising a dispute has been one of the methods used to support wait-and-see strategies. It takes several forms such as attracting bilateral support in a dispute, seeking allies in a regional organisation and media campaigns.[52] A dispute may also be internationalised through dispute processes in a multilateral organisation.[53] In the dispute between Lithuania and China over the title of the Taiwan Trade Office in Vilnius, Lithuania was removed as a China customs category, goods blocked in ports and restrictions placed on EU goods with Lithuanian component parts. The EU internationalised the dispute and took it to the WTO for consultations.[54] Further support for Lithuania came from the US,[55] Taiwan,[56] Canada[57] and Japan,[58] who also requested joint consultations. The main limitations of this type of method are two: the small power loses influence over the handling of the dispute, and the coercive initiator can turn the dispute into multiple counter panel complaints.[59]

In bilateral linkage, disputes the wait-and-see approach is generally built around diversification of markets and uses time to ride out pressure. For the targeted state, success in a dispute involving political issues (e.g. human rights, detention of nationals, diplomatic representation) relies on the political issues linked to punitive trade tariffs losing traction or relevance and becoming obstacles to bilateral trade.

External factors affecting supply or price may move in favour of a targeted commodity state.[60] For example, Chinese tariffs on Australian barley were removed less than a month after the termination of the Ukraine grain agreement.[61]

Moving to negotiations on removal or resuming normal relations involves difficult timing decisions. The standard method of resuming relations relies on visit diplomacy, media, communiques and other action for signalling changes in relations. Yet visit diplomacy is a blunt instrument which, if used too early in a dispute, may preface concessions or even lack of relevance, especially if bilateral trade with the initiating state has substantially increased in non-sanctioned sectors or generally benefitted from diversification. The economic grounds for normalisation may be less apparent and the corresponding political cost high.

An inbound visit by a smaller state may become part of the long-range strategies of a primary or major power to weaken an adversarial coalition or alliance by gradually detaching particular members through inbound visits.

## Asymmetrical counter diplomacy

Asymmetrical counter diplomacy is conducted by small or intermediate powers for similar purposes as other forms of counter diplomacy (block, defeat, takeover or remove opposition). Asymmetrical diplomacy goes beyond amendment of a resolution or revising parts of an agreement to encompass action to defeat major proposals. Most of the methods are at the "soft" end of asymmetrical counter diplomacy rather than the grey area between diplomacy and force which feature in other forms of counter diplomacy. Four main forms of asymmetric counter diplomacy can be distinguished: defensive, procedural, partner and alternative proposals.

### *Defensive asymmetrical counter diplomacy*

Defensive asymmetrical counter diplomacy involves the use of counter diplomacy by a small or weaker party to gather external support or international endorsement to defeat or overcome the policies of a larger power or group. It is different from other diplomatic methods in respect to calculations over uncertainty and risk. There is a high degree of uncertainty in asymmetrical diplomacy over the outcome and potential cost of failure. These risks tend to influence pressure in the initiating power for safer options involving negotiation and concessions.

### *Blocking multilateral resolutions*

In asymmetrical counter diplomacy, to block or defeat a resolution in a multilateral institution the methods primarily rely on intensive bilateral meetings and contacts with cross-membership groupings. The main function of media is to promote, support and refute counter narratives. More so than perhaps in other methods, accuracy, balance and up-to-date accounts are essential to support positions and undermine opposing arguments.

A rare diary of Sri Lanka's counter diplomacy by Sanja De Silva Jayatilleka against the EU and US (Western Bloc) proposals for a war crimes inquiry at Geneva UN Human Rights Council gives valuable insights into the concept and diplomatic practice of asymmetrical diplomacy.[62] Sri Lankan diplomacy by Ambassador Jayatilleka falls into two parts: the efforts to block the EU proposals from affecting the final military phase of the Sri Lankan military campaign against the LTTE and a post-war phase to defeat the revived proposals for a war crimes inquiry.

The success of phase one in achieving a majority to block the EU/US was based, against the odds, on several factors but three were particularly important. The first was careful bilateral diplomacy by the ambassador with individual counterparts in multiple meetings within a very short time frame under great pressure.[63] Second, the more independent and detached (at that period) Geneva-based nonaligned ambassadors facilitated a broader blocking coalition, which had empathy for the principled, outspoken non-career diplomacy, preventing the EU from putting together the necessary signatures endorsing a resolution. Third, recognition of the importance of supplying the embassy information staff with all available resources (such as Sri Lankan WHO and human rights specialists passing through Geneva for international meetings) to back up reasoned arguments and correct foreign reporting was seen as a critical component in winning the battle of ideas. The intensive information work – collating reports to embassies and media, constantly keeping on top of political and military developments in Sri Lanka, all in a measured and professional manner – gained trust for its accounts and sources, as well as corresponding political support.[64]

## *Procedural asymmetric counter diplomacy*

In the EU, procedural provisions have been used by individual and small groups of member states for asymmetrical diplomacy. Blocking or holding up approval of agreements has given individual members of the EU the opportunity to protect interests and attach modifications as a price of approval.

The ratification process accordingly is used to secure last-minute changes or the deferment of the agreement. The classic example of this development is seen in the Wallonia (Belgium) opposition to the EU–Canada (CETA) agreement, with the Canadian prime minister on standby at an airfield, unclear whether to fly to attend the signing ceremony.[65] The individual member or small coalition of small and large powers is isolated and under considerable pressure to withdraw objections.

The wide use of asymmetrical counter diplomacy in EU treaty practice has caused delay and shelving of agreements. In those cases in which an agreement is in effect shelved, the purpose of opposition is not amendment but to take the agreement off the table by creating a situation in which the agreement loses support or relevance (e.g. OACPS, MERCOSUR).[66] The agricultural and other terms of the most recent MERCOSUR negotiations concluded by the Commission had been long been contested by a coalition of France, Ireland and Austria opposing the beef provisions and others in the MERCOSUR agreement.[67] In EU mixed competence negotiations, national objections at ratification stage in effect put an agreement on hold, subsequent progress being linked to renegotiation of contested provisions, if at all. In practice, the delay introduces doubt over an agreement and questions over its validity – the classic purposes of counter diplomacy. In some instances, objections go beyond delay and aim to contribute to the demise of an agreement, e.g. the agreements to revise the Cotonou partnership with the ACP and create a new Organisation of African Caribbean and Pacific States. The main objections, led by France, questioned the EU's links with the ACP and relevance of the OACPS for the EU.[68] The ambiguous commentary on the OACPS was, in effect, counter diplomacy to block EU links with the new organisation, which was portrayed as too linked to the past.

## Finding a partner and backer

The efforts by small and medium powers to find backers or partners other than traditional large or primary powers has become an important part of the development of diplomatic methods. Finding new backers is more widely used by smaller actors looking for options for the financing of inter-regional logistics and development projects outside historical partners. Examples include the reorientation of the Solomon Islands.[69]

A different example is provided by the link up of Tanzania and DP World for exclusive port rights to run Dar es Salaam. Historically, Tanzania had found it very difficult to finance port development from multilateral agencies or agree new deals on favourable terms with its previous sovereign backer. Tanzania broke with its traditional project partner in favour of DP World, in a surprise counter diplomacy move.[70] The move extended DP World's reach further into Africa.

## Promotion of alternative schemes

Time is an important factor in different ways in all four methods available for asymmetrical counter diplomacy: the need for speed in completing lobbying before an opponent attracts support, procedural devices to delay entry into force of an agreement and moving decisively to secure a port development partner. In the fourth example, promotion of alternative proposals, time is an important factor partly because different or opposing ideas may quickly lose relevance or interest because of new issues, competing demands and events. Asymmetrical counter diplomacy is one of the areas through which small powers are able to seek redress and review with regards to issues which affect them but which have been addressed in plurilateral governance fora such as the G20, integration organisations and technical agencies from larger power perspectives. It is not a common method and depends on an earlier unfinished multilateral agreement or taking up an earlier neglected UNGA resolution.

The method relies on seeking amendment, for example, a plurilateral G20–OECD initiative through a UN General Assembly resolution to re-establish a UN multilateral process. In the dispute over establishing a global taxation scheme, the counter diplomacy was directed at reviving parts of the UN Model Double Taxation Convention and shifting the drafting of agreements to a UN Intergovernmental Negotiation Framework.[71]

The process is often lengthy, requiring intensive negotiation and lobbying. The results are not always evident but are part of a step-by-step process to establish points for change and the case for revising the OECD approach. Counter diplomacy is used in this process to project presence and to defensively counter threats to diplomatic and security interests.

The push back against the OECD G20 draft was led by Nigeria, Kenya, Pakistan and Sri Lanka on economic security grounds as part of proposals for a more powerful role for the UN in international tax policy. Analysis by the group suggested that the qualifying thresholds in the OECD two-pillar proposal were too high so that, for example, in the Kenya case, only 11 companies that operate in Kenya met Pillar 1 criteria, whilst the country has 89 companies currently paying digital services tax.[72] UNGA resolution 77/244 mandated the UN to monitor, review and set worldwide tax standards. It marked a major shift in methods to a UN intergovernmental process through the UN Secretary-General.[73]

## Flanking diplomacy: closing out options

Flanking diplomacy is unusual in comparison with other diplomatic methods in that it is forward-looking not about future plans, but rather anticipating the future action of another actor with a view to closing or blocking future moves. China's application for accession to the CPTPP was made the day following the announcement of the US–UK–AUS submarine cooperation agreement, making it one of the most striking strategic flanking moves, with potential to fundamentally alter geoeconomic trade by linking two competitive blocs.[74]

The aim of flanking diplomacy is to put an opponent off balance in order to create uncertainty over the best course of action or response. A possible move has been blocked off and an alternative is not clear. Merely duplicating an opponent's moves (aid, finance package, technical scientific cooperation) may seem dated and above all politically unproductive. A succession of high-level visits may be too little and too late to pull back relations when contrasted with an opponent's carefully tailored package of finance and technical cooperation.

Producing new policy initiatives at short notice is not a strength of bureaucratic politics. Further, the surprise element in flanking diplomacy relies on weaknesses in information capability and intelligence failure.[75]

On learning of the US–UK–Australia nuclear submarine deal, EU Commissioner Josep Borrel explained:

> I was not aware … we were not involved.. and I assume an agreement of such a nature was not brought together overnight.[76]

Information may not be shared of necessity but one of the diplomatic consequences of subsequent attempts at damage limitation with an excluded ally is over appropriate compensation, whether this should take the form of bilateral trade or political concessions, which may in turn create separate difficulties for other allies.[77]

Some of the main types of flanking diplomacy involve strategies aimed at closing off membership of international or regional organisations, exploiting contract negotiations, territorial and port acquisition.[78] The latter became a central component of the Belt and Road Initiative, extended into Europe with the foothold gained in the acquisition of the port of Piraeus by China Merchants Group, following its privatisation and extended via Arctic route initiatives. The group acquired an initial 25% holding, which was progressively increased to 70%.[79] It was unexpected and audacious, exploiting the sell-off of Greek utilities as part of the price of the Greek bail-out in the Euro financial crisis. A key role in the move was that of the Chinese ambassador to Athens, supported by extensive commercial intelligence operations, in a coordinated diplomatic effort directed at monitoring closely the internal Greek economy in order to support rapid exploitation.[80]

Not all flanking diplomacy fits neatly or precisely into these categories. An agreement may be presented as a scientific research cooperation agreement though its rationale or other purposes may not be initially clear. In this method the approach is step-by-step, beginning with a framework agreement and informal interagency MOUs, supplemented by educational links, moving to a formal agreement.

The development of Sino–Icelandic relations typified this approach in a six-year period built on a suite of coordinated agreements, symbolised by the passage of the Chinese-flagged research icebreaker MV Xue Long, funding of the China–Iceland Arctic Science Observatory at Kárhóll and the prize of gaining Arctic Council observer status.[81]

Disguised free trade agreements incorporating non-trade provisions are additional methods used to keep presence low key. For example, the China–Iceland bilateral trade agreement is styled as such but its provisions are much wider.[82] Its primary purpose is not promotion of China–Iceland free trade. The elaborate trade provisions in the agreement are quite out of proportion to the volume of bilateral trade more suited to a short standard agreement. Rather, it is intended to signal bilateral cooperation, which would go on to encompass non-trade areas and serve as a vehicle for arctic scientific cooperation and research designed to promote China's credentials as an arctic power.[83] Limiting the agreement to trade would not have helped those objectives. The title "Free Trade" was necessary to soften the label or mute domestic reaction, in which the arctic is a sensitive geostrategic area of conflict between China and western powers, played out through US high-level visit diplomacy and countered by China on Icelandic television.[84]

The intensification of geopolitical conflict and high levels of inter-national tension after 2022 influenced a major review in Nordic coun-tries of economic and security risks. Part of the subsequent shift to closer western bilateral security relations and alliance membership reflected an underlying sense of vulnerability, particularly for smaller members like Iceland. Nor could neutrality or similar orientations offer sufficient security certainty. The development of non western links discussed above through  trade , routes and other cooperation had too much risk and were accordingly curtailed or left to close.[85]

### Conditions for successful flanking diplomacy

Flanking diplomacy is a powerful and dynamic method in contemporary diplomacy. It fundamentally raises risks in conflict, shuts off options and sets limits.

There are three main contexts which favour the use of counter diplo-macy. First, counter diplomacy flourishes in end-run situations. These are found, for example, at the end of negotiations, near the run-out date of an agreement or in the lead-up to elections. A second context is one of policy drift. A new administration may have been slow in revising, devising and starting to implement changes to its predecessors' policies, leaving policy vacuums and the merits (or not) of continuity, which are debated as agencies contest role and respective influence over policy.

In alliances or groupings, a third related context is division over the scale of response to coercive action and force used by an adversary. Cracks in an alliance are exploited by adversarial states to probe limits and assess the risk of escalating the scope and level of coercive operations. Fourth, crisis provides an opportunity for flanking diplomacy, especially if an adversarial state is heavily involved in one particular problem, which then opens the possibility for exploiting that situation with pre-emptive moves.

# Conclusion

Counter diplomacy is a distinctive and widely used diplomatic method. A number of forms have developed including multilateral, blocking, denial, asymmetrical and flanking counter diplomacy. The development of these categories of counter diplomacy, particularly economic counter diplomacy, has created a substantial body of diplomatic practice dealing with methods which push diplomacy away from its traditional purposes of cooperation and contribution to international order.

Counter diplomacy is distinguished from other diplomatic methods in that it is positioned in the grey area between diplomacy and force. Its methods are directed to overturning key policies, establishing rival institutions, building alternative networks to defeat international sanctions, raising the level of risk in diplomatic initiatives and coercive action against individuals.

In most instances, these aspects set counter diplomacy apart from traditional conceptions of diplomacy based on values of diplomatic respect, cooperation and conflict resolution. In the UN Security Council, blocking action has progressively reduced the role of the Council in conflict and weakened its safety valve function. Its use as a platform or cover to buy time in civil conflict or create an alternative mediatory grouping highlights how the Council methods are challenged.

One of the main changes resulting from counter diplomacy is the greater use of indirect methods, including delay, non-attendance, limited participation and cancellation of meetings. Indirect methods cut away at diplomacy and reduce its multilateral use. The value and purposes of collective multilateral action is also called into question. This type of diplomacy is captured in the concept of disengaged diplomacy, which uses limited or selective international participation, observer status, extensive non-ratification of multilateral agreements and nominal multilateral obligations through second tier participation in less well-known multilateral agencies. Co-chairing conferences provides headlines. The public domain is backed by covert groupings, alternative alliance and selective bilateral relations.

Economic counter diplomacy has now developed as an established part of counter diplomacy covering institutions, projects, trade coercion, route competition and sanctions avoidance. The latter has impacted on the creation of informal groups, oil supply networks and new alliances. It has become a major driver in the development of cooperation between sanctioned states and entities.

Asymmetrical diplomacy has now received greater attention as a method used by a variety of small, weak and large powers. Large powers have used asymmetrical diplomacy in an alliance or regional organisation when in a minority position. Smaller powers have had some success in riding out trade coercion. Procedural counter diplomacy has found two uses: using blocking of signature to achieve amendments and a negative use to delay, undermine or terminate an agreement.

## Notes

1 See Inis L. Claude, Jr, *Swords into Plowshares: The Problems and Progress of International Organization* (University of London Press, 1965) p134.
2 Articles 23 and 27, UN Charter, Repertoire of SC Practice.
3 Jeremy Greenstock, *Iraq: The Cost of War* (Arrow Books, 2017) p144.
4 S/1441, 8 November 2002.
5 Greenstock, op. cit., p154.
6 Greenstock, op. cit., p148.
7 See "Timeline of nuclear diplomacy with Iran, 1967–2023", Arms Control Association at www.armscontrol.org/factsheets/timeline-nuclear-diplom acy-iran-1967-2023.
8 Note to Correspondents: Transcript of joint stake out by UN Special Envoy for Syria, Staffan de Mistura and Senior Advisor, Jan Egeland, 5 January 2017.
9 Russia, Iran and Turkey met initially in Moscow on 20 December 2016, and subsequently in Sochi (2017–19). The group also met at foreign minister level prior to the heads of state/government meetings.
10 On evacuation from Eastern Ghouta, see Jan Egeland, https://news.un.org/en/audio/2017/11/637941; Jordan border, https://news.un.org/en/story/2018/06/1013422; Idlib, https://press.un.org/en/2019/sc13956.doc.htm.
11 See S/PV.8697 (pp8–11) for Russian criticism of the German delegate.
12 See closing debate at S/PV.8697, 20 December 2019.
13 S/2019/961 (Belgium, Germany, Kuwait) and the second Russian resolution S/2019/962; cf S/PV.8623 and S/2019/756.
14 For example, on Kenya's handling of the security of Dr John Garang, leader of SPLA/M during its Sudan mediation role, see Boaz K. Mbaya, *Kenya's Foreign Policy and Diplomacy* (East African Educational Publishers Ltd, 2019) pp111–3.
15 For details of the diversion of Ryanair Flight 4978 (Athens–Vilnius) to Minsk, see *The Guardian*, 28 May 2021.
16 The position of National Security Advisor and Secretary of State in the United States system is almost inevitably a source of dispute over relative roles and responsibility. On the problem during the Biden administration of making visit arrangements for officials with China, see *Financial Times*, 29 August 2024; for Blinken-Sullivan roles in the off-radar strategic channel, see *Financial Times*, 30 August 2024.
17 In the UK–EU Brexit negotiations, Michel Barnier's preference was at offi- cial level for the detailed, granular style of lead negotiator Olly Robbins, rather than the broad-brush approach at ministerial level of David Davis. Barnier's communications to the UK prime minister was full of praise for Robbins on pro- gress. David Davis eventually resigned on 8 July 2018. See Barnier, *My Secret Diary*, op. cit., pp148–9. See *Financial Times*, 9 July 2018 for full text of Davis's letter and reply, setting out differences over decision-making and policy over EU withdrawal.
18 The Suez Canal was blocked between 23 and 29 March 2021, following the stranding of the Evergreen supersized container ship Ever Given (219.079 GT)

The Ever Given was salvaged and impounded for three months at Ismailia, pending a $550 million salvage claim. See James Baker, "Boxships begin to divert from the Suez Canal," Lloyd's List, 25 March 2021 at www.lloydslist. com/LL1136255/Boxships-begin-to-divert-from-Suez-Canal.

19 See *Financial Times*, 25 November 2011. For historical review of changing post-war involvement featuring US declining Arctic interest and corresponding expansion of Chinese and Russian presence, see report www.government.is/ library/01-Ministries/Ministry-for-Foreign-Affairs/PDF-skjol/Arctic%20Pol icy_WEB.pdf. See also the controversy over the attempted purchase of the abandoned military base at Grønnedal, p.63.

20 See RCEP, reservations Australia, New Zealand, Singapore. www.mfat.govt.nz/ en/trade/free-trade-agreements/free-trade-agreements-in-force; US–Mexico bilateral discussions held on US concern over projected China DFI electric vehicle/component manufacturing projects in Mexico for entry into the United States, *Financial Times*, 20 November 2023.

21 See Andrew Lambert, *Seapower States* (Yale University Press, 2018) chapter 9. The top ten shipping list is led by China, Greece and Japan (by ownership and registered vessels) and includes Singapore, Germany, Indonesia, Norway, Hongkong, Turkey, the Russia Federation (number of ships) and Korea. The US slipped out of the top 10 in 2022. See UNCTAD *Handbook of Statistics* 2023.

22 For the IPEF, see "US and Indo-Pacific Economic Framework Partners Announce Negotiation Objectives", Office of the United States Trade Representative, 9 September 2022. https://ustr.gov/about-us/policy-offices/ press-office/press-releases/2022/september/united-states-and-indo-pacific-economic-framework-partners-announce-negotiation-objectives.

23 See   https://maps.lib.utexas.edu/maps/middle_east_and_asia/schina_sea_ 88.jpg.

24 Vietnam agreed to pay substantial contract cancellation charges to Repsol (Spain) and UAE (Mahdah) following Chinese pressure to end their operations in disputed areas of the Vietnam EEZ. *Petroleum Times*, 20 August 2020.

25 Rosneft continued in Vietnam but regrouped its companies and retained interests in areas with differing scales of vulnerability.

26 See   www.chathamhouse.org/2022/01/new-alignments-are-looming-south-china-sea Chatham House, 12 January 2022.

27 R.P. Barston, "Port State Control: Evolving Concepts", in Harry N. Scheiber (ed.) *Law of the Sea* (Brill Nijhoff, 2000) pp87–102.

28 R.P. Barston, *Modern Diplomacy* 4th ed., op. cit, pp218–22.

29 The Tripartite Free Trade agreement linking the east and southern African economic communities (EAC, COMESA and SADC) was launched as a development-focused agreement in June 2015 at Sharm El-Sheikh (Egypt) but was challenged by a rival grouping favouring an African Union (AU) continental trade agreement of west and central African states, led initially by Nigeria then later South Africa). AfCFTA, which drew heavily on the tariff work of the TFTA, entered into force first on 30 May 2019, for 24 of the 55 AU members. This increased to 41 in 2022, partly through dual ratification by some east and southern African TFTA members (e.g. South Africa, Zambia). TFTA entry into force was also delayed by new members (South Sudan) and civil conflict (e.g. Libya). Although not in force, the strong development ethos of the TFTA is retained through the existing institutions (COMESA) and development projects. Implementation of priority tripartite instruments and programmes

including monitoring of non-tariff barriers (NTBs), transport facilitation, infrastructure development and SMS-based NTBs. Reporting systems do not require ratification and are ongoing. See on ratifications, www.comesa.int/ botswana-deposits-tripartite-fta-ratification-instruments/.

30 On the issues of links between the TFTA and AfCFTA and article 19 see "Concept Note Governing the Interface", https://archive.uneca.org/sites/ default /files/uploadeddocuments/RITD/2020/concept_note_interface_ between_the_afcfta_and_recs_ftas_issues_opportunities_and_challenges.pdf. For the text of the AfCFTA, see https://au.int/en/treaties/agreement-estab lishing-african-continental-free-trade-area.The text of the TFTA is at www.tra lac.org/ resources/by-region/comesa-eac-sadc-tripartite-fta.html.

31 The TFTA, linking COMESA, EAC and SADC, entered into force on 25 July 2024 with the ratification of Angola, reaching the threshold of 14 members. It was a major achievement for the COMESA secretariat and leading members in a lengthy negotiation. Above all, it perhaps symbolised the resilience of regional integration institutions against externally favoured continental models of trade and development cooperation. The members of the TFTA include Angola, Botswana, Burundi, Djibouti, Egypt, Eswatini, Kenya, Lesotho, Malawi, Namibia, Rwanda, South Africa, Uganda, Zimbabwe and Zambia.

32 On the 13th BRICS virtual meeting hosted by India, see www.youtube.com/ watch?v=KeWlSA0uuJk, 9 September 2021.

33 See Masoud Rezvanian interview at www.thehindu.com/news/national/mon ths-after-starting-chabahar-rail-project-without-india-iran-requests-help-with-equipment/article33048813.ece, 7 November 2021.

34 *Economic Times* (India), 14 December 2021.

35 https://indianexpress.com/article/explained/explained-global/history-of-iran-chabahar-port-india-9117732/.

36 See Chabahar Port project, India Council of World Affairs, 21 May 2024.

37 US–UK–Australia Trilateral Security Pact, 15 September 2021. *New York Times*, 29 October 2021. "The Secret Talks Behind the US Deal". See www.nytimes. com/2021/09/17/us/politics/us-france-australia-betrayal.html

38 "Reassurance and deterrence in the Mediterranean". Institute Montaigne, 17 November 2021. www.institutmontaigne.org>expression.>reass.

39 See *Financial Times*, 2 December 2021.

40 See, for example, on North Korea non-proliferation, the Final Report to the Security Council under resolution, UNSC 2569 (2021), S/2022/132.

41 UN S/RES/2627 (2022); S/2023/171, 7 March 2023, pp27–61.

42 On flag of convenience growth, see "An inconvenient truth: Flags failing" at www.lloydslist.com/LL1135690/An-inconvenient-truth-Flags-failing, 8 February 2021.

43 UN/SC/14841, 25 March 2022.

44 See Ralph S. Clem and Anthony P. Maingot (eds), *Venezuela's Petro-Diplomacy* (University Press of Florida, 2015) pp24–8.

45 https://lloydslist.maritime intelligence.informa.com/First, 10 November 2020.

46 *Financial Times*, 14 January 2022.

47 The UK bilateral trade negotiations with Kenya were attacked by Politico at a critical final stage and depicted as a threat to the East African Community (EAC). See www.politico.eu/article/uk-kenya-trade-deal-threatens-trade-in-east-africa/.

48  For differing perspectives on trade versus foreign policy interests, see *Financial Times*, 15 November 2022 on (Albanese's) change of government and review of Australia's relations with China; Reuters on "de-risking" trade decisions at G7, 20 May 2023.

49  On the Australia–China dispute, see https://lowyinstitute.org-the-interpreter-china-s; www.dfat.gov.au.trade.wto.wto-disputes. For arguments used for resetting relations, see extract of Prime Minister Albanese's address to the Australian Industry Group, 14 August 2023, www.aigroup.com.au/ news/speeches-transcripts/2023/ai-group-150th-anniversary-dinner-prime-ministers-address/.

50  China is the largest of the three main grain importers from Australia (China, Indonesia, Vietnam), with non-sanctioned wheat imports increasing by a factor of 6 to 6.4 million tons during sanctions to cover shortfalls and Ukraine-related market volatility.

51  The barley tariffs on Australia were withdrawn by China one month after the breakdown of the UN grain deal in July 2023.

52  See press release of meeting between Lithuanian Foreign Minister, Gabrielius Landsbergis and Australian Foreign Minister, Marise Payne, 9 February 2022. www.foreignminister.gov.au/minister/marise-payne/media-release/visit-australia-lithuanian-foreign-minister.

53  WTO dispute procedures distinguish between requests for dispute consultations (articles XX11 and XX111 of GATT 1994) and requests for the establishment of a WTO dispute panel.

54  WTO WT/DS 610/1, 11 February 2022.

55  WTO WT/DS 610/1, 11 February 2022.

56  WT/DS 610/5.

57  WT/DS 610/3.

58  WT/DS 610/2.

59  WTO Dispute settlement, press release, 28 February 2022.

60  www.abc.net.au/news/rural/2023-09-12/china-boom-agricultural-farm-exports-grains-record-high-wheat/102844300.

61  "China's tariff removal benefits barley exports". See www.awb.com.au/2023/china-tariff-removal-benefits-barley-exports.

62  Sanja De Silva Jayatilleka, *Mission Impossible Geneva* (Vijitha Yapa, 2017).

63  Jayatilleka, ibid., esp. pp91–7 on the Ambassador's intense schedule of bilateral meetings.

64  Jayatilleka, ibid., pp70–1.

65  "Canada–EU talks with Wallonia collapse", 21 October 2016. See www.cbc.ca/news/politics/canada-eu-ceta-brussels-friday-1.3815332.

66  Reuters, 12 September 2023. https://reuters.com/world/mercosur-splits-dampen-eu-outlook-trade-deal-window-narrows-2023-09-12/.

67  See www.euractiv.com/section/politics/news/french-farmers-ask-macron-to-stand-firm-on-eu-mercosur-agreement/.

68  See Elizabeth Morgan, op. cit., note 31. See https://caricom.org/statement-of-the-council-of-ministers-of-cariforum-on-the-ex-post-evaluation-of-the-cariforum-eu-epa/#:~:text=The%20evaluation%20shows%20scant%20regard, for%20cultural%20and%20professional%20services.

69  See www.rnz.co.nz/international/pacific-news/493661/solomons-pm-signs-new-deals-with-china-on-beijing-trip.

70  *Financial Times*, 10 August 2023.

71 Kuldeep Sharma and Raunicka Sharma, "The United Nations Intergovernmental Process: an opportunity for a paradigm shift", 31 May 2023. See www.southcentre.int/wp-content/uploads/2023/06/SV248_ 230531.pdf.

72 Sharma and Sharma, ibid., p2.

73 UNGA Res 77/244, 30 December 2022.

74 China applied for accession to the CPTPP on the day following the announcement of US–UK–AUS defence cooperation (submarine) agreement on 16 September 2021; Taiwan followed six days later.

75 See Graham T. Allison, *Essence of Decision: Explaining the Cuban Missile Crisis* (Little, Brown and Company, 1971) pp173–7.

76 *Financial Times*, 16 September 2021.

77 US relations with France remained difficult after defence cancellation. Efforts made to repair relations were made through a joint Council on technological cooperation. See chapter 4.

78 *Financial Times*, 21 September 2021. See also above N37 on the French use of US trade concessions to the EU on steel tariffs as linkage in the Northern Ireland Protocol dispute with the UK.

79 Jonathan Holslag, *The Silk Road Trap* (Polity, 2019) pp106–8. US strategy altered to involve some infrastructure port development with Sri Lanka in recognition of an area not given sufficient priority.

80 On the Greek port privatisation negotiations and links to China, see Finance Minister Yanis Varoufakis, *Adults in the Room: My Battle with Europe's Deep Establishment* (Vantage, 2017) pp138–9, 313–21, 364. See esp. pp314–15 on contacts with the Chinese ambassador; the Berlin counter diplomacy warning to China opposing China–Greek loans and participation in Piraeus port holdings until an all-EU package was resolved. Also p321, 527 and chapter 11 notes 6 and 8.

81 The China–Iceland currency swap during the international financial crisis concluded in 2008. China–Iceland Framework Cooperation 25 April 2011 with MOUs: Ministry of Foreign Affairs Government of Iceland. See, for example, the MOU on Chinese–Icelandic Cooperation on Arctic Issues between the Polar Research Institute of China and the Icelandic research Centre (section 5) on scope which consists only of very general headline topics (climate change, economic cooperation between Asian and Nordic countries and arctic strategy/legislation).

82 See Joint Statement China and Iceland on Comprehensively Deepening Bilateral Cooperation, Beijing 15 April 2013, para 7, which reaffirms Iceland's support for China's application for observer status in the Arctic Council.

83 China–Iceland Free Trade Agreement, 15 April 2013. www.government.is/topics/foreign-affairs/external-trade/free-trade-agreements/free-trade-agreement-between-iceland-and-china/.

84 For evolution of Iceland's relations with the US and China, see www.isdp.eu/pressure-in-the-arctic-china-iceland-relations.

85 https://www.defense.gov/..../us-allies-focus-on-partnerships. 9 October 2024.

## Chapter 9

# Logistics diplomacy

## Introduction

Logistics is an important but traditionally neglected branch of diplomacy.[1] Logistics issues feature in a wide range of transactions such as competitive port acquisition, threats to strategic routes, supply chain crises and geopolitical tension. The globalisation of trade has tended to accelerate differences between countries in terms of access to markets and capacity to manage supply chains. Periodic trade and logistic crises highlight access, supply bottlenecks and transport dependence. Yet a striking feature of logistics is that it remains, at least at the multilateral level, perhaps one of the least regulated areas of international relations. A central paradox of logistics is the tension between global commercial operations and the development of multilateral cooperation. The regulatory landscape is fragmented in terms of actors and agreements, distinguished by bilateral, small group diplomacy and ad hoc agreements.

In this chapter we will explore the definition of logistics: what kinds of activities fall within definitions of logistics? Where does diplomacy fit in? In what ways is logistics changing and how do these changes impact on diplomacy? Who are the main players in terms of states and companies? What are the characteristics of the multilateral institutional dimension of logistics diplomacy? In what ways have methods changed and how have these affected the conduct of diplomacy?

The main sections of the chapter cover five areas: logistics assets and players, the multilateral framework, port acquisition and geopolitical uses of logistics, developments in agreements and conferences, and developing methods in logistics diplomacy.

DOI: 10.4324/9781003204039-10

## Logistics: perspectives

Logistics is concerned with the movement of goods and services between and within countries, organisations and other actors. Central to this idea is transportation and the ability to move goods and services bilaterally and multilaterally through scheduled routes or as cargo of opportunity. Bilateral agreements between states frequently contain additional logistics provisions dealing with air, land or maritime transport, which provide for access and connectivity as part of a general cooperation agreement or as a separate sector agreement. Who provides those goods or services, frequency and routes has become not merely a technical aspect of bilateral or regional diplomacy but is a contested political issue in geopolitics.

From a trade regulatory perspective, logistics has been described as: "the glue which holds value chains together".[2] Underlying this definition is a WTO perspective of value chains and the importance of improving global supply chains. Linked to this definition is a second concept of "logistics gap" which is used to refer to issues of capacity and the problems particularly of smaller, landlocked and less developed countries in accessing supply chains.[3] The logistics gap perspective has fundamentally shaped several aspects of how multilateral logistics and trade facilitation agreements are framed, seen in disputes over provisions on financial support for less developed countries, in negotiations to incorporate exceptions in agreements to cater for different levels of logistic infrastructure reflecting levels of development, and in relatively weak multilateral agreements.

A third perspective brings out the central issue of the balance between international trade facilitation and logistics negotiations. From this perspective, international negotiations have not treated trade facilitation regulations (documentation, finance, simplified customs procedures, information flows, border procedures) and logistics (transportation, port access, labour, container return, security) from a holistic perspective but rather the balance has been too much on trade facilitation.[4] The freight transportation view was captured in a formative WTO forum in presentations by the transport and cargo representatives highlighting the need to shift the focus of multilateral negotiation to logistics issues.[5]

In the fourth perspective, logistics is viewed as part of emerging bilateral and regional agreements such as e-commerce and the RCEP.[6] This view, typified in international business assessments, puts logistics as part of market access agreements. At a bilateral or small group level, logistic agreements are presented as government innovation initiatives in technical political cooperation to improve supply chain connectivity.[7]

## Logistics and diplomacy

In logistics, diplomacy is used in five main contexts: acquisition of assets (ports, companies, real estate), defence of interests, coordination of transport services, negotiation and international regulation. Much of logistics diplomacy is conducted at bilateral and regional level, rather than through multilateral institutions. At a multilateral level, international regulation in multilateral institutions has tended to address transport-related trade from the standpoint of facilitation issues, i.e. documentary and communications aspects rather than logistics problems connected with movement such as supply disruption, container availability and vessel availability.

## Players and assets

Maritime trade accounts for over 80% of globally transported cargo by volume.[8] Three countries – Greece, China and Japan – own nearly half of the deadweight tonnage (dwt), whilst Singapore is the fourth largest, underlining the potential of small powers for entrepreneurial drive and creating global economic roles. The absence of the United States and Russian Federation directly from the top ten ranking is interesting in terms of global power and limited ability to influence many diplomatic aspects of logistics and international shipping.[9]

The leading flag registries by dwt are Panama, Liberia and Marshall Islands. Panama and Liberia are traditional open registers attracting varied tonnage, whilst Marshall Islands is similarly based in the US, but projected as a high-end flag, also available in crises such as Black Sea routes as an on-call flag of first resort for high-risk transportation.[10] International registers have been developed by Norway and Germany in an effort to retain their status as leading flag registration powers. Of the top three by dwt, only Panama has significant tonnage in all types of vessels, making it a general shipping register and, in terms of international agreements relating to shipping, a potentially important actor.

In addition, the Panamanian registry is extensively used in the fisheries sector, e.g. by China and others, for the registration of internationally trading fish factory support and freezer vessels, as discussed in chapter 5.[11] Liberia operates in most categories but with emphasis on oil tanker registration. Marshall Islands attracts bulk carrier trade registry as well as specialist vessel trades, including gas carriers, chemical tankers and a large segment of the US offshore vessels market. In terms of container vessels, Panama and Liberia are the leading flag registers. Four other flags – China, Hong Kong (China), Singapore and Malta – carry most of the remaining container traffic.

This group of seven states and ten operating companies has the greatest direct interest in the form and content of any international logistics agreement affecting transportation of goods. It is a disparate group which includes two major open registry states (Panama and Liberia), whose general diplomatic methods are largely defensive – defending non-compliance issues and adverse safety records – as against reformists or supporters of multilateral initiatives.[12] Moreover, China's approach to multilateral trade connectivity is similarly to rely on selective multi-lateralism, e.g. technical customs codes and indirect methods such as financial support for regional research projects on supply chains, to avoid commercially restrictive commitments or financial regulations. Its diplomatic methods use mainly bilateral relations at sub-national and regional initiatives, backed by selective headline media on logistics routes or ports and related environment or biodiversity declarations.

The absence of the United States from the top ten carrier group underlines the limits of US power and influence.[13] Maritime capability helps to project diplomatic power at all levels through port presence, transportation aid in emergencies and as part of implementation of trade deals. Presence in international negotiations is related to capabilities and initiatives as well as interests.

In logistics diplomacy, geopolitics puts a premium on speed, recognition of openings, and the use of maritime commercial power and multimodal transport to establish footholds, sustain the flow of maritime carried goods and services and retain influence by credible moves backing up declaratory policy. Alliances without implementation and ports without cargo are symbols of unfulfilled intent. Diplomacy serves to promote presence, whilst diplomatic visits serve to revive, symbolise and extend cooperation.

### Development of companies and groupings

In the container sector, the top five company groups (Maersk, MSC, CMA CGM, COSCO and Hapag-Lloyd), have over 60% of the market share. Maersk, established originally as A.P. Møller, has had a major impact on container trades, especially the transition of how cargo is carried, design of container vessels and route development.[14] It is, along with MSC and CMA CMG, part of a long-established European shipping carrier grouping, operating behind the scenes on technical and regulatory development in professional and multilateral fora, rather as an adjunct diplomatic driver of transport and logistics reform.

As a whole, the top 40 container operators include a varied range of companies, including the global shipping and multimodal groups, small state international companies such as Zim (Israel), as well as large, predominantly regional, operators such as Turkey and local transshipment companies.[15] The composition of the top five group has undergone frequent company realignments. One of the largest involved, state-owned COSCO (Shanghai), was formed from a merger of China Ocean Shipping Group and China Shipping Group. COSCO later acquired OOIL/OOCL and is fourth-ranked with over 400 vessels operating in and out of over 500 ports, with Maersk operating over 600 vessels.[16] The establishment of COSCO brought in coordinated capacity but also substantial differences of approach from other members of the top five, with shipping and port assets used as part of diplomacy and support of long-range foreign policy objectives.

The top five company groups coordinate route schedules and services through three alliances: Gemini (Maersk and Hapag); Ocean Alliance (COSCO, OOCL, CMA CGM and Evergreen) and Premiere (ONE, Yang Ming, HMM and MSC).[17] Their scheduled container services cover core routes such as Asia–Europe, Middle East and US east–west coast trades, using key ports.[18] The membership of individual groupings is fluid and alliance groups are periodically reconstituted.

The other notable area of change is the expansion of major shipping companies into terminal operations (by creating new terminal divisions or subsidiaries), and the acquisition of existing port terminal operators or joint ventures (as between Maersk and COSCO or COSCO subsidiaries in several areas). The expansion of leading operators into terminal and other logistics services has affected the scope of smaller operators. It has also introduced, for some states, the question of strategic dependence on one or two core carrier actors with their own differing agendas.

As regards other routes, unscheduled secondary routes using varying ports are maintained by the alliances and smaller independent operators. A third category of port/route development involves port operator initiatives or ad hoc group moves to diversify or test new market routes. Examples of the former include the initiative by the Port of Virginia to become a US port call in a Europe–Caribbean loop.[19]

In the specialised sector, Maersk opened the Costa Rica Express (CRX), a new refrigerated fruit service from central America to Southampton, with rotation via Antwerp (Belgium), Bremerhaven (Germany), Veracruz (Mexico), Big Creek (US), Manzanillo (Panama), Moin (Costa Rica), Cork (Ireland) to Southampton and return.[20] In other areas, New Zealand's supply chain vulnerability in pandemics to loss of port calls and high freight rates was partly reduced by Maersk's commercial decision to introduce an inter-island container service linked to its global network.

In contrast to these initiatives, the long-term goals of port acquisition and shipping services are more closely integrated in China's Belt and Road initiative through globally operating state-owned enterprises (SOEs) such as COSCO and China Merchants. These initiatives are driven by strategic political as well economic aims rather than largely commercial considerations. As such, they encounter higher political risk and are vulnerable to country and multisector project financial collapse, as well as threats to other key routes from climate factors affecting water levels and spill-over of regional conflicts affecting maritime transport and global reach. Port project failures are offset by rapid switches to other port-route options, multimodal options and offshoring using export zones, DFI projects on the periphery of economic blocs, or through joint ventures with individual regional organisation members.

The disparate membership of the owner-carrier groups impacts significantly on the nature and extent of regulatory and other wider cooperation, particularly the direct absence for the most part of primary powers. The movement of major carriers into terminal operations has also blurred the line between state and private interests, through cross-cutting joint ventures and equity participation.[21]

The scope of logistics diplomacy is affected by these developments in that multilateral cooperation remains limited by complex cross-cutting interests on the difficult logistics issues relating to supply chain crises, establishing obligations and procedures for container redistribution, guarantees of route security in war zones or agreements on shipment of cargoes and keeping ports open in conflicts on humanitarian grounds. The absence of primary powers in multilateral logistics negotiations affects the scope, agenda and overall implementation of proposals and agreements.

## Multilateral institutions and logistics

Transport logistics are covered by several international institutions normally as part of other policy areas such as trade facilitation. No single multilateral agency has overall responsibility for handling various logistics questions. The range of institutions includes IMO (safety, environment, trade facilitation), WTO (trade facilitation, services regulation, customs, subsidies, dialogue), UNCTAD (shipping and logistics data, port development, technical training), WCO (customs), World Bank (logistics data, connectivity index, port development, loans), ILO (seafarer crew welfare, working conditions).

The splintering of responsibility over logistics limits coordination between UN agencies, particularly over perspectives and pulling issues together. It also enhances the tendency for agencies and their sections to initiate and develop separate interests and agendas. WTO has focused on trade facilitation, UNCTAD on port and logistic services and IMO, as the lead maritime agency, has traditionally focused on technical regulation of navigation, safety compliance and marine pollution.

Separate agency agendas influence how negotiations are framed. Writing on the tendency of governments historically to focus on reducing barriers to trade for specific products and sectors (tariffs, subsidies, non-tariff barriers) rather than logistics, Bernard Hoekman notes:

> While these are all important areas of policy that give rise to trade costs to businesses, the lack of a 'whole of the supply chain focus' in trade negotiations and trade agreements means that key factors that impact supply chain efficiency are not addressed.[22]

Excluded are efforts to develop measures on supply chain breakdown and bottlenecks, and tackle problems such as lack of shipping services to developing countries, loss of services and blank sailings, and basic service issues such as container return.

There are also costs in terms of the methods and efficiency of international institutions. The splintering of logistics operations inevitably leads to duplication, for example, competing port projects and duplicated institutions. The WTO recognised the problem during the TFA negotiations over a trade committee with wide review functions in the Trade Facilitation Agreement (TFA) which would potentially duplicate the work of the World Customs Organisation (WCO). A formula was eventually found in the TFA which required close contact with the WCO to at least nominally address the problem.[23]

Other nominal areas of duplication may have wider diplomatic and commercial consequences, such as the creation of efficiency rankings by international institutions. Both the World Bank and UNCTAD produce connectivity indices.[24] Relatively small statistical shifts should be treated with some caution in view of the aggregate data construction. From a diplomatic perspective the value of these may be of some concern, in that low rankings on an index can be politically and diplomatically sensitive or have adverse commercial consequences for many less developed countries facing multiple emergencies. Withdrawing one or both might have diplomatic benefits. Ranking tables are not necessarily needed to promote or develop wider diplomatic and technical cooperation.

## Multilateral agreements on logistics: WTO and IMO

At a multilateral level both IMO and WTO have tended to approach connectivity in the Facilitation of International Maritime Traffic (FAL Convention) and TFA agreements from the documentary flow of goods angle.[25] The FAL focuses on the narrow technical area of standardised electronic transmission of ship/crew and cargo details to and from ports, e.g. the Maritime Single Window project and the TFA on supply chain facilitation (records of customs compliance, low physical inspection, financial guarantee requirements).

However, in response to COVID-19 supply disruption, IMO amended the FAL agreement with novel and potentially far-reaching provisions based on the concept of "public health emergency of international concern" (PHEIC). It was a groundbreaking concept requiring commitments to designate key strategic personnel to ensure ships and ports remain fully operational during a public health emergency of international concern. However, the entry into force date of the amendment and incorporation as an annex in the FAL agreement, rather than as an emergency binding resolution, suggested limitations to the multilateral consensus for the changes sought in the amendment.[26] Furthermore, the working procedures of the FAL committee meant the amendment was merely part of a lengthy agenda, with competing novel items such as regulations on unmanned drones dominating member interests and priorities.

## WTO Trade Facilitation Agreement (TFA): drafting exceptions and limits

The WTO Trade Facilitation agreement was completed at the Bali ministerial meeting in the final phases of the deadlocked Doha Round.[27] It was part of a package which was intended to salvage at least something from the failed Doha process. It is presented as a flagship agreement for trade facilitation, although in practice it reflects many of the weaknesses in method and style of operation which have come to epitomise the WTO multilateral process. Four aspects are worth noting. Although described as a multilateral agreement, the agreement actually uses an "opt in" formula. In this type of agreement there are provisions which allow parties to choose at what stage they might wish to participate, or adopt a particular provision.

Allowing parties to choose which set of regulations to apply is also found in other provisions on maritime transport which classify services products.[28] The TFA should be distinguished from WTO plurilateral agreements, e.g. civil aviation, which are sub-agreements only applicable to the signatories party to the specialist agreement. In the TFA these features contribute to the weakening of multilateralism allowing a patchwork of separate treatment which contributes to the progressive splintering of the perspectives and regulatory framework of the WTO.

Third are limitations arising from the drafting of obligations in the TFA. In general, there is extensive use of non-binding language, qualified obligations and recommendations. In the provisions, for example, on average release times for ships undergoing inspection, "members are encouraged to measure and publish details and share their experiences with the (Trade) Committee".[29] The capacity qualification formula removes much of the obligation: "Each member may determine the scope and methodology of such average release time measurement in accordance with its need and capacity".[30]

In article 7, a different aspect of variation occurs, in which the scope of special treatment for authorised operators is left to at least three measures from a list of seven. Three of these options are then qualified by the standard opt-out formula "as appropriate" which removes much of the meaning or intent.[31] Article 7.3 reads "three of the following measures:

(a) low documentary and data requirements, as appropriate
(b) low rate of physical inspections and examinations, as appropriate
(c) rapid release time, as appropriate"

Fourth, the implementation provisions in the TFA on special and differential treatment for developing countries are an attempt to find an innovative solution to the problem of uneven national capabilities in digital-based international trade facilitation.[32] The formula used in the TFA is based on a system of three categories of compliance with TFA deadlines, the third envisaging developing countries being considered for additional technical and financial assistance based on the applicant providing detailed identification of technical needs required to implement the TFA and independently securing sponsorship from a donor. The process is heavily bureaucratic and basically unworkable, with very few completed deals since the responsibility is shifted back on to the developing country via self-assessment.[33]

## Port development in logistics diplomacy

Port development has come to occupy a more significant position in economic statecraft, reflecting its central role in trade flows and geopolitical trade sources. It is a neglected area in the study of international relations and almost taken for granted by diplomatic practitioners. The scope is extensive, covering port acquisition, new routes, absorption of international rules, joint ventures, vessel design and other related areas. It draws in a wider range of actors in a representative and negotiating capacity to negotiate deals, finance and terms of partnerships than is traditionally understood as having responsibility for diplomacy. The methods used are standard ones of visit diplomacy, statements, negotiation and secret exchanges, but differ with high personal involvement at political, bureaucratic and company level, counter diplomacy and virtual absence of NGO or detailed domestic scrutiny backed by media support for projection and damage limitation. Maintaining and developing presence is a key function, which distinguishes port development diplomacy from other forms of diplomacy. Presence is evident in symbols – advertising, headquarters buildings, vessels, containers, news items, transportation services contracts. For example, the first vessel through the widened Panama Canal was the COSCO MV Panama, watched by a substantial crowd and global media.[34] The venue of an annual meeting, location of a signing ceremony for a major port project, or the port selection for inclusion on a cargo liner route are symbolically important.[35] These contribute to profile, construction of narratives and, above all, influence choice.

Presence is closely linked and dependent on the identification of opportunities (assessment of political and commercial scope, opportunities for government endorsement and negotiation of bilateral and other agreements). In this sense the requirement for success (or avoidance of failure) is higher in port development diplomacy than other types of diplomacy given frequently limited options.[36] Two further related features which distinguish port diplomacy are the use of counter diplomacy to block rivals or recover, and the use of defensive damage limitation methods to limit scrutiny or cover loss or decline.

## Port acquisition and infrastructure development

The increased importance of port development in economic statecraft is reflected in the national and regional diplomatic efforts to promote ports as part of bilateral relations (e.g. US–Vietnam),[37] revival of traditional ports (e.g. Morocco, Tanger Med 2),[38] regional forms of connectivity (ASEAN),[39] AfCFTA,[40] East Africa,[41] specialist ports, UK–Qatar gas trade,[42] Ghana,[43] new hubs (Piraeus, Durban) and transshipment ports (Kuantan, Vado).[44]

Many of the above developments followed the revival of shipping after the end of the international financial crisis in 2012.[45] The early model for global terminal operations was created by Dubai-headquartered DP World, actively pursuing the extension of its terminal operations globally.[46] Some of the difficulties associated with the takeover of foreign ports were foreshadowed in the controversy surrounding DP World's acquisition of six US terminals, which triggered opposition on national security grounds and lengthy domestic debate.[47] China drew on and expanded the DP World model with combinations of shipping, port construction, logistics, business park/economic zones and diplomatic functions.

The most striking of China's strategic port moves was the step-by-step acquisition of majority control of Piraeus port. It was a startling ingress, which established a platform for a multimodal bridge head at the heart of Europe's transport system, made possible during the Eurozone crisis by demands for privatisation of Greek assets as a condition for a European bail out. The fire sale of Greek assets enabled China to step up its earlier terminal holding at Piraeus (COSCO) to a majority equity control over Piraeus port.[48] As John A. Mathews noted on European policy:

> In a multipolar world there are limits to a strategy of imposing ideological driven austerity on a single country by squeezing its banks and enforcing fire sales privatisation.[49]

Piraeus subsequently formed a base for China's strategy of creating a central role in European transport via intermodal Euro–Asia land links and establishing shipping routes linking China via the Suez Canal and Italy–Greece.[50]

On ports, joint ventures are used with different combinations of equity, with the balance held by Chinese entities.[51] Concessions are generally for 30 years, with options for extension.[52] Finance is generally organised through the China Development Bank (CDB), special-purpose finance vehicles and channels for government financed contributions. Most do not involve a UN multilateral agency in the financing component. All the ports in this category are strategic ports in terms of location, linkage, impact on cargo delivery and the performance of neighbouring and other ports.

The rationale underlying port acquisition involves calculations of risk and advantage – deepwater feeder ports, e.g. Kuantan (east Malaysia), Vado Ligure (Italy) and Chancay (Peru) for geopolitical reach,[53] new ports, e.g. Lekki (Nigeria)[54] and corridor ports, e.g. Gwadar (Pakistan).[55] Risk is also illustrated by those ports which have moved into a borderline category of failing port, perhaps because of cargo uptake or decline in use. Examples of borderline ports include Kuantan (Malaysia) which has found it difficult to function as a major feeder port despite its proximity to the Gulf of Beibu (China).[56]

Despite their potential strategic locations, corridor ports are vulnerable to fail to attract in the set up or initial phases both cargo and shipping services. For example, Gwadar was selected in the China–Pakistan Economic Corridor framework (CPEC) as a corridor port, linking areas north of the Himalayas in a trade corridor to the coast of Gwadar. However, Gwadar's economically remote location from other Pakistan ports, and the fact that it is not on recognised shipping routes, limits opportunities to develop cargo and generate ship calls outside those potentially generated by other parts of the CPEC.[57]

In the final group of ports are borderline or failed projects. These include projects eventually cancelled (Melaka Gateway), altered through financial debt burden (Hambantota, Sri Lanka), commercial business park failure or loss of rationale (Chabahar, Gwadar).

## Geopolitical dimensions of port development

Piraeus has become a symbol of geopolitical tension over port acquisition, which continued through the progressive addition of linked subsidiary routes between Europe, Middle East and Asia. The dispute over Trieste port illustrated EU incremental policy failure and loss of strategic influence over European transport development. It underlined the inability of large regional actors to identify and respond quickly at a strategic level to critical moves by other logistics actors to acquire substantial stakes in port assets.

In the Trieste case, the Trieste–China MOU and related China Communications Construction Company (CCCC) agreement were intended to form the basis for China's European initiative. But European disquiet over Trieste and uncertainty among CCCC investors over Trieste's suitability (port depth and facilities) meant these agreements were not implemented. The Trieste option was later acquired for different objectives by the German logistics operator HHLA AG to develop Trieste as a sea-rail Adriatic hub.[58] The Italian government took the unusual step of withdrawing from the BRI.

The Trieste issues were not followed up by the EU and no further port-related counter diplomacy was carried out in response to COSCO's development of an alternative port at Vado Ligure as a new hub. It was a second European strategic error, following Piraeus, allowing the deepening of the logistic links to the Mediterranean, Middle East and Asia via Piraeus, Vado–Suez, using COSCO–APM port-terminal links.[59]

### Chabahar port: geopolitics

Competition over rival ports is illustrated in the India–China dispute over Chabahar port.[60]

Development of the port, located in Iran, was originally agreed between India and Iran, but was subsequently countered almost immediately by China in counter diplomacy with a $400bn, 25-year framework development deal which included Chabahar redevelopment. India revived ministerial talks with Iran using a window of opportunity provided by both the slowdown in the Chinese economy and Chinese over-extension on global projects to recapture some if its role.[61] But the project lost much of its rationale similar to Gwadar, as wider limitations on the BRI became apparent, on cost grounds and strategic relevance.

### Maritime cooperation agreements and logistics

Maritime cooperation agreements which contain logistics provisions fall into three broad categories: general cooperation agreements, special services and maritime security. All three categories have expanded, particularly logistics, security related agreements and service sectors because of factors such as supply chain breakdown, the Ukraine conflict and shifting levels of international tension.

The agencies and combinations of actors involved in concluding agreements have also become much more diverse. The line between diplomatic and commercial transactions has become blurred because of factors such as differing levels of government involvement in transportation and other maritime projects, regional authorities' external roles, the growth of SOEs and mixed consortia groups in port infrastructure, construction finance and logistics services. At bilateral level, digital trade-related agreements and innovation are more integrated into foreign policy and widely used to showcase innovation as part of dynamic and international e-commerce roles.[62]

Maritime cooperation agreements are used for several purposes: to establish a general bilateral or regional framework for regular dialogue on maritime issues,[63] open up new shipping routes,[64] promote trade,[65] protect trade access,[66] develop bilateral relations with neglected states[67] and foreign policy reorientation.[68]

## Memorandum of understanding

Agreements normally between two countries to develop maritime relations are often concluded in memorandum of understanding (MOU) format. It has the benefit of standardisation, relative simplicity and is an informal instrument making for ease of approval. MOUs are mainly concluded at interdepartmental or agency level. For example, the treaty framework for the China Belt and Road Initiative was created over a two-year period using a standard set of MOUs and cooperation agreements for speed and simplicity, and concluded with some 130 countries and 30 multilateral organisations.[69] The MOUs were part of the methods to showcase the project and give a sense of dynamic innovation and, above all, legitimacy. At a substantive level, however, it is notable that nearly all BRI projects have been concluded on a bilateral basis and have not involved multilateral institutions in finance or oversight.[70]

MOUs have traditionally been packaged as part of a bundle of agreements in leader visits to symbolise the content of bilateral relations. The implementation of the Belt and Road Initiative was unusual in the case of Trieste, because of location and level of visit, both showcasing presence and strategic challenge to the EU.

## Maritime security agreements

Maritime security agreements can be classified in three main areas: military logistics, routes and port access in conflicts. Military logistic agreements are a neglected but nonetheless important branch of diplomatic methods in the study of diplomacy. They generally cover reciprocal access to bases, logistics support, refuel supplies, repair, transport equipment, equipment for peacekeeping forces and humanitarian assistance operations.[71] Access to military weapons, ammunition and nuclear material is generally excluded.[72]

Military logistics agreements are symbols in bilateral and alliance relations. They are indicative of closeness and are highly valued in security and political terms. Conversely, to have requests for a reciprocal agreement avoided or turned down is not only a major security failure but also puts doubt over quality, scope and trust in bilateral relations.

Military logistics agreements are concluded as part of consolidating ongoing defence relations. They may also involve plans in alliances to improve interoperability, one of the most divisive aspects of alliance cooperation. Other reasons for military logistics agreements are their use as part of foreign policy orientation. Shifts to weapons supplies from an adversarial state may be part of an effort to signal changes in alliance relations or increase bargaining power.

A common reason for agreements is their use to gain geopolitical access. Djibouti provides China with a forward multipurpose commercial and advanced military base at the head of the Arabian Gulf, though the political and economic cost of this combination is high. For the US, Djibouti prompted added debate over the case for retraction in its role, especially from those commitments which have a very risk of pulling it into regional conflicts.[73]

A different set of reasons – greater international political presence, outlet for technology trade – shape India's aspirational foreign policy goal of securing recognition as an Arctic power. As part of that goal, considerable efforts were devoted without success to securing Russian agreement to defence logistic agreements, which would have opened up access to Russian Arctic bases and logistics facilities on the projected Northern Route.[74]

## Strategic routes in logistics diplomacy

Maintenance of the flow of trade on supply routes has been a traditional concern in foreign policy. How best to secure routes and continued access has become a more acute problem with the growth of supply chains, source dependence and spread of different types of threats to connectivity and supply chains. Issues have arisen over the arming of merchant vessels with "private" security guards on strategic routes, the limitations of intermediate oil storage agreements with petroleum states to offset long oceanic supply lines, and whether resort to bilateral or other trade deals or appeals to special allies are necessary or sufficient methods in supply crisis or global medical emergencies to offset threats to strategic routes.

The stability of South China Sea and Middle East strategic routes in particular present different difficulties over longstanding geopolitical claims (Taiwan, disputed offshore resources, naval base expansion).[75] These contrast with disputes involving the spill-over of regional conflict, Iran sanctions and threats to freedom of navigation from interdiction of oil supply routes such as the Strait of Hormuz.

For the US, the difficulty has been balancing pressure for retraction from its traditional global security role with selective military assistance to specific allies or partners. Bilateral maritime agreements covering logistics, infrastructure and supply chain security have increased with individual Middle East and Asia-Pacific states. For example, the US–Saudi defence equipment deal, which included supply of unmanned drone equipment for monitoring shipping in vulnerable straits, marked a major shift in the US approach.[76]


## *Port access in conflicts*

In regional conflicts, bordering and external states become involved in response to requests for transport, logistics for goods and support as a result of interdiction of supply routes, blockades and attacks on third country shipping. War risk premiums for shipping may become prohibitive, further extending the scope of conflict. For an alliance, the line between economic support and intervention is one of the blurred lines of risk, alongside decisions on weapons support and target use. The scope for diplomacy is narrow.

Partial agreements involving maritime links may break down because of unavailability of marine insurance, lack of suitable vessels or unwillingness of major carriers to redeploy shipping assets. Agreements may also serve quite divergent purposes for each party, with delay or diversion becoming apparent as implementation falters.

The Ukraine war illustrates a number of the difficulties associated with the use of logistics agreements in conflicts. For the EU, the Maritime Cooperation agreement with Ukraine and Moldova was part of signalling political support for Ukraine and a graduated economic response to the Russian blockade of Ukrainian Black Sea ports.[77] The agreement included provisions on mechanisms for maritime logistics and on a Danube economic corridor to facilitate inbound and outbound grain movement, which would significantly increase the level of risk and be unlikely to secure alliance agreement.

The second example, on the shipment of Ukrainian grain and related agricultural exports, illustrates the use of parallel negotiations to create a partial agreement constructed with two interlocking but contradictory agreements.

A temporary arrangement was reached on 22 July 2022 following UN and Turkish initiatives to allow exports of grain, related foodstuffs and fertiliser from specified Ukrainian ports subject to inspection, which lasted until Russian withdrawal on 17 July 2023.[78] The deal comprised two inter-related agreements: the first was negotiated by the IMO negotiating group on agreed products, routes and cargo inspection; the second, negotiated by UNCTAD,[79] provided for UN involvement in facilitating unimpeded exports of Russian food and fertiliser to world markets. These products would be excluded from sanctions or other measures on Russian products.[80]

The second UNCTAD negotiated agreement was a major concession which appeared to erode sanctions and provide multilateral recognition of Russian international trade in agricultural goods. Other limitations of the overall agreement stem from its construction as parallel diplomacy. Issues falling between the two sets of negotiations include detailed mechanisms for ensuring monitoring and compliance. The emergence of a dark Black Sea trade in grain, with unrecorded vessel movements, is a major area of difficulty.[81]

A second area concerns the critical omission of detailed provisions on cargo destination. In the debate on the grain export crisis, considerable emphasis had been placed on the impact of the crisis on food supplies for developing countries. This is perhaps because of the limited involvement of the FAO as an emergency food donor agency in the second set of negotiations led by UNCTAD and Turkey. The focal points of the first set (IMO group) of negotiations[82] were loading port designation, routes and inspection of vessels for weapons, topics falling within the IMO International Port and Ship Security (ISPS) Code,[83] rather than cargo destinations and end users.

## Development of methods in logistics diplomacy

Diplomatic methods used in logistics diplomacy have undergone several changes including the use of visit diplomacy, defence of interests, coordination of global transport services, negotiation and international regulation. Among the main changes in methods is the decline in the use of visit diplomacy as a result of factors such as the COVID-19 pandemic, reduction in diplomatic travel and shifts in supply chains.

In general, diplomatic travel has been curtailed as a method in promoting trade and political relations. Major deals and initiatives are often concluded and signed off at the headquarters of global NGOs rather than as part of a raft of MOUs presented at the end of a head of state visit, or as visit diplomacy, which is part of strategic power projection.

In terms of the coordination of shipping services, the role of shipping carriers has fundamentally changed, as a result of what services carriers offer and the closer coordination between two of the leading carriers. The shift of shipping groups into operating terminals as well as vessel services has received little comment, other than an anodyne reference in an annual report or paragraph in technical press, but is an ongoing development with widespread commercial and foreign policy repercussions.[84]

The major commercial implications of terminal acquisition affect choice and range of services, with regional and particularly smaller shipping lines and terminal operators squeezed out by principal operators and deployment of larger vessels. The foreign policy implications impact on national capacity, regional cooperation and national roles.[85]

For smaller powers, the impact of large fleet operator group expansion is similar to the earlier loss of national shipping lines fleets in the 1970s and 1980s. By the end of the 1980s, the maritime diplomatic agenda for smaller developing countries in the IMO shifted from national owner-ship to so-called capacity building and demands for seafarer training for developing country members. In the subsequent development of logis-tics, LDCs and other smaller logistics operators face loss of independence and absorption into corporate groupings.[86] Meanwhile, international institutions provide a continuing but distanced diplomatic narrative on technical projects and digital capacity building.[87]

## Soft power and influence in logistics diplomacy

The use of soft power in logistics diplomacy has tended to reduce the use of traditional methods such as visit diplomacy and MOUs. These have been replaced by greater use of mixed agreements involving government agencies, port operator authorities and finance consortia. The switch to soft power methods marked a major shift from traditional approaches. Central to these revised methods is decentralisation of government involvement, with greater reliance on soft power methods through SOEs, state-linked companies and mixed consortia of financial interests as pri-mary drivers.

The use of soft power is seen in other areas, for example, in diplomatic campaigns to secure nominations for heads of UN multilateral agencies such as WTO and less well known institutions such as UNIDO. Other trad-itional soft power methods in multilateral institutions use financial spon-sorship for environmental technical trials, investigations of accidents and technical assistance training. These are some of the central methods in the foreign policies of states which specialise in technical international diplomacy, such as Norway, Sweden, Finland, Germany, Japan, Singapore and the UK.[88]

The increased politicisation of multilateral institutions post-2012, following the end of the international financial crisis, has led to the devel-opment of additional soft power methods broadening the range of states involved in technical diplomacy to include states and other actors whose public foreign policy is predominantly concerned with operating as inter-national event organisers, PR facilitators and conference location hosts. In these cases, initiatives or host bids are more closely linked to particular issues and events rather than contributions to general funding or carrying out multilateral technical committee work, in order to maximise political benefit and media coverage.

Funding conferences or annual round table events, e.g. on LDC access to WTO[89] or Belt and Road forum[90] are now, for major and aspiring regional powers, low-cost methods of gaining profile, presence, distance from multilateral decision-making and, above all, avoiding exposure to political criticism and rule-making obligations. Convening or chairing a forum has the added advantage, particularly for a primary power, of gaining legitimacy for a project as well as serving, if necessary, as a platform for defusing or diverting criticism of financial or other implementation failures.

Soft power is used to build up external political capital and support, which may be needed in other contexts such as disputes to deflect criticism, building vote blocs in UN multilateral fora, or blocking international reports or proposals for investigative missions on matters considered within domestic jurisdiction or related to past events in armed conflict. This process is captured in the concept of transfer value; credit is gained which may be used in a different context.

Other indirect methods employed in soft power, such as trilateral diplomacy,[91] rely on using another partner or agency to front an initiative. Participation in trilateral diplomacy with other actors and multilateral institutions contributes to presence in a less visible manner. There may also be geopolitical advantages in some soft power initiatives in that a multilateral agency project may be used for bypassing the agenda of a regional institution, or detaching individual members to address bilaterally logistic, or other connectivity issues. For example, the China-funded research project in UNCTAD on ASEAN and SIDS connectivity[92] was a classic illustration of indirect diplomacy: providing a platform to bypass ASEAN, pursue follow-up bilateral meetings within the research report framework and geopolitical advantages in reinforcing its regional hegemonic role. Further benefits were achieved by extending the scope of the research project to small island developing states (SIDS). The SIDS portion of the project in effect became a small piece of long-range counter diplomacy in support of China's Pacific strategy of displacing United States, Australian and New Zealand regional influence in the Pacific.

At bilateral and plurilateral level, ad hoc conferences have developed as further methods for dealing with various supply chain crises and connectivity issues. At UN level, multilateral trade negotiations in WTO have become increasingly detached from bilateral and region level negotiations and exchanges on supply and connectivity questions. The lack of progress in WTO on a broad range of services negotiations has meant the WTO's role has been restricted to holding so-called dialogue conferences, as part of its mandate to promote international discussion.

Ad hoc arrangements can be divided into three categories: bilateral agreements on maritime cooperation (including logistics), ad hoc summit conferences on connectivity and alliance infrastructure. Ad hoc summit conferences include those called by regional organisations, e.g. ASEAN, CARICOM, EU.[93] In the ad hoc category of note is the Supply Chain Ministerial Forum (SCMF) crisis response group, the first of its kind, initiated by the United States, as an embryonic group of 18 members outside the UN multilateral framework, to address supply vulnerabilities, security and diversification of supply.[94] In response, the WTO deputy director general obliquely criticised the group's supply diversification objectives and called for enhanced multilateralism.[95]

How far the SCMF will develop as an international supply chain defence group is unclear, particularly in view of the absence of two of the lead cargo carriers and their respective governments from the forum. The overall emphasis of US policy has been mainly on internal measures relating to port efficiency in response to the logistics crisis. It has had to rely on maritime industry informal Shippers Councils on freight rate issues, rather than develop a lead global role on the broader logistic issues of carrier dependence and network services, liner availability and impact of ultra-large vessels, reflecting a lack of US-owned and flagged merchant vessels.[96]

Other ad hoc agreements have featured logistics as an additional dimension of diplomatic cooperation in connectivity and infrastructure agreements concluded by groupings and alliances. Examples of these are the EU–US trade and technology Council, Indo-Pacific Economic Framework and Americas Partnership for Economic Prosperity.[97] In response to the Belt and Road Initiative, the G7 agreed support for infrastructure projects.[98]

## Changes in diplomatic methods: managing risk and vulnerability

The differing way in which risk is handled and its importance in logistics diplomacy has had a major impact on changes in methods. Risk can be managed through four areas: composition of project group (finance, construction, implementation); contract terms; project redesign (revitalise business park, switch port to multimodal emphasis); and geographic refocus. As argued above, one of the important changes in methods has involved the broadening involvement of SOEs in logistics diplomacy. That aspect has been intensified in different ways. SOEs have become primary movers of deals, and that process has led to wider combinations of actors in financial consortia and port development.

The mix of an SOE and a large commercial terminal competitor was used by COSCO to extend its routes and acquire strategic presence. In the Vado Ligure port deal example, change of method was seen in the link up between COSCO and its competitor, APM terminals, in a joint venture to acquire holdings in the Italian port. As Port Technology noted succinctly: "APM terminal expands Chinese presence."[99]

The mix of actors is increasingly seen in lead SOE diplomacy to put together investor-manager groups for project finance, or additional consortia are formed for industrial parks backed onto port development. In Nigeria, the Lekki port development project had an unusual partner grouping, which drew in China Harbour Engineering Company (CHEC) with a Singapore conglomerate as a financial stakeholder and CGM, a leading European logistics company as port operator.[100]

Risk reduction is achieved in other areas, particularly port selection. Whilst some early port bids featured prominent ports for acquisition, many have tended to prefer relatively obscure or run-down locations. One example of the relative benefit of obscurity is the choice of Duisberg, at that point a little-known European inland backwater, for the end point of the Asia–Europe multimodal European terminus trade.[101]

Port selection facilitates project anonymity, helping to remove the project from domestic or international attention and reduce political exposure. Port selection is closely linked to media, to keep logistics as an opaque form of diplomacy in the background, typically using drip feed technical media reports on selected developments, projected timescales or first commercial vessel call photo-news, for high visibility impact.

Other significant classes of risk to supply chains arise from disruptions to strategic routes resulting from maritime accidents and political conflict. Limiting the impact of critical disruption from incidents such as the Ever Given six-day blockage of the Suez Canal, attacks on shipping in the Red Sea and other areas, as well as the impact of environmental factors on the Panama Canal and other strategic routes, have led to a variety of ad hoc meetings, summits and informal agreements.[102]

The long-term economic impact of incidents on freight rates has highlighted connectivity issues, the logistics gap for small and landlocked states and the ultimate concern of being written out of routes or isolated at the end of a logistics chain.[103] These factors have revived the debate over modernising the Liner Code Convention, with developing countries arguing for a multilateral conference to deal with logistics, instead of inappropriate foreign aid or technical assistance of benefit only to logistics carriers. They have also ensured that supply chain issues are a major element on the contemporary international agenda.[104]

## Implementation issues in logistics diplomacy

In logistics diplomacy, infrastructure projects generally take five to ten years to come on stream. The lengthy timescale from project concept to implementation tends to accentuate pressures to insulate the project and maintain high levels of secrecy around negotiations and operations in order to reduce vulnerability and possible commercial competition.

More than other forms of diplomacy, logistics negotiations and project implementation are highly vulnerable to external events, short-term financial crises and domestic economic factors in recipient states, deriving from loss of domestic output or inability to maintain high levels of debt repayment on infrastructure projects. Primary power donors may pause or scale back international commitments in response to domestic pressures, retraction from foreign commitments or international economic factors, as in the BRI projects. Large-scale projects are difficult to organise in loose western groupings.

In periods of long gaps or slow down before projects become operational, vulnerability to postponement or cancellation increases. Recipient states may find it difficult to respond to domestic pressure to break away from projects or terminate port concessions and reorientate because of debt pressure and lack of alternative public finance options. Recipient states move into a zone of high political security risk, e.g. Sri Lanka, Malaysia (Melaka Gateway). Alternative strategies based on switching contract partners introduces different risks for recipient states arising from lengthy international legal disputes over breaches of contract (Djibouti-DP World).[105] The Djibouti dispute had wider implications, influencing DP World to reposition its terminal strategies to focus on African gateway acquisitions in order to become a leading player in African hub logistics.[106]

## Negotiating mixes

Changes involving link-ups between leading competitor terminal operators and carriers, along with the composition of actors involved in consortia and finance groups (to mixes of SOEs, subsidiaries, affiliates and non-governmental players), have raised a number of issues concerning compatibility and conflict with other strands of foreign policy. The meshing of commercial interests potentially creates foreign policy difficulties in areas such as western sanctions, the Ukraine conflict, human rights, supply chain dependence and conflict over strategic goods.

The alliance between APM and COSCO over the acquisition of a stake in Vado port (Italy) helped extend China's wider European strategies and above all the creation of hubs to link the Middle East and Asia via Suez. The APM–COSCO link up had also wider transport services aspects with the tie-in to liner schedules operated on the EMA service giving an entry into US ports, nominally operated from Turkish ports (Iskenderun) to the United States but using COSCO vessels. The EMA service illustrates the expansion of transport mixes and connectivity link up.[107]

The closer meshing of economies between competitor and adversarial states impacts on the areas in which sanctions can be put in place and whether these extend to transportation services. In transport liner services, scheduled port start points give an entry option for the transportation of otherwise sanctioned goods and services.

Other effects of the expansion of terminal operators into other logistics services, including short sea shipping, can be seen with regards to impact on labour relations and crewing of ships and, indirectly, on foreign policy orientation. For example, the DP World acquisition of

UK short sea operator P+O led to crew replacement on commercial grounds of UK merchant navy officers and deck crew on P+O vessels by international crew on its ferry services.[108] This had a major impact on UK international orientation, part of which is based on an international maritime role through flag registration, maritime safety and regulation, survey and inspection, and active participation in IMO. It effectively removed a key shipping service as a training vehicle for UK officers and ratings, reducing considerably the ability to perform that role, with UK merchant navy officers becoming much scarcer, as also happened in the US.

### Finding the right mix of methods

Finding an appropriate mix of effective methods in response to issues arising in logistics is difficult for several reasons, including the continuing cross-meshing of economies discussed in the previous section. To be effective, counter diplomacy based on coordinated infrastructure projects requires high levels of economic and commercial intelligence, flexibility and sustained continuing follow up, rather than short-term responses.

Some methods such as summits are generally unsuited to dealing with logistics problems or threats, particularly if conducted between a single power and regional organisation. In this context, regional organisations are collections of competing interests, making shaping and implementing agreed policy on external economic threats difficult. For example, India attempted to engage ASEAN through on ASEAN–India Connectivity Summit to counter Chinese economic influence in Asia by setting up a special fund for ASEAN digital and physical connectivity with India. The idea never really advanced and gradually faded, given the differences of linkages between individual members and China.

The use of counter diplomacy by an alliance or grouping based on infrastructure logistics projects is a particularly difficult form of counter diplomacy suited more to non-democratic systems.

## Conclusion

The transportation of goods and operation of related services has become an increasingly important branch of diplomacy. Logistics has introduced a wider range of actors and pushes the boundaries of traditional conceptions of diplomacy. A central feature of logistics is the tension between global commercial operations and the development of multilateral cooperation and regulation.

Much of logistics diplomacy is conducted at a bilateral, small group or regional level on transport agreements, defence of strategic routes, developing ports and intermodal connectivity. Two factors in particular have altered the place of logistics from mainly a commercial activity: port acquisition as projections of state commercial power and geopolitical strategic factors.

The wider multilateral issues of distribution of routes and suspension of services, logistics gaps, breakdown of critical routes or supply chains remain areas of limited or little international agreement. The emphasis of multilateral diplomacy is on documentary and technical trade facilitation rather than logistics.

At a commercial level, the concentration of logistics carriers in the container sector centres around five company groups (Maersk, MSC, CMA CGM, COSCO and Hapag-Lloyd) with over 60% of the market share. This is a major factor in the dominance of commercial considerations at the expense of redistributive multilateral cooperation. Closing the gap remains a challenge.

At a multilateral level, the international institutional landscape is fragmented. UNCTAD was originally intended as a lead multilateral agency on development and shipping, promoting liner conferences and commodity agreements but its role subsequently declined, with the breakdown of liner transport agreements, to one of technical assistance and statistical reports. Other UN agencies, including IMO, FAO, ILO, along with the World Customs Organisation (WCO) retain specialist sectoral roles but operate as self-contained agencies, with varying phases and degrees of collaboration.

Institutional fragmentation limits regulatory development, as does the absence of the primary powers from regulatory driver groups in multilateral logistics diplomacy. In particular, the lack of a significant US all-sector merchant service is a major deficiency in US global power assets. Innovation in international regulation is limited or stifled, over issues such as commitments to retain critical port operations in global pandemics or supply disruption.

As regards changes in methods in logistics diplomacy, significant developments have occurred in five areas. Traditional methods have relied on visit diplomacy to promote, revive projects, protect interests or seal deals. Foreign ministers are now used more in a roving envoy role, including more extensive trade initiatives. Heads of SOEs have assumed a much more prominent international role. A related change is in the increased use of inbound official visits to the headquarters of an SOE or inbound official visit to formalise or promote a new deal.

The intensification of the role of governments in port operations or acquisition has underlined the importance of port strategies in external policy, commercial intelligence and the need to constantly monitor categories of strategic assets. These additional functions and organisational challenges raise major issues for external policy management with regard to the role of the foreign ministry, even in its reformed economic role, in port and logistics diplomacy.

Responsibility for these issues in most cases tends to involve unsatisfactory boundaries between several ministries. States with substantial oceanic interests require modernised maritime departments, linked closely to business, security and intelligence, with primary responsibility for issues in this area.

## Notes

1 Overviews of international maritime transport developments can be found in UNCTAD Review of Maritime Transport. Other useful review sources are publications of the International Chamber of Shipping Maritime (ICS) and individual chartered bodies. For a summary of the debate over the limits of multilateral governance, see Bernard Hoekman's essential article (World Bank) "A 21st Century Trade Agenda: Global Supply Chains and Logistics Services" at www.wto.org/english/forums_e/public_forum12_e/art_ pf12_e/ art5.htm. Transport issues are dealt with by several international institutions including IMO, WTO, UNCTAD, World Bank, ILO, FAO and WCO. In IMO trade facilitation, aspects of logistics are dealt with by the FAL committee (see www.imo.org/en/OurWork/Facilitation/Pages/FALCommitee-default. aspx#:~:text=The%20Facilitation%20Committee%20(FAL)%20deals,pers ons%20and%20cargo%20from%20ports.) whilst a useful summary of the documentation of other committees can be found on the IMO website (access IMO library for specific aspects).
2 For details of discussion in international institutions on supply chains, see establishment of the Global Supply Chain Forum, inaugurated in Barbados: https://unctad.org/conference/global-supply-chain-forum-2024.
3 Transport and Trade Facilitation News Letter, No 89, UNCTAD, para 73.
4 On the failure to treat facilitation and logistics in a holistic manner, see Bernard Hoekman, note 1.
5 See "Trade Facilitation-Impossible Without Facilitating Logistics", session 21, WTO Forum Trade Facilitation, 25 September 2008, presentation by Simon Bennett, Secretary, International Chamber of Shipping (ICS). The session included presentations by core NGO and INGOs – International Federation of Freight Forwarders Associations (FIATA), Global Express Association (GEA) International Chamber of Shipping (ICS) and the International Road Transport Union (IRU).
6 See nowthatslogistics.com.
7 www.gov.uk/government/collections/uk-singapore-digital-economy-agreem ent for the UK–Singapore agreement.
8 See UNCTAD annual review of maritime transport in: https://unctad.org/topic/transport-and-trade-logistics/review-of-maritime-transport.
9 The US nominally enters the top five by fleet commercial value because of the high number of cruise ships and other passenger vessels. UNCTAD Review of Maritime Transport, 2023, p35, table 2.3.

10 UNCTAD Review of Maritime Transport, 2023, p33, table 2.4.

11 See chapter 5.

12 Liberia, Panama and Marshall Islands vessels inspected in the Paris Memorandum (PMOU) area had deficiencies of 51, 60 and 49% respectively. Panama is listed in ships detained per flag exceeding the average percentage at 6.9% as a percentage of ships detained (number of inspections 1,830). The PMOU was set up 1982 as a marine safety inspection organisation and became the leading model of functional cooperation on maritime safety. The PMOU inspection area includes Belgium, Canada, Greece, Ireland, Italy, Malta, Netherlands, Poland, Spain, UK, Norway, Russian Federation, Romania, Germany, Denmark and Portugal. See PMOU Annual Report 2021, p37 and p41.

13 Relatively few US-flagged vessels operate in the PMOU area. Of 46 US flagged ships inspected, 26 had non-detainable deficiencies and were not detained. See PMOU Annual Report 2023, p26.

14 A.P. Møller, founded in 1904. See also on other Scandinavian entrepreneurs (Norway), Erling D. Naess, *Autobiography of a Shipping Man* (Sea Trade Publications, 1977) esp. chapter 16 on the formation of the Naess Group and chapter 37 on the International Tanker Owners' Federation for the international role in shipping regulation of the major carriers.

15 See www.marinedealnews.com/the-changing-nature-of-ship-ownership-in-turkey/.

16 Maersk had over 600 vessels owned or under charter in 2024. See Moody's Investor Service, A.P. Møller-Maersk A/S, 23 February 2024.

17 Review of Maritime Transport, UNCTAD, 2019, p47.

18 See Review of Maritime Transport, ibid., p18 for leading 20 global container ports. Nine of the top 20 container ports measure by container units were in China.

19 See www.joc.com/special-topics/top-40-container-carriers.

20 See https://container-news.com/dp-world-southampton-connects-central-america-with-new-service/.

21 Jonathan Holslag, *The Silk Road Trap*, Polity (2019) pp96–108.

22 See Hoekman, note 1.

23 Agreement on Trade Facilitation, Protocol Amending the Marrakesh Agreement Establishing the World Trade Organisation, WT/L/940, 28 November 2014, Section III, article 23.

24 See "Maritime connectivity: countries vie for positions" at https://unctad.org/news/maritime-connectivity-countries-vie-positions, UNCTAD, 17July 2019.

25 Agreement on Trade Facilitation, WT/L/490, 28 November 2014.

26 IMO FAL Committee, 9–13 May 2022.The entry into force date for the strategic workers amendment was 2024.

27 See WTO Trade Facilitation Agreement, https://wto.org/tradefacilitation#:~:text=WTO%20members%20concluded%20negotiations%20at,thirds%20of%20the%20WTO%20membership.

28 The failure to agree a collective maritime services agreement after WTO Services negotiations were resumed in 2000 resulted in WTO members using two different lists for classifying categories of services for tariffs and exemptions: the Services Sectoral Classification List (W/120). For further details of W/120, see www.wto.org/english/tratop_e/serv_e/guide1_e.htm.

29 TFA, op. cit., article 6.1.

30 TFA, ibid., article 6, footnote 6.

31 TFA, op. cit., article 7.3.

32 For a valuable survey of international transport agreements and trade facilitation, see the ECLAC transport research studies, including the report of Azhar Jaimurzina, "The future of trade and transport facilitation: Implications of the WTO Trade Facilitation Agreement", FAL Bulletin, Issue No 333/5, July 2014.

33 Out of 63 eligible states only 15 have notified arrangements in place. See WTO TFA database, https://tfadatabase.org/en/notifications/implementation/glo bal-status. The TFA entered into force in 2017.

34 www.theatlantic.com/news/archive/2016/06/panama-canal/488924/.

35 https://port.today/apm-terminals-expands-chinese-partnerships-in-italy/; www.apmterminals.com/en/vado-ligure/about/news/2022/220701-new-vado-express-service.

36 See Yanis Varoufakis, *Adults in the Room: My Battle with Europe's Deep Establishment* (Vintage, 2018) pp313–4, on limited Greek options.

37 US–Vietnam Maritime Cooperation Agreement, 3 October 2018. For the records of the US–Vietnamese consultations at Washington DC in 2019, see Agreed Minutes of US–Vietnam Maritime Bilateral Discussions, I July 2019.

38 For the development of Tanger Med as a leading port for African trade and its wider international operations see the annual reports of UNCTAD maritime review: https://unctad.org/press-material/review-maritime-transport-2023-facts-and-figures-africa#:~:text=Tanger%20Med%20port%20strengthened%20its, to%20about%2040%20African%20ports.

39 UNCTAD "Analysis of maritime connectivity in ASEAN and Small Island Developing States" (SIDS), draft, 24 May 2022.

40 See Arkebe Oqubay, "African industrial hubs and industrialisation: diversity, unevenness and strategic approach", Transnational Corporations, vol. 29, no 1, 2022, pp1–40.

41 Shippers Council of Eastern Africa.

42 www.gov.uk. Qatar agreement, 24 May 2022.

43 Africa Ports and Ships, 26 June 2022, pp7–8.

44 www.apmterminals.com/vado-ligure.

45 UNCTAD, Review of Maritime Transport 2015.

46 DP World returned to full state ownership on 16 February 2020.

47 DP World agreed in view of opposition in the US to withdraw its acquisition subject to financial return of costs. *The Guardian*, 10 March 2006.

48 See www.ftm.eu/articles/chinese-privatisation-greek-piraeus-port#:~:text= In%202016%2C%20the%20fund%20sold,an%20additional%2088%2.

49 John A. Mathews, Asia Pacific Journal, vol. 15, no 3, 2017. https://apjjf.org/wp-content/uploads/2023/11/article-1390.pdf.

50 See www.apmterminals.com. For Vado Ligure, see www.apmterminals.com/en/scct/media/news/2022/220701-new-vado-expr ess-service. The express service links Vado Ligure and Port Said East on the Suez Canal.

51 See https://lekkiport.com.

52 maukerja.my/en/company/158372-kuantan-port-consortium-sq-bhd.

53 Global Construction Review, 5 August 2022.

54 Lekki deepwater port project in Nigeria completed phase 1 in 2022 at a cost of $1.5 billion on a 45-year build and operate lease, involving Singapore (Tolaram Group), China Harbour Engineering and China Development Bank. There is

a range of financial and operating partners with the port managed by CMA-CGM Lekki Free Port Terminal, in a complex, blended and multilayered project. See on financing sections of the project, www.templars-law.com/news/templars-advises-project-sponsors-on-a-us629-million-project-financing-for-the-lekki-deep-sea-port-project/#:~:text=Lekki%20Port%20LFTZ%20Enterprise%20Limited,Chinese%20giant%2C%20China%20Harbour%20Engineering.

55 www.gwadarport.gov.pk.

56 See www.iaphworldports.org/memberports/kuantan-port-authority.

57 On Gwadar cargo uptake, see www.marinetraffic.com/aisdetails>ports.

58 Hamburger Hafen und Logistik AG (HHLA) acquired a majority stake in Piattaforma Logistica di Trieste in January 2021, developing it as a sea-rail Baltic, Adriatic and Mediterranean network. See www.hhla-plt.it.

59 www.port of genoa.com/en.

60 www.usiofindia.org/strategic-perspective/strategic-implications-of-chabahar-port.html.

61 The Indian role in Chabahar was revived at the visit of the Indian Trade Minister to Tehran in June 2022. *Business Standard*, 9 June 2022.

62 www.wionews.com/world/what-is-the-real-story-behind-chinas-400-billion-deal-with-iran-374134.

63 US maritime bilateral agreements have been concluded with Brazil, Korea, Russia, Japan, Philippines, Panama, Norway, EU. Other informal agreements include US–Taiwan. See www.maritime.dot.gov/economic-security/international-agreements#:~:text=The%20U.S.%20conducts%20bilateral%20maritime,not%20impair%20U.S.%20market%20access.

64 See www.porttechnology.org/news/nigerias-1-6-billion-lekki-port-nears-completion/ for implications of Lekki development for West African and other African ports. For further illustrations of routes and costs see www.icontainers.com/ship-container/africa. For niche route development see Zim ro-ro vehicle carrier service China–Italy (Trieste), metrans.en/new-weekly-connection-between-terminal-in-trieste-and-central-and-eastern-europe.

65 See US–Vietnam Maritime Bilateral Agreement 3 October 2018; agreed minutes US–Vietnam Bilateral Discussions, 1 July 2019.

66 Djibouti–Saudi Arabia Transport Agreement, 24 June 2022. The agreement reinforced Saudi Arabia's shipping and trade interests vis-à-vis Djibouti port. *Arab News*, 11 September 2022.

67 Kenya concluded ten agreements, including maritime cooperation, during the visit of President Uhuru Kenyatta to the Seychelles on 18 July 2022. The visit was the first by a Kenyan head of state to the islands.

68 Limited progress was made by Pakistan Prime Minister Sharif in reviving Pakistan–China relations, the Gwardar project and institutions dealing with CPEC. China's reluctant attitude was shaped by the diminishing importance of Gwardar, Pakistan internal economic and project security factors,  and support costs of competing BRI projects.

69 For the MOU between People's Republic of China and ADB, AIIB, EBRD, EIB, NDB and World Bank Group, 14 May 2017 see www.ndb.int/uploads/ 2018/ 09/MOU.

70 For World Bank defensive briefing on its links to the BRI, see https://openknowledge.worldbank.org/entities/publication/59486f09-600d-579e-b252-b2d5d06b88d6.

71 See Government of Japan and Government of India Concerning Reciprocal Provision of Supplies and Services, 9 September 2020, Article 1(b). www.mofa. go.jp/files/100091751.pdf.

72 See ibid., article 2 (3); also United States–Norway Defense Cooperation Agreement, 17 June 2022 (TIAS 22-617).

73 cfr.org/china-digital-silk-road.

74 *Hindustan Times,* 1 December 2021.

75 See https://news.un.org/en/story/2024/01/1145267es; see also https://unc tad.org/global-crisis/black-sea-initiativeurity Council Resolution S/RES/2722 (2024).

76 The Jeddah Communique: A Joint Statement between the United States and the Kingdom of Saudi Arabia, 15 July 2022.

77 https://news.un.org/focus/Ukraine.

78 The IMO Task force, including Martin Griffiths, UN Under-Secretary-General, dealt with shipments of Ukrainian grain through the Black Sea. See UN Secretary-General's remarks on signing the Black Sea Grain Initiative.

79 Secretary-General's remarks on signing the Black Sea Grain Initiative, 22 July 2022. www.un.org/sg/en/content/sg/speeches/2022-07-22/secretary-gener als-remarks-signing-of-black-sea-grain-initiative#:~:text=Ladies%20and%20 Gentlemen%2C,who%20helped%20make%20it%20happen.

80 See paragraph 2 in MOU between the Russian Federation and the UN in https://unctad.org/global-crisis/black-sea-initiative.

81 Lloyd's List, 21 June 2022.

82 R.P. Barston, *Modern Diplomacy* 5th ed. (Routledge, 2019) pp66–8.

83 International Port and Ship Code (ISPS Code) IMO (2003).

84 See UNCTAD Maritime Transport 2023, p29.

85 See, for example, DP World's expansion into terminals, including acquisition of Imperial, a South African major logistics terminal operator, www.dpworld.com/news/releases/dp-world-to-acquire-imperial South Africa. See also note 108.

86 https://theafricalogistics.com/2022/01/dp-world-boosts-logistics-in-sene gal-with-construction-of-port-of-ndayane/; www.thenationalnews.com/busin ess/dp-world-close-to-finalising-agreements-on-construction-of-new-port-and-economic-zone-in-senegal-1.976487.

87 See, for example, https://unctad.org/system/files/information-document/ ccpb_IGECOMP2023_PROG_Tech_Assist_Cap_Building_en_6.pdf.

88 Norway and Antigua–Barbuda bilateral agreement to trial single-window logis-tics documentation for SIDS, 8 April 2019–23, IMO.

89 www.wto.org/french/thewto_f/acc_f /g/_f.htm; wto.org/the wto/acc_e/ pillar1_e.

90 www.beltandroadforum.org/english/.

91 See chapter 5 on trilateral diplomacy and donor agendas.

92 "Analysis of Maritime Connectivity in ASEAN and Pacific Island Small States." See https://unctad.org/publication/analysis-maritime-connectivity-associat ion-southeast-asian-nations-and-small-island.

93 Chairman's statement 38th and 39th ASEAN summits, 26 October 2021. https:// asean.org/wp-content/uploads/2021/10/FINAL-Chairmans-Statement-of-the-38th-and-39th-ASEAN-Summits-26-Oct. pdf.

94 Office of the Spokesperson, media note, 20 July 2022, joint statement on Cooperation on Global Supply Chains.

95 For the WTO position opposing diversification and promoting supply chains, see "WTO offers unique forum for dialogue on global supply chains" www.wto.org/english/news_e/news22_e/miwi_21mar22_e.htm#:~:text=In%20her%20remarks%20to%20the,the%20production%20and%20distribution%20of.

96 See Journal of Commerce for US perspectives on logistics developments. https://www.joc.com>maritime.

97 state.gov/supply-chain-ministerial, 19 July 2022.

98 G7 Summit communique 26–8 June 2022, Schloss Elmau, Partnership for Global Infrastructure and Investment.

99 "APM Terminals Expands Chinese Partnerships in Italy". port.today, 18 October 2016, https://port.today/apm-terminals-expands-chinese-partnerships-in-italy/.

100 www.lekkiport.com/project-partners.

101 Annual report of the Duisport Group, www.duisport.de/pressemeldungen/publikationen/?lang=en_.

102 www.bbc.co.uk/news/business-56559073.

103 Bhagya Senaratne and Germana Nicklin, "Maritime Connections between New Zealand and Sri Lanka: Connected by Empire, Separated by Distance", National Security Journal, 1 May 2022, pp1–24.

104 See, for example, the supply chain forum at WTO and the UNCTAD Global Supply Chain Forum (note 2).

105 www.seatrade-maritime.com/ports/dp-wo.

106 See https://theafricalogistics.com/2022/02/dp-world-set-to-acquire-south-africas-imperial-logistics/.

107 "New vessel service connects Port of Vado Ligure with US ports", 21 September 2021. See www.porttechnology.org/news/new-vessel-service-connects-port-of-vado-ligure-with-us-ports/#:~:text=The%20first%20of%20a%20new, sea%20terminal%20on%2018%20September.

108 For the dispute over Saudi invitation to attend the London Investment Summit (2024 ) in view of the P+O Crewing  redundancy issues and Saudi financial stake in the London Gateway port .I, 15 October 2024. www.itfseafarers.org/newspo-sacking.

# Chapter 10

# An alternative architecture

## Introduction

Diplomacy involves choices over different approaches and courses of action. The decline of multilateralism, which had been one of the central approaches underpinning post-cold war order, opened up a governance gap, which has been progressively filled by the creation of an alternative order to multilateralism.[1]

Sustaining consensus for the collective action essential for multilateralism requires constant adjustment, concessions and innovation.[2] In contrast to strategies which drive consensus, restrictive strategies seek to limit the scope and pace of multilateralism. The boundaries of consensus may be cut back by strategies to reduce agendas, water down obligations, create exceptions and phase outs.[3] Nominal participation in collective action is obscured by apparent activism, projected through carefully timed statements, media releases on show projects, hosting conferences and participation in side events.[4] Conversely, the race to become the first state to sign or ratify a convention, common to all multilateral agreements, has been incorporated as a method for isolating and putting pressure on an opponent, by inferring that non-signature or ratification reflects poor track record, or lack of international commitment.[5] In these instances, early acceptance by a traditionally slow ratifying primary power may ultimately discourage participation by others or be used as counter diplomacy to question the intent and purposes of an agreement. A multilateral agreement may in effect become a plurilateral or small group instrument seen as of benefit only to larger powers or blocs.

The impact of the above factors is seen in four critical areas: declining use of multilateral methods, over-reliance on voluntary based long-range goals (MDG), limited progress in new agreements on core areas (climate, global development-based trade rules, resources, supply chain logistics), less recourse to UN peacekeeping and preventive diplomacy, and institutional fragmentation. Fragmentation of the international system is seen in areas such as the increasing compartmentalisation or detachment of

DOI: 10.4324/9781003204039-11

multilateral agencies, preference for non-multilateral methods including unilateral initiatives, bilateral and small group, high ambition alliances and geoeconomic shifts in foreign direct investment, and financial support to allied countries rather than wider or global safety net funding.[6]

The decline of multilateralism has shaped the scope of agreements by limiting obligations and precluding deep international commitments. Linking the above are two important additional factors: the loss of states or other actors committed to acting as regulatory initiators and drivers of reform which characterised pre-2000 diplomacy, and the effects on international order of changing levels of regional crisis and hostility between primary powers reducing their engagement in core regulatory processes.

## Alternative architecture

Alternative institutions are found in several areas of international relations, in which rival institutions or structures have been created in response to dissatisfaction with existing arrangements or as part of strategies of building up influence. In a diplomatic context, fragmentation is illustrated by rival sectoral programmes such as the World Food Programme, set up by a small group of powers, separate from FAO activities, to provide food aid to selected states.[7] At regional level, the creation of security groupings such as the Quad, or trade blocs such as RCEP and CPTPP have been part of the increasing splintering of the international system. In other areas of international relations, such as hosting sporting events, the growth of competing events and leagues in football, cricket, golf and motor racing are commercially driven but many have a political and diplomatic component. Event states use diplomatic and commercial channels to monitor opportunities, step in with bids, lobby and promote international presence.[8] Creating alternative institutions and events may also be a part of foreign policy reorientation to rebuild damaged political profiles, shift emphasis, or signal movement away from traditional links to create balance or hedge relations.

The term "alternative architecture" is used in this study to refer to the structure which emerged following the international financial crisis (2008–12), which is built around the Asian Infrastructure Investment Bank (AIIB), expanded Shanghai Cooperation Organisation (SCO), residual multilateral links and dark trade as a different framework to the existing multilateral order. It is not detached but exists alongside UN institutions and other institutions and procedures which constitute the contemporary multilateral system. The residual multilateral component is retained for three purposes: to acquire legitimacy, access to technical expertise and for supplementary financial resources using joint initiatives.

Although presented as multilateral or non-competitive, the essence of an alternative architecture is that it offers membership which is separate and of more value than that offered by multilateral organisations and agencies. It avoids the stigma of loan conditionality and offers indifference or minimal attention to domestic political structures and rule of law-style critiques associated with frameworks such as EU, G7 or G20.[9] It is an avenue for access to finance and the kudos of being part of a new developing order.

The long-term intention is to create separate institutions from current multilateral arrangements which can become alternative global hubs for trade and technical cooperation, accessing finance for development projects, commodities supply, port and logistical connectivity and cooperation with other like-minded actors. The outsider element is evident in cooperation over sanctions evasion, shipping transportation and commodity trades.

The underlying strategies are distinctive in that they rely heavily on flexibility, rapid exploitation of opportunities and constant re-evaluation of agendas and areas for building presence and influence. Rapid recovery narratives and initiatives in the event of reversals are also pieces in the ebb and flow of short-term moves and wider grand strategies.

Alternative architecture is distinguished by four indicators: creation of new alternative institutions, breakup of traditional groupings, dark trade and parallel diplomacy in conflicts.

## Development of an alternative architecture post-international financial crisis

A new alterative architecture challenging the multilateral international order emerged in the period of reorganisation and recovery following the international financial crisis (2008–12). Diplomatic methods evolved to take in the creation of new multilateral financial institutions, move away from traditional multilateral institutions and longstanding political and security relations to explore other structures. The institutional changes were not sudden or dramatic but, at least in the beginning, were technical and regional in nature. Nor were they all successful. Among the institutional changes were a new Asian development bank – Asian Infrastructure Investment Bank (AIIB) – which would focus on raising finance for regional infrastructure projects.[10] That a new regional development bank seemed necessary was influenced not merely by the vulnerabilities of the contemporary Bretton Woods international financial system, but by the failure to achieve sufficient reform of the institutions making up the international financial system to fully reflect changes in the relative financial and trade power of primary actors. It remains debatable, however, whether reform methods such as changes in IMF quotas and voting rights would have been sufficient enough to prevent China from moving onto a course which, in practice, was increasingly outside the Bretton Woods multilateral system.[11]

The IMF and G20 coordinated response to the international financial crisis, which included financial commitments from all major actors, was possibly the last major collective financial effort of its type, without a return to greater primary power cooperation.[12]

The extent of China's shift from multilateral institutions was blurred by the AIIB strategy of concluding multiple MOU cooperation agreements with existing multilateral development banks in order to nominally lessen the divergence and disguise the latent competitive elements. Doors were not closed but the new alternative architecture was sufficiently robust and politically independent to cope with shifts in primary power relations.

The fall out of the international financial crisis and the subsequent European financial bailout crisis provided context and rationale for new enterprises. In response to the perceived need for alternative approaches and financial lending, the BRICS created the New Development Bank (NDB), in parallel diplomacy to the multilateral institutions. The Chinese Minister of Finance, Lou Jiwei, commented at the launch of the NDB on the rigid and slow approach of existing multilateral institutions that "there is no such thing as best practice…but the NDB emphasis on development finance would be the next practice."[13]

The aim was for the NDB to become the premier lending institution for emerging economies and developing countries, complementary, but sufficiently separate, from existing UN multilateral or regional arrangements.[14]

Alongside this, the AIIB was a separate Chinese initiative announced shortly after the NDB, for an Asian infrastructure investment bank initially linked to the BRI as well as other infrastructure projects. Two such development bank initiatives, in many respects similar, would inevitably involve duplication and user uncertainty over which to identify with.

Within a very short period the AIIB moved from its initial regional and BRI mode into that of an embryonic global bank, potentially challenging the World Bank Group, Asian Development Bank and overshadowing the NDB. The NDB as part of BRICS made little progress in its first five years of operation. Creating a capital base from the very different economies of its five members made slow progress in difficult negotiations for a Contingent Reserve Arrangement (CRA), which foreshadowed later internal difficulties over the philosophy and management of the bank on issues such as types of loans.[15]

An ongoing core difficulty for the NDB was over its future membership. Expansion was opposed by the Russian Federation at meetings of NDB finance ministers and procedural obstacles over membership were used to slow down the process of admitting new members.[16] Expansion of membership raised the possibility of loss of influence in a five-member grouping, which the Russian Federation preferred to see undertake only very limited expansion and remain a small, restricted club. No new members were admitted in the first phase exploratory negotiations (2014–7), which were subsequently discontinued and later replaced by ad hoc initiatives.

Apart from membership issues, the growth of the NDB in the early period was affected by several clashes and crises involving BRICS members (e.g. India–China clashes in the Himalayas, sanctions on Russia over Crimea and the Ukraine war) which limited cooperation but also underlined the political weakness and image of the BRICS as an international development actor.

Paulo Nogueira Batista notes of the NDB five years on:

> An ambitious and expensive plan of creating an MDB of global reach had petered out into a five- member bank that basically receives capital from its members, makes small disbursements, pays staff and operational expenditures and deposits excess resources in well-reputed financial institutions and other safe and low-return venues.[17]

Whilst the NDB increased its membership in resumed negotiations as restrictions were intermittently removed, it has remained more limited in reach and influence than the AIIB.[18]

## The AIIB: a key part of an alternative architecture

The AIIB was initially depicted in public briefing narratives as a new organisation, feeling its way in a complex world.[19] In practice, its development suggested otherwise, with China as lead within the bank exercising discreet power. As a unilateral initiative, the AIIB had the advantage of escaping many of the BRICS limitations.

There were a number of indications which suggested that the intentions of the AIIB were to operate as a new leading global entity in line with its goals in its strategy plan.[20] The organisational style of the AIIB was that of a polished private commercial bank, headquartered in Beijing but with a mixed international strategic management staff,[21] glossy PR with regular bulletins on activities and rotating annual meetings in member locations.[22]

The strategy for internationalising the AIIB relied on four critical elements: financial legitimacy, political presence, international membership, and flexible and opaque decision-making to facilitate speedy response. Legitimacy was acquired by securing MOUs with primary development bank groups and international credit agency ratings. The conclusion of a general cooperation agreement with the World Bank was a key element in underpinning the international legitimacy of the AIIB.[23] That point became clear when a subsequent China–World Bank general MOU on cooperation with respect to the BRI was the subject of extensive criticism on why the World Bank was seemingly involved in the BRI negotiations.

It was sufficiently critical for the IBRD to issue defensive briefing in the form of a frequent questions section on its website.[24] The AIIB narrative subsequently shifted from BRI to mission statements on cooperation, sustainable social development and green infrastructure.

The second element in the AIIB strategy to acquire international financial legitimacy placed emphasis on acquiring triple A credit rating. The drafting in the Bank prospectus references the importance of rule of law, project management schedules, transparency and adopting World Bank environment impact and related procedures. These were later grouped in a slogan "lean, clean and green," and became critical in contributing to suggestions of well-ordered international practice. The AIIB gained triple A rating, unlike the NDB.[25]

Several methods were used to project the international presence of the bank including the rotation of annual AIIB meetings. Seeking observer status at the UN General Assembly[26] was a route pursued by both the NDB and AIIB. For the NDB it seemed a way of adding presence to its generally low key approach. The fit was much better for the AIIB, with its polished style and international approach, giving the AIIB a wide arena for contacts, meeting representatives of potential applicants and visibility. It also gave the AIIB a sense of the political agenda and calendar of multilateral institutions. The international financial presence of the bank was extended with an agreement for an overseas office within the UAE in Abu Dhabi, marking a quiet but significant shift in its orientation and operations.[27] By 2023, the AIIB had over 106 members, making it one of the largest development banks outside the World Bank Group.[28]

The AIIB was distinctive from traditional development banks in that it did not follow an all-projects approach used by most existing multilateral development banks (MDBs). A narrow emphasis focused on infrastructure and related projects with strict criteria on selection, scale and risk. Assessments of the financial viability of a proposal featured highly in the selective approach to projects. Projects were strictly assessed and monitored for compliance with financial feasibility criteria, assumptions about completion, social value and financial return. The cover narrative was connectivity, inter-regional development and sustainable green infrastructure projects. Most projects were chosen for small-scale funding opportunities rather than traditional mega infrastructure projects and were subsequently used as showcase examples of the work of the AIIB.[29] The loan distribution map gives an indication of the carefully selected spread of the bank: Turkey, Cook Islands, India, Bangladesh and Argentina.[30]

The orientation of the AIIB altered relatively quickly away from BRI to small projects linked to inter-regional connectivity, infrastructure and greening in part to counter negative perceptions of the bank as merely another vehicle for BRI. Sovereign and non-sovereign lending for port and infrastructure related to BRI projects (e.g. Brazil, Oman, Bangladesh) are channelled mainly through the NDB,[31] with some limited exceptions such as the Omani port of Duqm and so-called "dry" inland logistics hubs which are financed via AIIB loans.[32]

The AIIB has moved quickly and pragmatically on these and similar issues. In this respect it has been aided by an opaque, well-managed decision-making process, which has avoided the more cumbersome aspects of traditional multilateral banks.

The bank has been able to develop its portfolio and rapidly exploit opportunities such as digitisation, projects or cooperation with different financial actors.[33] As a development bank, maintaining a blue-chip image requires constant tracking of international banking regulation, cooperation with G20 and other financial institutions. Cooperation with the World Bank was further developed by the AIIB through the creation of a Multi-Country Guarantee Fund to back low-risk World Bank loans.[34]

An unusual feature of the decision-making process, which differs from a number of multilateral development banks, is the preference for a non-residential board of governors. European members of the bank had argued unsuccessfully for a residential board to facilitate policy discussion and access to decision-making. The AIIB was eventually headquartered in Beijing and the NDB in Shanghai. The use of a non-residential board reduces the role of the board of governors and increases the overall line management power of the AIIB president, linking the presidency to individual directors-general and project directors.

These four factors helped to rapidly move the AIIB into a decisive strategic position in the changing architecture of international order. It has above all moved flexibly, adapting its loan emphasis with new areas such as digitisation, reviving earlier projects and developing different forms of financial collaboration. These initiatives have sometimes put the bank into crowded areas such as smart cities or emerging project areas, but are part of its projection.[35] As a global development bank, it is also acutely aware of the need to maintain competitive collaboration with existing multilateral financial institutions.[36]

## Changing direction – the Shanghai Cooperation Organisation: building up the alternative architecture

The Shanghai Cooperation Organisation (SCO) is the second major pillar in the alternative architecture. The emerging links between the SCO and Middle East-Gulf states marked a strategic shift in groupings. Much of the groundwork for the expansion of the SCO was made possible through China's mediation in the Iran– Saudi normalisation negotiations, the summit meeting of Xi Jinping and King Salman, bilateral diplomacy with Gulf States and an inbound visit by the GCC Secretary-General. An indication of the importance attached to the China–Saudi summit was recognition by China of the need to avoid empty MOUs, by including at least one large operational project.[37]

The expansion of the SCO included Gulf States and Egypt; Iran's decision to seek full membership was a major signal in formalising existing cooperation with SCO members[38] and also one of moving into a grouping being built up as part of the leading alternative architecture.[39]

For Kuwait, joining the SCO as a dialogue partner reflected concerns over of its sovereign vulnerability, shaped by the lingering impact of the Iraq and Iran–Iraq wars, Iran–Saudi Arabia normalisation of relations, and doubts over future US security backing.[40] As a commodity power, open strategic maritime routes and continuity of supply line logistics are vital elements in its external strategies for trade security. The lessening of links with the US, implicit in the decision of GCC members to join the SCO, is potentially one of the major shifts in international alliance structures to an international order based around non-western influenced coalition structures.[41]

The continued expansion of the SCO in effect changed what previously had been a limited regional security club into a diversified international bloc of over 26 members.[42] The expansion of membership internationalised the SCO, marking a major political and strategic gain for China in the geopolitical competition over the shifting pieces which make up international order. Through careful and agile diplomacy, it brought into the SCO commodity powers including Iran, Saudi Arabia, Kuwait, financial actors and regional Middle East players, altering the capability, interests and projection of the organisation.[43]

## Multilateral links: a route closed off

Within the alternative architecture, residual links were retained with the World Bank Group and BIS on standards, loan procedures and asset recording, to a large extent for borrowed legitimacy, image and accreditation. Some residual institutional links lose their rationale, particularly if negotiated at an earlier period, or are attacked as outdated, especially in environmental agreements criticised as weak or ineffective.

The UN International Seabed Authority (ISA) is an example of an institution which is part of the residual multilateral links of the alternative architecture which has been potentially challenged by environmental coalitions and groups seeking a moratorium or abolition of deep seabed mining.

Set up under the 1982 UN Convention on the Law of the Sea (UNCLOS) and the 1994 agreement on implementing Part XI of the Convention, the ISA has a specialised mandate with respect to conservation and sustainable use of the seabed beyond national jurisdiction.[44] It has since become a multilateral institutional route, in which the Russian Federation and

China have built up a strong political and administrative position in the absence of US participation.

The ISA's status as an institution of the Law of the Sea Convention, and as a related organisation of the UN rather than a specialised agency, gave it a certain independence and separateness, which increased its value and fit in the alternative architecture as a remote and specialised dimension of diplomacy dealing with seabed mining.[45]

The stalled UN intergovernmental negotiations to draft an agreement on ocean biodiversity beyond national jurisdiction were reopened post-COVID,[46] by a France-led environment lobby, via parallel diplomacy, at the BREST Ocean Summit and the High Seas Alliance.[47] The French maritime initiatives illustrated the shift in diplomatic methods to small groups and coalitions as part of an evolving agenda for driving issues to conclusion. Other initiatives included proposals on ocean mapping and co-hosting with Costa Rica the 2025 UN Ocean Conference. The route used by the coalition for approving these was via a UN General Assembly resolution rather than a specific ad hoc multilateral conference. Institutionally, a third route in French diplomacy used extensive diplomatic involvement in the FAO to achieve a lead position in that agency for coalition initiatives and acquiring lead responsibility, working with the FAO on campaigns such a countering illegal fishing (IUU).

The move to resume the BBNJ negotiations, and the speed with which an agreement was concluded, caught China and the Russian Federation off-balance, diplomatically. For China and the Russian Federation, keeping the autonomy of the ISA and other regional resource institutions, coupled with accommodating elements of the Kunming–Montreal Declaration, were conflicting central negotiating aims.[48] Although an agreement on biological diversity beyond National Jurisdiction was concluded in 2023,[49] there were deep divisions on environment, size of marine protected areas, finance and mandates of existing institutions, including RFMOs, and the International Seabed Authority.

An indication of the extent of disagreement is illustrated by interpretive summary made at the consideration and adoption stage of the final documents of the BBNJ by conference president, Rena Lee (Singapore):[50]

(a) "In relation to article 18, entitled 'Area of Application', in part III the understanding was that the phrase 'the Conference of the Parties shall not consider for decision' means that the Conference of the Parties can look at a proposal but shall not decide on such proposals;

(b) In relation to environmental impact assessments, delegations were of the view that environmental impact assessments shall be State-led. In order to promote transparency, there are provisions in part IV that allow for another party to register its views on the impacts of a planned activity and for the Scientific and Technical Body to make non-binding recommendations. However, the understanding was

that it was the State that decided whether an activity under its jurisdiction or control should proceed."

The future of the ISA was nevertheless uncertain as a residual multilateral element in the alternative architecture, in view of the duplication of
mandates of the BBNJ agreement and ISA and the de facto creation of a
new parallel agreement backed by a coalition lobby.[51]

## Alternative architecture: dark trade

"Dark trade" is a traditional segment of international trade in which trade
transactions are disguised or hidden to avoid regulation, restrictions or
political exposure. The wider use of sanctions at national, regional and
international levels has resulted in the growth of dark trade to limit
or evade restrictions. Dark operations occur across a wide spectrum of
transactions in international trade, arms sales, illegal and unreported fisheries exploitation (IUU) and resource research. They have become a significant part of the emerging alternative architecture.[52]

Dark trade is increasingly sophisticated, networked and resilient to
countermeasures. Traditional methods relied on documentary fraud,
vessel registry and safe trade havens for diversion of transshipped
trade. These methods have become refined and carefully coordinated
as dark trade states and allied commercial actors continuously seek to
adapt related military technologies for evasion and communications
deception. One of the common uses of dark trade is shutting off electronic reporting equipment.[53] A key part of these methods is the disguise or alteration of identity and location of vessels and operators.
Switching off AIS and other mandatory IMO reporting systems, originally introduced to enhance maritime safety and emergency rescue
services, has become commonplace, backed by a standard "equipment
fault" narrative for vessels entering conflict zones or other areas for
illegal operations.[54]

The use of false identity has become an established method which
"borrows" the identity of another vessel (name, call sign). The vessel may
have been or is about to be scrapped, or in some instances is part of a
large fleet of similarly named or numbered vessels.[55] It is generally linked
to single ship and shell company operations.[56] False identity is used for
as long as possible before port denial indicates the identity has become
unusable for oil cargo shipments to or from sanctioned states or conflict
zones. The methods are very similar to those used in creating false identity in illegal fishing operations. Disputes over illegal fishing particularly
in and on the boundary of EEZs have centred on AIS cancellation, and
denial of identity and ownership of similarly named vessels or records of
port calls.

Other changes in methods have involved the adaptation of ship-to-ship cargo transfer (STS) for illegal oil transfer between large and smaller tankers at sea for transfer to or from sanctioned states in adjacent or compliant coastal anchorages off Spain, Greece, North Korea.[57] STS is also conducted inside territorial sea areas, similar to some fisheries transshipment operations,[58] rather than landed at port terminals in order to circumvent international sanctions or resource regulations. STS of crude oil is a specialised high-risk operation which, in the context of dark trade, indicates the enhanced technical and crewing networks as well as risk-sharing between dark state actors and allied commercial brokers.

The level of risk varies among the parties and is an element which is used to widen the number of those engaged in dark trade. Not all flags used in dark trade are blacklisted flags. Identity and cargo may be disguised by using cargo insurance and classification services from a regulatory power rather than a high-risk source to lessen attention on vessel and cargo. It is nevertheless a high-risk option, which highlights the limitations of national and commercial political and maritime broker scrutiny of cargoes with complex origins.[59]

## *Diplomatic dimensions of dark trade*

The diplomatic aspects of dark trade directly involve states in a consular capacity as a provider of maritime services for the registration of vessels and indirectly through classification and insurance of merchant vessels. The availability of registry services plays a key part in dark trade.[60] Expansion of flag availability, particularly from Africa (e.g. Gabon, Cameroon[61] and Mongolia).[62]

India, an SCO member,[63] became a key player in providing classification, cargo services and marine insurance and is the principal importer of Russian crude oil.[64] It is a fragile role, reflected in abstentions on key UN General Assembly votes on Ukraine and uneasy relations with the US, which casts doubt about its security relations based on the US-orchestrated Quad and Indo-Pacific Trade Initiative. Turkey provides a similar illustration of contradictory orientations and broker roles, although it is a long-standing member of an established western security alliance and has trade links with the EU which create perhaps greater limitations on the extent of its divergence.

The part of small powers is important in the development of the alternative architecture. For example, one of the less obvious aspects of China's Pacific visit diplomacy is the role of Palau and other Pacific microstates in providing flag registration services for dark state operations. The addition of Middle East oil states as dialogue partners in SCO marked a major geopolitical shift. It was reinforced by the decision of the AIIB to open a regional office in Abu Dhabi,[65] which signalled the new Asian–Middle East alignment. The addition of GCC states as dialogue members had several advantages for the SCO, including upgrading its diplomatic presence in the Middle East and formalising greater access to financial, corporate formation and maritime services, as part of the alternative architecture.[66]

## Multilateral resolutions and political support: choices

The strength of diplomatic support for dark trade is tested in the drafting of resolutions on investigations and sanctions at multilateral, regional or national level. At a multilateral level, mandates are a significant junction in resolutions in terms of the scope of investigation or enforcement action. At this point, states which have reservations about the remit of an investigative panel or scope of sanctions have an opportunity to present concerns or conditions in preparatory negotiations on the elements of a draft resolution. In a mandate renewal negotiation, conditions such as additional requirements on the work of an investigative panel may be stipulated in the draft. The introduction of conditions of this type, although seemingly small, on the frequency of reporting and review of the work programme, act as a kind of brake and are a procedural device to create openings for further criticism or grounds for blocking action for non-compliance and flawed procedures. It is a device especially for those states which oppose multilateral investigations or sanctions regimes, but who cannot afford politically to oppose a resolution for fear of being classed as opponents of arms control or other elements in the multilateral international order.

In the negotiations for the renewal of the mandate of the UN investigative panel on implementation of sanctions on North Korea,[67] the dilemma for China was how to criticise the panel without appearing obstructive. Chinese strategy was based on two procedural elements: using the brief formal session to question the credibility and bias of the panel; and to put in conditions in the text of the resolution requiring prior sight of the panel's work programme and frequency of reporting. These were major concessions which cast sufficient doubt on the findings of the panel without damaging its constructive international image in conflicts.[68]

## Implications of changes in dark trade for other diplomatic methods

The surge in dark trade following the introduction of sanctions by the G7 and EU highlighted the difficulties western powers have in creating effective counter methods.[69] Major weaknesses of the western scheme were allowing the continued flow of Russian oil subject to a price cap, and the corresponding failure to coordinate an effective response to the rapid creation of a shadow oil tanker fleet of over 400 vessels transporting sanctioned oil.[70]

Dark states improved logistics and maritime coordination across multiple sectors and laid the basis for an Asia–Middle East axis. The dark trade crisis also influenced closer India–Russia bilateral relations at the expense of the US–Indo-Pacific initiative. Whilst these two shifts in methods are not immutable, they introduce fault lines in traditional western relations and ability to create economic counter groupings. At bilateral level, India became a critical oil sales partner and pragmatic ally linked with China in networks of evasion and North Korea with the Russian Federation in Ukraine.

At a multilateral level, western diplomacy was channelled through the UN Security Council and International Maritime Organisation (IMO). The IMO provided a diplomatic platform for G7/EU pressure on registries (flag), classification and insurance societies. Over 14 dark fleet tankers were flagged to Cameroon; other flags used included Mongolia, for vessels run by single ship companies variously registered in Vietnam, Singapore and Marshall Islands. Classic cases, such as that of the tanker Turba raised by Spain in the IMO legal committee, drew focus on issues of fraudulent registration or breaches of safety regulations.[71]

Except for its work on ship safety and oil pollution, IMO remains a blunt instrument on issues of a political nature or involving operational commercial questions. It is unsuited to taking swift action as a consensus-based institution. The IMO legal committee relied on methods to slow inquiry down by using a suite of delaying moves to require more information on the problems of fraudulent registry, setting up a study group and moving the issue to another meeting or committee for action.[72]

Other limitations were a result of the use of indirect methods, such as relying on safety and insurance liability issues posed by dark fleet operations in STS passages from Baltic ports through the English Channel and other routes, as an agenda item on international insurance conventions. These did little to resolve the issues of EU sanctions exceptions, inadequacy of price caps, applicability of port state control of vessels avoiding port calls, or growth of STS hubs for vessels en route to Asia, off Greece, the Ceuta enclave and areas in Asia.

The use of port state inspection on vessels suspected of involvement in sanctions evasion has, on balance, merely diverted traffic into dark trade shipping and related logistics. Detained vessels or vessels denied port entry relocate to other available ports. Indirect western diplomacy has strengthened dark trade coordination in transportation and introduced an additional layer of covert level of cooperation into commodity supply and redirected trade.

## Conclusion

The post-2000 international system has been characterised by the splintering of the multilateral order. Part of that process has seen the emergence of an alternative coalition – the alternative architecture – made up of states and other actors operating independently as a centre of power, led by China. Four elements within the grouping can be distinguished: the Asian Infrastructure Development Bank (AIIB) and NDB, Shanghai Cooperation Organisation (SCO), residual multilateral links and dark trade cooperation.

The AIIB is the central component of the alternative architecture, built up at the expense of the BRICS's New Development Bank. There was not enough diplomatic space for two overlapping institutions, with the AIIB moving ahead separately under sole direction of China, detaching relations with the NDB. The split was a pragmatic recognition that the NDB BRICS-based model had become outdated as a vehicle for global development projects and projecting diplomatic power. Recurrent domestic difficulties in two of the BRICS members limited its regional and international roles. The NDB was also vulnerable to the impact of the Russian war against Ukraine on NDB operations. Rather than reforming or winding up the NDB, it was left to continue with marginal adjustments, whilst the AIIB carefully moved ahead to establish a global presence. The diplomatic methods used by the AIIB were unusual, following the initial exploratory discussions with the World Bank and possible European link-ups. It moved quickly to downgrade Belt and Road Initiative narratives, shifted its focus to green and sustainable Asian infrastructure project lending, and used negotiation to build-up membership, making the AIIB a global multilateral bank operating outside the World Bank. Particularly important was avoiding entanglements in the Middle East or other regional conflicts.

Along with the development of the AIIB, the second strand of the alternative architecture was based on the expanding membership of the Shanghai Cooperation Organisation. Residual links were retained with the multilateral development institutions for legitimacy and limited to financing, though the AIIB was very much an independent lead envoy of this alternative alliance.

# Notes

1 For debates on multilateralism within the UN Security Council, See Open Debate (Organised by Vietnam), 9 January 2020, President of the Security Council, Statement, 8,699ᵗʰ meeting, 7 May 2022 (China), 14 December 2022 (India), Statement 24 April 2023, UN Secretary-General, "Amid Strained Multilateral System States Must Recommit", https://press un.org / 2023 /sc15263.doc.htm. UN General Assembly, UNGA A/RES/76/1262, 26 April 2022.

2 See "Geoeconomic fragmentation and the future of multilateralism", IMF Staff Discussion Notes (IMF, 2023).

3 The WTO Agreement on Fisheries Subsidies was opened for acceptance after 20 years of intermittent negotiations, not as a freestanding WTO agreement but as a Protocol amending the original WTO Marrakesh agreement (Annex

1A, Agreement on Subsidies and Countervailing Measures) requiring a two-thirds majority of signatories under Article X, paragraph 3.

4 The resumed negotiations on a fisheries subsidy agreement could only reach a framework agreement. Subsequent negotiations prior to the WTO Ministerial conference in Dubai (Min 13) made little progress, with a heavily bracketed text. For a rare and valuable account of the differences and documentation by the negotiating committee chair, Ambassador Einar Gunnarsson, see WT/MIN(24)/W/10/add1.

5 The US was the fourth state to deposit an instrument accepting the Fisheries Subsidies Agreement, 11 April 2022, following Switzerland, Singapore and the Seychelles. A "race to entry" event was also organised to publicise the Fisheries Subsidy Agreement as part of the preservation of ocean resources deadline of the 13th WTO Ministerial Conference in Abu Dhabi. www.wto.org/english/news_e/news23_e/fish_21jun23_e.htm.

6 See IMF Staff Discussion Notes (2023), op. cit., p22.

7 The World Food Programme was established in 1961, following the World Food conference, drawing on US proposals (McGovern) for a new separate international agency for food emergencies and food assistance in conflicts.

8 www.chathamhouse.org/events/all/members-event/qatars-regional-and-international-role.

9 Anu Bradford, *The Brussels Effect* (OUP, 2020) pp XIV, XV1 and 67–91.

10 https://aiib.org.

11 Cynthia Roberts, Leslie Elliott Armijo and Saori N Katada, *The BRICS and Collective Financial Statecraft* (OUP, 2018) pp 92–6.

12 IMF Staff Discussion Notes, op. cit., note 2.

13 Cited in Roberts et al, op. cit., p95.

14 Agreement for establishing the NDB, BRIC summit Fortaleza, entering into force at the inaugural meeting of the Board of Governors, 7 July 2021. www.ndb.int /About NDB.

15 Paulo Nogueira Batista Jr, *The BRICS and the Financing Mechanisms They Created* (Anthem Press, 2022) pp29–30.

16 Batista, ibid., p54.

17 Batista, ibid., p62.

18 NDB new members included Bangladesh, 16 September 2021, UAE, 4 October 2021, Egypt, 20 February 2023 and Algeria, 31 August 2024. UAE is also a member of the AIIB and dialogue member of the Shanghai Cooperation Organisation (SCO). The AIIB opened a representative office in UAE in 2023. See www.ndb.int/about-ndb/members/.

19 AIIB Annual Report (2016) p6 and Preamble to World Bank Group. AIIB MOU, 23 April 2017, Section E and Article 1.1 on information and knowledge-sharing provisions.

20 AIIB Corporate Strategy mission: Financing Infrastructure for Tomorrow.

21 See resignation of Robert Pickard, Canadian Director-General for Communications, AIIB, over the decision-making process. *Financial Times*, 15 June 2023.

22 Annual Meetings of the AIIB were held in China (2016), Korea (2017), India (2018), Luxembourg (2019), Egypt (2023) and Uzbekistan (2024). AIIB meetings were held 2020–2 virtually because of COVID-19.

23 See MOU AIIB and The World Bank Group, 23 April 2017. https://
thedocs.worldbank.org/en/doc/412261495119092544-0260022017/origi
nal/OfficialDocumentsMemorandumofUnderstandingbetweentheMinistryof
FinanceofthePeoplesRepublicofChinaandADBAIIBEBRDEIBNDBWBGonCol
laborationundertheBeltandRoadInitiative.pdf>;
https://thedocs.worldbank.org/en/doc/412261495119092544-0260022017/
Official-Documents-Memorandum-of-Understanding-between-the-Ministry-
of-Finance-of-the-Peoples-Republic-of-China-and-ADB-AIIB-EBRD-EIB-NDB-
WBG-on-Collaboration-under-the-Belt-and-Road-Initiative.

24 See IBRD Q&A on Belt and Road. https://pubdocs.worldbank.org/BRI-FAQ.

25 Batista, op. cit., p63.

26 UNGA, A/RES/73/216, 20 December 2018, approving observer status of AIIB
at sessions and work of the UN General Assembly, and report of the UNGA 6th
Committee, A/73/464. The NDB application was approved by the UNGA on 1
November 2018. A/C 6/73/L4.

27 AIIB Notes to the Condensed Financial Statements, section C (Disclosure
Notes), C22, p30.

28 The membership reached 106 as of 2023, Annual Report (2023).

29 See AIIB (Projects) https://aiib.org. Shaanxi Ankang Green and Low-Carbon
Demonstration Urban Development Project proposal.

30 See AIIB (Projects) https://aiib.org. India: Tata Cleantech Sustainable
Infrastructure (project 0028).

31 See www.ndb.int/annual-report-2020/stories-with-impact.html. The Brazilian
project involved rail infrastructure and expansion of the Ponta da Madeira
Port Terminal, for Vale's transportation of iron ore for export.

32 Port of Duqm in Oman. www.aiib.org/en/news-events/media-center/blog/
2022/Diversifying-Oman-s-Economy-and-Promoting-Connectivity-and-Regio
nal-Cooperation.html.

33 G20 Working Group on Multilateral Development Banks.

34 AIIB Annual Report (2023) on the Multi-Country Guarantee Fund, creating
a $1 billion support facility as back up for IBRD projects. The new fund was
also part of the restructuring of the bank's loan portfolio to diversify sovereign
lending.

35 Christopher Humphrey, "From Drawing Board to Reality: The First Four
Years of Operations at the Asian Infrastructure Investment Bank and New
Development Bank". Working Paper of the G-24 & Global Development Policy
Center of Boston University, 2020, p3.

36 Co-financing provisions in the World Bank Group–AIIB MOU, 23 April 2017,
Preamble (section D) and Article 1, 1.1.

37 Aramco revived agreements for a petrochemical complex in Liaoning Province,
first signed as a framework agreement during King Salman's visit to Beijing in
March 2017, but stalled over uncertain markets. The Liaoning agreement was
backed up with other projects including a dual supply and long-term crude oil
investment deal with the Rongsheng Petrochemical Company in the eastern
province of Zhejiang, significantly expanding its refining presence and sales in
competition with the Russian Federation.

38 Iran was officially confirmed as a full member at the 22nd summit of the SCO.

39  Article 14 of the Shanghai Cooperation Organisation provides for either observer or dialogue partner status. UNTS, vol. 2896-I-50517.

40  Kuwait statement following application to the SCO for dialogue partner status, 19 September 2022.

41  The SCO was founded on 15 June 2001 as an intergovernmental organisation focused on regional security, combatting ethnic separatism and extremism, and regional development. By 2021, the SCO comprised eight members (China, India, Kazakhstan, Kyrgyzstan, Russia, Pakistan, Tajikistan and Uzbekistan), four observers (Afghanistan, Belarus, Iran and Mongolia) and six dialogue partners (Armenia, Azerbaijan, Cambodia, Nepal, Sri Lanka and Turkey).

42  Iran acceded as a full member in 2022 at the 22nd SCO summit. The summit also agreed to admit Bahrain, Maldives, UAE, Kuwait and Myanmar as dialogue partners. MOUs were also signed at the 22nd summit by Egypt, Qatar and Saudi Arabia for dialogue status. See *Tehran Times*, 19 March 2022.

43  "New Order in the Middle East", Foreign Policy, 6 March 2023. Ethiopia, Egypt and the UAE joined BRICS on 1 January 2024.

44  See UN Convention on the Law of the Sea, 10 December 1982, Part XI. For the background to the Agreement relating to Part XI of the United Nations Convention on the Law of the Sea, 28 July 1994, see www.un.org/depts/los/convention_agreements/texts/unclos/unclos_e.pdf. The 1994 Agreement entered into force on 28 July 1996.

45  See the defensive briefing note of the ISA to protect its UNCLOS responsibilities for seabed regulation from other international institutions and NGOs at www.isa.org.jm; www.isa.org.jm/wp-content/uploads/2023/03/ISA _secretariat_info_note_rev.1_27.02.23.pdf. For further details on the dispute, see https://demaribus.net/wp-content/uploads/ 2014/06/cropped-anonymous_the_noord-nieuwland_in_table_bay_1762.jpg; https://savethehighseas.org/isa-tracker/latest-news-and-updates.

46  On resumed fifth session of the ocean biodiversity IGC, see bbnj A/76/L46.

47  Brest Ocean Summit, 9–11 February 2022.

48  UN doc SEA/21282, 20 June 2023.

49  UNGA, A/CONF/24/2023/4.

50  A/CONF/232/2023/4. See section VI of the final report prepared by the President of the Conference (Singapore) on the meaning of article 17 (Area of Application) and the Part IV provisions on whether responsibility for decisions on environment decisions are state-led or not. The President's summary is heavily qualified as to be a source of continuing difference and dissent.

51  See statement of ISA Secretary-General to resumed 5th session of the IGC on biodiversity beyond national jurisdiction, 27 February 2023. The ISA was not able to directly participate in the negotiations but was invited by the President of the Conference, Ambassador Rena Lee (Singapore), to submit written statements.

52  For discussion of FAO agreements on IUU see chapter 5.

53  Hellenic Shipping News, 1 June 2022; Lloyd's List, 22 May 2023 (Dark STS). On loss of AIS of Russian and other vessels in the Kerch Strait on the Sea of Azov supply chain connecting the Black Sea to international trade routes, see Lloyd's List, 29 April 2023.

54 See report of the panel of experts (North Korea sanctions) on the use of the MMSI (communication call signs) of scrapped vessels, Section III, UN doc S/2020/668.

55 Lloyd's List, 9 February 2023. Other exchange points and anchorages include off Spanish and Greek coastal waters.

56 UN doc S/2022/618, paras 32.4–32.6.

57 UN doc S/2022/668, paras 39 and 43.

58 UN doc S/2022/668, para 39.

59 Insurance Marine News, 22 June 2023, "American Club hits back at New York Times article".

60 See Lloyd's List on ship registry "Dark fleet of tankers now comprises 10% of seaborne oil transport".

61 Lloyd's List, 31 March 2023, "Dark fleet: Out of mind but not out of sight".

62 Lloyd's List, 23 May 2023, on Gatik Ship Management (India), the largest dark trade vessels operator, reflagging four of its tankers to landlocked Mongolia, following removal from Lloyd's Register and loss of P+I insurance.

63 Lloyd's List, 13 June 2023.

64 Crude oil imports from Russia. *Financial Times*, 14 July 2023.

65 AIIB. Notes to Condensed Financial Statements (2022–3), Section C (Disclosure Notes) C 22, p30.

66 *Financial Times*, 20 July 2023.

67 UN Res 2627 (2022).

68 UN SC/14841, 25 March 2022.

69 Lloyd's List, 15 February, on EU port authorities detention of tankers linked to Russia oil trades.

70 Lloyd's List, 13 March 2023.

71 IMO, Legal Committee 110th session (LEG 110) 27–31 March 2023, p1.

72 IMO, Legal Committee, 110th session, pp2–3.

## Chapter 11

# Diplomacy in conflicts

## Introduction

Mediation is perhaps the most difficult of the diplomatic crafts. Its results are not necessarily immediately evident; they may sometimes be hard to establish or evaluate, at least in the short term, and evaluated differently by the parties. Outcomes, too, in many instances are short lived, contested or part of a long-running process. One of the central tasks of diplomacy at an international level is contributing to the peaceful settlement of disputes between states. The continued proliferation of disputes and armed conflict in contemporary international relations, many marked by their seeming insolubility, ethnic or nationalist nature and geopolitical dimensions, has meant almost constant pressure on diplomatic methods.

In this chapter we will provide a concluding overview of one of these methods – mediation – looking at the nature of mediation, the methods used in mediation and some of the limitations and successes of mediation efforts post-cold war.

Traditionally, the methods used in the peaceful settlement of disputes have included inquiry, monitoring ceasefires, negotiation, conciliation, arbitration, mediation and judicial settlement. These methods received formal recognition in both the League of Nations Covenant and the United Nations Charter and other instruments.[1] Those involved now in international mediation and dispute settlement processes, are far wider than envisaged by UN Charter-based processes to include bilateral, regional, plurilateral and individual actors and institutions alongside or separate from multilateral sourced mediation.

## Mediation: meaning and definitions

In a strict sense mediation should be distinguished from conciliation and arbitration, although there are a number of features common to all

DOI: 10.4324/9781003204039-12

three. The essence of conciliation is more on facilitating communication between the parties and clarification of opposing positions, rather than necessarily drawing out or proposing substantive solutions. Conciliation has been used particularly in domestic disputes.

Arbitration is distinguished from mediation in that it is generally juridical. Moreover, a solution proposed in arbitration may not necessarily be reached on the basis of a balance between competing interests but on criteria such as an arbitrator's interpretation and application of principles or precedents. Arbitration may be binding or non-binding. It is found as an option in some resource agreements.[2]

Mediation is distinct from conciliation or arbitration in that the mediator is directly or indirectly attempting to promote a temporary or permanent solution to a particular problem or issue, based on a conception of outcomes likely to receive joint or widespread acceptance by the parties in a dispute. A mediator is thus concerned with strategies to influence both the process and content of possible solutions. In other words, the aim of mediation is to change four elements: perceptions, approach, objectives and behaviour. In a definition of mediation, Henry Kissinger put these four elements as follows: "the utility of a mediator is that if trusted by both sides he can soften the edge of controversy and provide a mechanism for adjustment on issues of prestige."[3] In practice, however, the issues need not be ones of prestige but rather humanitarian access, creation or brokering a ceasefire, access for medical and food supplies.

Mediation is undertaken by third party representatives mainly from states and international institutions, but also by individuals, NGOs and informal actors. Mediators should in some sense be external to the dispute, though they could be an ally of one of the parties. In order not to broaden or make the concept imprecise, mediation by formal office holders and facilitators in multilateral conferences is better understood by other concepts such as the brokering of compromises, negotiation initiatives or facilitating roles.

Two further points concerning the definition of mediation can be made. The first concerns the perception of the nature, status and purpose of an envoy's mission. In some instances, one or more parties may misperceive the status or purpose of a visit or talks. For example, during the Chile–Argentine dispute over the Beagle Channel, with Argentinian and Chilean warships hours apart in the Straits of Magellan, the Pope's special envoy Cardinal Samorè made it clear that his mission to both countries was not to mediate a settlement but rather to seek restraint:[4]

> I speak rather of a mission and not of mediation, in a technical sense, because mediation is a juridical term that gives to the mediator, if not authority, the possibility of making proposals, not only to listen or to invite the parties but we're still not in that phase.

There may be multiple levels of mediation and contacts occurring in some disputes.[5] Multiple layers or types of contacts occur particularly in a multilateral conflict if one of the main protagonists is diplomatically isolated or has limited diplomatic machinery. In these circumstances there is a tendency to use multiple or perhaps informal channels of communication and conduct several levels of mediation negotiations. The levels and formats may switch for several reason, particularly changes of government which affect priorities, personnel and channels.[6] Again, in civil war cases in which there is an extensive range of external players, some disputants attempt to play off various mediation initiatives, linking them to battlefield developments, perhaps to delay mediation, pending battlefield progress or seeking other concessions.[7]

## Mediators

Mediation is caried out by a wide range of actors, including formal office holders of states, international institution officials, special representatives of the UN Secretary-General, envoys, groups and external diplomatic actors involved in implementation and monitoring.[8] The list of those in the informal category is extensive, comprising actors such as businesses, labour organisations, opposition politicians, aid agencies such as MSF, religious leaders and other citizen diplomats to perform on an invited basis (or not) mediation functions to varying degrees. It is not always clear what the status is of informal mediators and "unofficial" envoys, or their role in conflicts.

Other questions to do with the status of mediators and the purposes of initiatives occur because of the nature or circumstances of authorisation. Disputes over using an extant agreement as a source of authority for co-chair of mediation can lead to lengthy diplomatic wrangling, which may be used to delay or frustrate the start of a mediation process.[9] Similarly the resumption of longstanding frozen negotiations such as the Cyprus problem may be delayed by several factors, including the title and functions of a UN special representative. In the Syrian crisis, former UN Secretary-General, Kofi Annan, was appointed as a joint special envoy of the United Nations and League of Arab States to undertake a good offices mission. The authorisation was based on UN General Assembly resolution A/RES/66/253 and consultations between UN Secretary-General Ban Ki-moon and League of Arab States Secretary-General Nabil Elaraby,[10] following deadlock in the Security Council on the Syrian question as a result of a Russian and Chinese double veto on a draft resolution on the Syrian crisis.

The concept of a joint mission raised issues for opponents over the mandate, the mission and UN control.[11] Deadlock in the Council meant that support for the proposal was restricted to a statement issued by the

President of the Council.[12] Although a revised version of the joint proposal was subsequently agreed, reduced to an observer mission, the lack
of cooperation between the main protagonists and issues of humanitarian
access ultimately led Kofi Annan to resign.[13]

In mediation, the timing and space of an initiative is often critical for
its success. In conflicts such as Syria or Ukraine, the scope for mediation
is extremely limited or unlikely in the short term. Furthermore, confu-
sion can occur from the added complexity caused by the breakdown of
established diplomatic services and procedures during periods of high
tension, significant crisis and transition or civil war.[14] In other instances,
revolutionary or unstable regimes seem to attract foreign domiciled
nationals who inhabit the grey area or demi-monde of "representative" or
contact channels and thrive on intrigue, crisis and dark trade.[15]

Apart from questions to do with the type and status of mediators, it
should be remembered that although distinctions are made between
inquiry, conciliation and mediation, diplomatic methods used in conflict
are likely in practice to contain elements of all three, which are not easy
to disentangle.

## The development of categories of mediators

Whilst mediation is often conducted at a bilateral level, other forms
include trilateral and group envoys from regional organisations.[16] The
number of categories of mediators has expanded quite considerably, creating a diverse architecture of mediation and moving it increasingly from
its UN Charter-based origins. Five factors can be suggested as contributing
to the decentralisation of mediation.

One of the more important factors is the use of separate mediation in
conflicts by primary powers, either not, or only nominally, linked to UN
processes. The cumulative effect is to pull responsibility and management
of mediation away from international institutions.

Second, the growth of regionalism, particularly in Europe, Africa and
the Middle East, has introduced separate institutions and actors variously involved in mediation. External regional actors also see mediation
and security roles as part of strategies for extending presence and influence. Of the newer actors, the increasing international involvement of
the African Union has introduced the doctrine that regional conflicts
should be addressed as first call by regional organisations and managed
through regional institutions, rather than be primarily addressed at multilateral level.

The progressive shift into security, peacekeeping and conflict management by some economically based regional organisations has weakened
traditional responsibility for mediation. It has also to an extent weakened
multilateralism in terms of the role of the UN and functions of the

Secretary-General as a principal voice and agent of diplomatic persuasion in conflicts that threaten or weaken international peace and security.

Correspondingly, the differing conceptions of the role of Secretary-General and different perspectives which various Secretaries-General have brought to the office, have varied from the high active involvement of the cold war and early post-cold war period to a more public goods approach linked to promotion of collective action on climate and sustainable development goals, delegating security involvement substantially to the P5.[17]

Third, the traditional group of states with recognised roles as mediators and good offices – Norway, Finland, Sweden and Switzerland – has been augmented by newer actors, differently aligned or with mixed foreign policy orientation. These include Oman, Qatar, Saudi Arabia, Algeria and Turkey.[18]

Fourth, the number of NGOs with some degree of trade-related advocacy involved in humanitarian activities has increased.[19] One of the changes in NGO groups is the growth of less well-known agencies in various humanitarian sectors, supplementing established public advocacy groups. They tend to be more closely linked operationally to multilateral institutions such as UNCHR. Other food security and commodity-related NGOs operate off-stage as Geneva-based operations on the fringes of the UN specialised agencies. The funding of the latter and some other NGOs remains opaque, operating in effect as disguised states.[20]

Fifth, the informal category of mediator has increased partly as a reflection of the growth of the international commercial and financial sector as an adjunct of government, as states seek to improve relations, reduce political and trade tension or develop new financial and broker roles as part of foreign policy orientation. Informal mediators have also been more frequently used in cases of breaches of relations or periods of high tension (e.g. hostage release).[21] Another important use of informal mediators is in secret parallel negotiations outside formal exchanges or meetings, to convey messages, positions and hint at possible areas of agreement.[22]

## Mediation strategies

Mediation strategies are used to influence the setting, process and content of a dispute. Strategies related to the setting include choice of location, frequency and future locations, which parties to invite, the extent to which discussions are private and who else should be informed. Locations for mediation meetings have varied from a desert tent in no-man's land,[23] remote jungle to the Papal palace.[24] Most locations, though, are routine venues out of the need to avoid publicity. Often, initial or pre-negotiation contacts will be made at the margins of other international or regional conferences or meetings to settle initial organisation and location questions, with strategies to push through as quickly and conveniently as possible a wide range of initial questions.

Location can be a sensitive issue if a group has not met before. In other instances, review meetings between subsets of negotiators benefit from changing location, by moving to a delegation hotel. Change of location during a two- to three-day negotiation may be important psychologically for a sub-group to find a new setting, differentiating it from, for example, a UN multilateral setting, in order to determine differences, more easily establish areas of possible movement, or draft compromise text before rejoining the main location meetings.[25] Location becomes sensitive also in instances involving direct or indirect meetings between a primary power and an adversary. Oman has developed a longstanding role as a venue for private and sensitive diplomatic meetings and exchanges.

## Process

Mediation moves that address the process aspects of conflict are typically aimed at the perceptual and attitudinal approach of disputants. They seek to develop engagement and commitment to the negotiations. Mediation techniques in this area can be conceptualised as generally falling into two categories: procedure and approach. In the procedural category are questions to do with when and how to commence contacts and talks, who should be invited (or not) and suitable venue. Making first contact with rebel groups is difficult and unpredictable in civil war contexts.[26] Unpredictable meetings and cancellation make it difficult to sustain momentum.[27] In other instances, resuming mediation negotiations after long gaps is one of several difficulties in conflicts such as the Cyprus problem, which significantly limits relaunch.[28] Within the approach category, mediation techniques focus on developing rapport, framing problems, building agreements on possible sectors and creating common conceptions of what the negotiated outcome might broadly cover.

The routes for diplomacy in war and armed conflict are restricted and graduated in terms of the scale of possible mediation, good offices and negotiation, beginning with low-level or minimum areas including negotiated pauses in ground or air operations, limited humanitarian withdrawal, token prisoner exchange or hostage release, ceasefires through to cessation of military operations, agreed disarmament assembly areas, withdrawal and cessation of hostilities agreements.

In civil war and other military conflicts, the content of mediation is often limited to a fairly low level, linked to battlefield progress, covering token prisoner exchanges or small batches of humanitarian cases through border checkpoints. These may be symbolic for media purposes or politically grouped by nationality by the releasing party. They become, however, focal points in mediation, negotiation and good offices exchanges which seek to extend and expand released groups.[29]

Two further points on mediation content are necessary. Content issues occur during implementation, in framework agreements or because of revival of disputed constitutional provisions. An example of the latter is the conflict over the division of South Sudan into 28 counties based on old colonial boundaries, agreed in the negotiations to end the civil war, which became a source of ongoing controversy over boundary claims and administrative authority.[30]

## Mediation techniques

One of the main process techniques in mediation is that of clarification. For example, during the Beagle Channel dispute between Argentina and Chile noted earlier, the officially nominated mediator, Cardinal Samorè and his team devoted six months to the initial phase of the mediation, gathering information and hearing both sides' positions.[31] The use of clarifying and unpacking the main elements in the positions of the respective parties makes this aspect of mediation similar to conciliation but is distinct in that it is likely to be compacted and dispersed through brief good offices missions, visit diplomacy and diplomatic exchanges among a variety of parties.

Other methods used include process techniques that attempt to alter the pace of mediation negotiations, rescheduling talks, keeping talks going despite obvious lack of agreement, and deadlines. Deadlines have, however, not been extensively used by mediators for fear that undue use or failure to meet terms (cabinet construction, elections, legislation) might weaken the credibility of a mediator. Mediators, nevertheless, encounter deadlines set by the parties, arising from domestic or other contexts, such as a disputant's fear of running out of time, the perceived cost of failure or inability to complete mediation requirements because of an upcoming election. A mediation agreement may sometimes be signed as a face-saving measure despite critical reservations.[32]

Concern over establishing mediation and getting it underway is also evident in the use of "shuttle diplomacy". Shuttle diplomacy is based on a high-risk strategy, critically dependent on momentum to maintain the engagement of the principal protagonists. In the Israel–Gaza war, shuttle diplomacy by the US Secretary of State, Antony Blinken, relied on blending potential mediation with good offices to retain diplomatic links and influence with other states and organisations in a conflict in which diplomacy struggled to gain a role. That role depended on expanding the humanitarian and ceasefire elements and recovering from diplomatic setbacks limited following expansion of the conflict into Lebanon.

The focal points in the humanitarian negotiations centred on conflicting approaches between the concept of humanitarian pauses in military operations as against moving to a ceasefire. The related nego-tiation issues linked pauses or restrictions on military operations to the return of hostages and wider issues of foreign and dual nationals seeking exit through the southern border crossing point into Egypt from Gaza.[33]

The main risks in strategies of shuttle diplomacy are loss of ability to recover from setbacks and erosion of diplomatic space as a result of the splintering of humanitarian-ceasefire coalitions. These risks are reduced by backing up shuttle diplomacy in order to maintain momentum by shifting to covert bilateral and third-party mediation. For example, Qatar has specialised in finding diplomatic space for covert mediation to make progress in small steps to secure the release of hostages or exit of limited numbers of trapped foreign and dual nationals in civil conflicts.[34]

## Content

In wider and substantive mediation four types of initiatives can be distinguished: framework, integrative, incremental or compensatory.[35] Framework proposals aim to establish the overall basis for talks by seeking to agree general principles[36] and a timetable for conducting the negotiations.[37] In this type of approach, a high premium is placed on building rapport between opposing parties and promoting engagement with the process by refining or integrating opposing texts. Agreement is promoted by reducing the areas of substantive negotiation. Differences are narrowed[38] and outstanding issues are relegated to bilateral understandings or secret protocol.[39] Category three, incremental approaches, is the most widely used in mediation and good offices. It essentially relies on trying to build up areas of agreement following on from step-by-step initial mediation of partial ceasefire and humanitarian access, so as to contain the scale of conflict. It recognises, however, the limitations of what can be achieved in a highly polarised conflict.

Any gain is a small step forward, with the likelihood of periods of substantial reversal which test the cohesion of external actors.[40] The fourth category of compensation strategy is the least used in mediation as a main focal point for negotiation. Reaching agreement on provisions which redistribute benefits through compensatory measures (territory, political appointments, budgetary allocation) in peace agreements ending civil or other war, is one of the most difficult areas of mediation. In recognition of this, the tendency is for some elements of redistribution to be partly included in an agreement, along with forward-looking commitments in other areas, deferred to future institutions.[41]

## Constraints on mediation

Limitations on mediation can be grouped in three areas: who participates, how mediation is conducted and what is its scope. Questions over who participates affect a wide area of mediation including which states, or other actors, are invited to mediation groups, chairmanship of meetings and objection to those invited. Catherine Ashton, EU High Representative for foreign affairs and security, illustrates some of these difficulties seen in one early contact group set up during the Ukraine Maidan–Crimea crisis.

> (the meeting itself was chaotic)
> As well as all the countries I expected to be there, namely France, Germany, USA, Russia, Ukraine and the EU, there were lots of others claiming an invitation of sorts. Everybody gathered around a large table. It was shambolic. I was fed up with some European countries feeling they had to turn up at gatherings like this. It looked a mess. As a foreign policy actor, the EU was a twinkle in the eye of some countries and a plank in the eye to others who saw it as a threat to their role on the world stage. As the meeting began, it became obvious that the Ukrainians, Russians and Americans weren't there. They were somewhere else, making our meeting pretty pointless.[42]

One of the main factors which contributes to weakening mediation is the competitive expansion of those involved in initiating and conducting mediation. In a UN multilateral-endorsed mediation, the title of a UN special representative can be a source of difficulty, as in the frozen Cyprus talks, in that the use of special representative might imply limitations because of close links with the views of previous Secretaries-General or UN resolutions, in contrast to the neutral title of envoy. In UN mediation initiatives, who is invited to meetings or to conduct mediation is closely scrutinised by the protagonists. In the Cyprus case, Guterres made it one of three conditions after the breakdown of UN-mediated Greek–Turkish negotiations that the parties must agree on the title of the mediator prior to any resumption of talks.

Other protocol issues are problems associated with mixed actor meetings, which may comprise proscribed rebel leaders, which affect personal contact, seating and photography. These issues are not unimportant and can combine with other factors to affect the atmosphere of meetings and contribute to uncertainty.[43]

Questions to do with how mediation is conducted affect the scope of what is negotiated, its depth and traction, and levels of trust between the participants. Unsuccessful mediation contributes to adverse perceptions of the host state or organisation. The secret format of diplomacy remains a continuing feature of contemporary diplomatic practice and a source of difficulty over leaks. Much of mediation is conducted in secret, with a preference for bilateral formats. Movement from secret bilateral exchanges to include other groups is one of the major difficulties as in the US–Iran negotiations and relations with the P5, with the disclosure of secret bilateral exchanges to the P5 contact group. Subsequent difficulties also occur over aligning differing texts negotiated at bilateral and plurilateral level by different groups.[44]

Apart from these factors, mediation has been weakened by the competitive expansion of actors staking a claim to, or conducting, mediation. Institutionally, actors have proliferated as part of east–west détente in Europe following the ending of the cold war. The spread of regional conflicts in Africa and the Middle East has forced the African Union to assert an active interest in having primary responsibility for mediation and the establishment of African peacekeeping forces. Rivalry between the EU and US over Nagorno-Karabakh and Kosovo has resulted in duplication of meetings and undermined mediation. Separate European and US initiatives on the Armenia and Azerbaijan conflict were matched by Russian parallel meetings.

In addition, the creation of a new European forum, the European Political Council (EPC), made up of the EU and non-EU member states, at French initiative, added to the expansion of the machinery for mediation.[45] A change in EU diplomatic practice to allow member states to sit in on negotiations conducted by other EU office holders undoubtedly weakened the neutral status of the President of the Council. An additional difficulty was created by intra-EU external policy rivalry between the EEAS and Presidency of the Council.[46] Ultimately, the multiple mediation exchanges provided Azerbaijan with cover and, during the summer pause, an opportunity to use military force against Nagorno-Karabakh.

## Diplomacy and force

UN peacekeeping doctrine has undergone substantial change since 2010. A central feature of traditional UN doctrine developed during and after the cold war was that international security would be based on the idea that peacekeeping forces, especially those drawn from smaller members, would be responsible for contributing to international peace and security. Conflicts would be ring fenced by either an observer force or peacekeeping force. UN forces would not normally engage in offensive military operations and use of force would be strictly limited to self defence. Underlying UN peacekeeping doctrine in the cold war era was the concept of preventive diplomacy: keeping the great powers out of local conflicts.[47]

The abandonment of peacekeeping forces and preventive diplomacy after 2010 has significantly reduced the contribution of the UN to maintaining international peace and security. Differences in the P5 meant that generally no new traditional peacekeeping forces were deployed after 2010 in areas of major competing interests. Existing forces have been challenged or withdrawn as in Mali, Chad, Central African Republic (CAR) and Democratic Republic of Congo (DRC). Mandates have been reduced, reporting requirements to the Security Council increased and termination of mission provisions set via review requirements, using diplomatic methods which chip away at the operational effectiveness of existing

UN forces. Other missions have been periodically authorised under the doctrine of stabilisation and political transition, mainly without a military component.

Central to the doctrine of stabilisation is the promotion of development and political transition through elections and mediation with different internal groups to establish electoral and governance institutions, supported by good offices contact groups. For example, the CARICOM Eminent Persons Group for Haiti is a good offices mission formed to support regional and international efforts to return Haiti to political stability.[48] In essence, stabilisation doctrine shifted the emphasis from peacekeeping based on a UN military and police presence to internal political integration in unstable states, supported by electoral processes. The Emergency Security Mission for Haiti, led by Kenya, approved under chapter 7 of the Charter, was time limited and even retained provisions on resumption of elections.[49]

The ideas were augmented by UN Secretary-General Guterres in the New Agenda for Peace Policy, which argued for greater focus on implementing the UN Sustainable Development Goals (SDGs) as part of a holistic platform in conflict reduction.[50] The traditional doctrine of preventive diplomacy is revised and reinterpreted into a formula which is premised on security being related to putting emphasis on the achievement of the Millenium Sustainable Development Goals.

The stabilisation doctrine has been challenged in UN mandate renewal debates in cases such as the CAR, DRC, Haiti and Somalia. In the counter view, greater importance is attached to enhancing the capability of a sovereign authority to maintain internal order, rather than establishing electoral processes or rebel group dialogues. Lack of international agreement over peacekeeping doctrine opened up scope for unilateral internal security initiatives by adversarial primary powers as part of gradual geopolitical expansion into new or established areas in Africa and the Pacific.

## Mandate and force

Trying to reverse the perception that peacekeeping forces are merely damping down or containing conflict, inevitably raises issues over strengthening UN mandates to include switching to offensive military action by a peacekeeping force and the impartiality of a UN force. Only rarely has a UN force commander been replaced. Nevertheless, the distinction between ensuring internal stability and impartiality is finely drawn. A UN force risks being drawn into allegations of bias and loss of impartiality if force is used operationally to retain order or, in the case of expanded mandates, limit cross border incursions or regain territory (e.g. DRC). In these types of context, efforts to provide domestic security and stability may not be a viable enough platform for associated transition initiatives to promote internal political mediation. Stabilisation missions in nearly all instances are constrained by acute internal disorder and factionalism in the host state, rendering concepts of order promoted by dialogue and electoral processes as unobtainable. The causes of political instability are so fractured and ethnically based as to render political resolution extremely difficult.

A third factor which creates limitations on the use of mediation occurs in civil conflict in which priority is given by an adversary to battlefield developments for control of territory, retaking specific towns or geographic features. In these contexts the primacy of military objectives over diplomacy is reflected in the repeated vetoes over humanitarian access for convoys into conflict areas including Syria, Sudan and Gaza.[51]

## Conflicts: diminishing options for resolution

The scope for mediation in contemporary diplomacy is restricted by the continued mix of conflicts shaped by deep-seated historic legacies, prevalence of proxy wars and endemic instability in weak states. Progress has been made in a few historic legacy conflicts such as the Japan–Korea Camp David summit to normalise relations, which gained momentum as part of the United States' counter diplomacy supporting its Indo-Pacific strategy.[52] Other historic conflicts remain largely unmoved by diplomatic initiatives and continue as points of high international incident and tension. Normalisation between ideological adversaries, which is primarily economically driven or is at an early stage of restoring carefully framed political relations, is vulnerable to third-party counter moves such as incidents, border clashes or military incursions aimed at halting mediation or normalisation.

In civil conflicts in weak states, factors such as external intervention, political collapse and inter-ethnic clashes have made mediation in areas such as humanitarian supplies, ceasefires and re-establishing political governance structures difficult or impossible. Environmental factors linked to climate change have introduced added security problems associated with extended drought and nomadic movement across boundaries in search of water and support of livestock. The increase of weak states with collapsed administrations and failed mediation has prompted questions over the appropriateness and effectiveness of mediation and conflict resolution mechanisms in conflicts, such as in Somalia, Libya, Sahel and the Central African Republic.[53]

First, the office of special representative of the UN Secretary-General is a critical role in respect of contributing to lessening tension and finding ways of resolving conflicts. The frequent short-term rotation of representative adds a sense of instability and uncertainty over the mission. Regular changes of representative also raises issues of negotiating priorities and continuity within the way of proposals.

Second, the balance of how the role is carried out in stabilisation missions has shifted operationally from dialogue and mediation to standardised reporting and assessments of the internal situation mixed with appeal for internal order to New York.

The doctrine of dialogue and extending institutional governance to remote areas (e.g. in the CAR) has been at the centre of some of the approaches to the transition from peacekeeping. In situations of collapsed governance or contested territory, it is doubtful if that approach on its own is sufficient to create conditions for stability. Similarly, modifications of UN doctrine include an emphasis on achieving sustainable development as a route for stabilisation rather than security stabilisation and causes of instability.

Third, it has proved difficult to recruit or retain UN special representatives, e.g. for implementation of the Ukraine grain deal or to relaunch new mediation initiatives in cases of stalled historic conflicts. For example, in the Cyprus dispute, the office of administrative responsibility for the UN peacekeeping force (UNFICYP) is jointly responsible for relaunching a mediation mission.

## Loss of credibility and bias in international negotiations

Mediators may lose credibility for one or more of the following reasons: technical deficiencies, challenges to status, charges of partiality and loss of secrecy. Challenges to status, apart from blocking action to defeat an initiative, are used commonly to delay the start of talks by credentials issues, grounds for participation or reasons for invitation. As regards other factors, mediation and negotiation depend critically on secrecy.

If elements of secret negotiations are leaked to opponents of the process, difficulties occur in that possible concessions by one party are brought out publicly, weakening its position. The credibility of the mediator may be called into question, an incorrect or misinterpreted version of "contact" discussions or negotiations may be presented in the media, which require correction or denial, all of which can reduce freedom of action or set back progress. Above all, mediators may cease to be effective if they lose the confidence of any of the parties to a significant extent through perceived undue partiality.

Mediation efforts may be either implicitly or explicitly rejected. Implicit rejection most frequently occurs when mediation is allowed to run down and become ineffective and drift into stalemate. The longer that continues, the less likely it is that they will be constructively resumed. Frozen conflicts often become symbolic instruments in the battle for ideas and influence. Formal rejection of mediation is, however, relatively rare because of concerns over image and potential damage to the validity of a case.

## Successful mediation

Three main factors can be put forward to account for success in mediation conflict negotiations.

First, the maintenance of secrecy is essential in facilitating the construction of new proposals, continued momentum and avoiding the effects of leaked proposals such as mistrust and possible breakdown of contacts.

Second, the use of informal mediators and outside powers with limited or no direct stakes can be a useful means of breaking sterile, long-running ritualised meetings. In other cases, limited or short-run success may be achieved by ad hoc envoys as channels of communication or as means of last resort. Outcomes in this category, however, are often temporary and subject to revision, serving propaganda or diversionary purposes.

Third, an important element in successful mediation and negotiation is the role of overarching formulae that are used to construct agreements. Examples of these are definitions of areas of military disengagement, composition and functions of a joint administrative regime for a disputed territory or, in bilateral disputes, formulae to leave aside or "suspend" decisions on sovereignty or parts of a disputed frontier, concentrating instead on functional areas of practical cooperation such as air services, bilateral transport and economic cooperation.

Success for states which specialise in offering conflict services in ending or reducing instability in long-running civil wars can run out. Service roles may become exposed or transition into a public phase of institution building, as in most post-2000 conflicts. The special representatives of multilateral institutions are frequently the backstop or mechanisms of last resort. In lengthy transition negotiations, external service states can become focal points for attack and counter diplomacy by external powers. Political contexts, governments and contacts change. Past success as a service provider in conflict management is no guarantee of future replication.

## Conclusion

The role of diplomacy in limiting or resolving international conflicts is increasingly challenged in post-2000 conflicts. The axis for mediation has shifted from the UN and, in particular, the Secretary-General to a diverse and extended range of other actors, spread across primary powers, regional organisations and informal envoys. The reduced role of the UN in political and security mediation has removed one of the symbolic points which offered good offices, mediation and a Charter-based collective view on international conflicts. The changed role of the UN is reflected in mediation rivalry, and the shift in responsibility for mediation and joint missions of varying effectiveness to regional organisations in Europe, Africa and the Middle East. Underlying the changed role is the shift in UN peacekeeping doctrine to a revised doctrine of preventive diplomacy, built on the premise of meeting Sustainable Development Goals as a foundation for security.

The scope for mediation is restricted by conflicts shaped by deep-seated historical legacies, prevalence of proxy wars and endemic stability associated with weak and fractured states. In historic conflicts mediation is often limited to building ceasefires and temporary holding agreements. Normalisation agreements are brittle and easily overturned by shifts to violence. At some point though, diplomacy may re-emerge to undertake its central functions of conflict resolution and contribution to international order.

## Notes

1 Article 12 of the League of Nations Covenant identified three techniques in the event of a dispute: arbitration, judicial settlement or enquiry by the Council. Chapter 6, Article 53 of the United Nations Charter requires parties to resolve disputes through "negotiation, enquiry, mediation, conciliation, arbitration, judicial settlement, resort to regional agencies or arrangements or other peaceful means of their choice".

2 See Sydney D. Bailey, *The United Nations: A Concise Political Guide* (Palgrave Macmillan, 1989) pp45–6.

3 On the changing composition of primary and other powers in mediation groups, Portugal, the Russian Federation and United States constituted the mediation-contact group on Angola. See SC/5982, 12 August 1994. On Syria, see UNSC 2254 and 2336, Statement of UN Special Envoy for Syria, Staffan de Mistura and Jan Egeland, 5 January 2017.

4 Thomas Princen, "Mediation by the Vatican", in Jacob Bercovitch and Jeffrey Rubin (eds) *Mediation in International Relations* (St Martin's Press, 1992) pp154–5.

5 On the difficulties Brazil encountered in developing a diplomatic role on Middle East issues, see Celso Amorim, *Acting Globally* (Hamilton Books, 2017) pp226–3.

6 Amorim, ibid., p234 on Brazil and the Obama administration.

7 For Sri Lankan counter diplomacy tied to battlefield developments against the Tamil Tigers (LATTE) to stall or prevent an emergency meeting on human rights sought by the EU, see Sanja de Silva Jayatilleka, *Mission Impossible Geneva* (Vijitha Yapa Publications, 2017) pp112–4.

8 See, for example, the wrangling over the formation of the Joint Monitoring and Evaluation Commission (JMEC) under the South Sudan peace agreement which, apart from domestic interests, included external players (UK, US, Norway, EU, China) with individual representation and an additional miscellaneous group of countries (IGAD Partners Forum) supportive of the

African Union's group mandated for negotiating an end to the conflict in South Sudan.

9  See Robert M. Cutler, "The US Role in the International Meditation of the South Caucasus Peace Process", Analytical Articles, 26 June 2023. The resumption of talks was delayed over whether the US could act as a co-chair on the basis of the long-defunct Minsk Group. Other difficulties included whether guests could be invited (e.g. President Emmanuel Macron who had put forward the European Political Cooperation (EPC) initiative) to trilateral meetings (Armenia, Azerbaijan) chaired by Charles Michel, President of the European Council.

10  See UN Secretary-General, SG/SM/14124, 23 February 2012 and joint statement at www.un.org/sg/statements/index.asp?nid=5880.

11  See UNSC 2042 (2012), 14 April 2012 (annex).

12  UN Press release SG/SM/14179.

13  UNSC 2042 (2012), 14 April 2012. Algerian diplomat Lakhdar Brahimi replaced Kofi Annan and Nasser Al-Kidwa (Arab League) continued as Joint Arab League-UN Special representative for Syria. See SG/SM/14471. Kofi Annan resigned on 12 August 2012.

14  See John E. Hoffman, Jr on the several competing and self-contained channels during the Iran hostage crisis between Iran and the United States, in Warren M. Christopher, *American Hostages in Iran* (Little Brown, 1982) pp251–2. These included an informal envoy channel, banking channel and the German counsel to the Iranian Ministry of Foreign Affairs, via the Iranian embassy in Bonn.

15  The grey area channels between Iran and the United States in this crisis were finally merged in December 1980. See Christopher, ibid., p255.

16  See UN General Assembly, A/72/115.

17  On the transitional role of the UN in conflicts, see Brian Urquhart, *A Life in Peace and War* (WW Norton and Co., 1987) esp. hp XXI (Watershed).

18  For membership of the UN Group of Friends of Mediation, see https://peacemaker.un.org/friendsofmediation.

19  The Ukraine–UN grain deal shed light on the NGO commodity sector groups.

20  For details of the concept of disguised state see R.P. Barston, *Modern Diplomacy* 5th ed., pp163–5.

21  On Qatar's hostage mediation role in the Israeli–Gaza war see UN Secretary General, SG/SM/22011, 28 October 2023.

22  William J. Burns, *The Back Channel* (Hurst and Co., 2019) pp356–77.

23  James C. Jonah, "The UN and International Conflict: the Military Talks at Kilometre Marker-101", in Bercovitch and Rubin (eds) *Mediation in International Relations*, op. cit.

24  Thomas Princen, "Mediation by the Vatican", in Bercovitch and Rubin (eds), op. cit., p162. In the Beagle Channel mediation, the location (i.e. the Vatican itself) probably made a difference. The negotiators were constantly surrounded by the impressive ambience.

25  See Catherine Ashton, *And Then What?* (Elliot and Thompson, 2023) pp163.

26  For the first meeting in 20 years of the UN at senior official level and the LRA, between Jan Egeland and Joseph Kony, at Ri-Kwamba in a remote abandoned jungle village on the border of south-western Sudan and north-eastern Congo, see Jan Egeland, *A Billion Lives* (Simon and Schuster, 2010) pp200–8.

27 On the abortive Nagorno-Karabakh cancelled negotiations, see Robert M. Cutler, op. cit., p1.

28 "How to reinvigorate the Cyprus talks" Crisis Group, 2023.

29 For details of the issues in the first temporary ceasefire, 24–30 November, following the Hamas attack on 9 October 2023, and the role of Qatar in facilitating these negotiations, see Reuters 21 November and 1 December 2023. On the resumption of ceasefire talks in 2024, see *The Guardian*, 11 July 2024 and *Washington Post*, 24 August 2024. For details of the issues, including territorial questions (e.g. Israeli demands for control of a strip of territory on the Egyptian–Gaza border known as the Philadelphi corridor), see AP News, "New Gaza cease fire talks – why is a deal so elusive?".

30 Nicholas Coghlan, *Collapse of a Country* (McGill-Queen's University Press, 2017) on the issue of the division of South Sudan into 28 states by the Kiir government, pp209–11.

31 Henry Kissinger, *Years of Upheaval* (Little, Brown, 1982) p811 on avoiding setting time limits.

32 For discussion of South Sudan President Salva Kiir's reluctant signing of the Agreement on the Resolution of the Conflict in South Sudan (ARC), creating a transitional government of national unity based on a mediated complex power-sharing formula which favoured the opposition (SPLM/A-IO, Riek Machar) but postponed elections, see Coghlan, op. cit., p207.

33 *Financial Times*, 26 October 2023.

34 On incremental methods that break a dispute into particular subparts, see J.G. Stein, "Structure, Strategies and Tactics of Mediation: Kissinger and Carter in the Middle East", Negotiation Journal, vol. 1 (4), 1985, pp331–47.

35 In the Aswan talks between Israel and Egypt, Kissinger, who mediated the talks, initially tried to get agreement on general principles as the basis for the agreement but the approach was rejected by Sadat who wanted definitive agreement. See Kissinger, *Years of Upheaval*, op. cit., p799; Ismail Fahmy, *Negotiating for Peace in the Middle East* (Johns Hopkins, 1983) p55.

36 Establishing an agreed timetable for key phases or stages of conflict resolution (e.g. ceasefires, holding areas, weapons collection, elections) is an important but difficult method to apply, especially in civil war and fragile political systems. See Muriel Asseburg, Wolfram Lacher, and Marieke Transfeld, "Mission, Impossible? UN Mediation in Libya, Syria, and Yemen", SWP research paper, 8 October 2018.

37 Roberts B. Owen, in Christopher, *American Hostages in Iran*, op. cit., on the role of Algeria in narrowing the differences between the United States and Iran; the talks alternated between Algiers and Washington over a period of two months.

38 In the 1973 Israeli–Egyptian disengagement negotiations on withdrawal of forces, the issue of reopening and rebuilding the Suez Canal was extracted from the main negotiations and dealt with in a side letter between Israel and Egypt. See Kissinger, *Years of Upheaval*, op. cit., p835.

39 The precise terms of the Israeli–Egyptian agreement, concluded in parallel negotiations to the UN "Kilometre 101" talks, were not known to UN negotiators. See Kissinger's account in *Years of Upheaval*, op. cit., p835.

40 See Jan Egeland, *A Billion Lives* (Simon and Schuster, 2010) pp203–8, on the meeting with the LRA, the first of its kind for the UN.

41 See Coghlan, *Collapse of a Country*, op. cit., pp225–31.

42  See Ashton, *And Then What?*, op. cit., p200.

43  Mark Salter, *To End a Civil War* (Hurst and Co., 2015) p104 on peace negotiation issues over participants.

44  Ashton, op. cit., p175.

45  Cutler, "The US Role in the International Meditation of the South Caucasus Peace Process", op. cit.

46  Cutler, ibid., p2.

47  Inis Claude, *Swords into Plowshares* (University of London Press, 1971) pp208–233; David M. Malone (ed.), *The UN Security Council* (Lynne Rienner, 2004) pp2–6; David Hannay, *New World Disorder* (IB Tauris, 2008) chapter VI, pp75–117.

48  For details of the initiatives of the Caribbean Eminent Persons missions to Haiti mediate an internal political agreement, see https://caricom.org/statement-eminent-persons-group-following-third-facilitation-visit-to-haiti/. On the internal security police support force for Haiti, see https://reliefweb.int/report/haiti/joint-statement-multinational-security-support-mission-pre-planning-conference>.

49  UN S/RES/2699 (2023), 2 October 2023.

50  UN Secretary-General, New Agenda for Peace, 2023, SG/SM/21885, 20 July 2023.

51  On Syrian negotiations in the Security Council on ceasefires and humanitarian convoy access, see chapter 7, Parallel Diplomacy.

52  Japan–Korea Camp David Summit, 18 August 2023, joint statement at www.whitehouse.gov/briefing-room/statements-releases/2023/08/18/the-spirit-of-camp-david-joint-statement-of-japan-the-republic-of-korea-and-the-united-states/.

53  For the CAR, see report of the Special Representative to the Secretary-General and debate, SC15466, 26 October 2023 on the internal situation in the CAR and what the future involvement of the UN in the CAR might be. In this context, pressure to get the UN peacekeeping force (MINUSCA) out of the CAR, and the wider struggle for external influence to displace residual western presence, is reflected in the subsequent report of the SRSG, 27 June 2024, which draws attention to identified sources conducting a disinformation campaign against MINUSCA and appeals for UN member support against.

# Conclusion

The evolution of diplomacy post-2000 has been shaped by contested conceptions of international order and disengaged diplomacy. The problem of defining and securing wider agreement on core issues is reflected in the progressive decline of multilateralism. Relatively little attention has been given to disengaged diplomacy. This study has highlighted it as one of the important areas in diplomatic methods, giving insights into how it has affected the management of resources and regulatory functions of diplomacy. Selective non-attendance by heads of state/government at multilateral climate and other conferences is now a practised device, especially used by adversarial powers for media attention, delay or to disguise non-involvement. Similarly, withholding inbound ministerial visits, or cancellation whilst not, are now developed and extensive methods for controlling the pace of relations and an integral part of wait-and-see strategies from the sidelines of major conflicts. The extent of disengaged diplomacy in these different forms as part of orientation constitute a significant negative set of diplomatic transactions which limit detailed cooperation and weaken multilateralism.

In terms of other aspects of orientation, diplomatic methods have largely involved sectoral change to deal with disputes, problems of adjustment, opening up new relations or trying to reduce dependency by trade diversification. Major shifts in orientation have been relatively rare and, for the most part, unsuccessful. Mixed orientation, however, has become increasingly used by states to conduct a form of dual relations with adversarial states or blocs, testing the boundaries of alliance to conduct political, trade or security transactions. Trying to maintain alliance credibility, value and acceptance is a constant difficulty in balancing interests. It is a high-risk form of diplomatic method which may bring uncertain or temporary gains but which still appears attractive to a larger number of states.

As regards content, the evolution of contemporary diplomacy has been distinguished by the density of issues, fragility of power and influence. These have impacted on the different skill requirements for bilateral and

DOI: 10.4324/9781003204039-13

multilateral diplomacy.[1] This study has underlined the continued changes in density of diplomacy, especially in bilateral relations and impact on methods. In trade diplomacy, for example, the changes in methods are reflected in three areas: creation of new groupings such as the RCEP and CPTPP, types of agreements and the growth of dark trade to evade sanctions. The new groupings have also become platforms for bilateral side agreements with third parties. Trade agreements have generally become more informal as framework instruments or MOUs, with the exception of complex EU multisector bilateral or inter-regional governance agreements. An important change in EU multisector agreements is the expansion of the content to include fisheries governance and other resource access provisions to EEZs in partner cooperation agreements, as part of a wider EU maritime presence strategy linking regional organisations.

Other developments in methods include innovative modular framework agreements for promoting bilateral technology and supply chain connections. Keeping ownership of bilateral agreements is inherently difficult as other states monitor and seek access to trade benefits. As a result, defensive diplomacy has developed new treaty forms to defend negotiating territory and stake prior claims through advance notification of the outcomes of preliminary negotiations, or setting out areas of agreement in principle. Detailed monitoring of other state trade operations has become an important diplomatic function.

In negotiations, one of the major developments is the movement away from consensus-based procedures to plurilateral, bloc and other methods in multilateral negotiations. Consensus had been the bedrock of multilateral conference negotiation, with the UN Convention on the Law of the Sea becoming the standard consensus-based model for collective diplomacy in the multilateral era. Within the WTO, the breakdown of the Doha Trade Round influenced the shift to finding other non-consensus-based methods. The likelihood that the talks would fail to develop a comprehensive agreement accelerated the importance of alternative bilateral trade negotiations as an alternative, and more generally bilateralism as a preferred form. These were supplemented by the spread of regional agreements, of which the RCEP and CPTPP, as mega trade blocs, symbolised the fragmentation and competition as critical features of diplomacy after the international financial crisis.

In terms of content, the scope of negotiations has been reduced with the decline of primary power summits and, in the UN, the cancellation of periodic large-scale event conferences, including Habitat and Information Society, as outmoded forms of multilateralism. The movement away from ad hoc conferences was accelerated by the COVID-19 pandemic, though the general sense of the need for redirection was already evident for an overall reduction on multilateral conferences. Problems of finding hosts, split sites and funding, together with finding more UN members willing to host in order to provide greater sustaining influence, to that of the New York–Geneva or Dubai–Astana axis, remain significant issues for diplomatic methods.

Further changes in the conduct of diplomacy are notable for the use of parallel and counter diplomacy, which reflect the expansion, competitive moves and instability of the contemporary international system. Parallel diplomacy is a key feature in diplomacy post-2000. It aims to create separate or competing institutions to existing multilateral or regional agencies as alternative ways of operating, leveraging influence and projecting interests and influence. In the early phases of establishing a parallel institution, relations may initially appear cooperative rather than competitive. This generally is to aid acceptance or acquire legitimacy. In some instances, parallel diplomacy can become counter diplomacy, in which the opposing agency is taken over or superseded, organisationally. Parallel diplomacy typically creates alternative institutions and breakaway groups, and contributes to fragmentation of the international system.

Counter diplomacy has continued to increase in use and significance.[2] Its assumptions and modus operandi are inherently negative: to block, delay or undermine alternative or competing ideas and initiatives; to gain control of regional and other institutions; or to assist in blocking or negating other actors and individuals in areas such as mediation and arms control. Much of counter diplomacy fits into the "grey area" on the boundaries of acceptable norms and notions of diplomacy, mixing with coercion, deception and covert action. Its use reflects and resonates with competing conceptions of international order, weakening of multilateralism and an emerging alternative architecture.

In the final sections of the book, attention turns to logistics, the emerging alternative architecture and diplomacy in conflicts. These three chapters provide insights into processes and methods as perspectives on critical areas of diplomacy. Of these, logistics is a little-examined area of diplomatic methods. It offers insights into state commercial-diplomatic groupings, port acquisitions, geopolitics and supply chains as part of national agendas and the new international agenda. The chapter, An Alternative Architecture, continues those ideas with discussion of the emergence of an alternative grouping (the Alternative Architecture) as one of the changes in the structure of the international system and the diplomatic methods used to develop that emerging alliance. Together, these give an indication of the range of changes in methods as diplomacy is used and adapts to the contemporary international system.

The challenges for diplomacy remain significant in a setting of declining multilateralism, mega trade blocs, regional conflicts, splintered coalitions and the ongoing task of creating stability in a contested international order.

## Notes

1 Yolanda Kemp Spies, *Global South Perspectives on Diplomacy* (Palgrave Macmillan, 2018) pp251–2.
2 R.P. Barston, *Modern Diplomacy* 5th ed. (Routledge, 2019) pp48–50.

# Index

For Product Safety Concerns and Information please contact our EU
representative GPSR@taylorandfrancis.com
Taylor & Francis Verlag GmbH, Kaufingerstraße 24, 80331 München, Germany

www.ingramcontent.com/pod-product-compliance
Lightning Source LLC
Chambersburg PA
CBHW050632280326
41932CB00015B/2617